8/11/02

With compliments

H. P. Achebe

Where Others Wavered

The Autobiography of Sam Nujoma

Where Others Wavered

The Autobiography of
Sam Nujoma

PANAF

Where Others Wavered
The Autobiography of Sam Nujoma

Copyright © 2001 Sam Nujoma

The moral right of the author has been asserted.

First published in 2001 by Panaf Books

All rights reserved. No part of this publication may be reproduced, stored in retrieval system, or transmitted, in any form or by any means, electronic, mechanical, photocopying, recording or otherwise, without the prior permission in writing of Panaf Books, nor be otherwise circulated in any form of binding or cover other than that in which it is published and without a similar condition including this condition being imposed on subsequent purchaser.

A catalogue record for this book is available from
The British Library
The Namibian National Library
The OAU Library

ISBN   0 90 1787 57 4 (Hb)
ISBN   0 90 1787 58 2 (Pb)

Jacket design, volume design and typesetting
Myrene McFee

Panaf Books
75 Weston Street
London SE1 3RS

◆◆◆

*This book is dedicated to
the gallant sons and daughters,
heroes and heroines
under the leadership of
their vanguard SWAPO,
and to those who struggled
and sacrificed their precious lives
for the total liberation
of Namibia.*

◆◆◆

Acknowledgements

I wish to express my sincere thanks to the numerous Comrades, former commanders of the People's Liberation Army of Namibia (PLAN), friends, family and acquaintances who gave freely of their time to make the writing of this book possible despite the heavy national duties entrusted upon me by the Namibian nation. Although it had been always my idea and commitment to write a book, it was Mr. Randolph Vigne, founder member and President of the then Namibia Support Committee in London who contributed a great deal in helping me to draft the initial version, and I am greatly indebted to him. Also, special thanks are due to Comrade Jerobeam Shaanika who worked with Mr. Vigne in the early stages of the project.

I am equally grateful for the input and valuable contributions I received from the following Comrades: Hage Geingob, Theo-Ben Gurirab, Hidipo Hamutenya, Hifikepunye Pohamba, Andimba Toivo Ya Toivo, Dr. Libertina Amathila, Dr. Iyambo Indongo, Dr. Zephania Kameeta, and the Omugulu-gOmbashe veterans, to mention but a few.

I am also indebted to Dr. Lazarus Hangula from the University of Namibia Multidisciplinary Research and Consultancy Centre, and Mr. Vilho Tshilongo, a historian of traditional history, who provided me with valuable information on our traditional chiefs and kingdoms; and Comrade Monica Nashandi, the Namibian High Commissioner in London and her Staff for kind assistance.

Much appreciation is also due to the following offices and institutions which provided me with photographs and other illustrations: Office of the President — Media Section; SWAPO Department of Information and Publicity; New Dawn Video; Namprint; National Archives; the Embassy of the Republic of Cuba; and numerous other individuals.

When I started this book, I thought it would be a matter of a year or two to complete, but this has not been possible. In order to work on this book and at the same time do justice to my other duties and responsibilities, the only time available has been from 3a.m. to 7.30a.m., before the start of official working hours. Thus I am grateful to Comrade John Nauta who has always been at my disposal at these odd hours to record and do the typing. I also wish to thank all my Office Staff members who have provided me with the support I needed.

My publisher and I would like to acknowledge the contributions of several readers, including Professor Shula Marks, School of Oriental and African Studies, University of London; Jill Scott, Staffordshire University; June Milne; and Marc Keech, University of Brighton.

Finally, I would like to thank my publisher, Panaf Books, for their diligent editing and dedicated support in bringing this volume to completion.

~~~~~~~~~~

Contents

List of Abbreviations xi
List of Illustrations xiii
Foreword by David Meroro xvii
Introduction 1
Map of Africa 2

1   Background and Early Years 3
2   Walvis Bay and Windhoek 31
3   The Formation of the Ovamboland People's Organization (OPO) 45
4   Political Confrontation: the Popular Windhoek Uprising 71
5   Escape from South West Africa 83
6   Ghana and the United Nations 97
7   The Establishment of the SWAPO Office in Dar-es-Salaam 113
8   Preparation for Armed Liberation Struggle 121
9   Sixteen Hours in Windhoek 135
10 The Hague Court — A 'Mockery of Justice' 143
11 From Caprivi to Omugulu-gOmbashe 157
12 The Struggle Intensifies on All Fronts 185
13 Workers' Struggle and Diplomatic Advance 197
14 Worldwide Recognition 205
15 Waldheim Initiatives 215
16 The Collapse of The Portuguese Empire in Africa 227
17 SWAPO — Home and Exile 239
18 Resolution 385 and the Kissinger 'Shuttle' 251
19 The Western Contact Group 261
20 US Policy towards Namibia in the 1970s and 1980s 277
21 Geneva and the Reagan Years 291
22 At the Height of the War, 1980–1985 315
23 From Strength to Strength, 1985–1989 339
24 In Sight of Victory 365
25 Final Days of the Struggle for Independence 387
26 Return to Windhoek, Independence and a New Beginning 413

Appendix 1	Inaugural Speech, 21 March 1990	445
Appendix 2.1	Letter: 14 March 1989, Javier Pérez de Cuéllar to Sam Nujoma assigning cease-fire date of 1 April 1989	448
Appendix 2.2	Letter: 14 March 1989, Javier Pérez de Cuéllar to Botha (as copied to Nujoma) assigning cease-fire date of 1 April 1989	449
Appendix 2.3	Letter: 18 March 1989, Sam Nujoma reply to Javier Pérez de Cuéllar accepting cease-fire date of 1 April 1989	450
Appendix 2.4	Letter: 21 March 1989, Botha reply to Javier Pérez de Cuéllar accepting cease-fire date of 1 April 1989	451
Appendix 3	Resolutions of the United Nations Security Council, pertaining to South West Africa / Namibia	
	Resolution 385 (1976) 30 January 1976	452
	Resolution 431 (1978) 27 July 1978	453
	Resolution 432 (1978) 27 July 1978	454
	Resolution 435 (1978) 29 September 1978	454
	Resolution 439 (1978) 13 November 1978	455
	Resolution 532 (1983) 31 May 1983	456
	Resolution 539 (1983) 28 October 1983	456
	Resolution 566 (1985) 19 June 1985	458
	Resolution 601 (1987) 30 October 1987	460
	Resolution 629 (1989) 16 January 1989	461
	Resolution 640 (1989) 29 August 1989	463

Photograph Acknowledgements 466

Index 467

List of Abbreviations

ANC	African National Congress
CANU	Caprivi African National Union
CCB	Civil Co-operation Bureau
CDM	Consolidated Diamond Mines
CIA	Central Intelligence Agency
DMZ	De-Militarised Zone
DRC	Democratic Republic of Congo
DTA	Democratic Turnhalle Alliance
FAPLA	People's Armed Forces for the Liberation of Angola
FCN	Federal Convention of Namibia
FLN	Algerian National Liberation Front
FNLA	National Front for the Liberation of Angola
FRELIMO	Front for the Liberation of Mozambique
GRAE	Government of Angola in Exile
ICJ	International Court of Justice
JMC	Joint Monitoring Commission
JMMC	Joint Military Monitoring Commission
KADU	Kenya African Democratic Union
KANU	Kenya African National Union
MPC	Multi-Party Conference
MPLA	National Front for the Liberation of Angola
NAM	Non-Aligned Movement
NAMPA	Namibian Press Agency
NANSO	Namibian National Students Organization
NATO	North Atlantic Treaty Organization
NDP	National Democratic Party (Southern Rhodesia)
NNC	Namibia National Convention
NNF	Namibia National Front
NPF	National Patriotic Front of Namibia
NUNW	National Union of Namibian Workers
OAU	Organization of African Unity
OPC	Ovamboland People's Congress
OPO	Ovamboland People's Organization
PAC	Pan-African National Congress
PAFMECSA	Pan-African Freedom Movement of East, Central and Southern Africa
PAIGC	African Party for the Independence of Guinea and Cape Verde Islands

PEDE	Policia International Defence d'Estate
PF	Patriotic Front
PIM	Pre-Implementation Meeting
PLAN	People's Liberation Army of Namibia
RSAC	Radio South African Corporation
RTZ	Rio Tinto Zinc
SADCC	Southern African Development Co-ordinating Conference
SADF	South African Defence Force
SANP	South African Nationalist Party
SAR	South African Railways
SWALA	South West Africa Liberation Army
SWANLA	South West Africa Native Labour Association
SWANU	South West Africa National Union
SWAPO	South West Africa People's Organization
SWATF	South West Africa Territorial Forces
TANU	Tanganyika African National Union
UDF	United Democratic Front
UDI	Unilateral Declaration of Independence
UN	United Nations
UNHCR	United Nations High Commissioner for Refugees
UNIP	United National Independence Party
UNITA	National Union for the Total Independence of Angola
UNTAG	United Nations Transitional Assistance Group
US	United States
WENALA	Witwatersrand Native Labour Association
WHO	World Health Organization
ZANU	Zimbabwe African National Union
ZANU-PF	Zimbabwe African National Union — Patriotic Front
ZAPU	Zimbabwe African People's Union

List of Illustrations

1	Namibia in Southern Africa	4
2	Herero tribesmen, during imperial German occupation	7
3	Chief Hendrik Witbooi; Chief Samuel Maharero	9
4	Chief Nehale lja Mpingana of Ondonga (c. 1900)	12
5	Chief Mandume ja Ndemufajo of Uukuanjama (1893–1917)	12
6	Chief Iipumbu ja Tshilongo of Uukuambi (1873–1959)	15
7	Tate Daniel Utoni Nujoma	21
8	With mother, Mpingana-Helvi Kondombolo, 14 September 1989	23
9	The young Sam Nujoma. Walvis Bay, 1948	32
10	With Cousin Johannes Ushona, 1954	32
11	Aaron Kapere, the Reverend Michael Scott, Katjikuru Katjiongua and Fritz Zaire, 1947	35
12	Wedding, Windhoek — Old Location, 1956	39
13	Theopoldine Kovambo Katjimune holding daughter Nelago; Utoni Daniel; Sakaria Nefungo; John Ndeshipanda, 1958	40
14	Route of Sam Nujoma's "escape from South West Africa"	94
15	President Kwame Nkrumah (Ghana) and President Gamal Abdel Nasser (Egypt), 1964	98
16	Chief Hosea Kutako	106
17	Sam Nujoma, March, 1961	116
18	Jacob Kuhangua and Sam Nujoma crossing the Zambezi River, 1964	127
19	PLAN combatants crossing Cuando River from Zambia into the Caprivi part of Namibia, 1973	137
20	SWAPO members in Dar-es-Salaam, 1964	148/149
21	Tobias Hainjeko, first Commander of South West Africa Liberation Army (SWALA); Peter Nanyemba, first SWAPO Secretary for Defence. Mbeya, Tanzania, 16 April 1965	161
22	Veterans of the 26 August 1966 attack at Omugulu-gOmbashe, 26 August, 1990	165
23	Monument at Omugulu-gOmbashe, 26 August, 1990	165
24	"R1000 reward offered for notorious SWAPO leader", 8 June, 1970	167
25	Patrick Iyambo (Lungada), 26 August 1990	169
26	Andimba Toivo Herman Ya Toivo (pictured in May 1984)	176
27	Sam Nujoma at Rome Airport, 24 July 1968	186

28	Attendees of the Tanga Consultative Congress, 1969–1970	190
29	Moses Garoeb, Peter Nanyemba, with Mishake Muyongo, December 1970	191
30	Seated as a speaker at UN, 5 October 1971	206
31	With Sean MacBride, September/October 1974	221
32	PLAN combatants inspecting captured weapons and supplies	223
33	With President Neto, 4 February 1976, Luanda	233
34	Dr. Antonio Agostinho Neto	233
35	Strategic planning over a map	235
36	Addressing the UN Security Council, 30 May 1975	252
37	With Henry Kissinger, 29 September 1976	255
38	Addressing the UN Security Council, 28 September 1976	258
39	With Sean MacBride and Theo-Ben Gurirab, 28 September 1976	259
40	With Hidipo Hamutenya, Theo-Ben Gurirab, and SWAPO delegation to the UN, 1977	262
41	Iyambo Indongo addressing the WHO Assembly, 4th May 1978	264
42	Victims of the Cassinga Massacre, 4 May 1978	265
43	Western Contact Group members, 27 July, 1978	269
44	Henry Kissinger, 1973	278
45	Western Contact Group members, 27 July 1978	280
46	SWAPO delegation at the United Nations, 7 January 1981	298
47	SWAPO delegation at the United Nations, 7 January 1981	299
48	Anti-SWAPO propaganda leaflet, 1980s	301
49	Anti-SWAPO propaganda cartoon, mid 1980s	302
50	Anti-SWAPO propaganda leaflet with "safety guarantee"	303
51	With Yasser Arafat; Indira Gandhi; Najma Heptulla; March 1983	308
52	Indira Gandhi; Fidel Castro; Natvar Singh, 7 March 1983	309
53	With Javier Pérez de Cuéllar, Luanda, Angola, 26 August 1983	310
54	Peter Nanyemba, 1970–1983	311
55	Dimo Hamaambo; David Meroro; Sam Nujoma; Moses Garoeb; Peter Nanyemba, 1981	316
56	Captured South African soldier, February 1978	317
57	South Africa's military buildup	319

58	PLAN combatants together with Cuban military advisers, 17 August 1982	320
59	Aircraft brought down by PLAN, southern Angola, 1982	320
60	PLAN shooting range in Lubango, Angola, 1982	324
61	Victims of Oshikuku massacre, 1982	327
62	Preparation of a mass grave, March, 1982	327
63	Weapons used by PLAN combatants	330
64	With Hu Yaobang, Peking, 16 March 1985	333
65	With President Fidel Castro, Havana, Cuba, 1977	333
66	With Hendrik Witbooi and Toivo ya Toivo, April 1984	345
67	With Rajiv Gandhi, August 1986	346
68	Julius Nyerere; Samora Machel; Robert Mugabe, March 9, 1985	346
69	Inauguration of the first SWAPO Embassy, 24 May 1986	348
70	With Kenneth Kaunda; Bishop Makulu, 4 May 1987	351
71	The parading of corpses by South African security forces	357
72	Passport of "Mr. Sam Mwakangale"	359
73	Diplomatic Passport of Mr. Sam S. Nujoma	360
74	With Arnaldo Ochoa Sánchez; Jorge Risquet Valdès; Raúl Castro, April 1987	362
75	With President Fidel Castro, 1987	363
76	With SWAPO Secretary for Defence Peter Mueshihange, 28 December 1987	368
77	Nghilifavali Thomas Hamunjela (1987)	368
78	Technicians servicing a MIG-23, January, 1988	372
79	Arrival of helicopters in Cuito Cuanavale, January, 1988	372
80	MIG-23 being readied for a mission, January, 1988	372
81	Addressing the NAM Summit, 1986	382
82	Bernt Carlsson, 26 August 1987	385
83	With Peter Mueshihange, 18 February 1989	393
84	SWAPO troops gathered at a rally, 31 March 1989	394
85	With Ottilie Todenge and Laimi Uunona, 31 March 1989	394
86	With Pedro Mutindi and Hidipo Hamutenya, 31 March 1989	395
87	Speaking to SWAPO star rally, 4 November 1989	407
88	With Louis Pienaar, 24 September 1989	408
89	With General Opande of Kenya UNTAG, 20 April, 1989	408
90	With Hage Geingob, 18 June 1989	411

91	With Libertina Amathila; Nahas Angula; Patrick Ijambo (Lungada), 18 June 1989	411
92	With Lucas Hifikepunye Pohamba; Hage Geingob; Hidipo Hamutenya; Toivo ya Toivo, November 1989	423
93	Thirteen Administrative Regions of the Republic of Namibia	427
94	The Namibian Constituency Assembly	428
95	Signing of the Constitution of Namibia, 9 February 1990	432
96	With Toivo ya Toivo; David Meroro; Hendrik Witbooi, 9 February 1990	432
97	During Constitution ceremonies, with the new Namibian flag, 9 February 1990	433
98	On the steps of the Tintenpalast, Windhoek, 2 February 1990	433
99	The Cabinet of the Republic of Namibia	434/435
100	Arrival of heads of state for the Independence Day ceremonies, Windhoek	440
101	With UN Secretary-General Javier Pérez de Cuéllar, 21 March 1990	442

Foreword

I am honoured to introduce the Autobiography of Sam Nujoma, the life story of this great son of Namibia and Africa. Over the last few decades I have had the honour and privilege to know and work with Sam Nujoma, the man, the leader of the national liberation movement, SWAPO, and the first President of the independent Republic of Namibia. Sam Nujoma dedicated his whole adult life to the achievement of Namibia's liberation from apartheid and colonial domination. He did not rest until Namibia's independence and sovereignty were celebrated on 21 March 1990.

This narration takes the reader through the life history of a remarkable man who drew his inspiration from Namibia's heroic forefathers such as Chief Hendrik Witbooi and Chief Hosea Kutako, and from the great pan-African leaders Gamal Abdel Nasser and, especially, Kwame Nkrumah. As a youth Sam Nujoma witnessed and experienced first-hand the racist oppression of colonial police and 'contract' administrators. As a young man he educated himself in the English language, and in history and world politics.

During the 1950s, Sam Nujoma participated in and was a primary force in the political awakening of the Namibian people. With other leaders, he joined in petitioning the United Nations to bring pressure to bear on the South African colonial administration to adhere to UN mandates which were designed and intended to progress Namibia's independence. But such peaceful protest alone did not prove a sufficient force to break the colonial chains. On 10 December 1959 at the Windhoek Old Location, 12 unarmed peaceful protesters were killed and more than 50 people were injured by colonial South African police. The incident sparked Sam Nujoma's decision to go into exile in order to intensify the struggle on behalf of the people of Namibia. His exile lasted 29 years, from 1960 to 1989.

During those years he travelled every corner of the world, mobilising support for the liberation struggle of Namibia. He was instrumental in the formation of, and always at the head of, SWAPO. He lobbied Western and Eastern capitals to persuade them to talk to the intransigent South African colonialists to see sense. He hung about the conference corridors and stalked the leadership of the Non-aligned Movement for political and diplomatic support.

SWAPO for several years concentrated on the political and diplomatic fronts of the liberation struggle, both internally and internationally. When all peaceful means to achieve Namibia's independence were exhausted, SWAPO, with Sam Nujoma as its leader, launched the armed liberation struggle, on 26 August 1966, while all the time maintaining the political and diplomatic endeavours around the world.

On 21 March 1990, the armed liberation struggle ended with victory when Namibia's flag of independence was hoisted in Windhoek, and South Africa's colonial flag of racism, oppression and exploitation was lowered forever.

Sam Nujoma was elected to be the first Namibian Head of State by the Constituent Assembly, and was sworn in as President on 21 March 1990. In 1994 and 1999 he was popularly re-elected as President by the Namibian people in recognition of his wise and dynamic leadership.

Through SWAPO's policy of national reconciliation under the slogan of ONE NAMIBIA, ONE NATION, he has united all Namibians into a peaceful, tolerant and democratic society, governed by the rule of law.

In this book, His Excellency President Sam Nujoma invites us on his journey of courage, commitment and determination towards building a steadfast Namibia in an assertive, prosperous and peaceful united African continent.

David Meroro

Publisher's Note: David Meroro

David Hosea Meroro is a grassroots Pan-Africanist who has known the author for a very long time. He was born on 1 January 1917 in the Keetmanshoop District, close to the Blouburg mountain in the Karas Region of Namibia. In the 1940s he joined the African Improvement Society which had its roots in the Universal Negro Improvement Association (UNIA), founded in 1914 in the United States by Marcus Garvey to promote the interests of black people.

In the 1950s, he worked closely with the Herero Chief, Hosea Kutako, Nathaniel Maxuilili, Clemens Kapuuo and Sam Nujoma. Together they petitioned the United Nations against the incorporation of Namibia into South Africa and for an end to South African colonialism in Namibia. He is a founder member of SWAPO and was elected as its National Chairman in 1962.

At the end of 1971, the UN Security Council held a special session in Addis Ababa and passed a resolution calling the Secretary General, Kurt Waldheim, to establish negotiations towards self-determination for the people of Namibia. This led to Dr Kurt Waldheim's visit to Namibia in March 1972. The SWAPO petition to Dr Waldheim was handed over by David Meroro, who also was the leader of the SWAPO delegation.

On 17 February 1974, David Meroro was arrested by South African security police and kept in solitary confinement for nearly six months. During that time he was tortured, and eventually charged under the 1967 Suppression of Communism and Terrorism Act. Eventually, due to lack of evidence on other charges, he was only found guilty of possession of the illegal publication, *The African Communist*. He was sentenced to a three-year suspended term, and fined R500.

With the death of Chief Phillemon Eliphas in 1975, a number of SWAPO leaders such as Othniel Kakungua, Eliphas Muniaro, Alfred Naruseb, Aaron Mushimba and David Meroro, who was the most wanted person, were arrested. He was forced to go underground and as the search for him intensified was eventually forced to leave Namibia. He went into exile on 1 September 1975, journeying through Botswana to Zambia.

In 1987 he received the Omugulu-gOmbashe Medal for Bravery and Long Service.

❖ ❖ ❖

Introduction

I am Sam Nujoma ja Nujoma, born on the 12th May 1929, the first of my parents' eleven children, in an area then known by the world as colonial South West Africa, now the independent Republic of Namibia.

Like the broad history of any one man's life, mine could be told in a few sentences. As a child I listened with pride to the stories of my parents' and grandparents' lives, grew in strength and learned responsibility in herding my family's cattle and guarding them against natural predators — the lion, leopard and jackal.

As a youth and young adult I gained experience of the world through education, work and travel. Through those experiences I learned that predation also existed in the racism, oppression and injustice of the colonial governments and the attendant structures of apartheid — that these unwanted, iniquitous regimes were predators, too, feeding cruelly on the lives of the African people and on the riches of their land.

I became a participant dedicated and committed to the political and military struggle for freedom and independence that has long been the story of Namibia. The people's goal achieved at last, I have been honoured to serve the Republic of Namibia as its first President.

Now, in the year 2000, I pause not merely to reminisce over the first seventy years of my own life, but — more importantly — to recount how the path of my life has joined with others on the road to independence for Namibia. How that goal was accomplished is the real story of this book.

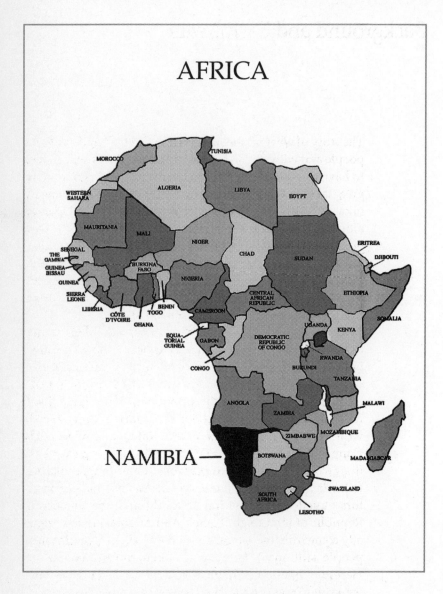
Namibia and the countries of the African Continent (2000)

1

Background and Early Years

The story of what is known today as Namibia begins with the people and with the land. Many of our ancestors are believed to have migrated to the region many centuries ago from the great lakes in Central Africa, such as Lakes Victoria, Tanganyika and others, particularly in the region of Uganda, although for some indigenous people our land has been their home since time immemorial. Their means of livelihood included cattle farming and cultivation of millet, sorghum, groundnuts and beans, which are highly nutritious crops still found in Southern Africa, East Africa, right across Sudan, Egypt and beyond the Red Sea, up to India.

Languages like my own, Oshiuambo, and others similar to the Herero language, are today spoken around Lubango in Angola, among the Mwila and Kipungu people of Matala, up to Bailundo of the Iimbundu people. Crossing over to the Democratic Republic of the Congo and Zambia, you will find Lunda people who are situated in Mwinilunga (northwestern Zambia), and Katangese in Katanga province of the Congo and into Bembaland (Zambia) stretching over Lake Bangweulu, Lake Mweru (Zambia), Lake Tanganyika and Lake Victoria. Some of our historians believe that our ancestors travelled from Central Africa through the Democratic Republic of the Congo, Zambia and Angola, having originally come from the Mountains of the Moon in Uganda where people still speak languages similar to Oshiuambo and Herero of Namibia, Shona of Zimbabwe, Kalanga of Botswana and Tonga of Zambia. These ethnic groupings have, to this day, similarities of language, culture, farming and land

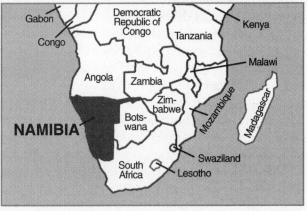

1   NAMIBIA in Southern Africa

cultivation. They may have merged with the Damara people, having met them on the long migration southwards, and settled in the region of south western Africa, now the Republic of Namibia. Eventually, they settled, many centuries ago, on a sandy plain, with mopane (Omisati) forests and savannah grasslands, in the western sector of what is known in English as Ovamboland. The region as a whole was home to nine ethnic groupings, all originally ruled by powerful chiefs.

Pre-colonial and colonial eras — alienation and dispossession

Before I begin to speak of my personal history, I must devote space to the story of the last several hundred years, when the ages-old history of the African people was so drastically diverted from its traditional path.

In the late 1400s, even before the explorer Christopher Columbus set off in the direction of the 'new world' of the Americas, exploration of the Namibian coast had begun by Portuguese, Dutch and English explorers who were, like Columbus, in search of sea routes to the Indies. Later, American and British whalers and sealers operated along the coast in the 1700s, but white settlements inland were first established by missionaries in the early and mid 1800s. Missionaries and traders would befriend the Chiefs, offer them gifts and ask for land. Those given land to settle carried out surveillance and exploration, and sent back information to their countries of origin. In the wake of these foreign 'guests', then, soon came a flood of military reinforcements, and whole territories which offered material or strategic value to the Europeans were claimed by them. In 1793 the Dutch claimed areas including the whaling port of Walvis Bay, which in 1795 came under the control of the British. Rich copper lodes were discovered in the 1800s, and in 1843 a small island near what is now called Lüderitz Bay was found to be a source of valuable guano. The copper regions and Walvis Bay were formally annexed by Britain in 1867 and 1878 respectively.

So the purpose of colonial conquest of the African continent by the western imperial powers was to acquire wealth, and the way to acquire wealth was, of course, to acquire land. For the indigenous people of Namibia, as elsewhere on the continent, the result of what has been called the 'scramble for Africa' by England, France, Germany, Belgium, Italy, Portugal and Spain was drastic and tragic. From the late 1800s to the time of the first World War, German traders in particular resorted to methods which varied from cunning 'trading' deals to the unilateral imposition of boundary 'agreements', as well as subjugation under force of arms. In 1883, coastal lands were acquired by the German merchant Adolf Lüderitz, and soon after that vast inland areas of Gobabis, homelands of the Khaua Namas and eastern Hereros were lost to a German land settlement syndicate. This led to the tragic battle of Otjunda, and to the eventual obliteration of 80% of the Khaua population. When the Herero Chiefs Kahimemua Nguvauva and Nikodemus Kavikunua went to Okahandja to protest, they were arrested, court-martialled and shot as rebels. All this was in line with the avowed German intent and strategy that the indigenous populations should be simply wiped away in order to make room for the colonisers.

After World War I, when 'South West Africa' was subjected, under Mandate, to the rule of South Africa, more and more valuable land passed into the hands of South African settlers. The local black populations were driven, sometimes literally, into 'native reserves', where resources were scarce and subsistence was meagre. This intentional strategy of displacement of blacks from their traditional lands also served to create a supply of cheap labour for the whites, since natives would be forced off their farms to look for work in mines and on white-owned farms.

In the 1920s, the South African Union government continued the land allocation schemes initiated by the previous German colonial rulers. The Union land allocation was much more extensive, an outright give-away scheme that dumped illiterate poor white Afrikaners onto, to all intents and purposes, free Namibian land. They were additionally supported by the government with cash loans, supplies, boreholes for water, cattle and seeds, and schools were built by the government for their children. In the 1930s, the Union government simply looked the other way when loans were not repaid or when farms were not developed.

After World War II, returning white soldiers were rewarded with yet more freeland stretching along the coast of Lüderitz to Walvis Bay. By the mid 1950s all the usable farmland of Namibia was largely in the hands of white Afrikaners. Then in the 1960s came the further intensification of apartheid as the official form and principle of the white South African regime, with its establishment of 'buffer zones' between the established white areas, especially around Kavango and Bushmanland, and the so-called 'homelands' (nefarious invention of the apartheid South African regime) — but all of these are subjects for the following chapters of this book.

2   Herero leaders, chained and awaiting execution, during imperial German occupation

Resistance

Of course, from the beginning of the various colonial occupations, the stories of resistance by the indigenous people are many. In this book it will have to suffice that only some of them can be related, and those only briefly. In short, events would proceed as follows: when the indigenous people resisted colonisation, troops armed with modern weapons would then fight and conquer, and declare the whole country a British or German colony. The people would then be told that they were now under the 'protection' of British or German rule; that they were subjects of the British or German Crown, and would henceforward be expected to obey the laws of their 'protectors'.

Thus over the years, the indigenous people lost not only their traditional homelands, but also control over the natural resources that occurred there. They were herded off their homelands and into 'native reserves', which were the creation of the colonial administrators. In addition to their land, they were also robbed of their individual freedom, their self determination, and even their individual personal dignity, as they were turned into a captive workforce of labouring slaves.

German colonial occupation of the Namibian lands began 'officially' in 1884 as a prelude to the decisions of the infamous 'Berlin Conference' (1884–1885), at which the imperial powers sought to prevent European war over the riches of Africa by dividing the lands officially amongst themselves. On 24 April 1884, the German Chancellor Otto von Bismark declared the Namibian lands to be a German 'protectorate'. In the following years, Namibians suffered greatly under the brutal and destructive colonial German rule.

That the people should resist the capture of their lands, the disruption of their traditional livelihoods and the loss of their ancient freedoms was inevitable. By 1884, Germany had established a number of colonies in Africa: German East Africa Tanganyika (Tanzania), Ruanda, Burundi, Togoland (Togo), Kameruun (Cameroon) and German South West Africa (Namibia). In all these areas, the indigenous peoples attempted to resist the German colonialization.

During the 1880s, the Nama people, under the leadership of Hendrik Witbooi, launched a popular uprising against the German occupation. Hendrik Witbooi was one of the first black men to actually engage in armed resistance against the occupiers. This early resistance was against relatively small German forces, and when Witbooi refused to sign a peace treaty, reinforcements were soon sent from Germany. Nevertheless the resistance continued into the 1900s against ever increasing German military force, during which Witbooi was able not only to attack and kill German soldiers, but also to capture their weapons, supplies and horses.

During the war, Witbooi was for a time forced across the Orange river, which formed a border between the then German South West Africa (now Republic of Namibia) and the British Cape Colony, where he was amongst Nama speaking people. He bought guns from Boers who were retreating towards the north of the Cape during the Anglo-Boer War, pursued by the British troops. He clandestinely returned to Namibia, continuing the campaign of resistance against the German troops, which were steadily increasing in numbers. During one of the many battles between German colonial troops and Nama warriors which Chief Witbooi led, he was finally killed in action at a place near Vaalgras on 29 October 1905.

After the death of Hendrik Witbooi, the resistance by the Nama people continued unabated, this time under the leadership of Jacob Marenga (whom the colonialists referred to as Morenga). Jacob Marenga was also forced out of the country by the now heavily increased

3   (L) Chief Hendrik Witbooi; (R) Chief Samuel Maharero

German troops. Where German forces in Namibia had numbered only in the hundreds at the beginning of Witbooi's campaign of armed resistance, by shortly after the turn of the century there were 17,000. In exile, Marenga gave a press conference, where he clearly stated that, "so long as an inch of South West Africa was occupied by the Germans, the Nama people would continue to attack the Germans wherever they encountered them, until the land conquered by the Germans is returned to the rightful owners". Jacob Marenga also died in one of the fierce battles. It was reported that while he was in the British Cape Colony, the Germans connived with the British about the movements and hideout of Jacob Marenga and his warriors. It would appear that the Nama people were subjugated by the German soldiers with the active participation of the British Governor in the Cape Province.

The Germans went on further inland and encountered the Hereros who were found around Windhoek (known by the Hereros as 'Otjomuise'). Chief Samuel Maharero's palace was situated at Okahandja. The Germans went there and asked Maharero to give them land. This was interpreted in Herero as "ehi", meaning sand, so Maharero thought they were asking for sand, and told his people to give the Germans a bucket of sand. The Germans said 'No! No! We want the land to settle on'. But the somewhat comical confusion was explained, and Chief Maharero agreed to allow the Germans to settle — as he thought, temporarily — on a certain piece of Herero land. This was a genuine gesture of hospitality by Chief Maharero, meant to express respect for the strangers and to treat them as human beings. Also, it must be said that when one offers accommodation to a guest, it is not expected that the guest will occupy the whole house, and then remain there permanently! It became clear that the Germans did not intend themselves as guests, but rather that their settlement was to be permanent, and that they considered themselves to be the owners of the Herero land. This became a cause of war between the Hereros and the Germans. Of course, Chief Maharero would at first have had no understanding that the Germans were desperate for land, and would be willing to cheat, rob and kill Hereros in order to get it.

German missionaries and merchant-traders who were already in the country reported to their government that the central region was well suited to European-style agriculture and cattle farming. Then more German troops and colonial settlers were sent from Germany. They forced the Hereros from their land and confiscated their livestock. Chief Maharero was left with no alternative but to wage a popular war against the German colonial occupiers. As the struggle continued, more and more German troops arrived, this time through the port of Swakopmund where the Germans had already settled. The war intensified from both sides, and the Hereros were suppressed with superior German weapons. Some Hereros went into exile in the then British Bechuanaland, through the Omaheke region where the German Governor Von Trotha issued an extermination order that "every Herero man, woman and child must be killed". At the battle of Ohamakari, when the Hereros retreated towards Omaheke and then crossed into Bechuanaland, German troops threw poison into water-wells knowing precisely that Hereros would drink from them, resulting in a mass murder of the Hereros. Some of the Hereros retreated north to Ovamboland — especially in Oshikoto, Oshana and Omusati Regions — and requested assistance from their Ovambo cousins. Chief Nehale lja Mpingana of Ondonga sent reinforcements to the central region, and battles took place, particularly in the districts of Outjo and Amutuni (currently known as Onamutoni) where many German troops were killed by Ondonga warriors. To the present day, a monument can be seen there, where names are inscribed of German soldiers who died at Onamutoni battle. The names of the dead Ondonga warriors remain unrecorded.

The struggles in Namibia were paralleled in neighbouring countries, where resistance also continued, unabated, to the colonial occupiers and their practices of subjugation and exploitation. In Portuguese colonies, such as Angola and Mozambique, the colonialists had acquired African slaves by sending police to the native chiefs to round up all young and able-bodied men to go to work in sugar and coffee plantations, mines and farms, as well as for domestic servants. If a worker violated the rules or was considered simply to have been rude to his master or mistress, he would be beaten with a 'palmatoria' (piece of wood with protruding nails) underneath the feet, at the palms of the hands and buttocks. To make matters worse, fine salt would be put on the flesh wounds. A person beaten with this infamous weapon would be unable to sit or use his hands, but could only lie on his stomach.

In the early years of the twentieth century, the Portuguese who were advancing in southern Angola towards northern Namibia encountered popular resistance in many battles led by Chief Mandume ja Ndemufajo of the Uukuanjama tribe. The Portuguese were defeated and asked help from South Africa. The combined Portuguese and South African troops fought against Chief Mandume who was killed in action in 1917 at Oihole, which is today part of the Kunene province of the Republic of Angola.

The Portuguese-Ombadja hostilities go back to the time of the Portuguese intrusion into Onghumbi and the occupation of its capital, Omutano, in the early 1880s. To pre-empt Portuguese advances into Ombadja territory, the combined forces of the two Ombadja kingdoms crossed the Kunene River and attacked the Portuguese garrison at Omutano in 1885. But the Ombadja attack on the Portuguese was not successful, and the combined forces of kings Shatona of Omhungu and Haikela of Onaluheke had to retreat. In winter 1891 the Portuguese invaded Ombadja through Onaluheke with the intent of ruthlessly strangulating guerrilla activities and the resistance of the king of Onghumbi, Luhuna, who had found support from the two Ombadja kingdoms. In July 1891 the Portuguese suffered a humiliating defeat at Ondobeyofenge, and their surviving troops retreated to Onghumbi.

4   Chief Nehale lja Mpingana of Ondonga (seated on the right) (c. 1900)

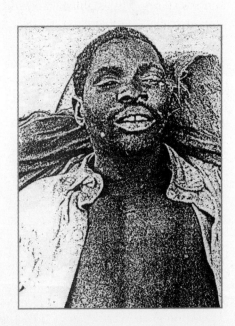

5   In death, Chief Mandume ja Ndemufajo of Uukuanjama (1893–1917), killed in battle of Oihole, 6 February, 1917

In 1904 the Portuguese organized new military expeditions and, after crossing the Kunene River, got involved in battles with the Mbadja warriors at Omwandiwoshivandje, Ouhekeweenghenghe, Omakunghu, and at the famous Evelo la Pembe (also called 'Portuguese Adowa' by some historians because of the catastrophic defeat inflicted on the Portuguese; Portuguese history refers to it as the 'Pembe Disaster').

The reign of King Shihetekela Hiudulu of Ombadja [b.1860–d.1934] was an apocalyptic period which coincided with the third big Portuguese invasion of Ombadja. Shihetekela's warriors were armed with spears, bows and arrows and a few firearms against the first and most sophisticated war machinery in modern colonial history. Because of the thunder of the modern weapons, his allies of the first Anti-Portuguese Greater Ovambo Coalition (1904, in regiments from Ombalantu, Ongandjera, Uukualuudhi and Uukuambi) entered the annals of oral history as having said *"aambadja otaa lu nomvula!"*, meaning literally "The Mbadjas are fighting with the rain".

Some of the most famous battles fought against the Portuguese by Shihetekela and his allies in the Coalition took place at Onhundayevala (1904); Eloveya la Nanghanga, Omufilu (1907); Omukoyimo (1907); Omufitu uaNdeiteja, Oda yanangeda (1907); and Onangovo (1907). After all his defence lines were broken and Omhungu was taken by the Portuguese, Shihetekela retreated to Oukuanjama to organize the resistance. He established himself in Onangodji, near Ombuba yomanyoshe. As relations between Ombadja and Oukuanjama during most of the Hedimbi dynasty were not at their best, Shihetekela had to wait for the Mandume period to step up Ombadja resistance. When Mandume (of whom he was political mentor) ascended to the Oukuanjama throne, Shihetekela organized the Ombadja guerillas. This led to his comeback in 1914 when, after making a blitz attack on the Portuguese flank at Oshihetekela, he progressed eastwards, retaking Ombala yaMhungu, which he found with brick houses built by the Portuguese during their six years of occupation. Thus, in 1914, Shihetekela started what local historians call *"Ouhamba weengulu"* ("reign of palace of bricks"), later also known as *"Ouhamba woihehelela"* ("reign of bad augury"). Shihetekela's arrival was unexpected and the Portuguese had no time to put up any resistance or even pack their belongings. They beat retreat in a disorganized way, leaving everything behind. King Shihetekela sent a big consignment of the arms and ammunition captured from the Portuguese to his ally, King Mandume.

Shihetekela's *Ouhamba weengulu* was very short. It coincided with the outbreak of World War I in 1914 and with the political alignments between Portuguese, British and South Africans in this part of the African sub-continent. Soon Ombadja and, subsequently, also Oukuanjama, found themselves sandwiched between three allied powers of World War I — Portugal, Britain and South Africa — who considered these African kingdoms sympathetic to Germany, their arch-enemy in World War 1.

Still unsettled and faced with the war machinery of World War I advancing into Ombadja in form of an inverted V, and on many fronts in 1915 from Onghumbi, Shihetekela was once again forced to retreat into Oukuanjama. The Portuguese continued with their march and attacked Oukuanjama. Once in Oukuanjama, Shihetekela advised Mandume. Later, when the Kuanjama defence lines broke down after the famous battle of Omongua (called 'Kuanjama Armageddon' by historians because of its ferocity and duration), Omongua and Ondjiva fell. Mandume retreated to Oihole to organize the Kuanjama resistance and guerrilla forces, while Shihetekela settled at Etomba.

Shihetekela was considered to be King Mandume's 'right hand' by colonial authorities at Ondangua, and by King Martin Kadhikwa. He was therefore the 'most wanted man' after Mandume's death in February 1917. Because of his political connection with Mandume, and for being considered a 'danger' to the whole of Ovamboland, Shihetekela was imprisoned by the British Military Government in South West Africa and ostracised to Nkurenkuru *reclusion* in Kavango in 1918, thus inaugurating this first 'Robben Island' on Namibian soil. His old friend King Iipumbu ja Tshilongo would follow him there later in 1933.

In defiance of the colonial authorities, King Shihetekela left the Nkurenkuru *reclusion* prematurely and returned to Ouamboland. He was, however, detected and expelled from Oukuanjama by C.N. Manning. He then settled temporarily in the *bushveld* ('no man's land') between Oukuanjama and Uukuambi at a place called Oshikwiyu (or Akwashika) and which later became known as Onawa yaShihetekela. His friend, Iipumbu, offered him a place to stay at Uuvudhiya. However, Shihetekela declined the offer by saying that the area has no trees and that *ovambadja* are not used to live in *ombuwa* (i.e. desert).

Written sources in the National Archives in Windhoek have it that in 1928 King Shihetekela left Oshikwiyu and went to the 'no man's land' (*ofuka*) of his own country, Ombadja. He became one of the first settlers of Onambome village in Okalongo. King Shihetekela Hiudulu died on 13 September 1934 at the age of 74. His grave is on his former homestead and *omahangu* field at Onambome in Okalongo. A big palm tree rises from it.

6   Chief Iipumbu ja Tshilongo of Uukuambi
    (1873–1959)

In 1932, Chief Iipumbu ja Tshilongo of Uukuambi refused to obey colonial orders from the South African Commissioner Hugo Hahn "Shongola", and also refused to pay taxes to the colonial authority. Commissioner Hahn considered this an act of rebellion and ordered the South African air force to bomb the Chief's palace at Onatshiku. Chief Iipumbu was captured and forcefully exiled in Kavango region. He was later brought to Uukuanjama, then to Uukuambi where he died in 1959.

'Mandate'

During World War I, Germany's Namibian holdings were lost to South Africa, and in 1920 the League of Nations granted South Africa mandatory powers, ostensibly to 'administer' our country and 'prepare us towards self-determination'. Article 22 of the Covenant of the League of Nations did not allocate the former German colonies to the mandatory powers. This was done by the Supreme Council of the Principal Allied and Associated Powers, to which Germany handed over its colonies under the Versailles Treaty (1919). Although the Allies decided who would receive which mandates, no mandate was assigned to any ostensibly qualified 'outsiders'. Article 22 provided that "the degree of authority, control or administration to be exercised by the Mandatory shall be explicitly defined in each case by the Council [of the League]". In fact, the Allies submitted to the Council draft agreements for the 'C' mandates, and these were accepted with minor changes.

The Mandate for German South West Africa read as follows:

"Whereas by Article 119 of the Treaty of Peace Germany signed at Versailles on 28 June 1919, Germany renounced in favour of the Principal Allied and Associated Powers all her rights over the overseas possessions, including therein German South West Africa; and

Whereas the Principal Allied and Associated Powers agreed that, in accordance with Article 22, part 1 (Covenant of the League of Nations) of the said Treaty, a Mandate should be conferred upon His Britannic Majesty to be exercised on his behalf by the Government of the Union of South Africa to administer the Territory aforementioned, and have proposed that the Mandate should be formulated in the following terms; and,

Whereas His Britannic Majesty, for and on behalf of the Government of the Union of South Africa, has agreed to accept the Mandate in respect of the said territory and has undertaken to exercise it on behalf of the League of Nations in accordance with the following provisions: and

Whereas, by the aforementioned Article 22, paragraph 8, it is provided that the degree of authority, control or administration to be exercised by the Mandatory, not having been previously agreed upon by the Members of the League, shall be explicitly defined by the Council of the League of Nations."

South African rule continued from then, on through World War II, all the time increasing and intensifying the oppression and apartheid laws of the regime. In 1946 the League of Nations itself dissolved, and the United Nations assumed negotiations with South Africa to place South West Africa under the trusteeship of the UN. But the new body, dominated at the beginning by Western powers, was unwilling to apply sufficient pressure to make South Africa, their war-time ally under General Smuts, place our country under its trusteeship system.

Instead, South Africa — in order to convince the international community that she had the support of the majority of the South West African people — used dirty tricks. A bogus referendum was held in which the puppet chiefs, mainly from Ovamboland (whom South Africa considered to represent the majority of the population) voted on behalf of their people to incorporate South West Africa as a fifth province of the Union of South Africa. This ploy might have succeeded had it not been for the actions of Chief Tshekedi Khama of British Bechuanaland, and paramount Chief Frederick Maharero of the Hereros, who was living in exile in British Bechuanaland. They sent the Reverend Michael Scott to South West Africa to see Chief Hosea Kutako in 1947. Chief Maharero also wrote a letter warning Chief Kutako about the danger of incorporating South West Africa into the Union of South Africa as the fifth province.

Struggles against oppressive colonial regimes continued to be intensified all over the African continent after World War II. More than thirty years after its end, the still-colonized peoples of Angola, Mozambique, Cape Verde, Guinea-Bissau and Sao Tome & Principé fought heroically to help liberate the European people of Portugal oppressed by the Salazar/Caetano dictatorial regimes. On 25 April 1974, young Portuguese officers, who were often sent to fight and suppress the people's war in Portuguese colonies, decided that enough was enough and launched a military coup which overthrew the Caetano regime and brought freedom and democracy to the European people of Portugal. Credit must be given where it is due — to the heroic and popular armed resistance to Portuguese colonialism by the African patriots in the former Portuguese colonies.

In Angola and Mozambique, migrant labourers had been reserved especially to be recruited to go to work in South African mines. However, there was an agreement between the Anglo-American Corporation and South African authorities to pay British pounds sterling for each labourer recruited from these two Portuguese colonies. The money was exchanged in gold to maintain the Portuguese regime in Europe. Workers were treated like slaves, ill-treated and paid starvation wages, and many of them died, without compensation to their families.

Migrant workers were recruited in Central Africa (then Belgian Congo, Southern Rhodesia, Northern Rhodesia and Nyasaland) and further in East Africa (Kenya, Tanganyika and Uganda). They were transported by Witwatersrand Native Labour Association (WENALA) Transport Planes, which had special aircraft purchased by Anglo-American Corporation. Workers from Kenya would be transported by road to Mbeya in Tanganyika and then to Broken Hill in Northern Rhodesia, thereafter to Mungu in the then Barotseland (now Western province of Zambia). Then they would be flown to Francistown in British Bechuanaland, where they would be transported by railway to Johannesburg.

What must be recognised is that slavery had been abolished by law throughout the world. But in the British colonies of Southern Rhodesia, Northern Rhodesia, Nyasaland, Uganda, Kenya and Tanganyika, and also in the Belgian Congo and in the Portuguese colonies, the slave contract system nevertheless continued until those countries achieved their independence. I recall that immediately after Tanganyika achieved her freedom and sovereignty, Prime Minister Mwalimu Julius Kambarage Nyerere banned the WENALA slave contract system from operating in Tanganyika and WENALA offices closed down at Mbeya.

~~~~~

My family

My maternal grandfather, Kondombolo ka Kambulua, grew up in Uukuambi during the reign of Chief Nujoma ua Heelu [w,Eelu], who was a very popular Chief in the Uukuambi district. Kondombolo was trained as warrior and also as a herbalist. He knew all types of roots that could cure certain diseases including venom from dangerous poisonous snakes like the mamba. He was a fast runner and also a brave warrior. During the Portuguese advance in southern Angola towards northern Namibia in the 1880s–90s, there were fierce battles between the Portuguese invading forces and Mbadja warriors led by Chief Shitekela sha Hiudulu, of whom I have spoken already. My grandfather Kondombolo was among the reinforcements sent by the Chief of Ongandjera. The warriors were armed with spears, bows and arrows, and fought heroically to prevent the Portuguese advancing into northern Namibia, which might otherwise have become part of Portuguese occupied Angola were it not for their brave resistance. With a spear, Kondombolo killed a Portuguese soldier and captured a carbine gun which he brought back to Ongandjera. He was considered to be one of the heroes in the district and was presented with many cattle by the Chief of Ongandjera. As a boy, I was proud that I had been born into such a respected family.

My parents, both father and mother, like my grandfather and many generations before them, were also born in Uukuambi, and were both from the royal families of that region. My father was Utoni Daniel Nujoma —

> Nujoma ua Mutshimba
> Mutshimba gua Kandenge
> Kandenge ka Negumbo
> Negumbo lja Koongoti

— being his grandparents' names. All these names are of a generation of chiefs of Uukuambi. He was later baptized Daniel Utoni Nujoma.

It was said that in ancient times our chiefs were fetched from a very distant place by envoys who would go away for three to four years to the north, where they would find the new Chief among people who spoke a language similar to our own. The new Chief-to-be would be brought back after a time to live among beautiful women who had been specially chosen within the tribe. From them he would learn the language, and he would then succeed as the Chief.

During my parents' childhood, however, the young ones from the royal clan, particularly the boys, were always at risk of being eliminated because they would have been trained to defend the Chief's palace and might be in the way of others aspiring to the throne. So at one point in my parents' early years the Chief died and there was, of course, conflict to decide who, from among the royal family members, was going to succeed to the throne. My father therefore had to be rushed with his parents to the Ongandjera district, while he was still a small boy, as he would have been caught up in the power struggle. The same happened to my mother's family, the Kondombolos.

Traditionally, as elsewhere in the world, when a son of the Chief of an ethnic grouping in the north, whether from Uukuanjama, Ondonga or one of the other groupings, goes to settle among another ethnic grouping in another part of the north, he is still respected and considered to be from the royal family. Thus, my father was brought up in the royal family of Ongandjera and he was given the task of looking after the Chief's horses, often staying 30 km away from the residential areas, or homesteads where people lived, at a cattle post in the forest where grazing was plentiful.

My father grew up together with the San Community (Bushmen), from whom he learned how to prepare poisons which were cooked for 24 hours, fermented and put on the arrow heads to shoot and kill antelopes such as Kudu or Oryx. An animal struck with such a poisoned arrowhead will die quickly, thus assuring the hunter of fresh meat. He learned also which types of snakes were not poisonous and were edible, such as python, and also how to cook them and to prepare a good meal. This was done by digging a hole, wrapping the meat with mopane tree leaves, making a fire and putting the meat in the hole with hot sand on top of the leaves and covered with charcoal that had been burning in the fire. After two or three hours there would be very delicious cooked meat, as if it had been grilled in the oven.

During those days, my father used to be active in hunting, especially of giraffe and eland. The large skin of the giraffe was specially prepared and always worn by the chief's senior wife. When my father was a boy he would never ride a horse, but always ran alongside while more senior members of the family of the Chief, his councillors or warriors would ride on horseback. Later, when hunting on horseback himself, he would make sure that his mount went where the giraffe or eland he was chasing had just passed through, before the branches of the trees closed up. My father's body was marked with great scars, where the flesh had been torn off in the chase by thorns of trees or branches.

7   *Tate Daniel Utoni Nujoma*

My father was known to be one of the best runners in the whole district of Ongandjera, and he was also a famous hunter. If a beast such as a lion caused trouble or attacked cattle or goats in the surroundings, my father was often one of those who were called to deal with it because he was a sharpshooter with bow and arrows. No animal could get away if it ran in front of him — once he had taken aim he would shoot to kill, often with a single arrow. He was also a sharpshooter with firearms. Having grown up at the Chief's palace, he knew all about these weapons and was well versed in their usage.

My mother was also from the Chief's family. In my mother's family, my mother is:

Mpingana–Helvi ja Kondombolo
Kondombolo ka Nakathingo
Nakathingo ja Kaambulua
Kaambulua ka Hango
Hango ja Ndjuluua
Ndjuluua ja Kiinge
Kiinge ka Mukongo
Mukongo gua Tshijala
Tshijala tsha Namundjanga
Namundjanga gua Nambala

These names were also all from the Chiefs of Uukuambi ethnic grouping in Omusati Region. When my mother was grown she was baptised Helvi Kondombolo. I can still remember her father, my grandfather Kondombolo ka Nakathingo. I saw him when I was about four years old. He would have been born before the missionaries from Finland came to Ovamboland in 1870, which was itself before the Germans took the southern part of Namibia as a colony in 1884.

Of my immediate family with whom I grew up at my parents' home, I was the first born. I was born on 12 May 1929 in Ongandjera district. My sister Maria, who was immediately after me, died when she was a small child. Then came Frieda, who lives with my mother now as a widow. We were 11 children in all and all at home together, but now we are only six — three boys: myself, Hiskia and Noah, and three girls: Frieda, Sofia and Julia. We lost five. One was my younger brother Elia (Kanjeka), who joined us in the struggle for liberation in Zambia through Angola. He was among hundreds of the Peoples' Liberation Army of Namibia (PLAN), SWAPO military wing volunteers who were given intensive military training in Zambia and returned to the northeastern front, where he died in battle on 1 January 1976.

As the eldest son, I had to look after them all, even carrying the little ones on my back. In our tradition, the mother would work on the land cultivating mahangu (millet), groundnuts and other crops, together with the father. I had to look after the cattle and goats, separating the calves from their mothers to prevent them from sucking milk from the cows before my father and I had milked the cows to provide milk for the family. I had a tough time having to do this with a baby on my back — sometimes also holding another by hand. Other boys used to laugh at me, calling out, "Look at this one! Why is he carrying a baby on his back

8   With my mother, Mpingana-Helvi Kondombolo, on the day of my return to Namibia from exile, 14 September 1989

like a girl?". But as I was the first-born, even though a boy, I had to do it. I would drive our cattle in a different direction so that my fellow cattle herders would not see me and laugh at me. In the evening we were supposed to milk the cows, put the milk in a calabash, produce butter and keep the milk, too.

My mother remembers how she once heard me singing, very loudly near our homestead, a song I had learnt from other boys when we were looking after cattle: "I'm going to make a problem with the whites". She threatened me with her belt to make me stop as it was a taboo for a child to sing so loudly. I had learnt the word 'problem' somehow, but did not know what it meant. In those early days boys knew they would grow up and be recruited into the contract labour system. Some of the elder boys who went to work in the South told us dreadful stories of cruelties committed by white masters, of workers who were beaten or even shot to death. Horror stories were told that some white employers fed their pigs with the flesh of black workers who would then be reported as having escaped. When we were old enough to be recruited we used to prepare ourselves against the possibility of being employed by a cruel Boer who would assault or beat workers with a whip. We trained ourselves in the art of hitting back, and the song my mother heard me singing was about how to fight the white man in self-defence.

My boyhood

My mother was in charge of the household, and worked in the fields (as she continued to do well into her nineties, although she could sit at home and do nothing if she so wished). As I was the eldest son, I sometimes had to assist my mother by pounding the millet when she was not feeling well because otherwise we would have had no flour for the porridge which we normally ate during lunch or dinner time. I would also help to fetch fresh water, as well as looking after my young sisters. One of my main duties was to look after cattle, 'the profession' I enjoyed very much, like all other boys of those days.

Near the houses, where there were many cattle, there would not be enough grass to keep the cattle in good condition, so I would have to go far, and my companions and I would stay together with the cattle. When summer came and grazing was most scarce, I would sometimes have to go to the cattle posts, perhaps 20 to 30 km away. There grazing was to be found, especially from September to December, and I would stay as long as three months.

We boys would have to know how to sharpen arrows for our bows to be ready to defend the cattle from being attacked by lions. In those days, there were still lions in some places, because the area was not as densely populated as today. The further one went from people, the more lions and leopards one encountered, but this was the only way we could find good grazing. We had to make sure that the cattle were kept fat so that they could produce enough milk, and more calves. At the cattle post we lived mainly on milk and also on wild fruits, which made us healthy.

I remember during the early 1940s there was a very severe drought so there was hardly any grazing. When it eventually rained somewhere, the cattle could smell grass and fresh water far away and would move rapidly in that direction, and I would have to drive them there. This way of life really taught us to be self-reliant and tough.

My father made sure that I was properly trained and prepared both mentally and physically. I had to go through all the ethnic and tribal rituals, with the clear purpose that as a man I would be able to undertake initiatives and succeed in the most difficult missions. My father often told me that I must be responsible and be able to look after myself, even if he was not there to take care of me.

It was the custom every year, about the month of June when the rains had just ended, for the elders and fully grown boys to journey to the salt pan in the district of Ongandjera (locally known as Ekango ljo

Mongua). From there fresh salt would be fetched which would be processed and stored for home consumption. The salt was also important and valuable because it would be used for barter, along with other goods, with neighbouring districts of Ombalantu and Uukwanjama, and sometimes over the borders in Angola where there were no salt pans available. According to our tradition, when a boy first went to fetch salt, it was expected that he would go all the way on foot as a sign of maturity and strength.

One day in 1942, I learnt that my family's acquaintance — whose last born I am named after — was going in a donkey wagon to the salt pan, and that I was to go along. Before the journey began, though, I expected that since I was really under age, and since the adult was my father's friend, my main task on the journey would be to look after the donkeys when we rested for them to graze, and that I would be allowed to ride on the wagon now and then. We set off after lunch one day, and at first I was allowed to ride on the wagon. But as soon as we entered the thick forest, I was told in no uncertain terms that I had to walk on my two feet all the way to our destination. I jumped out of the wagon and took a lead, holding and pulling the front donkey when we moved through the deep sands. I also looked after the donkeys so that they were not attacked by lions that were plenty in the bush and were very fond of donkey meat. I was a little bit concerned when I saw what resembled a grey cat, and the donkeys became nervous, probably after the smell of a lion blew in their direction. I reported to the elders what I had seen in the dry grass, and was told to gather wood quickly, make fire around the wagon and bring the donkeys nearer to ensure that they were safe. I was later on told that lions often fear to come close where there is fire burning.

We continued the next morning, walking for five days and nights. During the long journey, it was for the first time in my life that I had ever been so utterly exhausted. I fell asleep and dreamed even while moving alongside the wagon. The older person I was with threatened to whip me with a fresh mopane branch if I did not move along quickly, and at one point I was almost overrun by the wagon. Nevertheless we finally arrived back home. When my mother saw me she started sounding traditional words of praise. She instructed the girls to slaughter a big cock, which was then cooked in special gravy extracted from marura tree nuts — a feast normally prepared for very important guests in the house. My father presented a goat as a sign of gratitude to me, a small boy who had brought salt to the family. This female goat produced many young ones, and I was very happy and proud to possess goats of my own. I felt well rewarded after the long hard journey to fetch salt, and I learned the value of undertaking difficult missions in one's life.

During my boyhood, looking after the cattle was my main activity, and schooling came second or even third in my mind. I started to go to the Finnish Missionary Society School at Okahao, near Ethiya Ombupupu, at about the age of 10. [The school is still there, but if one visits it today one will see how it had been shelled by South African troops during the war of liberation. Even though the South Africans claimed to be civilized and committed Christians, if one goes to Okahao, the modern church there also bears the holes of machine gun bullets. These were fired from the South African military base which was deliberately established close to the two Secondary Schools and the Church building to harass the students, and the population in general during Sunday church services.] Eventually though, I finished my Standard Six, with Wilhelm Amutenja as my teacher. Though I was still young, I could not go for Standard Seven as it was not provided at that school. The only option open for me in order to proceed with education then was to be prepared to be a clergyman, and again, I was too young to be considered. Procedurally, one had to be mature and allowed to take Holy Communion. Only then one could be considered to go to a seminary school where boys could be trained to become clergymen.

When World War II had just ended, my aunt Julia Gebhard Nandjule, who was my father's cousin, married to my father's relative Hilma Mushimba, came to the north from Walvis Bay to visit her parents. She was a widow, and in our tradition she could not be expected to live alone. Though she had lived with a girl, a daughter of her elder sister who passed away, it was thought in the family that the girl, Magdalena Shimbambi, was too young to provide the necessary support to Mother Julia. I was a little bit older and had just finished my Standard Six. Mother Julia asked my father if he could allow me to go and live with her in Walvis Bay, in place of Magdalena. My father reluctantly agreed. Magdalena then remained with her grandparents in Ongandjera, and I went to Walvis Bay in December 1946.

It might now seem a simple, private, family matter that I should travel a few hundred miles to another town, to live with my aunt. But during the apartheid regime even such private decisions were under the force of law. Boys of my age fell under the contract work and travel restrictions of the apartheid regime, so my departure was delayed until a friend of Mother Julia, Meme Aune Katangolo, who had the names of many children endorsed in her travelling pass, could include my name. I was still young, but I was told to join them and we departed from Ondangua through Tsumeb to Grootfontein. There we caught the train to Swakopmund where we spent a few days before continuing our journey to Walvis Bay. While we were travelling in a third class compartment, I saw a group of men being transported in cattle trucks. I asked Mother Aune Katangolo why these people were travelling in cattle trucks. She told me that they were contract workers going to the places of their employers. It shocked me very much but there was nothing I could do at that time.

As young boys looking after cattle and gathering firewood, we always talked about strategies and future plans to get engaged to girls and get married. But before one could get married one had to work in order to accumulate some wealth. In those days one way of preparing to build one's own homestead was to look for employment in southern Namibia. For blacks, travelling required a pass issued by the colonial authority, and finding employment was also heavily restricted by law. The only option, if we wanted to work in the south, was to become a contract labourer.

Boys in rural regions such as Ovamboland, Kavango and Kaokoland were recruited by SWANLA (South West Africa Native Labour Association). This was a notorious South African government-sponsored organization which took young boys and able-bodied men to work for the white settlers as near-slave labourers in mines, farms, factories and as domestic servants in towns like Windhoek, Omaruru and others in central and southern Namibia. We heard stories of abuse and humiliation of the contract workers at the hands of white employers. But only later in my education did I personally come to learn the full history of the system. It had begun in the 19th century when the African continent came under the control of the various colonial powers. It was for this source of cheap labour that the white German and South African colonial administration had come into Ovamboland then, sending people like Native Commissioner Major Hugo Hahn "Shongola" to see to it that men were forced, by economic pressure such as taxation and by order of the traditional Chiefs and Headmen who collaborated with the colonial administrators, to go to the south for long periods of 'contract' employment. Stories were well known to us of workers paid starvation wages and being badly treated, especially on the Boer farms, even to the extent that some of them never returned home.

Each of the various colonial governments had instituted different systems of slavery and forced labour. In northern Namibia, indigenous people in Ovamboland, Kaokoland and Okavango were not allowed to freely seek employment in the central and southern regions, except through SWANLA. Workers from these regions were not allowed to leave the country to look for employment in other neighbouring countries such as South Africa, even though Namibia was a South African colony. They were exclusively restricted in order to provide cheap labour to minority white settlers in Namibia, except the Caprivians who were recruited by WENALA to work in South African mines.

Workers recruited through SWANLA were systematically humiliated: for example, transported in a cattle truck with tags around their necks on which the names of their masters-to-be were written. For instance, a worker who was going to work on a farm in the district of Gobabis had to travel through many other districts, during which a train conductor would go through the cattle trucks reading out his master's name. When reaching the destination he would be told to follow the road leading to his master's farm.

Since the white settler employers paid a certain amount of money to SWANLA in order to be provided with cheap labourers, such whites would normally consider that they had actually bought the workers and considered them as slaves. Young boys could be sent away to work for as long as two years before the contract expired, without leave to visit families, and entitled neither to sick leave nor to be accompanied by any family member, including even a wife. Families would not be allowed to visit, even in the event of terminal illness. And in the event of injury or death of any worker, there would be no compensation paid to the family.

I personally witnessed the results of the cruelty of white employers while working at the railway station in the late 1940s. It happened one day, early in the morning, that I found a young boy of about 15 years who had been dropped off at the station by a train that had come in from the south. This boy was paralysed as a result of having been beaten with a whip by his white master. He was naked and had only a sack which he carried in his arms. I rode my bicycle home and fetched a shirt which I gave to him. Afterwards, I saw to it that he was taken to hospital by the railways' police. Luckily, he was young and able to recover from his wounds. His master reported to SWANLA that the boy had run away and demanded, therefore, to be supplied with another worker.

This slavery went on in South West Africa after it had long been abolished in other parts of the world. But many minds and hearts, including mine, had by now been set to fight and put an end to the contract system, and to achieve genuine freedom and independence.

~~~~~

This is something, then, of the background against which both my personal and political history began. It seems clear to me now that, from such beginnings and in such surroundings, there could have been no other path for me than to take up and continue the people's struggle for freedom and independence, which has culminated in the creation of the Republic of Namibia.

The words of King Mandume ja Ndemufajo were inspirational to me as a young man of awakening political awareness, about to join in battle, on many fronts, against colonialism.

> *Oililima jokongulu itai dulika.*
> *Oifendela jokongulu ojeehama.*
> *Oupika nefjo shimuaashike.*

> The payment of capital tax to the colonial master
>   is a tiresome exercise.
> And colonial vassal reporting is unbearable.
> Death and slavery are one and the same thing.

And the prophetic challenge of these words, spoken by King Iipumbu ja Tshilongo, could not be ignored.

> *Nande mu kuate ndje;*
> *Oohiinina taa ja tshito*
> *je mu tse otshiti.*

> You can hold me hostage; but the day will come
> When our children will take revenge
> and teach you a lesson.

◆ ◆ ◆

2

Walvis Bay and Windhoek

On my arrival in Walvis Bay in December 1946, my aunt Julia Gebhard Nandjule welcomed me with open arms and was happy that I had finally joined her. She loved me very much, and frequently she would return from work with a piece of cake or other treat for me. We lived a happy life.

In 1947, at the age of 17, I began work, for a monthly salary of 10 shillings, at a general store owned by Hugo Ludwig, a German national. Hugo Ludwig and his brother Peter had not identified themselves during the war as pro-Nazi, and now, unlike other Germans who were pro-Nazi and had been interned, they were allowed to carry on with their business. By the end of 1947 my salary had increased from 10 shillings to one pound per month. However, this was still too little, so I left and sought employment at a Whaling Station run by a Norwegian (Walvis Bay actually means 'Whale Bay').

The Norwegians used to go far into the South Atlantic Ocean to hunt whales. These would be harpooned from small boats, and would then be towed to the accompanying larger factory ships for processing. My Norwegian employer had a shore station for repairing small boats, and there I earned a little money to buy clothing for my brothers and sisters, and later on a sewing machine for my mother, which pleased my parents very much. My life in Walvis Bay had taught me to be self-reliant and was enjoyable, with much of my social life centred around the family.

In Walvis Bay I made friends with people old and young, and I enjoyed working, particularly with Salatiel Nghaamua

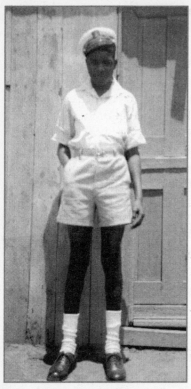

9 (Left) The young Sam Nujoma. Walvis Bay, 1948

10 (Below) with Cousin Johannes Ushona, 1954

who was a bit older than I. Both of us were fascinated by the South African, British, Norwegian and other European soldiers who were still stationed in Walvis Bay. Although the war had ended in May 1945, there was suspicion that German U-boats remained at large, and soldiers continued to man the artillery emplacements at Rand Rifles, the Lagoon and at Pelican Point. Most of the infantrymen had been discharged and were returning to South Africa and other countries of their origin, but some of those manning long range artillery, and the Navy, and at the air force base at Rooikop, stayed until 1948. At the end of 1946, when I had just arrived there, rumours went round among the residents of Walvis Bay that a German spy had turned into a jackal and had been seen at the Cold Storage near the harbour. Of course, this proved only to be one of the ordinary jackals which, as normal, prowled the coast scavenging dead fish and seals.

Salatiel and I were always looking at soldiers with great admiration, especially when they drilled, making about-turns and saluting. Salatiel and I bought some military boots from the soldiers which cost us about five shillings and we used to practise with those boots, kicking other boys when playing football. At times, we kicked some white boys who referred to us as 'Kaffirs'.

At this time I was not yet politically aware that Walvis Bay was an enclave of South Africa. World War II had just ended and the National Party had not yet come to power in South Africa. The United Party was still in office, led by General Smuts, who during the World War II had fully collaborated with the British against Nazi Germany. The National Party, which came to power in 1948, led by Dr. Daniel François Malan and Dr. Hendrik Fresch Verwoerd, had supported Nazi Germany and had sent their Boer commandos to fight on the side of Hitler against the Allied Forces. All Namibians who lived in Walvis Bay at that time considered Walvis Bay to be part and parcel of the hinterland South West Africa, as it was known by its colonial name.

In Walvis Bay, I was exposed to modern world politics by meeting soldiers from Argentina, Norway and other parts of Europe who had been brought there during World War II. I remember a particular instance when a British warship arrived at the harbour, and the public was invited for an inside tour and observation. My friends and I went on board and were shown around the ship, down below in the engine room, the Captain's cabin and the big guns on the deck of the vessel. We were served with tea and cakes in typical British fashion. Many South African Boers turned up but, as was their practice, refused to tour the ship while blacks were still present. Those Boers who waited for the blacks to come ashore were disappointed when they were told that it was too late for them to board the ship.

As young people we were not afraid of the whites, and certainly did not feel inferior to them. We, however, as Africans, knew first-hand and were concerned about the oppression and racial discrimination, the pass laws which restricted the movements of the indigenous people, SWANLA's modern slavery contract labour system, and the starvation wages paid to the Africans in their own country. Nevertheless, the idea of South West African politics was still developing as this was the year, 1947, when Chief Hosea Kutako — the Herero paramount Chief who became the father of modern Pan-African politics in South West Africa — was visited by the Reverend Michael Scott, who worked as a British clergyman with the Anglican church in South Africa, and spoke genuinely to indigenous South West Africans as equals.

The Reverend Michael Scott became our first link with the outside world where he helped to start the long struggle for South West African freedom and independence, by petitioning the United Nations on behalf of Chiefs Hosea Kutako and Samuel Witbooi.

I worked for another year in Walvis Bay until the sad news of the death of my aunt Julia, who died from tuberculosis at the end of 1948 while visiting her parents in the north. The death of my aunt Julia shocked me greatly, and since I was still young, I had to find another home in which to stay. I then went to Windhoek at the beginning of 1949 to join my uncle, Hiskia Kondombolo, the last-born in my mother's family.

In Windhoek I worked by day, and at night attended adult school where classes were taught in English. I had finished primary school at Okahao, but there we had not been taught English, only Afrikaans. In the north at that time, English was taught only at Odibo, at St. Mary's Anglican Mission about 100 km north-east of my home district. People would travel long distances to attend St. Mary's School. So despite the fact that I left school before the Bantu Education Act came into force in South Africa in 1953, and imposed later in South West Africa, the syllabus of the Finnish Missionary Society primary school had still been inadequate. Consequently, in Windhoek I concentrated hard on learning English.

I was introduced to St. Barnabas Night School by Tate Aaron Hamutenya, who was working for the South African Railways in the locomotive yard. He was a very kind man (who was the father of our

11 [L to R] Aaron Kapere, the Reverend Michael Scott, Katjikuru Katjiongua and Fritz Zaire. Partners in opposition to colonial rule over South West Africa. 1947

current Minister of Trade and Industry, Honourable Hidipo Hamutenya) who helped me a great deal. Every night we would go together to classes, from 7 p.m. to 10 p.m. I rode my bicycle to work early the next morning to start at 6 a.m., cleaning the Boers' offices before they arrived at 8 a.m. to commence their daily office work.

In Windhoek, lies were circulated to discourage us from learning English. For instance, it was repeated that 'all those people who are being taught English should watch out: it is a language of mad people, and they will soon go mad. You will see them standing, speaking English to an anthill or a pool of water'. Much nonsensical propaganda against English was spread about, but this did not discourage us, as more people continued to learn English.

The authorities saw how many Africans were attending St. Barnabas Night School, and that they included members of the Roman Catholic and Lutheran churches. They realized that all of us attending there, despite our separate religious denominations, were interested in learning a foreign language which would arm us with knowledge. So, while I was in Standard Five, English was prohibited as a medium of instruction and Afrikaans was imposed.

I had already learned to read English at St. Barnabas School, but after the ban on teaching English, I left and took private study by enrolling as a student at the Trans-Africa Correspondence College in Johannesburg, again with the encouragement of Tate Aaron Hamutenya. We both joined the correspondence college, and paid the fees for our lectures. We sat for private examination at the Anglican church hall with the Anglican clergyman serving as invigilator. One still had to take Afrikaans as a subject, but all subjects were taught in English. This was how I improved my English, and I still continue to study wherever the opportunity arises.

~~~~~

My uncle Hiskia Kondombolo lived in the Old Location in Windhoek where he was the so-called Advisory board-man, appointed in accordance with the old South African apartheid system.

I started working as an office sweeper with the South African Railways (SAR) in Windhoek, immediately after getting my working-pass from the Native Commissioner in March 1949. With a starting salary of £5 per month, I continued to support my parents, and brothers and sisters who were at school. They still lived outside the 'cash economy', and for them money was very hard to obtain although they had enough food throughout the year, such as millet, sorghum, beans and groundnuts. Our family led a happy life and had adequate food at home.

From Windhoek, the SAR catered not only for South West Africa but administratively also for South African districts such as Upington, Springbok and Prieska in the northern Cape Province. The System Manager was always appointed from Pretoria. I began to learn about the racial discrimination that existed in an extreme form on the railways where Afrikaners predominantly occupied supervisory positions. Posts of many kinds were reserved for whites only, even for those who lacked any education. The drivers of motor cars used by railway officials, for example, were all white and it was forbidden for a black person to be a driver. Even while cleaning a vehicle, blacks were not allowed to touch the steering wheel. That was taken as a threat to the job of a white man, and a cleaner could be fired with immediate effect for such an offence. Painting was equally for white men: the blacks could climb up the ladder to clean the old paint but a white person would come and do the painting.

Such demeaning practices had existed before the National Party came to power, but the situation became more serious when the National Party won the general election in South Africa in 1948, under Daniel Malan, with Hendrik Verwoerd as his Minister of Native Affairs from 1951. Verwoerd later introduced innumerable repressive laws to govern the lives of blacks. He even instructed that trousers worn by blacks should have one leg shorter than the other so that blacks would be seen to be different from whites even in their clothing. Similar discrimination was also applied to cemeteries and residential areas.

We saw how the Boers, now that they had their own government, looked after their own people — at the expense of blacks. Hundreds of Boers came from as far as south of De Aar to work on the railways. Some of them were very poor, even bare-footed, and all were given jobs superior to the highest paid black railway employees, who were considered inferior. This reflected the superior position the Boers considered themselves to have in relation to the English and other whites in South Africa.

In my job at the railways, I became an office cleaner at the System Manager's offices, and when Mr. C. S. Middlewick was the System Manager and travelled by private coach I went along to serve him. He was quite a good person and I was a hard worker, so we got along very well. When he was transferred back to South Africa we went to Pretoria in a private coach (later used by the Administrator) to fetch his successor, J.P. Hugo, a Boer. I served as a waiter and somebody else was a cook. The Boers liked everything shining, and when the new man and his wife came on board they found that everything satisfied their high expectations. They were extremely happy with the food we served them, though I was amused at the way the new man and his wife ate: they finished everything and left nothing for us workers who could not normally eat before our 'bosses'.

My co-worker, the cook, spoke Afrikaans, which pleased the System Manager. On his birthday he and his wife entertained the Administrator, the South African Chief Executive Officer in South West Africa, to dinner. The System Manager often invited me to serve his guests, which I did, so we again got on well together, in our two different worlds. To me, he was a reasonable human being, but nevertheless, in general the Boers working on the railways were very oppressive.

Windhoek railway station was a good example of apartheid in practice: whites bought their travelling tickets inside the station, coloureds (mixed race) outside but under the cover of some shade, and blacks out in the open where they had to purchase their tickets from behind a wooden screen so that they could not see the white ticket clerk. This was insulting, but trivial compared to the treatment of contract workers on the railways. I saw much of this myself, as I could volunteer for overtime to boost my earnings, doing work on the line, especially after the railway lines were washed away in the south.

Contract workers were brought in to work in the goods shed and on the construction of the railway itself, where we could work side by side in my overtime. In the event of an accident, causing a man to have a leg amputated or lose an arm, SAR would simply send him back to the north through SWANLA, and recruit a new worker. No compensation whatsoever was paid. It was from seeing this happen that I learned — more than from anything else — that we had to do something in order to change the situation.

~~~~~

After living with my uncle Hiskia Kondombolo, I bought a house of my own in the Old Location in Windhoek. Exactly like Katutura — which succeeded it as the segregated home to which the Boers forcibly moved black Namibians from Windhoek — the Old Location had been divided into so-called tribal units. The houses in the Herero section had a capital "H" on the door, those in the Ovambo section were marked "OV", Damaras were labelled with a "D" and Namas with a capital "N". If you were not a Herero, you could not get a plot and stay in the Herero section. This was all part of the system of apartheid, and its policy of divide and rule.

In 1956 when I was earning a little more on the railways, I got married to Theopoldine Kovambo Katjimune. She was called Kovambo, to signify her as an Ovambo child because her mother was a Herero and

12   Wedding, Windhoek — Old Location, 1956

her father was an Ovambo. She was born in Windhoek and our families were connected on her stepfather's side. Her stepfather was Johannes Mushimba and closely related to my father and my aunt at Walvis Bay, all being part of the Aakuambi royal house.

They visited us in Walvis Bay as they were friends of my aunt and so we were children together. I started writing to Kovambo when she returned to Windhoek and our relationship developed in that way. Our wedding was in the Old Location. It was the first attended by a white photographer from Ottilie Nitzsche photo studio in Windhoek, to whom I paid six pounds.

13   Theopoldine Kovambo Katjimune holding baby daughter Nelago;
     Utoni Daniel (standing); Sakaria Nefungo (seated L);
     John Ndeshipanda (seated R), 1958

Our three sons, Utoni Daniel, John Ndeshipanda and Sakaria Nefungo were born in 1952, 1955 and 1957 respectively. Our daughter Nelago was born in 1959, and was only 18 months old when she died, sadly while I was in exile. I could not attend my only daughter's funeral without being arrested by the Boers.

My job at the railways made it easy for me to travel in a country where everything possible was done to prevent blacks from getting passes to travel and see how others lived. In 1955–56 I was thus able to visit Cape Town where there were already Namibians living. Our meeting place was a barbershop in Somerset Road, run by Timothy Kambonde.

I was also able to gain insight into the political outlook of the whites by being in the System Manager's office. It surprised me that white employees of the National Party and United Party only read their own party newspapers, *Die Suidwester*, *Suidwest Afrikaaner* and *Windhoek Advertiser* respectively. They could be shocked to see their fellow members reading the other party's newspaper. For me and my friends, newspapers were not only a vital aid in our effort to learn English, but also an important source of political information. Apart from reading the local *Windhoek Advertiser* I also used to read the *Star*, *Cape Times* and *Cape Argus*. These South African newspapers seemed to us, by South West African standards, very progressive, mainly because they carried news about the outside world. We knew about Indian independence in 1947 and were inspired by the seizure of power by Sukarno of Indonesia in 1945, by Abdul Nasser's victory against Britain, France and Israel for control of the Suez Canal in 1956. The most important of all these press reports, however, were those of Ghana's independence in 1957, which had a tremendous impact and provided a ray of hope for the future of our own liberation.

The pattern of my life had completely changed by then, through the chain of events that began in South West Africa in 1947 when the Reverend Michael Scott, on behalf of Chiefs Hosea Kutako and Samuel Witbooi, commenced the petitioning of the UN.

In 1957, at the age of 29, I resigned from the SAR with the purpose of devoting my time to politics. However, I had to face the problem that, by law, an African not employed or in the service of a white man would not be allowed to live in Windhoek or elsewhere in the urban districts. My solution was to seek employment with the Windhoek Municipality doing some clerical work. But when I found myself doing the work of lazy Boers, with too little money as my salary, I resigned and found employment with Hurbert Davis, a subsidiary of a Cape Town company which supplied and fitted electric cables in new buildings. The manager liked my work, but other whites did not, so I left and moved to another job with Carsten Veld, a South African manufacturing representative and wholesaler.

On the 2nd August 1957, the Ovamboland People's Congress (OPC) was formed by Namibians who were working in Cape Town, South Africa. Its aims and objectives were to petition the United Nations to force the South African regime to agree to surrender South West Africa to the Trusteeship Council of the United Nations and also to terminate the inhumane contract system under which Namibians from the north and north-east were forced to work for meagre wages. Comrade Andimba Toivo ya Toivo, one of the founder members, personally worked on such a contract from 1944–45. During that whole time his wage was equal to only N$10 or N$11 a month.

In 1958, Comrade Ya Toivo sent a message to the UN through Mr. Mburumba Kerina who was a student at Lincoln University, and also the first Namibian petitioner at the United Nations, together with the Reverend Michael Scott. The message was a request to the UN to exert pressure on South Africa to relinquish its administration over South West Africa and allow the Trusteeship Council to take over the administration of the Territory. For security reasons, Comrade Ya Toivo sent the message both as a tape-recording concealed in a copy of the book *Treasure Island* by Robert Louis Stephenson, and as a letter. The letter was the first to reach its destination, and Kerina read it to the Fourth Committee of the General Assembly. When the tape arrived, also safely, Mr. Kerina proposed to the members that they listen to the tape, but they declined because they had already heard its contents from the letter. Nevertheless, this message made the headlines in the *New York Times*, and it led to Ya Toivo's expulsion from Cape Town. He was given 72 hours, and left Cape Town on the 4th December 1958, together with Mr. Jariretundu Kozonguizi, deported to Windhoek and then to Ondangua.

In 1959, while still working with Carsten Veld, I received a letter from Comrade Ya Toivo informing me that he had been threatened with deportation to Angola by the Boers who normally collaborated with the Portuguese at Oshikango border post. I sent a telegram to the UN Secretary-General, urging him to stop the South African regime from sending Comrade Ya Toivo to Angola. Within a few hours of sending the telegram, two Special Branch policemen came to my work place pretending that they wanted to see me because I had applied for employment with their company. I knew I had never made application seeking employment with any such company. Nevertheless, I went out and saw their vehicle parked in front of our office, in it one white policeman whom I had never met before, accompanied by a native policeman by the name of Martin Nangombe. As soon as I approached the vehicle, Mr. Blaauw, who was a chief of Special Branch recently transferred from South Africa to South West Africa, asked me if I was Sam Nujoma who sent a telegram to the UN Secretary-General telling lies that Ya Toivo was being threatened with deportation to Angola. I answered affirmatively. I informed him that I had received a letter from Ya Toivo, whereupon he began insulting me and saying again that I was telling lies. Mr. Blaauw was short and thin, and since I did not know who he was I caught him firmly and threw him back in the car. There were white onlookers at a grocery place nearby who laughed at what happened between me and Mr. Blaauw as I walked away.

Incidents such as this only served to cement my dedication to changing the political situation. Things became worse after Verwoerd succeeded J. G. Strijdom as South African Prime Minister in 1958. Many of the extreme laws of apartheid were experimented in South West Africa, where the Boers' actions went unquestioned — unlike in South Africa where there was frequent criticism from the English and also from Afrikaner members of the opposition United Party.

Most serious, of course, was the situation developing in Windhoek, as the apartheid regime instituted the forcible removal of black people from their traditional Old Location within Windhoek, to an area outside the town, known as Katutura, in order to create a buffer zone between black and white residential areas. That was one of the main factors that led to the black uprising in Windhoek Old Location on 10 December 1959 [the full story of this event is told in Chapter 4], to my departure from my country [Chapter 5], and my joining with Chief Hosea Kutako and Samuel Witbooi in petitioning the United Nations to demand the placement of South West Africa under the UN Trusteeship system [Chapter 6].

◆ ◆ ◆

3

The Formation of the Ovamboland People's Organization (OPO)

There was a new spirit taking hold in the 1950s, especially among the young men and women with whom I associated in Windhoek. The same spirit was also taking root in other regions, in factories and mines, and in the rural areas where people were even more strictly controlled by the apartheid South African colonial regime and its puppet chiefs than they were in the urban locations. This was true not only in our own country but also in South Africa, where some of our compatriots were working.

To us, the most important international political development after the end of the Second World War was the struggle for the independence of Ghana, which was finally celebrated on 6 March, 1957. Ghana's fight for freedom inspired and influenced us all, and the greatest contribution to our political awareness at that time came from the achievements of Ghana after its independence. It was from Ghana that we got the idea that we must do more than petition the United Nations to bring about our own independence, and so on 19th April 1959 we formed our own liberation movement, the Ovamboland People's Organization.

As we were stimulated by the political developments in Ghana, we learned that Julius Nyerere and Sylvanus Olympio, later to become the founding Prime Minister and President of Tanganyika and Togo respectively, were also petitioning at the United Nations. The UN Trusteeship System had taken over the work of the Permanent Mandates Commission of the League of Nations, which had supervised the mandate given to Britain and France to rule over

Tanganyika. By 1945, Rwanda-Burundi, Cameroon and Togoland had also, like what was called German South West Africa, all become United Nations Trust territories. Julius Nyerere and Sylvanus Olympio were both petitioning directly at the Fourth Committee hearings in New York in 1958 and 1959.

Stirred by these events and by an awareness that we must achieve our inalienable rights — over which World War II had apparently been fought! — we, the youth, set out to break the system of ethnic segregation, even by intermarriages, and by the close alliance we from the north had formed with the Herero Chiefs' Council, and with the Damaras and Namas United Front. It was our generation who first effectively attacked the tribal system to destroy tribalism and to get rid of white colonial rule, following a successful inspiring struggle by the people of Ghana under the leadership of President Kwame Nkrumah.

South West Africa was often described by the Boers as a large country with relatively few people but with many ethnic groups and different cultures, languages and traditions. To build a nation from this diversity — which the South Africans had tried to emphasise and exploit so that they could keep control — we had first to form a national organization. We started to do this in Windhoek in the middle of 1950s. We encouraged the youngsters to see that tribes, ethnic groups and cultural differences did not matter. We spread the idea that the liberation of Africa and of our own country was more important. We simply took no notice of these differences in our social lives, political work and even our marriages. The idea of African liberation was spread also by publications like *Ghana Today*, which we read and passed around, and it politically enlightened us. We all gathered together to read it, usually in town outside the Post Office where we used to meet. One of the most memorable issues contained a picture of Kwame Nkrumah dancing with the Duchess of Kent who was representing Britain at the celebrations of Ghana's Independence on 6 March 1957. Angry Boers noticed this and shouted at us, using abusive language, but we just ignored them and continued with our political mobilization.

The leader who above all inspired us to make our way in modern politics in South West Africa was Chief Hosea Kutako, already a very old man. He was a Namibian who had stood up with his stick and opposed the white oppressors. He had led his people in their war against the Germans from 1904 to 1907. He was wounded in one of the battles and bore the scars of his wounds until his death. He had confronted the white South Africans from the days of General Smuts, through Malan,

Strijdom and Verwoerd. To us he was unquestionably our leader. Although he was the Chief of the Hereros, he had followers among all the other ethnic groups, and he was a strong advocate of unity among them. Many who should have known better were afraid to be seen supporting him for fear of attracting the attention of the Special Branch police. He himself was fearless and continued leading the struggle.

With him, of course, there were others, like the principal of St. Barnabas School, Batholomeus Himumuine, who was really the man behind Chief Hosea Kutako. Himumuine was our teacher and he encouraged us. He had completed his own matriculation through private study. Through the efforts of the Reverend Michael Scott, he was offered a scholarship to study at Oxford University. But the Boers refused him a passport to travel to England. He was very frustrated by this, his health broke down and he died not many years later while still young and brilliant. Himumuine was fearless too. There were times when he could physically fight back against the Boers. One such instance was at the police station in Windhoek when he was asked to produce a night pass — a demand which he considered to be an insult to his integrity. Now we know that he could have just walked across the border into the then British Bechuanaland and got himself into Southern Rhodesia for scholarship. And with his scholarship he could have boarded a plane to England. South Africa was still a member of the Commonwealth and he could have entered Britain without any problem. We thought at the time that one could not travel without a passport.

I myself had first became aware of the United Nations through Chief Hosea Kutako. I came to meet him through such friends as Gabriel Mbuende (the father of the first Deputy Minister of Agriculture, Water and Rural Development later to become Executive Secretary for Southern African Development Community [SADC], Dr. Kaire Mbuende), and the late Clemens Kapuuo, a teacher trained in South Africa, then acting as Secretary to Chief Kutako. They not only brought us to Chief Kutako-Katjikururume, 'wise elder' as we called him; they were also, along with Himumuine, our teachers. Around Chief Hosea Kutako, we were able to talk about how we would achieve our first objective, the ending of the slave Contract system. We also discussed the repressive pass laws, and how we could obtain our freedom with the assistance of the United Nations, which we then thought was possible.

It was the cruelty of the Contract system and other oppressive laws that convinced me that we absolutely had to do something, that we could not allow this oppression to continue unchallenged. It was that situation which motivated me to embark upon a political campaign. Again Chief Hosea Kutako, paramount Chief of the Hereros, was the man who politically influenced me and my friends and colleagues from the start of our campaign. With him, we took our first steps of petitioning the United Nations, as he and Chief Samuel Witbooi had been doing since their first encounter with the Reverend Michael Scott in 1947. Since that time Chief Hosea Kutako continued to send petitions, and now we joined him. I was also busy organizing the workers underground, but in the open our work was focused on the activities of Chief Hosea Kutako and petitioning the United Nations.

The Good Offices Commission

In 1958, Chiefs Kutako and Samuel Witbooi petitioned the United Nations against the UN Good Offices Commission, which had been given the task of consulting with the apartheid regime about a possible solution to hand over South West Africa to the UN. The British member of the three-man commission, Sir Charles Undery, spent only a couple of hours at a meeting in Keetmanshoop. The commission eventually proposed to the UN a partitioning of South West Africa so that the whole of what was still called the Police Zone, where the whites lived (fully 85% of the area), would become part of South Africa, while the remaining northern and eastern regions which provided a cheap labour reservoir for the minority white employers (including the Kaokoland, Ovamboland, Kavango and the Eastern Caprivi) would come under a trusteeship agreement with the UN which would be administered by South Africa. Needless to say, our opinion of this 'solution' was that it was no solution at all.

At that time, the Americans, who were represented on the three-man commission, were prepared to leave southern African matters to the British. At the General Assembly, the recommendations of the commission were rejected, but the records show that no fewer than 21 voted for them, 40 against and 11 abstained. That was, of course, before the African bloc began to build up its numbers at the UN, and we had to rely on India, Ethiopia, Egypt and a few others to fight for us. India had been a strong supporter of our cause ever since the foundation of the UN at San Francisco, when General Smuts showed up in his Field Marshal's uniform. Smuts expected everybody to recognize him, only to find that both his and South Africa's days were already passing, and hardly anyone took any notice of him.

Nevertheless, the apartheid South African manoeuvres and the Western complicity which was behind the Good Offices Commission were closely followed by us young people who were close to Chief Hosea Kutako, and his response encouraged and strengthened us.

The Good Offices Commission was opposed by the petitioners at the UN, too. The *Windhoek Advertiser* reported the Reverend Michael Scott's speech, in which he said: "Conditions could lead to an explosion which human history never had seen before when channels of constitutional change had been blocked. There were no such channels in South West Africa and such an explosion was all the more certain."

Chief Hosea Kutako also proved himself as the father of modern South West African politics when he broke tribal barriers by signing petitions to the United Nations jointly with the Nama leader, Chief Samuel Witbooi and, from 1959, with myself as President of the Ovamboland People's Organization. This was a major political development. I had mobilized the Contract workers from the north and could speak on their behalf, while their chiefs in the north were still collaborators, supporting the activities and manoeuvres of the whites, particularly in continuing to recruit Contract workers through SWANLA slave contract system.

Continuing influences of apartheid

We were aware that other former German colonies had become trust territories of the United Nations, while we remained under the rule of South Africa. The white South Africans thought that most South West Africans, and particularly the Ovambos, would be content, because they were without modern education. One Dr. Vedder — who had been a German pastor and was later in the white-only South African Parliament, ostensibly 'representing the interests' of the natives of South West Africa — used to say, "Do not give education to the South West African natives, because if you do so it would be as if you were giving the white man a razor blade to cut his own throat". That was why, at that time, no South West Africans received higher education. The single exception was Fanuel Kozonguizi, who managed to matriculate in South Africa and went on to Fort Hare University, where so many African leaders — not only of South Africa origin but also from eastern and central Africa — were educated. A few others, like Reverend Theophilus Hamutumbangela and Clemens Kapuuo, managed to get teaching qualifications at Junior Certificate level (for primary school teaching) in South Africa, but the rest were denied permission to study in South Africa.

The South African government was determined to hold us back in every way possible. In 1959, when we realized that we needed our own lawyer in South West Africa, we took one of our youngsters, Onesmus Shikongo Akwenye, and sent him to Cape Town to attend a Cape Coloured school, for which we paid sixty pounds per annum. We wanted him to go to the University and become "our" lawyer. Somehow the Boers found out, and the police went to the college where he was studying. He was arrested and deported back to South West Africa. Akwenye subsequently went into exile and obtained the education the South Africans denied him. He is currently the Deputy Permanent Secretary in the Ministry of Health and Social Services.

One of our contemporaries, Mburumba Kerina, got to New York and studied at Lincoln University, and another, Hans Beukes, was offered a scholarship in Norway. Beukes was smuggled out of the country by Allard Lowenstein, then an American student leader, who came to South West Africa with two friends and wrote a factual book about South West Africa, called *Stolen Mandate*. Lowenstein also gave evidence with us before the Fourth Committee of the UN General Assembly in the early 1960s. His life ended tragically in 1988 when, as a US Congressman, he was murdered in his New York law office.

Another American who wrote about South West Africa was John Gunther. His book, *Inside Africa* (1954), which I read during my private studies, told us a lot about what was happening in Africa in the early 1950s. Beside the ancient Ethiopia Empire, there was only one independent republic in Africa until Egypt became one in 1953, and that was Liberia, which Gunther called "an American stepchild". Gunther wrote that "even a sympathetic observer has the feeling that many Liberians, backward and eccentric, are children playing at state craft". He described Liberia as "a perverse advertisement for imperialism", as its people lacked "the advantages in education and similar fields that 'enlightened colonialism' provides". There was, however, nothing of 'enlightened colonialism' in South West Africa.

Contract system — the most urgent evil

For us in South West Africa, though, neither the lack of schooling nor the knowledge that other former colonies like Ghana were becoming free nations were the most pressing motives for action against the colonial authorities — with or without the support of the United Nations. Overriding all other concerns were the oppressive semi-slave

Contract system and the pass laws which restricted the movement of Africans in the land of their birth.

The Contract system was the most urgent evil to be dealt with. I had seen examples of the physical attacks on Contract workers even as a young child at home. I had seen on the railways that employers considered their Contract workers as less than human beings, as mere objects that could be thrown away when unfit for work, even because of injuries suffered at their work. I took direct action on behalf of young men who were beaten by Boers. For instance, whenever I met a young boy while working at the railways, I would throw his Contract papers into the toilet and take the boy to school in the Old Location where the teachers were my friends.

There was also WENALA (Witwatersrand Native Labour Association), which recruited migrant labourers from what were then British Bechuanaland Protectorate, Northern and Southern Rhodesia and Nyasaland up to Tanganyika, Kenya and Uganda. This was how South Africa's economy was built up, through the mines, by the blood and tears of almost the whole of the sub-continent. Workers were recruited from Angola too, at Rundu in South West Africa, but the South West Africans were reserved only for the mining industry inside South West Africa itself, as well as for the government and white farmers and domestic service. The system had in fact originally been established by the Anglo-American Corporation, whose aircraft flew from Francistown all the way to Senanga and Broken Hill in Northern Rhodesia to take the workers from there and bring them to Francistown. The last part of the journey was by train to South Africa. The East African workers were brought in by truck to Mbeya in Tanganyika and flown to the South African mines.

The attitude of the whites who ruled us was unchallenged, except by Chief Hosea Kutako inside the country and by the Reverend Michael Scott at the United Nations, where he was attacked by Eric Louw, Malan's South African Foreign Minister, for claiming to speak for the people of South West Africa. It became essential that they be confronted.

One who had tried to do this, inspiring many people in the north, was an Anglican priest, the Reverend Theophilus Hamutumbangela. While working at Onekuaja Anglican Parish in Uukuanjama district, he received many complaints from workers coming home at the end of their contracts. They were paid appallingly low wages. White shift bosses in the mines were paid R375.00 per month, while monthly pay for the black miners varied from R17.00 to R45.00, construction workers from R7.50 to R18.00, and farm workers from R3.75 to R10.50. Black workers were often contracted for 18 or sometimes even 24 months without annual leave for visits to their families. There was so-called payment in kind (worth R15.25 per month in the mines), but the living quarters were terrible and food was sometimes disgusting, unhealthy and inadequate. Workers could neither choose their own job nor visit or be visited by their families, and no sick leave or annual leave was granted to them, not even in the case of death of their loved ones. In the days of slavery it was in the master's interest to look after his slaves, since they were his own property. But under the Contract system, the employers did not suffer if their workers were sick, injured or even if they died: they simply asked for a replacement from SWANLA and had no responsibility for the worker's personal interest being replaced or to his dependents' compensation.

In addition to the starvation wages, bad working conditions and other maltreatment, Contract workers were made to feel inferior in relation to white workers — not only because of the difference in their wages, but also by the contemptuous attitude of the whites to them. The Contract workers deeply resented this and also were bitter because they were worse off than the other Africans in the country, who, though also oppressed, were not subjected to the semi-slave Contract system.

Reverend Hamutumbangela and our first victory

Though they received so little money, the workers still managed to send money home and carry back to their families what they had bought in the way of appliances, utensils and clothing, and other items such as scented soap and perfume. At Namutoni, which was considered as the border between Ovamboland and the so-called Police Zone — the area where the whites settled — the very crude Boers there, mainly policemen, used to rob the returning Contract workers of such goods, particularly soaps and perfume, saying that these items were not suitable for Africans. They simply confiscated them and shared the goods amongst themselves.

When the Reverend Hamutumbangela learned about this, he sent a petition to the United Nations. Chief Native Commissioner Blignaut conspired with the Anglican Bishop Vincent (the Bishop of Damaraland, as his position was then known), and in 1957 Reverend Hamutumbangela was deported from his Onekuaja Parish, to Windhoek. In Windhoek, he conducted services every Sunday at St. Barnabas. We knew he had been deported from the north because he was influencing the people against the South African white oppression. Early in 1958, Fanuel Kozonguizi and I decided to confront Vincent, the Anglican Bishop. He agreed to see us.

Early one Tuesday evening, we went to him at his house next to the Anglican Cathedral. We told him: "You, an Anglican Bishop, have collaborated with the Native Commissioner to remove Reverend Hamutumbangela because he petitioned the United Nations, opposing the injustices being done and the robberies of the Contract workers' properties". Kozonguizi was then a student at the University College of Fort Hare in South Africa and we put our case strongly. The Bishop was plainly alarmed. This was most likely the first time in his life that he had been confronted in this way by Africans. We told him, "We are going to denounce you unless you make sure that Reverend Hamutumbangela is returned to his parish, and that you stop collaborating with the Boers". The Bishop had recently come back from the international meeting of Anglican Bishops at Lambeth in London and had perhaps been made aware there of the changing attitude to colonialism. He had said in London that the whites worshipped separately in the Anglican Church in his diocese because "Ovambos and other indigenous people would be unhappy to worship together with Europeans in one church", which must have raised some criticism among his audience.

Then Wednesday and Thursday passed, and during those two days Vincent bought a train ticket for Reverend Hamutumbangela, and told him to return to his Onekuaja Parish in the north. Members of the country's youth as we were, this was our first victory.

Late in 1958, I also visited the north, the last visit I made there before I went into exile. I took my whole family to visit my father and mother. After staying at Ongandjera with them, I went to visit Reverend Hamutumbangela at his Onekuaja Parish in Uukuanjama district, to which Bishop Vincent had returned him. We spent four days together in December 1958. My main purpose was to greet and pay tribute to him and to ask him how he was settling down back home, but we went on discussing future political strategies. We agreed that he would have to be even more active, and to create a flow of information so that we could keep in touch with what the white South Africans were doing in the north. Reverend Hamutumbangela was a committed person in his own right who politically inspired many of our young people, both in Windhoek and in the north. He continued his work as a priest in the north for many years until his death in 1990. He will always be remembered as one of the pioneers of our freedom struggle.

The year of the Ovamboland People's Organization

I then returned to Windhoek, at the very same time as Comrade Andimba Toivo Ya Toivo was being deported from Cape Town for, like the Reverend Hamutumbangela and others, having sent a petition to the UN. I knew of his work in mobilizing our Namibian workers in Cape Town, but I missed him, as our trains crossed each other at Jakkalsberg railway siding, the first stop on the railway line south of Tsumeb. I heard afterwards that he was arrested when his train reached Tsumeb. It appeared that the police had been following him after he left Windhoek. The Boers held him there and later left him to travel to Ondonga, his home district in the north. On arrival in the north, he was detained by Chief Johannes Kambonde, the Chief of Ondonga. Andimba Toivo Ya Toivo and I did not meet until many years later after he was released from Robben Island prison in 1984, though before his arrest in 1966 we had corresponded regularly.

Our Comrades in Cape Town, including Andimba Toivo Ya Toivo (my former Minister of Mines and Energy), Jacob Kuhangua (now deceased) and others had been working with the African National Congress (ANC) of South Africa, the Congress of Democrats, the Communist Party of South Africa, with leading progressives like Professor Jack Simons and his wife Ray Alexander, and with Liberals like Patrick Duncan and Randolph Vigne. They had become involved in political activities in South Africa. This was why Ya Toivo, their leader, was deported. He had also sent a tape to Mburumba Kerina, who was already in New York with Reverend Michael Scott, appearing before the UN Committee on South West Africa. This tape exposed the evil of the Contract system and the repressive South African apartheid policies in South West Africa.

In Cape Town, Ya Toivo and his colleagues formed the Ovamboland People's Congress (OPC) and sent us a copy of the OPC Constitution. On 19 April 1959, we formed here, in Windhoek, after Ya Toivo had been deported, the Ovamboland People's Organization (OPO). Our chief objectives were the end of the South African colonial administration, and the placing of South West Africa under the UN Trusteeship system, but the end of the Contract system was our first priority. We were determined to destroy the Contract migrant labour system which was the most humiliating type of oppression against our people.

In the same year, there was a move to send back all the Namibians in Cape Town, with the excuse that there was a labour shortage in South

West Africa. This was reported in the *Windhoek Advertiser*. But we knew that the main reason was because of the tape-recording that Ya Toivo had smuggled to Kerina at the UN.

We were fighting against the lack of education, the slave Contract system and the pass laws. Everyone had to carry at least three — a monthly pass which was renewable, a night pass signed by one's 'master', and a travelling pass. Further, one had to carry a hut tax receipt. If you did not have these papers, which you had to carry on you every day, you could be arrested and locked up. Contract workers from the north working as domestic servants were not allowed to go into the street, or to the location or townships, unless they had a pass from their masters. How can a human being be confined, like a dog, to his master's yard? It was the worst insult and humiliation to blacks as human beings.

I had already sent a petition to the UN General Assembly in February 1959 with six other Ovambo workers from Windhoek, on the subject of the arrest of Andimba Toivo Ya Toivo and his detention at Okaloko as the prisoner of Chief Johannes Kambonde. From April 1959 we could now petition as the Ovamboland People's Organization (OPO). Though formed by a group of individuals, it already had a solid base among the Contract workers of the Windhoek area, in the Old Location and the Pokkiesdraai Compound. I was the founding President, with Louis Nelengani as Vice-President and Jacob Kuhangua as Secretary-General. To form the OPO Constitution, we adapted a copy of the OPC Constitution, changing it only slightly to suit the political conditions in South West Africa. I myself typed it out on a second-hand typewriter I had bought from an old German lady in Windhoek. Our stated aims and objectives were:

1. To fight relentlessly to achieve United Nations Trusteeship and ultimate independence for the people of South West Africa;

2. To serve as the vigorously conscious political vanguard for removing all forms of oppression, and for the establishment of a democratic Government;

3. To secure and maintain the complete unity of the people of Ovamboland, Hereroland, Damaraland and Namaland;

4. To work with and in the interest of the Trade Union Movement, and other kindred organizations, in joint political or other action in harmony with the Constitution and standing orders of the OPO;

5. To work for a speedy reconstruction of a better South West Africa in which the people and their chiefs shall have the right to live and govern themselves as free people;
6. To promote the political, social and economic emancipation of the people, more particularly those who depend directly upon their own exertion by hand, or by brain to improve their lives.

We had international aims, too, which declared that we would work with all nationalist, democratic socialist movements in Africa and elsewhere to abolish "imperialism, colonialism, racism, tribalism and all forms of racial segregation, oppression and economic inequality amongst nations, races or peoples, and to support all actions for world peace". We also supported the "demand for West African Federation and Pan-Africanism by promoting unity of action among the peoples of Africa and all people of African descent". Membership was open to all persons over 18 years who accepted what we stood for, provided "he or she is not a member of any other political party with policies inconsistent with those of OPO".

Thus we combined the goals of independence, democracy and an end to the slave Contract system and unity of the South West African people. It must be remembered that at that time there was no Damara bantustan or homeland as such, and all African indigenous people lived in their traditional and historical regions of Ovamboland (the north), Hereroland (the midlands) and Namaland and Damaraland (central and south), even if in enclaves like the Reheboth reserve, or in towns where whites dominated and we were forced to live in designated locations, usually on the outskirts. People from the Kavango region soon joined us, and a little later the eastern Caprivians, who at that time had almost no contact whatsoever with other Namibians. We recruited members for OPO very quickly and in large numbers, in spite of the difficulties involved in moving around the country in order to meet and speak with leaders and organizers and with groups in workplaces and churches.

As I have said, in those days no native could move in the country without a pass signed by his master showing that he was allowed to travel. He would have to get a pass from the local pass office or police station, and when he reached his destination he would have to go first to the pass office to report his arrival and get yet another pass, permitting him to stay in that town or village — all this before seeing his relatives or friends. A five-day or a two-day permit might be issued, but usually for a shorter period than had been asked for.

As I related in Chapter Two, because I had worked for the railways and travelled with the system manager, I knew how to get about the country without being noticed and without any 'pass'. As I knew the system, I would book myself in a reserved single first-class compartment. No natives normally travelled in that comfort, so I would simply lock myself in knowing that the ticket conductor would only look for blacks in third class compartments. I was thus able to defeat the travel restrictions and get to places like Walvis Bay to the west and Tsumeb far to the north, to form branches of OPO and to mobilize the workers.

We held many rallies after our formation of OPO in the Old Location in Windhoek. We also formed a very big branch far to the south in Oranjemund — which was done by simply sending membership cards to the branch secretary. I would not myself have been allowed to go there as it was in the 'Sperrgebiet' and forbidden to all except for those authorized by the Consolidated Diamond Mines of South West Africa.

When I went to establish the OPO branch in Walvis Bay, it was a trip that, as usual, required me to avoid being arrested for travelling without a pass. I left Windhoek late on a Friday night, in a reserved first-class single compartment. I simply got off at Walvis Bay when the train reached there at about 6 a.m. the next day, and walked to the location with my suitcase. I spent the Saturday organizing meetings 'underground'. On Sunday morning at about 7 a.m., I went to the railway compound. There was a railway policeman at the gate checking passes. So I put on a jacket and a white shirt turned back to front, and carrying a Bible and hymn book so that they would think I was a pastor, I just walked in alongside those night-shift workers who were coming back without even saying 'good morning' to the policeman.

I started singing a hymn from the hymn book, and workers gathered around and joined in. I then began to explain why I had come to see them, and told them that Jesus came to the world to save mankind. After all, mankind was born free but we Africans were not free, so we must unite and work together, form an organization to protect the interests of the workers, and demand higher salaries and better working conditions. I explained to them that since World War II ended, all nations were becoming free and that only we in South West Africa were not getting our freedom, although we too were supposed to be free. I told them our country was supposed to have been ruled under a mandate of the League of Nations, but the mandate was never implemented and so we were still not free. The crowd grew bigger and became interested and many of them joined OPO from there. In the railway compound that day

I met Comrade Augustus Nghaamua "MacNamara", who later on joined me in exile and became PLAN Chief of Communication, but died in one of the many battles.

I met Comrade Vinia Ndadi on that visit and appointed him secretary of the Walvis Bay OPO branch. He did a lot of work and collected more membership fees and donations from the workers. At one point we asked Vinia Ndadi to seize the chance and go to the UN, stowed away in one of the ships which had called at Walvis Bay. He managed to get on board but the only place he could hide was down below deck. He was suffocating and had to leave his hiding place while the ship was out at sea. The captain turned the ship back and put him ashore at Walvis Bay. The Boers were furious and demanded, 'What do you think you were doing, to go to the "VVO"?' (as they always referred to the United Nations). They put him in prison and information quickly got to the workers that Ndadi had been arrested. In his book, *Breaking Contract*, he tells the story of that event and other trials we had to go through in the early days of OPO.

A political mission

In August 1959, I left Windhoek and travelled to Tsumeb clandestinely to open an OPO Branch Office there. On my arrival at the train station I was met by the late Leevi Muashekele who was working at that time at Tsumeb Corporation LTD (TCL) mine. Before I disembarked from the train, he quickly whispered in my ear that the police were looking for me. They had noticed that I was not in Windhoek, and had sent cable messages to all train stations in the whole of South West Africa to arrest me. However, since I knew Tsumeb railway station, I remained in my train compartment and told Muashekele to take my belongings to his house. This he did, and later I disembarked from the train and went to the bus station where passengers travelling to Ondangua were normally picked up by buses from Grootfontein to Ondangua via Tsumeb. After an hour or so, some passengers who had arrived in Tsumeb from Walvis Bay left on foot from the bus station, and I joined them. As we were approaching the centre of the town, there was a police road block and two black policemen came and asked us to show our passes and identify ourselves. The others with whom I was walking produced their passes which stated that they were returning to Ovamboland. The two policemen also asked me where my pass was. I simply said that I had a pass like the others, and therefore there was no need to show it. The two lazy policemen allowed me to continue to the centre of the town.

I went straight to Ackerman Hotel to see my cousin David Uushona, who was employed there. In the evening when it became dark, Leevi Muashekele sent his daughter Kathrina to fetch me from the Hotel to his house in the township. I met with Muashekele to draw up plans and strategies, and we quickly decided to convene a meeting during the church service. There I was given the floor to explain in detail the aims and objectives of OPO. I urged the residents to mobilize the people and establish an OPO branch in Tsumeb. I gave them application forms for OPO membership and copies of the OPO constitution. Old man Leevi Muashekele was a patriot and hard working. He mobilized the workers in Tsumeb mine, which became another OPO stronghold.

After the church service we went to his house and had our meal. However, he was worried about the movement of the police and thought that while he was at work they might search his house and find me there. He quickly worked out a plan to send me with his daughter Kathrina to hide at the mine hospital where there was a male medical assistant by the name of Luanda, originally from Nyasaland (now Malawi). Luanda was quite friendly and worked together with Leevi Muashekele. Luanda welcomed me and kept me in his room during that day and brought me food. We discussed politics and the need to mobilize the African people to liberate our continent. Many African nationalist leaders were struggling for freedom during that period, and Luanda was a member of the Nyasaland African Congress, led by Dr. Hastings Kamuzu Banda.

While I was in Tsumeb a telegram was sent to me from Windhoek warning that I should be extra careful because the police were looking for me. They had come to my house after midnight and asked my wife where I was. Although my wife knew I was on a special mission to Tsumeb, she told them that I was probably in the location with some girlfriends. (Comrade Nelengani, the Vice-President of OPO, was communicating all this information to Leevi Muashekele.)

In the evening, I decided to leave Tsumeb by the goods train which carries copper to Walvis Bay for shipment to North America and Europe. There was only a small conductor coach which I entered. The train conductor came and saw that I had reserved a first class ticket. He asked why I was travelling in the goods train when I had an expensive passenger ticket. I said I was rushing to Otjiwarongo because I had received news that my mother was very ill. The conductor was sympathetic and invited me to sit next to him until we reached Otjiwarongo.

In Otjiwarongo I disembarked from the goods train and went to the location where I visited Aaron Iipinge, a teacher. We started talking about politics and the struggle for liberation, and also went to the workers' compound to mobilize the workers. Since I had no travelling pass for Otjiwarongo, I decided to take another goods train to Omaruru and continue to Usakos. On my arrival in Usakos, I went directly to the OPO branch Secretary who was a worker on the railways, and again held a meeting with workers and community leaders. The same morning I embarked on the train from Walvis Bay to Cape Town via Usakos, Okahandja and Windhoek.

I went into the reserved single first class compartment, ordered breakfast and continued my journey to Windhoek. As soon as I arrived at Okahandja, the OPO Branch Secretary came to see me and told me that he had received advice from Windhoek that I should get off the train there to avoid further travel in the daylight. I was afraid, however, that I could be arrested, since Okahandja was a very small town and any stranger could be easily identified. Thus I continued on the train to Windhoek.

The train arrived at Windhoek main station in the afternoon, and through the window I could see policemen moving around. I remained in my first class compartment. As usual the porters were busy changing bed sheets and fresh water was being put into the train. The water normally spilt around, and in all the mess and bustle the policemen went away. While sitting in my compartment I saw a taxi owned by a person by the name of Kauhuepuku who came to fetch passengers and take them to the Old Location. I had him pick up my suitcase and take it to his taxi while I casually went to have some refreshment at the kiosk which was specially built to serve the Africans at the railway station. After a while, I went to join Kauhuepuku who drove me to my house.

So I arrived home safely without being arrested. My wife related that police had been at our house three times looking for me. The same afternoon I went to see policeman Maritz at the Municipality office which was about five hundred metres from my house. I found Maritz in his office and I asked him why he had to bother my wife and children three times during the night. I also asked him whether he did not look through the record to find that my house was paid three months in advance. He replied that Special Branch policemen had been looking for me and he had simply brought them to my house. I urged him to stop coming to my house after midnight, disturbing my family.

Policeman Maritz then asked me a question. If we ever succeeded in placing South West Africa under UN trusteeship, what would happen to him, an uneducated white person? I told him in clear language, "If you are a citizen of our country, you will remain in your employment, provided you give up arrogance and harassment of the people". He looked at me with sharp eyes and I went out of his office and returned home.

A week later I met a black Special Branch policeman by the name of Andreas Nangolo who told me that a Special Branch policeman by the name of Van der Watt wanted to see me at the CID Special Branch Headquarters in Windhoek. After another two weeks, I went there early in the morning and went straight to Van der Watt's office. Since Special Branch policemen were known to be arrogant towards Africans, I sat down in front of his desk. There was a coat on the chair and I leaned over it. When at last he came in he shouted at me and asked me who had given me the right to sit in his office. I shouted back at him, telling him that he did not call me to stand all day in his office. Misunderstanding and argument ensued. He said that he was not the one who called me but that I had been called by the Special Branch chief Captain Blaauw — the same little man who had harassed me outside the Carsten Veld offices around August 1959. I replied that I did not care who called me at the Special Branch office, and that I had no intention to go there. Van der Watt then said, "let me direct you to his office". I asked him to lead me to that office!

In the meantime, the Boers planned to attack me physically. When we entered Captain Blaauw's office I saw three policemen lined up, dressed in black uniforms similar to those of the railway policemen. Blaauw was sitting behind a long desk like a reception counter. He ordered me to be quiet because I was in the police station. I told him that he had no right to shout at me. Then he stood up and tried to push me towards the three policemen. Since he was short and looked as though he suffered from malnutrition, I pulled him over the counter and he appeared to be hurt on his shoulders. I told him that I wanted to teach him a lesson. At that point, Johannes Muleko — a black Special Branch policeman from Kavango also known by the nickname of 'Warmgat' — jumped in and attempted to interpret for me from Oshiuambo to Afrikaans, but I rejected his mediation. Meanwhile, the three policemen in black uniforms never said a word, nor did they make any attempt to attack me as they had clearly planned.

As I was about to walk out, Captain Blaauw told me that I was wanted by the Magistrate in Tsumeb who had learned that I had been there without a pass and without reporting to the pass office. I simply walked out of the CID Headquarters and went home.

Apparently, after my departure from Tsumeb, a certain Mr. Conradie, who was working at the travelling pass office in Tsumeb, had picked up information from the medical assistant Luanda, with whom I had spent a day. Luanda told Conradie that I was there and he had seen me with his own eyes. Conradie argued that if Sam Nujoma was here, he himself would have been the first person to see him as he ought to have reported and registered himself at the Travelling Pass Office. The medical assistant, to prove his point, replied, "Sam Nujoma came to my place with Kathrina, the daughter of Leevi Muashekele". The policeman then arrested Kathrina, interrogated her, and beat her.

Later she confessed that her father had instructed her to take Sam Nujoma to the hospital to spend the day in hiding with Luanda, and that I left Tsumeb the same evening by goods train and went back to Windhoek. Of course, I never went back to Tsumeb for trial before that arrogant magistrate. He was the same man who, a few months earlier in December 1958, had ordered the illegal arrest and detention of Comrade Ya Toivo while he was travelling from Windhoek to Ondangua via Tsumeb.

After one month, I sent five pounds to Captain Blaauw, which he had demanded from me as a fine for being in Tsumeb without a travelling pass. Then the case was closed.

The point here is that it was routine practice for the Boers at the CID Special Branch to physically assault blacks: some suffered serious injuries and ended up being hospitalized. I was aware of this and of what could be the consequences of being beaten up by the three policemen dressed in black uniforms. I was determined to defend myself, and made sure that they did not attempt to assault me.

Blignaut's failed plot

OPO had grown from strength to strength very quickly, and in August 1959 a confrontation with the Boers' Ovambo puppet Chief took place in Windhoek. This incident was of great consequence in turning a large number of Ovambos away from the chiefs, to support the liberation movement that was to become SWAPO.

The Native Commissioner, Brewer Blignaut, realized that OPO had become deeply rooted in the masses of the people so he decided that I must be dealt with. He did not send Uushona Shiimi, the Chief of my district, as he knew Shiimi used to stay with my uncle when he visited Windhoek, and that my father was a popular man in Ongandjera district. So he sent, instead, the Ondonga Chief, Johannes Kambonde, a far more ruthless man. This same Kambonde had tied Ya Toivo to a pole outside his palace at Okaloko.

Chief Kambonde arrived in Windhoek on a Wednesday and stayed with Nikanor Shikuambi, one of the black policemen in the Old Location (OV 2 Section), whom I knew through my uncle. Traditionally, on such a visit the people would come to pay their respects to their Chief, bringing gifts, and there would be beer drinking — but this time they did not come. People learned that the Chief had been sent by the Boers to suppress our struggle to eradicate Boer apartheid colonialism. They knew he had been told to order us to stop our political activities and that OPO should cease to exist.

Information reached me from Nikanor Shikuambi that the Chief wanted to see me so I went, with some of my companions, on Sunday, 23 August. I took along two bottles of mellow-wood brandy, since traditionally one must bring a gift when visiting an Ovambo Chief.

The Chief became excited when he saw the liquor and called the Advisory Board men, led by Ananias Shipena, to 'warm themselves up', which they did so carelessly. Kambonde quickly lost his sobriety and demanded: 'I want to see Sam Nujoma!'. However, not all the chief councillors supported him: some of them knew me personally and clearly understood that he was wrong, so they sided with me against Kambonde. One of them, who had been deported from Walvis Bay in 1947 and had gone to work on Contract, was Kali Ki' Israel, and though he was Kambonde's very close councillor, he opposed the Chief's demand that I must be arrested and taken away to be imprisoned at his palace together with Comrade Ya Toivo. People started to gather outside Shikuambi's house, Contract workers among them, and the place quickly filled up. I told Chief Kambonde in the presence of all that our aim was to eradicate the shameful slave trade contract system carried out through SWANLA by the white colonialists.

The Chief told the councillors with him, "I am specifically here to fetch this young man Sam Nujoma. His Chief, Uushona Shiimi objects to him because he does not want the white man in this country". I stood up to reply, and said, "No! this does not mean that we do not want the white men here. What we do not want is the white domination in our country". He said, "Well, what do you want?". I replied, "We want to rule ourselves in the land of our birth. We want equal rights". He asked further, "Where have you seen a black man ruling himself?", and I told him that Tanganyika, which was about to have elections, was well into the process of achieving independence and self-rule. The black man there would soon be ruling himself. He said, "If I sent you there, would you go?". I answered, "Yes, I would happily go there, where a black man will be ruling himself". Little did I know at that moment that in only six months time I would in fact go into exile, in Tanganyika itself, to carry on the struggle.

Chief Kambonde then ordered all his people from Ondonga tribe to leave OPO and demanded the membership fees and donations they had given to OPO. Then a commotion ensued, started by Johannes Henock who was drunk and attacked another Ondonga man for being an OPO member. Fighting began and the Chief ran into the house. He was afraid because of the size of the crowd, but as yet there was no real hostility towards him. White policemen were present but did not see what had happened. They nevertheless reported that I had started the fighting. I denied this and was supported by a black policeman, who had been present on the scene. The police had no grounds, so they did not charge me. In fact, I was the one who said to the crowd, "Let us disperse! Let us leave this old Ondonga Chief and let him go with his Boers!".

The following morning Kambonde was supposed to address the Contract workers who were starting to build new houses at Katutura. Early that Monday morning, he went to the office of Blignaut, the Chief Native Commissioner, to report that I had insulted him. He said he wanted the colonial authorities to hand me over to him, so that he could tie me to the back of his vehicle and pull me all the way to his palace at Okaloko in northern South West Africa. I would probably have arrived there without legs.

Blignaut said to Chief Kambonde, "No, this is now a hot potato and a political issue. There would be headlines and reports that you came here at the expense of the government, and yet this is what happened!". They certainly could not hand me over to him. I had the full support of the people. OPO was popular in the country and we had over one thousand pounds in the bank — a lot of money in those days. Workers would give as much as five pounds, which represented a huge amount of their wages, they desired so strongly to be free. The response was tremendous — even in areas where there was no OPO branch, people would contribute money and send it through the post office. By contrast, a puppet Chief like Johannes Kambonde had to be subsidized by the government to visit Windhoek. We obtained information from our African agents in the police force that Chief Kambonde got petrol from the police at Ondangua, Okaukuejo, Outjo and Otjiwarongo before he finally reached Windhoek. We went to the press to denounce the colonial authority and its use of this puppet Chief. So our side of the story was published, and Chief Native Commissioner Blignaut, we learned, was shocked that this abuse of authority had all become public.

My meeting with Chief Johannes Kambonde had an influence on people's attitudes towards their traditional rulers, who were almost all puppets of the Boers. His ignorance and unpatriotic acts as well as his behaviour in front of the crowds were shown up: our argument about Tanganyika, a former German colony, made people see where he stood. At night, children from all sections of Old Location, spontaneously threw stones at the house where he was staying. The tradition was that Ovambo women should go to where the chief was and brew traditional beer to celebrate his presence, but this time nobody paid respect to him.

Chief Kambonde's next meeting with workers in the Pokkiesdraai Compound, near what became Katutura, was meant to turn them away from OPO, but it had the opposite effect. Before he arrived, many people had sharpened pieces of iron bar into spears and there was an angry mood. His own Ondonga people stood behind Aangandjera, Aakuambi, Aakuanjama and others so that Kambonde and his councillors could not identify them. I saw the danger in this and thought that our movement, which was still young, could be suppressed. If the Chief was attacked and harmed, the Boer authority would act excessively against us. I sent a message to the Chief warning him of the danger, and tried to calm the workers, which was a difficult thing to do when they had become angry. The meeting that day was hostile to Chief Kambonde, but not violent, and from there on wherever he went, he was boycotted. In Walvis Bay, where Aandonga workers would normally have brought him presents and had a feast in his honour, nobody went to receive him. Johannes Nakanjala, who was the treasurer of Ondonga Chief Association, collected money meant for the Chief and gave it to OPO instead. Chief Kambonde went home a very disappointed man.

Blignaut was very disappointed, too. Having brought the Chief down to arrest me and stop the OPO, he had totally failed in his attempt to suppress our movement.

The press and publicity campaign

During those early days, whenever I made a statement to the newspapers it would become a headline. The local newspapers were keen to publish my statements in order to bring a confrontation between the indigenous people and the colonial administration. For the first time in the history of South West Africa, the white authority was being challenged by indigenous people. We found that the *Die Suidwester*, the Nationalist Party owned paper, and the German *Allgemeine Zeitung* also reported my statements with almost exactly the same headlines. They sent their reporters to pick up whatever news there was, whether it was anti-government or not.

An example was my response to a news item, printed at the bottom of an inside page in the *Windhoek Advertiser* on 30 July 1959, under the headline, "Ovambo Chief tells of loyalty to SWA". This described a meeting at Ondangua between a party of foreign correspondents who were touring the country and Chief Johannes Kambonde of the Ondonga and Uushona Shiimi of the Ongandjera. The latter was reported as having said, "The Ovambos have no desire to have the administration of their land placed in the hands of another authority. The South West Africa Administration and the Union Government were good to them".

My reply on 11 August filled a full column on the front page, under the main headline of the newspaper: "Native Commissioner attacked by Sam Nujoma." The article simply printed my letter in full, refuting Kambonde's and Shiimi's assertion that they could not co-operate with the Hereros who wanted "a change in the administration of South West Africa". I made the point as plainly as I could:

> "The foreign correspondents addressed the Chiefs in English and, as the Native Commissioner [through an Ovambo puppet] was the interpreter, we leave it to the world to guess what actually took place at that meeting."

The newspaper went on, "Johannes Kambonde is the Chief of the Ondonga tribe. All these tribes co-operated with the Hereros and are opposed to South West Africa being controlled and administered by the Union of South Africa and they want South West Africa to be placed under the United Nations Trusteeship System".

The newspapers did the work for us by printing the rest of the letter which included the list of "our grievances", as follows:

"1. After 39 years of administration by the Union of South Africa, all the natives in South West Africa have no right to vote in the land of their birth and have no representatives in all the councils of the State. They are represented by self-appointed whites and European settlers who do all in their power to retard the progress of the Africans.

2. Twenty-one million hectares of the total land in South West Africa have been allotted to the Africans whose population is 472,000 while 37 million hectares of land have been given to the 66,000 Europeans living in South West Africa.

3. The Government spends R781,000 annually on European education while they are less than 12 per cent of the population. The Government expenditure annually on Native education is R190,000.

4. The Ovambos are employed under the hated slave Contract System which does not allow them to choose employers for whom they are going to work, while the rate paid is 1s, 3d per day.

5. The oppressive laws, such as the Pass laws and other laws which have relegated the Africans to the status of slaves.

The above five points are a challenge to any person who defends the Native policy of the Union Government.

All that one can say about South West Africa, is that her prospects look duller each year and it will be in the interest of the white community if the Chief Native Commissioner and other government officials make honest and serious attempt to solve the above mentioned problems rather than to play the role of dishonest interpreters.

(Signed) Sam Nujoma, President of the Ovamboland People's Organization."

On 1 September 1959, the *Windhoek Advertiser* again gave front page coverage to an account of the meeting with Johannes Kambonde. 'Native Affairs' officials were unable to contradict our statement that I, along with Kuhangua and Nelengani, had been threatened with deportation to Ovamboland. They were also unable to contradict our statement that Comrade Ya Toivo, who was a member of OPO, was being held as a prisoner by Chief Kambonde. The *Windhoek Advertiser* story continued:

"Officially Chief Kambonde of the Ondonga tribe came to Windhoek to visit his people who were working in the Police Zone under Contract. Natives, however, alleged that he was brought to Windhoek to counteract the Ovamboland People's Organization."

On 23 September 1959, we were again on the front pages, under the headline, "Native Leaders write to UNO [United Nations]: Further protests about Union laws". The *Windhoek Advertiser* reported and quoted in full the letter sent by Chiefs Kutako and Witbooi and myself to U Thant, the Secretary-General of the United Nations.

"On September 18, Chief Samuel Witbooi (Nama People), Chief Hosea Kutako (Herero people) and Sam Nujoma (Ovamboland Peoples Organization) wrote the following letter to the Secretary-General of the United Nations:

We strongly object to the proposal made by the South African delegate to the United Nations, Mr. Eric Louw, that the debate on the question of South West Africa be postponed to another session. This statement is unwelcome seeing that the Africans are faced with mass removals from their lands in order to make room for European settlements. It is most unwelcome because, judging by the situation in South West Africa, the Union of South Africa has no intention of abolishing the oppressive laws designed to preserve white supremacy and which have relegated the Africans to the status of slaves. We make our often-repeated proposal that seeing all other measures to bring the South African Government to obedience have failed, the question of South West Africa be referred to the "International Court of Justice" for its compulsory jurisdiction.

We consider that a period of 14 years of the United Nations debates and resolutions on South West Africa, and the Union government's infringement and violation of international obligations, all necessitate the United Nations' immediate take-over of the Mandate."

~~~~~

It is regrettable that, apart from a few cyclo-styled copies of the Ovamboland People's Organization Constitution in English and Oshiuambo, there are almost no records in existence, even photographs, of OPO's year of activity. Even my old typewriter was hidden by my colleagues in the mountains near Rehoboth after I had gone into exile. Their concern was that if the police found it, they could use it as evidence against OPO members in the country.

OPO was in existence from April 1959 to 19 April 1960, when its aim of uniting all the people of South West Africa was reflected in its change of name, and it became the South West Africa People's Organization (SWAPO).

Yet the issue which was to change everything was not our fight against the Contract system, nor our demand to come under UN Trusteeship but our struggle to achieve self-determination and independence as a united people in South West Africa. This transformation happened because of a historic event which changed all our lives at the end of 1959 — the Windhoek Uprising.

With terrible irony, the catalytic event came about as a direct result of South Africa's own attempt at an intensified enforcement of the apartheid policy: the threat to take away from us our homes in Windhoek, poor as many were, and to forcibly remove us to a new 'township' in the outlying area. This place was called "Katutura", a word which means literally "a place where we shall never settle". In Katutura the racist regime could maintain the colonial system of divide and rule. They now struck deep at the ordinary lives of a people living in the centre of their own political awakening.

As this threat began to become a reality, the day of the final reckoning which was to turn our confrontation with the colonialists into deadly conflict drew near.

◆ ◆ ◆

4

Political Confrontation: the Popular Windhoek Uprising

The Windhoek Uprising of 10th December 1959 was a direct result of oppression by the National Party minority white government led by Daniel Malan, Hendrick Verwoerd and J. G. Strijdom. These and others made law in the all-white Parliament in Cape Town, deliberately based on the principles and practices of apartheid. Among these forms of racial discrimination was the insistence on a buffer zone between white residential areas and those of the indigenous people in South West Africa and South Africa.

We who lived in Windhoek Old Location were told to move to Katutura, which was about 5 km away from the centre of the town of Windhoek. We, however, insisted that if it was a question of improving our houses, they must be built on the same *erven* where our ancestors lived and were buried. Our wishes were rejected by the colonial authority, as the sequence of events at the end of 1959 shows.

Prelude to the Uprising

On Sunday, 13 September 1959, at a meeting convened by the Advisory Board and attended by Nel de Wet, the Superintendent of the Locations, the residents categorically rejected their removal to Katutura. Six weeks later, on Thursday, 29 October 1959, another public meeting was called by the white authorities. The representatives of African communities — comprised of OPO, SWANU (South West Africa National Union), Chief Hosea Kutako's Chief Council and the Damara's Chief Council — reiterated the same case against their removal.

The Windhoek Municipality deliberately ignored the people's objection against their removal from the Old Location. On Friday, 4 December 1959, policemen and Superintendent de Wet began to register people by force in Damara Section five (D 5), where they assaulted Advisory Board member August Gariseb for refusing to collaborate with the white authorities. Since this was during the daytime when the majority of men were away at work, it was the women who came to his rescue. They attacked the police and set them running. Within a short time, however, the police returned with reinforcements and arrested the four women leaders. This unjust arrest precipitated a historic and popular women's demonstration and march to Daan Viljoen (then colonial Administrator), first to his office and then to his residence. Dan Viljoen first tried to play hide-and-seek, and then later showed up but refused to talk to the women demonstrators, referring them to the Magistrate, C. L. Hager.

Magistrate Hager said to a huge crowd of demonstrators, "You must accept that if the authorities want to give you good houses for the good of yourselves and your children, you should be thankful. You should thank the Municipality for the money spent on your behalf". Watja Kaukuetu (the then Vice-President of SWANU), who was at the scene, replied to the Boer Magistrate, "The authorities have the wrong idea, if they think we believe that anybody's life can be bettered if you build him a place and give him nothing else. We look upon the move as not being in the spirit of the mandate, but in the spirit of the apartheid policy. We are not worried about the money the Municipality has spent to build Katutura. That is their own trouble".

Magistrate Hager carried on, "The building of Katutura shows what Europeans are doing for you natives. My final advice to you is don't take the law into your own hands, behave like law-abiding citizens. It won't help you if you hit your heads against the wall". Kaukuetu replied, "What do you mean by hitting our heads against the wall? We won't move to Katutura. What about the people you arrested?".

On Saturday, December 5, 1959, the women militants paid fines of about £3 each, imposed on them by the colonial magistrate.

The residents of the Old Location had long been segregated into the so-called ethnic sub-sections — Hereros, Ovambos, Damaras, Namas and Others — the location itself was part of Windhoek and was administered by an all white municipal council, where decisions affecting the social welfare of indigenous people were made without their consent. These decisions were communicated to the residents of the Old

Location by the Superintendent of the Old Location, Nel de Wet, through the elected Advisory Board members.

There was, however, a loophole in the municipality regulation that there should be an election to elect new Advisory Board members. This election was also held on the basis of ethnic representation. For example, an Advisory Board member in Herero Section 1, or Damara Section 5 or Ovambo Section 1 could only be elected by the residents of that section on verification that they were permanent hut tax payers.

We, the youth, seized on that opportunity and carried out clandestine election campaigns to put our own candidates in all the ethnic sections of the Old Location. In Ovambo Section 1, our candidate was Thobias Akuenye; in Ovambo Section 2 was Fanuel Kampala; in Herero Section 1 was Frans Shiguedha. All our candidates were elected with a two-thirds majority. In Damara Section, the incumbent Advisory Board member was a patriot and was unanimously re-elected. The new Advisory Board members, elected by the people, were to campaign to oppose the forcible removal of the residents to Katutura.

The Katutura residence would be run by Verwoerd's new Ministry of Bantu Administration and Separate Development, as it was the practice that laws were made in Cape Town and experimented in South West Africa before implementation in South Africa itself. The relocation to Katutura meant that the former residents of Windhoek Old Location would be subjected to complete control. Further, they would be compelled to pay monthly rent ten times the amount of the Old Location service charge of 3 shillings and 6 pence per month. The difference was that we owned the houses in the Old Location, whereas in the new township of Katutura the houses would belong to the municipal authorities. There, if one disagreed with the Boers, one could simply be removed from one's house by the stroke of a pen.

When we realized that the colonial authority was determined to implement its diabolical policy of forcible removal of the residents of Old Location to the segregated Katutura, we took the initiative and launched a boycott of all municipal activities and services in the Old Location.

I hired a vehicle mounted with a loud speaker, and we drove around the whole location announcing through the loud speaker in Nama-Damara, which was done by Comrade Moses Garoeb (later SWAPO Secretary-General and Minister of Labour). Willy Watja Kaukwetu and Nathaniel Mbaeva of SWANU announced in Otjiherero, while I announced in Oshiuambo, calling on all residents of the Old Location neither to go to the municipal Beer Hall, nor the municipal Cinema Hall, nor to use the Municipality buses.

The boycott was fully backed by Chief Hosea Kutako's Council. It was successful, and led to the standstill of all municipal services in the Old Location. The people were happy to hear their own languages spoken through the loud speaker for the first time.

10 December 1959

Early in the morning of 10 December 1959, de Wet, the Superintendent of the Old Location, convened a meeting of Advisory Council members of the Old Location. Also present at that meeting were the Chief Native Commissioner Blignaut, the Chief of Police Major Lombard, Mayor of Windhoek Snyman, and other municipal and government officials. Major Lombard attempted to threaten us by saying; "Bantu, I want to tell you a story. If there is a wounded lion don't follow it or go near it, otherwise it will attack you". We all challenged him to explain what he meant by that. Then Blignaut responded, saying "We have not come here to discuss with you, but to warn you to stop the boycott of municipal services". At that stage he and other white officials walked out. Mayor Snyman — an ex-policeman and former wrestler who owned a bottle store and was known for his aggressive attitude towards blacks — drove back into town to collect the Sten-gun that was to be used against the crowd, and also bought a new pistol for himself.

That night on 10 December 1959, I went to address a rally at the Pokkiesdraai Compound where the present Katutura is situated. We went by car driven by Mr. Gezemba, a friend of mine, accompanied by Kurundiro, a young niece of Clemens Kapuuo who was interested in politics and wanted to see how I was addressing the workers.

Luckily, we did not use the direct road. We took the main road leading to Okahandja and then turned into the compound. We were met by our supporters, who told us that there were two policemen hiding somewhere in the rooms within the compound, ready to shoot me. In the meantime, marching beneath the Hill where the railway line passes to Okahandja, was a large contingent of about one hundred soldiers, armed with rifles.

Their officers had read the placards announcing the rally that I was going to address. I was determined to go on and hold the rally despite the attack threat. But we had to consider the safety of this young girl, who was only about 19 years old. So we drove back so that she would not be caught up in the conflict, and the speech was not delivered. We then went to Kapuuo's house where we found Zedekia Ngavirue (who later became my first Director-General of the National Planning Commission) and Levi Nganjone, a teacher, both of whom had been active in the campaign against the forcible removal to Katutura. We paused there and discussed strategies on what to do next. Ngavirue was then a social worker at the municipality. Kapuuo and I decided to escort Ngavirue to his residence at the municipality offices.

While I was still at Pokkiesdraai Compound to address the workers, the police had made a deliberate arrest of somebody walking where people had gathered at the municipality offices in the Old Location, claiming he was one of those preventing the people from drinking at the Beer Hall. He was in fact a perfectly innocent man. So people, knowing the man was innocent, started to gather around and demand: "Release the man! He is innocent!". That was how the conflict started. Meanwhile, the Superintendent and government officials ordered the police and soldiers to be ready to attack people who gathered at the municipality offices in the Old Location.

The crowd continued to demand the innocent man's release, and Major Lombard responded by giving the crowd five minutes to disperse. Kaukuetu intervened but Lombard refused to withdraw the police, and instead ordered them to fire live bullets into the crowd.

All they could do against the hail of bullets, which killed 12 people and wounded over 50 others on the spot, was to gather stones and throw them at the municipality offices where the police and the Superintendent de Wet and other white officers were inside.

Meanwhile Kapuuo and I reached Ngavirue's residence. Just as we went into the house, shooting started, so we had to lie low and take cover as the house was near the gunfire. After a while the shooting stopped, so Kapuuo and I left, Kapuuo to his house and I went to my home which was only about 500 metres from the municipal offices where the shooting took place — shots had hit the roof of my house. Ngavirue was later expelled from the municipality employment.

Thus ended 10 December 1959, the day the United Nations had proclaimed as Human Rights Day, the Universal Declaration of Human Rights having been passed on that day in 1948. I might add that South Africa was one of the few countries that did not sign the Declaration of Human Rights.

The aftermath of the massacre

The next morning David Meroro, another active campaigner (and later National Chairman of SWAPO), Aaron Kapere and others came to see if I was alive. I was so enraged at the massacre of our people that I seized a gallon of petrol that was in the house, intending to set fire to one of the white-owned shops near the Location, but my wife and my brother prevented me. We had in fact been caught quite unprepared for the shooting by the Boers. Had we known what was to happen we would have organized our young men to counteract, and we would have carried the fight into the centre of Windhoek itself. The time was simply too short to prepare an effective counter offensive to the whites' aggression against our people.

That same morning, members of the Herero Chief's Council and OPO went to the police station to count those who sacrificed their lives on 10 December 1959. I was threatened by one of the policemen, who was carrying a Sten gun. He said I was a troublemaker and I should have been lying dead with others. I was talking to him with my hands in my pockets, and he shouted at me, "Hey! Take your hands out from the pockets, or I'll shoot you!". I told him not to threaten me. Of course, this was the first time I had seen a Sten gun, and I imagined that bullets would come at me from all holes of the barrel. I was later to get much used to the sight of the gun, during our war of national liberation — the idea of which was born that day, when we all knew that, in the end, the only effective way the enemy force could be met would be with the same fire power.

There were many heroic deeds that night, even though our people were so taken by surprise. One of those killed was Bernhardt Gutsche, who was Kerina's step-brother. He was a teacher and a popular man living right next door to the scene of the uprising. The police were determined to kill him in his house because they hated Kerina, who was then in New York petitioning at the UN. Bernhardt Gutsche was shot a second time in the head after the first bullet failed to kill him.

Another victim was Ms. Anna Mungunda, popularly known to us as Kakurukaze Mungunda. During the shooting she attempted to set fire to the Superintendent's car and was then shot dead while doing so. She was one of the heroines of that night's events, and a very beautiful woman. When I went with the National Chairman Meroro, Kapere and many others to see the dead bodies at the police station, I was very moved to see her body. I knew her of course. She seemed to be shining even in her death. We knew when we saw those bodies of innocent people that we had to find a way of fighting against those Boers. It was what really inspired me and others to leave the country, to prepare ourselves for a protracted armed liberation struggle.

The South African Administrator, Daan Viljoen, who was the highest Executive Officer in the country, gave orders that those Africans who were injured during the uprising should not be given medical assistance. I recall that the wife of Dr. Kiwi, who was the President of the then South West African Red Cross, refused to donate blood to the wounded residents of the Old Location. Similarly, all the white doctors at the Windhoek Native Hospital refrained from attending or giving medical treatment to the victims. However, Meekulu Putuse Appolus, who was working as a nurse in that hospital, and other black nurses treated the victims in darkness and saved their lives. She was later deported from South West Africa to South Africa after it was discovered that she and other nurses had helped the victims during the Windhoek Old Location uprising.

A state of emergency was declared and a curfew imposed, and armoured cars and police with sub-machine guns patrolled the streets and perimeter of the Old Location. Even though there was a curfew, we still managed to meet in the Herero Section, making our way there singly and secretly under cover of darkness. The only people given passes to enter the location were those attending church services and relatives who were allowed to attend the burials of those killed by the police. The South African Congress Alliance magazine, *Fighting Talk*, managed to get a black reporter to the funeral. He took pictures and interviewed Nathaniel Mbaeva and myself. Otherwise the press was strictly excluded.

The struggle against the removal to Katutura went on for another seven years. The last of those who had withstood all the South African attempts to move them had to go when the area was 'proclaimed', making it illegal for them to live there. My wife was in that last group who stayed to the end. The houses were demolished and the area was cleared. I was proud to go there in 1990, as the first President of a free non-racial Republic of Namibia, to unveil a memorial tombstone in honour of those who lost their lives as a result of the South African police massacre on 10 December 1959.

Continued appeal to the UN

Chief Kutako, Kaukuetu and I telephoned our colleagues, Kozonguizi, Kerina and Rev. Michael Scott at the UN, and they urged the UN Secretary-General to send a commission of enquiry to investigate the cause of the shooting and massacre of the innocent people of South West Africa.

On 22 December 1959, as President of OPO, I signed a letter together with Chief Hosea Kutako and Samuel Witbooi, reporting the deportation order (at 72 hours notice, with no reason given), against Kuhangua, Mbaeva, Bathlomeus Shimbama and myself. One part of our letter read that our faith in the UN was already being tested by these events:

> "We ask the United Nations to tell the Union Government to desist immediately from these repressive acts of deportations.
>
> We find it very difficult to have our cases defended in courts in South West Africa where there are only white lawyers who are not keen at all to defend Africans. For that reason we asked Mr. Oliver Tambo, a well known African lawyer from the Union of South Africa, who, on his arrival by air from Johannesburg, was not granted the necessary permit to enter South West Africa. [Oliver Tambo left South Africa the following year and later became the President of the ANC of South Africa, in exile.] In South West Africa, Africans had no lawyers to defend them. Windhoek has just become a war camp. The Location is being patrolled day and night by armoured cars and armed police jeeps with machine guns. We strongly request the United Nations to urge the Union Government to withdraw its police and defence forces from South West Africa.
>
> The Union Government appointed Mr. Justice Hall, Judge President for South West Africa, to investigate the cause of the uprising in Windhoek Old Location. But as we have no faith in the Union Government we do not trust any commission appointed by the Union Government. We are afraid that such a commission will not be free from partiality, taking into account the atmosphere in which the commission will investigate. We therefore ask the United Nations to send an impartial commission to South West Africa to investigate the recent killings and shootings of Africans in the Windhoek Old Location by the Union Government forces.

It is absolutely necessary that a United Nations Commission should visit South West Africa immediately because the absence of a United Nations Commission in South West Africa has created the impression among Government Officials in South West Africa and the Union that the United Nations is far away in New York and will never set its foot in South West Africa to prevent them from further carrying out their repressive acts against the indigenous people."

The debates on South West Africa at the United Nations during the past 14 years would have been effective had the United Nations sent a commission during that period.

We first sent a letter that read: "We earnestly request that the question of South West Africa be taken to the International Court of Justice without any further delay for compulsory jurisdiction." A week later we sent another letter reporting on the police raids on the homes of eleven people, including Chief Kutako, Louis Nelengani, Nathaniel Mbaeva (already deported to the Epukiro Reserve), and Bernhardt Gutsche, Kerina's step-brother. The police also raided the houses of Comrade Ya Toivo and the Reverend Mutumbangela in Ovamboland.

We also reported the deaths of three Africans, shot by unidentified whites on the Okahandja Road, and the purchase of more than 200 rifles and revolvers by the white community in Windhoek as the result of the South African government's deliberate creation of hostility between black and white. We appealed to the UN, in the light of this grave situation, to treat this matter as urgent.

Attempts to arrest and deport activists

In the days after the uprising, two armed white CID policemen were employed to follow me. Their plans were to find me alone, interrogate me and then shoot me on the pretence that I was running away from them. OPO members volunteered to guard me 24 hours a day, even in my house. That protection saved me.

We also learned from a worker employed by the Lutheran Church that there was a meeting at Pastor Diel's house attended by the Chief of the CID, the Commander of Police, the Chief Native Commissioner and other officials. The meeting was called, with their puppets such as Ananias Shipena who were members of the Old Location Advisory Board, to plan how to deal with the situation in the Old Location.

Shipena told his bosses that, if they wanted politics to stop in South West Africa, they must first remove this young man Sam Nujoma — "He is everywhere; he organizes the people and is very effective. He must be removed." Again I was in danger of being deported to the north, where like Comrade Ya Toivo I would have been placed in detention at Chief Kambonde's residence at Okaloko. But I found a lawyer to defend me, and once again they failed to arrest and deport me, as they had also failed to do the previous August.

On 15 December 1959, I was served with a deportation order, as was Bathlomeus Shimbama. I was accused of inciting violence and hatred against the whites and of being an undesirable person to be in the Police Zone. Employers had already been warned not to employ Sam Nujoma as he was considered to be a dangerous person for the future of white people in this country. My lawyer, Lucian Goldblatt of the law firm of Block and Co., told me that he could do little to defend me as a black person in court, since the law of this country did not recognize a black person as a human being. Thus a black person could not be tried in accordance with the law. I was his client so he did appear for me on 30 December 1959. The magistrate simply said, "Your case has been withdrawn". I left the court only to be re-arrested on the same charge. I was taken again to the police station and had to pay bail of £10. On 10 January 1960 I appeared again, and again the case was withdrawn. I was served with deportation orders for a third time.

From 27 to 31 December 1959, Chief Kutako's house, mine and others' were surrounded by the police and searched for documents. They first came to my house before dawn, waking us up and frightening our small children. My wife's young sisters, who were staying with us, bravely went out as if to fetch water from the common tap, taking my papers with them to Aaron Hamutenya to hide. So the police got nothing from my house. Elsewhere, letters from Michael Scott and Kerina, as well as petitions to the UN — which were anathema to the Boers — were taken, some of which came to be used by the police in the Court of Enquiry, which began on 11 January 1960.

I was among many people who had been rounded up and accused of organizing the uprising. OPO hired the law company of Tambo and Mandela in Johannesburg. As we had told the UN, when Oliver Tambo flew to Windhoek he was held up at the Eros Airport by Native Commissioner Blignaut, because the magistrate did not want to be confronted by a black lawyer, and Tambo was deported back to South Africa the next day. We brought food to him at the airport. Later on, advocate

Van Niekerk was sent from Johannesburg to defend us. He was a very effective lawyer. He squashed the case after a very lengthy trial.

Decision to leave South West Africa

Now into February 1960, the case had already cost us £125 — a very great deal of money at that time. We realized that we were spending too much money and getting nowhere, so it was decided that I had to get out of the country, to reinforce Kozonguizi, Kerina and the Reverend Michael Scott in their petitioning at the UN. The decision was taken by both OPO and the Herero Chiefs' Council, and OPO provided me with £500 sterling to cover the expenses of my journey to New York. We knew this would be a hazardous and roundabout affair, as I had no passport. I was technically still on trial and I would have to jump bail and travel through countries that were still British colonies.

At the time it was decided I would leave for New York, we still trusted that the UN would assist us to achieve freedom. I had already spoken for OPO by petitioning in writing, together in a broad front with Chief Samuel Witbooi of the Namas, Chief Hosea Kutako and the Herero Chief's Council. Now I should petition at the UN itself.

My objective was to achieve the removal of the South African colonial administration, and the placement of South West Africa under the United Nations trusteeship system, so that while under UN trusteeship our preparation for self-determination and independence could be achieved. We took it for granted that our petitions would be effective and that the UN would assist us towards self-determination and genuine independence.

However, much disappointment and frustration were to follow.

I said good-bye to my wife and small children, whom OPO had undertaken to support during what we thought would be my one or two year absence. I had a final meeting with Chief Hosea Kutako on 26 February 1960. We had been meeting very frequently before that, so at the end he merely gave me his blessing and told me that I must be prepared to be away for a very long time and if necessary not to come back until South West Africa had won genuine freedom and independence.

Chief Hosea Kutako was right, for the two years I thought I would be absent stretched in the end to 29 years before I was able to come back and play my leadership role in ensuring the creation of a free and independent Namibia.

◆ ◆ ◆

5

Escape from South West Africa

From Windhoek to Francistown

I commenced my long journey on the morning of 29 February 1960. I was driven from Windhoek Old Location to Gobabis by Johannes Karuaihe who was going to Otjinene and Epukiro. From Gobabis we then continued after midnight to the border between South West Africa and British Bechuanaland Protectorate. I was given a lift in a truck, driven by a man named Stanley who was originally from South West Africa but was then living in Bechuanaland. Around midnight, Stanley dropped me near Kanaindo, about 20 km from the border post. I went on foot until I had to crawl under the border fence into the British Bechuanaland Protectorate. Thus, on 1 March 1960, I found myself for the first time beyond the reach of our South African oppressors. Ahead of me were many British colonial territories to pass through, before reaching Dar-es-Salaam in Tanganyika, which was then still one year away from independence.

At that time the nearest independent African states were Egypt, Libya, Morocco, Ethiopia and Liberia, and the more recent ones Sudan, Guinea-Conakry, Mali and Ghana. Though my own country was little known, not being part of one of the empires of the western powers but occupied by South Africa, the uprising in Windhoek Old Location and the massacre of its people less than three months earlier had been in the headlines. My own name and face were well known from the local press reports, at least in South West Africa and across its borders.

Furthermore, the leading politicians in the countries I was hoping to cross on my journey to the UN would know about the petitioning of the Reverend Michael Scott, with Kozonguizi and Kerina at the UN.

There were people from the Herero section of our population who had been living at Omakunda since their grandparents had escaped from the genocide inflicted on the Herero and Nama by the Germans in the 1904–07 war. They knew about me, and it was arranged through Chief Hosea Kutako that they would assist me after I had crossed the border. I went first to Omamuno on the Bechuanaland side. It was the middle of the night so I saw no one and went on foot all the way to Omakunda, an area predominantly inhabited by our Herero people.

It was before dawn and people were still sleeping when I reached this village. I went to one of the huts and knocked. A lady came out and I spoke to her in Herero. She probably thought I was one of the local people and invited me in. It was chilly, being the beginning of March, and it was raining. She asked me whether I did not feel cold. I said "no, I have an overcoat, so I would prefer to stay outside". I asked her about people I knew, or whose names I was given. She told me they had gone to a wedding ceremony somewhere nearby in one of the villages, and they would be back in the morning. She again asked me to come in though that was the only hut she occupied, and she offered me some milk. I thanked her and said I carried a flask and had just had some tea. She was a very good lady and her kindness cheered me. I waited with her until the people whom I was expected to meet arrived.

During the day I met those I was looking for. I was still close to the border, so, that same day, we arranged that I would ride with them on horseback deeper into the interior. We reached a place where I bought a goat and we had a barbecue. The next day a truck arrived which belonged to some local white farmers. I wore my trousers with one leg longer than the other so that I would look like an ordinary local villager. With my Herero companions, I travelled in the truck with my suitcase concealed under sacks. We had to pay 2s 6p each for our lift, sitting at the back of the open truck.

The owner of the truck was going only as far as his farm, so at that turn-off we had to wait for another truck. This took us to a place called Kai, where the farmer who owned the truck had a store. He had been in South West Africa before, farming near Grootfontein. Some of his workers were from the Kavango Region, and had come with him to Bechuanaland. When the daughter-in-law of the owner of the store saw me, she noticed the marks on my face and said, "Oh! I know this man is an Ovambo", and ran out from the store. I felt very scared for a moment, until I realized that she had gone to call one of the Kavango workers. When this Kavango man came to look at me, I quickly said, "No, my mother is Herero and my father was an Ovambo, but I have never been in that part of the country". So the Kavango man lost interest in me and went back to his work. I was very relieved, having thought suspicion would be aroused and that I might be held by these people and returned to South West Africa.

I bought some biscuits at the store and ate with my companion who had accompanied me from Omakunda to this place. We stayed there waiting for transport, but the local people told us that the next transport from here to Sehitua might not come for a week. The farmer also owned an aircraft which he used to ferry tourists. We knew this would cost us a lot of money, and instead we went to ask him if he could take us by car. It was exactly 100 miles from Kai to Sehitua and he charged us £1 sterling per mile. I had no choice. I could not risk staying there for a week because of this lady who had identified me as an Ovambo.

The farmer dropped us at Sehitua where I made contact with the late Daniel Munamava, whom I had met when he used to accompany Chief Munjuku Nguvauva of the Mbanderu during his visits to Windhoek. His family were related to my wife, so he used to visit me in Windhoek and knew me very well. From Sehitua, Munamava and I went on to Maun where he got places for us in a truck that was transporting contract workers, mainly from Angola, through Rundu in South West Africa where they were recruited by WENALA, and on to Francistown to work in the South African gold mines.

Meanwhile my companion who accompanied me all the way from Omakunda had to return home as he was going to get married in a few days. I paid for his journey back.

From Francistown to Salisbury

Munamava and I travelled with the contract workers to Francistown, the first small town I had reached since I left home. There was no single political party in the whole of Bechuanaland at that time, so there was nobody in Francistown I could make contact with. For the whole week that we stayed there, the only people I met who were really politically conscious were from Nyasaland (later to be known as Malawi). They were returning from the South African mines after completing their contracts and were waiting to go back home by WENALA Air Line from

Francistown via Broken Hill in Northern Rhodesia (now Kabwe, Zambia). We discussed politics because, with Dr. Hastings Banda in prison, like Dr. Kenneth Kaunda, politics was hot in the so-called Federation of Rhodesia and Nyasaland and they were politically conscious.

The day they were to leave I asked them popular names of people in their area and they told me that 'Chipinga' was one of the most common names. I decided to assume the name 'David Chipinga'. Then I drafted a telegram, gave them enough money and told them to send the telegram back to me once they got to Broken Hill. It read: "Your Uncle Chipinga is very ill and there is no hope come soon". I received the telegram the same day, and later that afternoon I took a passenger train which was passing from Johannesburg to Bulawayo in Southern Rhodesia. With that telegram I passed through Plumtree, the Border Post between Bechuanaland and Southern Rhodesia, and began the next stage of my journey.

I worked out a new plan. I bought pyjamas, a smart dressing gown and slippers, and a number of newspapers — *Cape Times*, *Cape-Argus*, the *Star* and *Rand Daily Mail*. I laid the papers out neatly on the little table in my single reserved first class compartment, and locked myself in. When we reached the Southern Rhodesian border, a Rhodesian Boer knocked several times before I let him in. I could see he thought I was a well-to-do man, and I said to him, "You woke me up!". He replied, "Yes, but I wanted to find out whether you have a permit or visa to enter the British colony of Southern Rhodesia". I told him I was a teacher in British Bechuanaland Protectorate and I was on my way to my uncle Chipinga who was very ill in Broken Hill. I was making a very quick visit after which I would have to rush back to school. He read the telegram which the Nyasa workers sent me in Francistown. He said he would let me through, but that next time I must have a visa. When he left I laughed to myself with satisfaction that my plan had worked.

Daniel Munamava still accompanied me since he knew the way by train to Bulawayo station. Because he was travelling on a British passport, he had no problem. He sat in a different compartment so as not to draw suspicion. It was best for me to handle my situation alone.

When I left Windhoek our National Chairman, Comrade David Meroro, had bought me a travelling rug and six very good white shirts, what we used to call 'cutaways'. When we arrived at Bulawayo station after midnight we saw the notice 'Goods to declare' and went there because of the new shirts. An official took the shirts and the rug, but said the Customs officials had closed for the night and told us to come back the next day. I could not risk returning to the train station to claim my belongings, because of the great danger that Southern Rhodesian immigration authorities would recognize me and send me back to South West Africa. The political situation in March 1960 was very tense in Southern Rhodesia.

I rushed early in the morning to Bulawayo Airport and bought a ticket to Mbeya in Tanganyika, via Salisbury and Ndola in Northern Rhodesia. From Bulawayo that same morning I flew to Salisbury (now Harare).

From Salisbury to Mbeya

I was now well and truly on my own — however, in a strange country that was in a state of political turmoil. In the airport lounge I heard some African women talking in the local language — a form of Fanakalo called Lapalapa. This was the 'Lingua-Franca' spoken in South African mines, a little of which I had picked up, while I was working at the whaling station in Walvis Bay, from someone who had worked in South African gold mines. I asked the women if they knew of any politicians I could meet. They said "Yes, we know". I said "OK!, take me there by taxi and I will give you money to come back to your work".

They took me to a member of the Liberal Party of Southern Rhodesia, which had backed the Rhodesian Federation, led by Sir Roy Welensky. This man was a Southern Rhodesian who had worked in Cape Town where he married a South African lady, and they had children. His name was Muamuka and he had a small general store in the location called Highfield. I told him who I was and asked him a lot of questions. He said he knew about South West Africa, and told me all about his work in South Africa and that he got married there, and was altogether sympathetic to our cause. I asked him to introduce me to the local politicians. He arranged a meeting for me with the President and Vice-President of the National Democratic Party of Southern Rhodesia (NDP) [this later became ZAPU, which then came to be known as ZANU (PF)].

The President of the NDP was Michael Mawema, and the Vice-President was Morton Marianga. We had a lot of discussions about future plans and strategies on how to liberate Africa from white domination. Our discussions carried on too long and I missed my flight to Ndola. I went back to Mr Muamuka who was kind enough to provide me with meals and overnight accommodation.

The next day I managed to get a flight to the Copper Belt town of Ndola, but in Ndola I missed my connecting flight to Mbeya in Tanganyika. I found I would have to spend a week in Ndola, waiting for the next flight. I decided to leave my belongings at the terminal, and walked about the streets of Ndola.

Eventually, I found some African children, aged between 12 to 14. I talked to them and bought them some sweets. I asked them where their teachers lived and they took me to the house of one of them. Luckily, this teacher had been to Ghana to attend one of the Commonwealth Teacher's Association meetings in Accra. So he knew something about the political developments that were rapidly changing Africa.

At that time Dr. Kenneth Kaunda was in detention in Salisbury, as well as Hastings Banda in Gweru. Sir Roy Welensky, British Colonial Administrator, was trying to maintain the white domination in the Federation which was under attack by Banda and Kaunda who were struggling to liberate the Federation. Kaunda, particularly, was referred to as a terrorist and as the 'Black Mamba' by the white settlers. Political activists were closely monitored.

The teacher told me that there was a guest house for black members of the Liberal Party, so I made my way there, paying in advance for a week's stay.

While staying in the Guest House I asked for members of the United National Independence Party (UNIP) and finally found them during the week. One of them was Fines Bulawayo, who became a Minister in Kaunda's government, later a member of the Central Committee, and Provincial Political Secretary in Luapula Province. He was then Publicity Secretary of UNIP in Ndola for the whole Copper Belt. They told me I was staying at the wrong place, and that the security police of Sir Roy Welensky would find out I was there and report my presence. They moved me out to one of the African shanty townships where I stayed with the Vice-President of the UNIP Youth, Daniel Chitunda.

With UNIP member Fines Bulawayo we crossed the border at night from Ndola into Katanga Province of Belgian Congo (now DRC). We met with members of the Conakat Party of Moice Tshombe who, together with Patrice Lumumba and Josef Kasavubu, were still fighting against the Belgian colonial occupation of their country. We discussed how we could coordinate our political activities in order to get rid of colonial occupation of Africa in general and of our countries in particular. Those were the days of practical solidarity and Pan-Africanism taking roots among the African people on the continent.

We also met Tshombe's legal adviser. I had doubts as to his credibility as a lawyer, as he did not even know where South West Africa was. I already knew from home of the struggle in the Congo against Belgian colonialists. Bulawayo and Tshombe's legal advisers knew each other as they were both members of the Lunda tribe who are found in Katanga Province and in Northern Rhodesia's Copper Belt (and some are even found in Angola), and they conversed in their local language. Most people were satisfied by our political discussions, though I had to be a little careful with everyone I talked to.

That same night we crossed the border back to Ndola in Northern Rhodesia. The next day someone went to Ndola Airport with my ticket and kit-bag and a small suitcase containing my thermos flask and other basic items that I needed since I sometimes did not know where I was going to spend the night. He checked-in my bags and brought me the boarding pass. I waited until the very last announcement of the flight, and then appeared with my boarding pass. The custom officials asked me where I was going and where my passport was. I told them I was a teacher and I was going to Mbeya and then back to Broken Hill by road. As I was talking I was already moving towards the aeroplane, just as the air hostess was beginning to close the door. While the Rhodesian Boers kept on questioning me I simply passed them and got into the plane.

I was the only black person in the plane with a lot of British passengers. Though I had seen a few British before, this time I was struck by their long moustaches and long feet.

From Mbeya to Njombe

When we were just approaching Mbeya airport we were given an immigration form to complete, on which was written that anybody who entered the British Protectorate of Tanganyika Territory without a visa or permission would be liable to pay a fine of 50,000 East African shillings or serve three months imprisonment, or both. So I became rather alarmed, tore the form up and discarded it.

We duly landed at Mbeya Airport which in those days was not fenced off. There were long grasses around it and bushes. When the British passengers got out I decided to remain in the plane. I then disembarked and looked around, thinking I might run into the bush and hide in the long grasses. But I decided, No! I must keep my dignity, I would not run. But then how would I get through the customs immigration without a passport? This was the worst moment of my journey since I left home.

There were some African and Indian children spectators watching the flights that were arriving. The British started to go through the immigration officials, so I started to read one of the newspapers I had brought from Bechuanaland and moved towards the group of children. I had to plan how to get my kit-bag and briefcase, but I could not come up with any idea at all. Then suddenly, with amazing good fortune, an Indian man, a driver of an East African Airways station wagon, came to me and said, "Are you Mr. David Chipinga?". I said yes, and he said, "Your suitcases are over there! Will you fetch them or can I bring them to you?". I replied, "Yes, please bring them". He did so and asked whether I had a place to stay. When I said no, he asked me whether he could take me to Mbeya Hotel, to which I agreed and off we went. At Mbeya Hotel, I registered myself as 'David Chipinga' and was given a bungalow far from the main hotel building, with a warm bathroom. And so for the first time in my life I found myself staying in a hotel.

I unpacked my suitcase, ordered food, ate well and waited there until dark. I then went out, following a long avenue until I reached the African township. When I found children at a playground, I bought them some sweets and started to talk to them in simple English. I asked them if they knew where the Tanganyikan African National Union (TANU) Office was and they said yes. I asked them to take me there, which they did. As it was already very late in the evening, I went back to my hotel. The next morning I went to the TANU Office where I found the Regional Secretary of TANU, by the name of Ali Chande. He was a very good man, who later became the first Chief of Protocol in Nyerere's government. I told him who I was and he told me how he and his colleagues were struggling for their independence. Nyerere was, at that time, in New York petitioning at the UN.

It was now Monday, 21 March 1960, three weeks since I had crossed the border, and a day that was to become our Independence Day.

I got the impression that the TANU members were well in control of the situation. I drafted a telegram to the Chairman of the United Nations Committee on South West Africa, requesting an oral hearing. I went together with Ali Chande to Mbeya Post Office and sent it, feeling that I had taken a major step towards my destination, but not knowing that obstacles were still to come.

The British had a good intelligence network wherever they were. Those who were working for the colonial authority were well trained. They saw this telegram and sent it to the police to check whether I had a permit to enter the British Tanganyika Protectorate. I had no idea of this. I then fell ill, suffering from malaria, which I must have picked up in Bechuanaland during one of the nights when I slept in the bush.

Ali Chande took me to the Catholic Hospital where his wife was working as a nurse, and I was given an injection against the fever. I went home and took the sleeping tablets which I was also given to take. Ali Chande went to town on some party business but came rushing back to tell me that he had met a British policeman who was new in town, transferred from Tabora. The policeman asked him whether he knew someone called Sam Nujoma who was trying to get to the United Nations, and that they wanted to check on him. Ali Chande told me that he knew how the British system operated, and he was sure they were going to ask the magistrate to issue a warrant to search the houses of TANU members, including his own.

Chande also knew that all British officials including the police would go for lunch at 1 p.m., and so he arranged for me to leave Mbeya at that hour, in a taxi. Again I had avoided discovery, but had to pay a lot of money for the 100 mile journey from Mbeya to Njombe.

From Njombe to Dar-es-Salaam

Njombe was a small town with a Lutheran Mission, a big church and a good hospital. When Ali Chande and I reached Njombe the police saw us in the car, but we were not recognised. Meanwhile, as I learned later, the British had telephoned all the police stations in the whole of Tanganyika to watch out for me.

At Njombe we proceeded to the house of the Regional Secretary of TANU. While we were there they prepared some food for us, but Ali Chande and the Regional Secretary went away to the TANU office. While they were away, two black CID police officers came to the house, but they only saw the two children, who were between 10 and 12 years of age. They asked the children if there was a strange person in the house and when the children said no, the CID policemen left. Ali Chande saw the CID police officers on their way to the house and rushed, thinking they had discovered me. But by the time he arrived the CID officers had already gone.

Ali Chande and his colleagues, for tactical reasons, had arranged with an African Medical Doctor to have me admitted to the Lutheran Hospital. I was taken there that afternoon and spent the night in the hospital. But the black medical doctor had to go off duty the next day and was replaced by a white doctor. So he had to discharge me from the hospital, and I was taken to the local Chief's court and hidden there. Chief Josef was also a supporter of TANU and a friend of Nyerere. No one would suspect that anybody was in a courtroom if there were no court proceedings going on, so I was hidden there until dark, and they brought food for me there. Some time after midnight, when the policemen on the beat were moving slowly, I was taken from the courtroom.

A taxi carried us from Njombe to Dar-es-Salaam. We arrived there the next morning after an eight hour drive, during which we had to stop for petrol at Iringa and Dodoma. I was able to pay for all this as I had still had funds remaining from those provided by OPO for my long journey to the United Nations.

Ali Chande had accompanied me all the way from Njombe to Dar-es-Salaam. From there he went back to Mbeya where he found a positive reply telegram from the UN Committee on South West Africa, granting me an oral hearing. He had to travel all the way back to Dar-es-Salaam again to bring it to me.

From Dar-es-Salaam to Accra

I felt I was another step ahead, and even more so when in Dar-es-Salaam I met Julius Nyerere, who was the president of TANU and a member of the Legislative Council of Tanganyika. He had just arrived from New York where he had been petitioning at the UN. He addressed a rally in Dar-es-Salaam informing the public of the result of the petitioning. I met Nyerere then and we discussed at length our plans concerning the liberation of the African continent. After our discussion he asked me if I had money. The Mau Mau State of Emergency was still in force in Kenya, and he told me that the only way to get out of East Africa was to travel to Khartoum in the Sudan, and that I should try to cross the continent to Accra — Ghana. He arranged for me to stay at Mangomeni Mukumi with his friend Mr. Mbakbenja, and said he would talk to the British Governor about me being in Tanganyika and my intention to proceed to New York to petition at the UN.

I stayed about for a fortnight in Dar-es-Salaam while we planned my journey. Since I had no passport or legal document, the British Overseas Airways Corporation (BOAC) refused to put me on board unless I had a Dar-es-Salaam—Nairobi—Khartoum return ticket. In the event the Sudanese refused me entry at Khartoum airport, they would have to fly me back to Dar-es-Salaam. There was also the problem of me being illegally in Tanganyika, while 'wanted' by the colonial authority back home. Nyerere, as he had promised, went to the Governor and told him who I was and that I was intending to go to the UN. The Governor, Sir Richard Turnbull, was a good man. He said, "So long as he is leaving the country it's quite all right having him here until he finds his way out".

Following the State of Emergency in South Africa, after the Sharpeville massacre on 21 March 1960, the South African apartheid regime banned the national liberation movements, the African National Congress (ANC) and Pan Africanist Congress, on 8 April 1960. Just before this, Comrade Oliver Tambo, President of the African National Congress, and Ronald Segal, editor of the magazine *Africa South*, had chartered a plane to Bechuanaland and they came on to Dar-es-Salaam and found me there. After we met they flew on to London. I stayed to continue on by BOAC from Dar-es-Salaam to Khartoum. The flights of those days were not direct so we made a stopover at Nairobi Mbakasi Airport. I saw the British soldiers there, the King's African Rifles, drilling smartly. The security was very tight, so the BOAC officials put me in a small room, and brought me tea. I waited for two hours until we flew on to Khartoum, leaving about 9.30 p.m. and reaching Khartoum at about 7 a.m the next morning.

When we arrived in Khartoum I found that there was a Muslim Conference taking place. I saw people wearing long white dresses: I had not expected to see this in what had been the Anglo-Egyptian Sudan, which had only just become independent in 1957. Again I was the only black person on the plane, so as before I waited until all the British got out and then went into the airport building. At the immigration counter I met an elderly Sudanese who was a very stout man. I said "Uncle, I am from South West Africa, and I am going to the United Nations to petition". He was alone and listened to me attentively. He asked me whether I had money and when I told him I had, he told me that he had also been in prison here during their struggle against the British.

I showed him the money I had, and he said he would keep it with him in his safe, and that I should take about £3 which would be enough for me to pay for hotel accommodation. He booked me into the Hotel Acropole, run by a Greek businessman. It was a nice hotel with nice food. While I was in the hotel I contacted the Ghanaian Embassy, and after discussions the Ambassador sent a telegram to Accra. My flight to Ghana was quickly arranged with Air Liban, but at that time Nigeria was still a British colony, six months away from independence, and the danger and tension of my journey was still on.

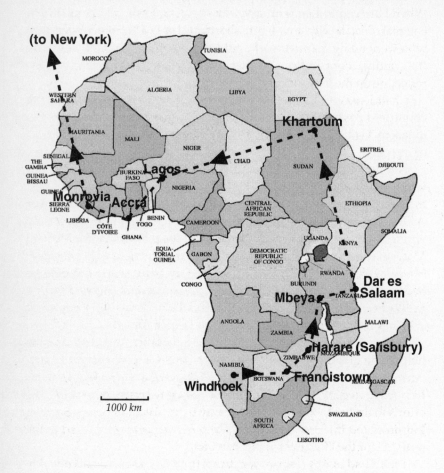

14 Route of Sam Nujoma's "escape from South West Africa" (showing present-day names of countries)

The good fortune that got me to Dar-es-Salaam, and on through Kenya and Sudan, stayed with me. Air Liban flew every Thursday across the continent, from Khartoum to Lagos and from Lagos to Accra. When I arrived in Lagos on my way to Accra, I saw plenty of British colonial officials with their white shorts, and only a few black Nigerians who were doing manual work, but I did not talk to them. I went into the waiting room and stayed there until my aircraft was ready to fly, reflecting on the long journey behind me.

I had learned much from my journey. I was a stranger in all the countries I passed through and often had to make up my mind on who to talk to. I was always friendly to the children, and they were often part of my plan.

Another thing that I learned was that ordinary people did not know much about South West Africa. The Windhoek Uprising and massacre the previous December had been in the headlines all over Africa, but nevertheless many people did not even know precisely where South West Africa was. It was only the politicians like Michael Mawema and the UNIP and TANU members who were well informed. Many of the Zimbabweans had worked in South Africa and some had been to school there, like Herbert Chitepo, one of the first advocates in Southern Rhodesia who studied at Fort Hare University. Only a few scholars and politicians knew about South West Africa.

It was these leaders of the National Liberation Movements who helped me greatly on my way. In some cases we were extremely successful in our cooperation, such as in Tanganyika where TANU members frustrated the British Criminal Investigation Department in their efforts to find out who I was, all the way from Mbeya to Dar-es-Salaam. I appreciated their solidarity and the positive part they played in the struggle for the liberation of our continent.

I felt I had at last reached the free Africa which we would one day join. Sudan had been a foretaste, but Ghana led by Nkrumah was a real inspiration.

◆ ◆ ◆

6

Ghana and the United Nations

I had escaped from South West Africa and finally arrived in a free and independent Ghana in April 1960. I found myself in the centre of the campaign for African independence and unity, in which OPO and my fellow countrymen in the Herero and Nama chiefs councils and SWANU were engaged. When I arrived in Accra, there was a Positive Action Conference in progress, organized by President Kwame Nkrumah, against the French Government's testing of the atomic bomb in the Sahara desert at the time when the Algerians were fighting for their freedom and independence. The same Conference also condemned South Africa's apartheid policy and its refusal to place South West Africa under the UN trusteeship system.

Accra held much in store for me and for our struggle. This was a time of tremendous historic occasions in Africa. Following on our own Windhoek Uprising was the Sharpeville Massacre, and the decolonization of many African states, with the former Belgian Congo also on the brink of independence.

My arrival in Accra was expected and I was warmly welcomed. I found the Reverend Michael Scott and Fanuel Kozonguizi there, who had left South West Africa early in 1958 and gone to New York to petition the UN. While in Accra, I met African leaders from different liberation movements in the continent including President Kwame Nkrumah himself, Patrice Lumumba, Josef Kasavubu, and Frantz Fanon, representing the Algerian National Liberation Front (FLN).

15 The great leaders of African independence
    (L) President Kwame Nkrumah (Ghana) and
    (R) President Gamal Abdel Nasser (Egypt)
    in Cairo for 2nd OAU Summit, 1964

These were leaders who made great contributions to the liberation of the African continent. I gave an eye-witness account of the Windhoek Old Location Uprising and the unprovoked police massacre. We had cabled the UN about the killings and Chief Hosea Kutako and I had jointly sent a written account to the United Nations, but there had never been a first-hand oral presentation, and I was at last able to tell the whole story. I also addressed the Conference, which supported our demand for the placement of South West Africa under the UN trusteeship system as the first priority. Tambo, Segal and Dr. Dadoo were there too, as well as PAC representatives, and South Africa was also deliberated upon. At that early stage, we had to make it categorically clear that we were not part and parcel of apartheid South African territory but a different and separate country altogether, demanding our inalienable rights.

I remember clearly Nkrumah's words at the Conference. His theme was that the continent was awakened: the giant that had been asleep was aroused. The whole continent was represented, from South Africa to Algeria, and Nkrumah himself gave the Keynote Address. I had personal talks with Nkrumah on several occasions, at which he urged me to "Keep on! The Ghana government is behind you". It was immensely encouraging to know that a free African country was supporting us; so far I had been receiving assistance, but always from people whose countries were still ruled from Europe. Nkrumah did not only encourage us, but his Government also spent a lot of money in publicising the cause of the oppressed people of Africa. This effort greatly contributed to the awakening of the people of Africa to demand their freedom and independence.

Despite being the architect of his county's independence, subsequent political manoeuvrings against him resulted in Kwame Nkrumah spending the last years of his life in exile in Conakry, Guinea. He died 27 April 1972 in Bucharest, Romania, where he had been receiving medical care. His body was first sent to Conakry, where a state funeral was held (14 May 1972). He was then buried in Ghana, not in the capital city Accra, but in the town of his birth, Nkroful, on 9 July 1972. Twenty years later, in 1992, I attended a ceremony of reburial in the new Kwame Nkrumah Memorial Park, in Accra. This ceremony marked a renewed recognition, in his own country and around the world, of the importance of this great leader. It was in a spirit of sincere gratitude that, at the invitation of Ghana Head of State Flight Lieutenant Jerry John Rawlings, I was present at the ceremony as the only visiting head of state, together with Oliver Tambo (President of the African National Congress), and I addressed the solemn proceedings at the ceremony.

In Accra, Kozonguizi and I contacted the Special Representative of President Gamal Abdel Nasser of Egypt, who came to attend the Positive Action Conference. He gave us a very sympathetic hearing which I was soon to follow up. Egypt's first practical help came from President Nasser's Special Representative who gave £100 sterling to each of us. With part of the money I was given, I bought an Olivetti portable typewriter, which I used for many years during the struggle and which I still have.

At that time, Liberia and Ethiopia, on behalf of African independent states, had initiated legal proceedings against apartheid South Africa at the International Court of Justice in The Hague, charging the apartheid South Africa for failing to fulfil the mandate over South West Africa, with which it had been entrusted by the League of Nations in 1920. To assist in the preparation for the case, I went to Liberia and met Ernest Gross, the American attorney who was preparing the legal proceedings.

Between 1950 and 1956, the International Court of Justice had given three advisory opinions on South West Africa, all of them favourable to the people of South West Africa. But these were ignored by South Africa, who defied the United Nations resolutions that resulted from these rulings. After a thorough preparation, on 4 November 1960, Liberia and Ethiopia, the only African members of the League of Nations, applied to the Court, under Article 7 of the mandate, which laid down that:

> "If any dispute should arise between the mandatory or another member of the League of Nations relating to the interpretation or the application of the provisions in the mandate by such dispute, if it cannot be settled by negotiation, shall be submitted to the Permanent Court of International Justice."

The International Court of Justice under Article 37 of its own statute took over some of the functions of the Permanent Court. If South Africa failed to act upon the judgment of the court, the Security Council could be asked to act so that the judgment was given effect. Even if there was a veto in the Security Council, a two-thirds majority in the General Assembly could bring about sanctions in the interests of 'international peace and security.'

So the case being brought by Ethiopia and Liberia was of very great importance to us. After seven years of petitions, resolutions and three advisory rulings, the United Nations would at last have to consider serious action against apartheid South Africa — if the Court ruled in our favour. We were strongly in support of the court action and gave the lawyers, led by Ernest Gross, all the help we could. While in Monrovia I met Mburumba Kerina, who was working at the Liberian mission at the UN. We planned to strengthen our petitioning strategies at the UN and decided that the name 'Ovamboland People's Organization' (OPO) gave the impression that we were only a regional organization and not, as we really were, a national one. So we sent a message back to Windhoek to change the name to 'South West Africa People's Organization' (SWAPO).

Another thing that held us together, across the tribal barriers the Boers tried to perpetuate, was the inspiration we got from what was happening elsewhere in Africa — not only in Ghana but in Guinea-Conakry, the Belgian Congo, the Central Africa Federation of Northern and Southern Rhodesia and Nyasaland led by Kaunda of UNIP, Banda and Mawema, and the Mau Mau armed struggle led by Jomo Kenyatta in Kenya. And Tanganyika led by Nyerere was on the verge of independence. The whole process on the continent gave us moral encouragement to continue with the struggle to fight against the apartheid South African regime in South West Africa.

Inside South Africa, the apartheid regime was aware of this growing spirit of unity and wanted to make sure we did not call ourselves 'Africans', so they had previously introduced the word 'bantu'. For decades by this time the apartheid regime had implemented numerous pieces of oppressive legislation incorporating this term. Among these was the invention of the so-called 'bantustans', which were the least hospitable extenses of land, without economic or strategic value to the white South Africans. These had been designated as 'native homelands', while the white farmers appropriated the rich traditional homelands. Restricted to the bantustans, the people could only live in poverty because of the unsuitability of the land for agriculture, and the general lack of natural resources such as water, grazing and fuels. Additionally, 'natives' were effectively, if not directly, prevented from owning land in the 'bantustans', or otherwise becoming prosperous. Having thus created a poverty-stricken population and a pool of cheap labour, the diabolical apartheid regime then held out the opportunity for work through the semi-slave contract labour system.

Incredibly, in view of all that, I remember the leader of the South West African colonial administration in South West Africa, the counterpart of the opposition United Party, being quoted in the papers as saying that the introduction of the term 'bantu' was a mistake, because it would make the 'natives' in South West Africa think they were the brothers of blacks in South Africa! So in his fanciful view, the possibility that 'natives' might prosper, even from the word 'bantu' itself, would be a bad thing. In South West Africa, of course, we already knew we were brothers and sisters of blacks in South Africa, and that we must not allow ourselves to continue to be isolated.

To New York

From Liberia we flew to New York, together with a remarkable lady, and ally of SWAPO, the Honourable Angie Brooks. She was Assistant Secretary to the Liberian Foreign Minister, James Grimes, and later become Vice-President of Liberia. She was to make a statement at the UN on South West Africa and to spearhead the campaign on our behalf. The Liberian government paid for my ticket from Monrovia to New York and back to Dar-es-Salaam via Monrovia, Accra and Lagos. Pan-American Airways was the only passenger airline which normally flew from New York to Monrovia, Leopoldville (now Kinshasa) and Johannesburg and returned to New York via the same route. There were some white South Africans in the plane who recognized Angie Brooks, as we could hear from their conversation in Afrikaans, but they did not know who I was — though my name was soon to become undesirable to them!

On that 16 hour flight from Monrovia to New York in an old DC-6 four-engine aeroplane, one really felt that one was travelling from one continent to another. All one could see was blue sky and blue water, hour after hour, before we landed in New York.

It was now June 1960, and I petitioned before the Sub Committee of the Fourth Committee of the General Assembly for the first time, and before the Committee on South West Africa on 5 July, giving my firsthand account of the Windhoek Uprising and the massacre. I appeared twice again, on 8 and 11 July, to answer questions from the committee, and also reported by letter on the situation in Ovamboland on 7 July. With Kerina I put in another letter about the Windhoek Uprising on 2 August, and a request for a meeting on 8 August, and appeared again to answer questions the following day. It all needed great concentration and fast learning on my part, as I was unfamiliar with the UN procedures.

I found the Ghana Mission to the United Nations very helpful, and benefited greatly from their advice. I stayed with Kerina, who was living in New York, having just completed his studies before joining the Liberian Mission to the UN. I also stayed with Herbert Whiteman, an African-American, very highly politically conscious, being one of W.E.B. Du Bois's followers, those early Pan-Africanists. When Kwame Nkrumah was a student at Lincoln University he also stayed with Whiteman's family, as did Ako Adjei, Nkrumah's first Foreign Minister. Herbert Whiteman died in 1990. He was a very good old man from whom I learnt much. I was proud to be made to feel a part of a great tradition of struggle for the rights of the people of African descent.

I then had to petition the General Assembly again, so I stayed in New York until November and December. We were demanding that South West Africa be placed under the trusteeship of the United Nations in preparation for our independence, which we asserted could be achieved by 1963. Some UN members asked us questions like how many educated people we had, and whether we were capable of running a country. I would reply that man was born free and did not need to be educated to demand self-determination and freedom.

When I first attended a General Assembly session in 1960, there were only 10 independent African countries: Ethiopia, Sudan, Egypt, Libya, Tunisia, Mali, Morocco, Guinea-Conakry, Liberia and Ghana. Before the end of that great African year, the Belgian Congo [renamed Zaire in 1960; then DRC in 1999] also became independent on 30 June 1960, and Nigeria in October 1961. Many African countries followed them into the UN, and the national liberation movements received tremendous support in their fight against colonial oppressors in Africa.

We were invited to petition before the Fourth Committee but, as petitioners without the special status of 'observers', we were required to withdraw after answering questions. Also, we were not allowed to come in through the delegates' entrance but had to go through the non-governmental organizations entrance. Furthermore, petitioners were not allowed to enter the delegates' lounge area unless we had been invited by a delegate.

We had to contend all along with the attempts of the white South Africans to stop us petitioning at the UN. But I was able, at my oral hearing on 5 July 1960, to quote from a letter the SWAPO branch at Walvis Bay had received from the Secretary of the South West Africa

Administration, refusing us our right to petition the UN and saying we could petition the Union Government only, but that they would not transmit such petitions to the UN. The South African treatment of Comrades Ya Toivo, Hamutumbangela and Hans Beukes put them in an even worse light and greatly strengthened our case before the United Nations.

Liberia and Ethiopia informed the UN at that 1960 Session that they were starting 'contentious proceedings' against apartheid South Africa at the International Court of Justice. Because of earlier discussions with Ernest Gross in Liberia, we were confident of their success in proving that apartheid South Africa had failed to fulfill its League of Nations mandate over South West Africa.

Over the years we struggled hard and finally gained recognition, with observer status for SWAPO in the General Assembly. We were also able to address the General Assembly directly and there was even more support, in the form of facilities, allocated to us. But before we were able to have our own representatives at the UN we were greatly helped by Marcus Garvey's African Pioneer Movement, and by George Houser of the American Committee on Africa, who remained our friends throughout the long and bitter struggle.

As petitioners to the Fourth Committee, we were treated by the British and others in support of the apartheid South African regime as very unimportant compared to the delegates and even the officials. But Africa was at the centre of activities and we were able to inform world public opinion. There was a very good response to our cause, and we gained support from many corners of the world. In New York, our number increased when Kuhangua was deported to the north after the Windhoek Uprising and managed to get to Angola, Zambia and Tanzania. In August 1960 he was able to travel to Addis Ababa and to New York where he joined Kerina, Kozonguizi, the Reverend Michael Scott and myself.

Others who petitioned at that time were the Reverend Markus Kooper, the pastor of the people of Hoachanas who was evicted in 1958, Hans Beukes and Ismail Fortune. Moses Garoeb and Zedekia Ngavirue reached the UN the following year and then we acted as a group, not as representatives of different parties. We were thus a symbol of unity and exposed the lie in South Africa's propaganda about tribal divisions in South West Africa. The South African regime really hated the UN, and even blamed it for the success of the African freedom movement that reached its climax in 1960. In 1954 the first Prime Minister of the Afrikaner Nationalists, Dr. Malan, had accused the UN of giving "the immature and in many cases barbaric races of Africa the idea that they are oppressed, and if they are an oppressed people they must use all possible means to obtain freedom". There was 'unrest' in Africa, he said, because the people were brought up with the impression fostered by the United Nations that they were oppressed.

The apartheid South African whites tried to convince the UN that the Ovambos were not unhappy with the situation by sending Blignaut, the Chief Native Commissioner, whom we had strongly opposed, to the UN as adviser to Eric Louw. Blignaut had been stationed at Ondangua at one point and was said by the South Africans to 'know the natives better'. He was there to tell the UN that the 'natives', particularly the Ovambos, were happy under South African rule. The Hereros and Namas were said to be trouble-makers, but the South Africans always claimed that the Ovambos, who were the majority, were satisfied with South African rule. They later tried to build up Mr. Peter Kalangula, so-called Minister of the Ovambo Legislative, in which even the Germans supported them. This underestimated the intelligence of the oppressed people, and certainly did not fool most of the representatives at the UN.

I spent six months in New York and met many leaders from National Liberation Movements, as well as delegates from newly independent countries with whom we talked about international politics, especially with regard to the liberation of the oppressed people in the colonies in Africa, Asia and Latin America. While in New York City, I was able to make contact with leaders of the African-American Civil Rights movement who were also struggling for equal opportunity and rights in the USA. I got to know New York City very well, travelling in the subways to Brooklyn, Long Island, Queens and many other parts of New York City.

The most famous UN session

The year 1960 was the year of the most famous of all the General Assembly sessions, where, together with our companions, we were given the opportunity to petition before the Fourth Committee of the General Assembly. In this session, Fidel Castro, who led the successful Cuban revolution in 1959, made his historic speech of five hours without reading or repeating what he had already said. Also in this session, Harold Macmillan, the then British Prime Minister, repeated the 'wind of change' speech which he had first made in Cape Town at

16   Chief Hosea Kutako

the beginning of the year. And Nikita Khrushchev, the then General Secretary of the Communist Party of the Soviet Union, hammered on the desk with his shoe, in protest against imperialists and colonialism. It was a very historic General Assembly because it had acknowledged and reaffirmed the rights to freedom and independence of colonial countries and peoples, under General Assembly Resolution 1514, which was a crucial move forward in support of the oppressed peoples throughout the world.

Our petition at the UN General Assembly was strongly supported by Chief Kutako from inside South West Africa. He had already reported the Boers' actions against me and others to the Secretary General of the UN. He had even sent an open letter, dated 10 March 1960, to King Baudouin of the Belgians, Harold Macmillan, Prime Minister of

Great Britain, and President Charles de Gaulle of France. He put it thus to those western leaders, all of them of leading imperialist powers, who were relinquishing their colonies in Africa:

> "After 41 years' rule as a mandate, we have no secondary schools for the vast majority of our population. When the Europeans covet our lands, we are told to move on. We have no security, no hope for the future. Is this what the Principal Allied and Associated Powers intended by their conception of a Sacred Trust, when the indigenous people would be helped to stand on their own feet? We implore your respective governments, now, to be true to the ideals that have moved you in the reforms brought into those other countries in Africa. We too are your responsibility!"

Also in March 1960, the OPO executive had sent a full report to the UN Secretary General describing the repressive actions of the apartheid South African regime in Uukwaluudhi district, when Blignaut had installed a puppet chief against the wishes of the followers of the old ruler, Chief Muaala, who had always opposed the apartheid policy. They also reported the treatment of those associated with the Windhoek Uprising, such as Nathaniel Mbaeva, Jacob Kuhangua, and myself, all of whom had been served with deportation orders. Later more than 100 people were deported from the Windhoek district. This was a general repressive law against blacks who lost their right to remain in Windhoek after armed police raids on their premises, while white employers resorted to the dismissing of their employees and deported them to their so-called native reserves (bantustans).

Chief Hosea Kutako's March 1960 report to the UN also dealt with specific cases of cruelty to Ovambo Contract workers, with deportation orders of others to Rehoboth, and the deportation of a staff nurse from South Africa, Miss Putuse Ntshona (later Mrs. Appolus), who was working as a nurse at a local hospital (she later joined SWAPO in exile and became a founder member of the SWAPO Women's Council, as well as one of the founder members of the Pan-African Women's Organization).

OPO's information to the UN dealt with the realities of life in South West Africa by exposing as lies the South African claims that Africans were well treated. A case in point was that of J. G. van der Wath, the then South African colonial governor, who paid his contract labourers only 10 rand after 18 months work, with a ration of a gallon of maize-meal a week.

When SWAPO was formed on 19 April 1960 and I was elected President *in absentia*, SWAPO continued to appeal to the UN to remove the territory of South West Africa from the Union Government and place it forthwith under the UN trusteeship system. We further requested that a UN Commission be sent to investigate the Windhoek massacre, the forcible removal of African people from their lands, as well as their living conditions. I gave evidence to the Fourth Committee of the UN again at the end of November 1960, and exposed some of the terrible facts about labour conditions in the country, as the Cape Town liberal paper *Contact* stated in a report devoted to my part during the hearings. I singled out SWANLA and revealed in detail its monopoly of migrant labour from the north.

On 6 December, 1960, by 67 votes with 11 abstentions, the Fourth Committee passed a resolution which seemed to us as another step forward in the campaign for our independence. It resolved to send members of the UN Committee on South West Africa into the country, with or without the consent or co-operation of the South African regime, with a view to ascertaining and submitting a report to the General Assembly on the conditions for restoring a climate of peace and security for the indigenous people of South West Africa, to achieve a wide measure of internal self-government, and to lead them to self-determination and independence as soon as possible.

The plenary General Assembly session adopted the resolution by 78 votes, with 15 abstentions. We felt that we had moved from petitioning and backstairs diplomacy to a direct demand for our independence. This UN resolution gave us a further determination and encouragement to continue with the struggle both politically and diplomatically at the international level.

Resolution 1514

This historical year ended with the adoption, by the General Assembly, on 14 December 1960, of Resolution 1514 which upheld self determination as a legal principle. Eighty nine states voted in favour. None voted against, but 9 abstentions were recorded from Australia, Belgium, Dominican Republic, France, Portugal, Spain, Union of South Africa, United Kingdom, and United States. The text of the Resolution is as follows:

Declaration on the Granting of Independence to Colonial Countries and Peoples, Adopted by the UN General Assembly Resolution 1514 (XV), 14 December 1960

Preamble

The General Assembly,

Mindful of the determination proclaimed by the peoples of the world in the Charter of the United Nations to reaffirm faith in fundamental human rights, in the dignity and worth of the human person, in the equal rights of men and women and of nations large and small and to promote social progress and better standards of life in larger freedom,

Conscious of the need for the creation of conditions of stability and well-being and peaceful and friendly relations based on respect for the principles of equal rights and self-determination of all peoples, and of universal respect for, and observance of, human rights and fundamental freedoms for all without distinction as to race, sex, language or religion,

Recognizing the passionate yearning for freedom in all dependent peoples and the decisive role of such peoples in the attainment of their independence,

Aware of the increasing conflicts resulting from the denial of or impediments in the way of the freedom of such peoples, which constitute a serious threat to world peace,

Considering the important role of the United Nations in assisting the movement for independence in Trust and Non- Self-Governing Territories,

Recognizing that the peoples of the world ardently desire the end of colonialism in all its manifestations,

Convinced that the continued existence of colonialism prevents the development of international economic co-operation, impedes the social, cultural and economic development of dependent peoples and militates against the United Nations ideal of universal peace,

Affirming that peoples may, for their own ends, freely dispose of their natural wealth and resources without prejudice to any obligations arising out of international economic co-operation, based upon the principle of mutual benefit, and international law,

Believing that the process of liberation is irresistible and irreversible and that, in order to avoid serious crises, an end must be put to colonialism and all practices of segregation and discrimination associated therewith,

Welcoming the emergence in recent years of a large number of dependent territories into freedom and independence, and recognizing the increasingly powerful trends towards freedom in such territories which have not yet attained independence,

Convinced that all peoples have an inalienable right to complete freedom, the exercise of their sovereignty and the integrity of their national territory,

Solemnly proclaims the necessity of bringing to a speedy and unconditional end of colonialism in all its forms and manifestations;

And to this end Declares that:

Declaration

1. The subjection of peoples to alien subjugation, domination and exploitation constitutes a denial of fundamental human rights, is contrary to the Charter of the United Nations and is an impediment to the promotion of world peace and co-operation.

2. All peoples have the right to self-determination; by virtue of that right they freely determine their political status and freely pursue their economic, social and cultural development.

3. Inadequacy of political, economic, social or educational preparedness should never serve as a pretext for delaying independence.

4. All armed action or repressive measures of all kinds directed against dependent peoples shall cease in order to enable them to exercise peacefully and freely their right to complete independence, and the integrity of their national territory shall be respected.

5. Immediate steps shall be taken, in Trust and Non-Self-Governing Territories or all other territories which have not yet attained independence, to transfer all powers to the peoples of those territories, without any conditions or reservations, in accordance with their freely expressed will and desire, without any distinction as to race, creed or colour, in order to enable them to enjoy complete independence and freedom.

6. Any attempt aimed at the partial or total disruption of the national unity and the territorial integrity of a country is incompatible with the purposes and principles of the Charter of the United Nations.

7. All States shall observe faithfully and strictly the provisions of the Charter of the United Nations, the Universal Declaration of Human Rights and the present Declaration on the basis of equality, non-interference in the internal affairs of all States, and respect for the sovereign rights of all peoples and their territorial integrity.

~~~~~

Return to Africa and SWAPO

This declaration boosted our morale, and put SWAPO in a leading position to forge ahead with the struggle for our liberation by initiating other forms of tactics than merely petitioning the UN.

The time had come for me to return to Africa. I had been continuously in touch with the SWAPO leadership in Windhoek by letter and telegram, and they managed to send me money. With that and the support of the Liberian Government I was able to return to Africa after that historic UN General Assembly session was over. Early in January 1961 I flew from New York to Monrovia and Lagos where I started planning to open SWAPO external offices. The end of my journey took me back to Dar-es-Salaam and I knew I must now consolidate SWAPO in exile, as a viable organization to campaign and champion the cause of South West Africa's liberation struggle.

❖❖❖

7

The Establishment of the SWAPO Office in Dar-es-Salaam

I was alone in Dar-es-Salaam after returning from New York early in 1961. One of the first to join me from South West Africa was Mrs. Putuse Appolus, a nurse who had been deported from South West Africa to South Africa by the Boers, and escaped via Southern and Northern Rhodesia. She had spent some time in Katanga Province before coming to Dar-es-Salaam, and becoming active in SWAPO.

Tanganyika did not become independent until 9 December 1961 (thereafter the United Republic of Tanzania), but it achieved internal self-government in May of that year, and that made SWAPO's development, and the conduct of our campaign from there, somewhat easier.

All-African People's Conferences

The General Assembly's passing of Resolution 1514 at the end of December 1960 had certainly strengthened SWAPO's position as a viable political entity. But we also felt empowered to forge ahead with the struggle through tactics other than petitioning the UN. We adhered to the resolution which had been passed by the first All-African People's Conference, launched by Kwame Nkrumah in 1958 which, crucially, had affirmed the fundamental moral right of Africans to engage in all means of resistance against the foreign colonial powers, including armed struggle.

This historic Conference was followed by the Second All-African People's Conference, in Tunis in January 1960, attended by Mburumba Kerina. At that time we had hoped

South West Africa would be freed through the negotiations and interventions of the United Nations. However, as I have related, due to the continued oppression of the people of South West Africa by the apartheid regime, Liberia and Ethiopia initiated legal proceedings at the International Court of Justice in November 1960, charging apartheid South Africa with having failed to fulfill its mandated responsibility to advance the people of South West Africa towards self-determination and independence.

At the beginning of March 1961, I attended the Third All-African People's Conference in Cairo, hosted by President Gamal Abdel Nasser of Egypt. With other representatives from other national liberation movements, I left Dar-es-Salaam on BOAC, via Nairobi and Aden to Cairo, Egypt. In Nairobi we were joined by Tom Mboya who was then the Secretary General of the Kenya African National Union (KANU), and James Gichuru who was the Acting KANU President (representing Mzee Jomo Kenyatta who was still in Kapenguria Detention Camp), Ronald Ngala who was President of Kenya African Democratic Union (KADU) and Martin Shikuku who was the then Secretary General of KADU. [At that time Daniel Arap Moi, who was not part of the delegation to Cairo, was the Vice-President of KADU and was Ngala's successor after the latter died.]

We spent a night in Aden, still a British colony with a large military base, in those dying days of Britain's 'East of Suez Canal'. The next day we arrived in Cairo, the capital of Egypt, and received a warm welcome from government and party officials.

I met many other Pan-Africanists from both the Brazzaville Group, which emerged from a conference of the former French colonies in December 1960, and the Casablanca Group, led by Ghana, the United Arab Republic of Egypt and the Algerian Provisional Government which was formed in January 1961. To many people, South Africa's refusal to hand over the South West Africa mandate to the UN trusteeship system was being dealt with by the World Court and it was not always easy to win support for the liberation movement of the country. SWAPO gained many friends nevertheless, and we began slowly to build up our reputation as a credible liberation movement.

During the course of the Conference I met a representative from the Yugoslav Government who extended an invitation to me to visit his country. So, I made my first journey to Europe from Cairo to Belgrade, Yugoslavia where I had a meeting with President Josip Broz Tito and other party and government officials, where I briefed them thoroughly about the apartheid oppression in South West Africa. Tito, being a revolutionary himself who fought against Nazi Germany, clearly understood what was meant by oppression of a people by a foreign power. He authorized his officials to give me all the necessary assistance. I was offered scholarships and the first group of students from Dar-es-Salaam went to Yugoslavia at the end of 1961. Later Yugoslavia became a very active supporter of SWAPO during our liberation struggle: rendering scholarships, military training and military hardware.

At the Third All-African People's Conference in Cairo, my growing realisation was fully confirmed — that South West Africa was not known and that many still thought it was part of apartheid South Africa. I knew therefore I must mobilize world public opinion about South West Africa. The real leaders like Nkrumah and Nasser fully understood the importance of the South West African issue. Nkrumah, for example, told the Commonwealth prime ministers in London that South West Africa was their responsibility because the mandate had been given to South Africa as a member of the British dominion after the First World War. And Nasser warned the Cairo Conference that the UN was being used as a tool by the imperialist powers because of Africa's lack of unity, and that this disunity was the cause of the inability to enforce its will to liberate the rest of the African colonies. He cited the UN's influence over South West Africa as the best example of the influence of Western powers in support of the South Africa white minority in the Security Council.

International mobilization

In March 1961 in Cairo during the Third All-African People's Conference, I requested President Nasser to offer the opportunity of military training to SWAPO members. Nasser assured me of such opportunities if I could get a group of SWAPO members from South West Africa. He urged all African independent countries to render the necessary assistance to the national liberation movements, including military training, in order to free their countries from colonial occupation and foreign domination. He also urged the Independent African States not to allow the imperialist powers to maintain and promote neo-colonialism and disunity among the African countries.

After returning to Dar-es-Salaam, I wrote to Peter Mueshihange in Cape Town, and to other colleagues in South West Africa, inviting them to come out of the country and join me in Dar-es-Salaam, Tanganyika.

17 Sam Nujoma, at the Third All-African People's Conference in Cairo, Egypt. March, 1961

As the years progressed our numbers in Dar-es-Salaam increased. In the meantime, I had to travel alone, attending international conferences in order to mobilise world public opinion to support the cause of the people of South West Africa. I always carried my portable typewriter in order to type my speeches on the flight. I had to economize on everything, and for quite a while had to manage with meagre resources.

Dar-es-Salaam offered other opportunities for us to present the case of South West Africa to the international community and mobilize material support, whereas at home our SWAPO members were suppressed and isolated from the international community. Nevertheless, their resistance from within the country continued with vigour and determination. It began to make sense for me and my colleagues in Dar-es-Salaam to establish SWAPO Provisional Headquarters, from where to carry out the struggle for national liberation.

From our Provisional Headquarters, we began for the first time to make contact with many countries. I managed to arrange scholarships for students, first to Yugoslavia, and we worked hard to find scholarships for the increasing numbers of new arrivals. Peter Mueshihange, my first Minister of Defense, obtained a scholarship for a teacher training course combined with his studies in political economy at Kivukoni Training College in Dar-es-Salaam. From there he went on to Ghana where he studied political science and the ideology of Nkrumaism at the Winniba School of Ideology in Ghana. After completing his studies in Ghana, he rejoined us in the struggle for liberation in Tanganyika.

Meanwhile, Putuse Appolus got a nursing post at Muhibili Hospital in Dar-es-Salaam. Nevertheless, life was very difficult for the rest of us. Some had to wait for scholarships, like Moses Garoeb, who went to study later at a University in the United States of America, while the rest of us depended on the generosity of TANU and its government, whose people, under the leadership of Julius Nyerere, encouraged us to continue with the liberation struggle.

UN Committee fiasco

The link between Britain and apartheid South Africa was weakening. In 1961, South Africa left the Commonwealth as a result of pressure from Prime Minister Nehru of India, President Nkrumah of Ghana, the Canadian Prime Minister Diefenbaker and Malaysian Prime Minister Tung Rahman. Apart from our petition at the UN General Assembly and the UN report at the hearing at the International Court of Justice in The Hague, the Western powers, especially Britain, continued to support the apartheid South African occupation of South West Africa.

But with the Court hearings continuing and increased unpopularity at the UN over the barring of the Committee's visit to South West Africa, South Africa saw danger ahead. In 1961 South Africa made a gesture to the UN by inviting a delegation to investigate, in South West Africa itself, the accusations against its rule.

In 1962, the UN Committee on South West Africa, led by Professor Febregat of Uruguay, failed to enter South West Africa because, first, South Africa opposed their visit. Then the British colonial administration withdrew the Committee's visas to enter Bechuanaland for the purpose of interviewing our Herero people who were living in exile there in the Maun and Ghanzi districts. The Committee refused to give the British an undertaking that they would not try to enter South West Africa from British Bechuanaland. This was a setback to our plans. Chiefs Hosea Kutako and Witbooi, together with SWAPO, sent a letter of protest to the UN Secretary-General, expressing their bitter disappointment at the failure of the UN Committee to enter South West Africa.

This May 1962 visit by the Chairman of the UN Committee on South West Africa, Victor Carpio, the Philippino and the Brazilian respectively and his deputy, Salvador Martinez de Alva, was an undignified farce, which brought home to the people in the country what we already knew, that the UN was ineffectual when it came to pro-South Africa stance especially by some of the Western powers.

Those who petitioned before the UN Committee on South West Africa were Emil and Putuse Appolus, Solomon Mifima, Peter Mueshihange, and others who represented SWAPO, along with Ngavirue and Konzonguizi who represented SWANU. At that time, Daniel Munamava, who had guided me out of British Bechuanaland, was in Dar-es-Salaam to appeal to the Committee for the return of the Hereros in British Bechuanaland to South West Africa, "as soon as South Africa ceases to have control over the Territory", as the UN report read. Munamava was able to return to British Bechuanaland as he had a British passport. Ismail Fortune and Louis Nelengani gave evidence in Cairo, as did Moses Katjiuongua and two other SWANU members.

In December 1962, in response to South Africa's objection, the World Court voted that it had "jurisdiction to adjudicate upon the merits of the dispute. Article 7 of the Mandate gave Ethiopia and Liberia, as former members of the League, legal right or interest in the observance by the mandatory of its obligations". This opinion was carried by only eight votes to seven, but it successfully confirmed the advisory opinion the Court had given as far back as 1950 that the UN had taken on the League's responsibilities over the mandate.

As a result of the report by the Committee on South West Africa to the General Assembly, the UN passed a resolution which set up a Special Committee charged with responsibility for organizing a conference which would prepare a constitution for an independent South West Africa, and with responsibility for training the oppressed people in many fields, and establishing a UN presence in the country itself.

Progress for SWAPO

In September 1961, I travelled to Belgrade for the second time — joined by UNIP official Kamalondo, who was the Chief Representative to Britain and a representative from FLN of Algeria — to attend, as an observer, the launching of the Non-Aligned Movement hosted by President Josip Broz Tito of Yugoslavia. The initiators of the Non-Aligned were Tito of Yugoslavia, Kwame Nkrumah of Ghana, Modibo Keita of Mali, Jawaharlal Nehru of India, Sukarno of Indonesia, Nasser of Egypt, Sékou Touré of Guinea-Conakry, Mrs. Banderanaike of Ceylon and Arch-Bishop Makarios of Cyprus. At all international forums, the Movement of the Non-Aligned countries championed the cause of the colonial occupied and oppressed people of Asia, Africa and Latin America.

In December 1961, SWAPO and SWANU members as a united group again jointly petitioned the Fourth Committee of the UN General Assembly, protesting against the exploitative foreign companies operating in South West Africa. Kozonguizi was also present with the Reverend Michael Scott and Reverend Markus Kooper.

I returned to Africa via London, where Ngavirue and I spent Christmas 1961. It was my first visit to the country upon whose king, George V, the League of Nations mandate had been conferred in 1920, "on behalf of the Union of South Africa".

Inside the country SWAPO had been very deeply rooted in the masses, and the South African apartheid regime thus found they could not suppress SWAPO, though they did everything short of banning it. Various manoeuvres were undertaken; members were threatened, arrested and tortured but they never gave up.

Reports reached me about the Boer attempts to discredit SWAPO and myself in particular. One such was a meeting at Ondangua, addressed by the Colonial Administrator Daan Viljoen and Chief Native Commissioner Blignaut who called on the puppet chiefs to work with the apartheid regime as Chief Kambonde of Ondonga tribe had done. They said:

> "There are some who go about talking nonsense to the people like Sam Nujoma, who takes the Ovambo people's money away — about £10,000 and runs away, taking a wife from Bechuanaland. He is the biggest thief who has been among you people, and we want to work together with you."

They offered to increase the salaries of the workers employed in mines and railways and in domestic service as an incentive for them to remain in the country, and not join SWAPO in exile. Viljoen said he could tell the whole world that it did not matter if there was an Ovamboland Peoples Organization that would not work with him. Here were the people who wanted to work with him.

However, the Boers were not aware that hundreds of the people in the north were already leaving, making their way to join me in exile in Dar-es-Salaam.

◆ ◆ ◆

8

Preparation for Armed Liberation Struggle

Tanganyika achieved its independence on 9 December 1961. Early in 1962, Julius Nyerere — at the time serving as the new country's first Prime Minister — assisted us further, as he had already done in so many other ways. (In 1962, one year after independence when Tanganyika became a Republic, Nyerere was its first President, and remained President when in 1964 Tanganyika and Zanzibar together formed the new nation of Tanzania.) The British had started on a policy of uniting Kenya, Uganda and Tanganyika in the late 1940s. Nyerere broadened this in the spirit of Pan-Africanism, by bringing in other East African states as well as Nyasaland, Northern and Southern Rhodesia (later Malawi, Zambia and Zimbabwe). They had formed a joint association, with Pan-African ideals.

Pan-African consolidation

When I returned to Dar-es-Salaam from New York in January 1961, I got together with representatives of other national liberation movements of east, central and southern Africa — UNIP, KANU (Jomo Kenyatta was still in detention), ANC, PAC of South Africa, ZAPU (Southern Rhodesia), SWAPO and SWANU (South West African National Union). TANU had already formed a government.

We fitted together those ideas Julius Nyerere had already brought to form the Pan-African Freedom Movement of East, Central and Southern Africa, known as PAFMECSA. As an organization, PAFMECSA played an important role by uniting the African liberation movements and consolidating the ideals of Julius Nyerere.

We always kept in touch with our people inside South West Africa. To launch an effective struggle you need a constant inflow of cadres to be trained. That was a headache for us and made it even more necessary to keep in touch with the party back home.

I lost no opportunity to maintain links with SWAPO members in the country. For example, returning to Dar-es-Salaam from Cairo on one occasion, I found I was travelling with an elderly German lady, Mrs. Ursula Schultz, whose bag, I had noticed when we were at Khartoum airport, had a Windhoek label on it. On the plane, I greeted her, telling her who I was. We sat together and talked all the way from Khartoum to Dar-es-Salaam. She told me that her parents had come to Tanganyika, where she had been born before the World War I. Her father had been deported by the British to Germany, but in due course they returned and settled near Kilimanjaro, only to be sent back to Germany again when the World War II broke out. In the 1950s they emigrated to South West Africa and kept a zoo at Okahandja. She had been to Egypt to buy zoo animals, especially a very beautiful type of rabbit. It was 22 December 1961, and she was rushing back to Okahandja to have Christmas with her family. We talked and talked about many issues. I then gave her some money to take to Windhoek, directing her to Comrades David Meroro and John Ya Otto, giving her their house numbers in the Old Location. She duly met them in town and delivered the money. Mrs. Schultz was very sympathetic because of the sufferings of her own family in the two world wars. She knew we were struggling for our country's independence and wanted to help us as much as she could. I took such opportunities to mobilize wherever I could.

PAFMECSA was strengthened by the activities of Mbiyu Koinange, who was one of those who had been detained with Kenyatta, and was his personal secretary. He had spent many years in England and was not allowed in Kenya because Kenya was not yet independent. The British had allowed him only to land at Nairobi airport and then proceed to Dar-es-Salaam, where he became secretary of PAFMECSA. We had a little office, which we shared with SWANU, ANC, PAC, UNIP and the liberation movements from Ruanda-Burundi, Kenya and Uganda. Zambia was in the process of moving towards elections, and Kenneth Kaunda, who was the chairman, played a leading role in PAFMECSA.

Much effort was made at this time to unite the liberation movements. We were brought together in a United Front with SWANU and the South African ANC and PAC. But internal differences were too great and the

ANC and PAC parted company very early on. SWAPO worked with SWANU at the UN and a 'Liberation Front' survived for a brief while.

The African countries were on the increase at the UN as more were achieving independence. The Non-Aligned countries totally supported the African countries and we achieved a situation in which all the resolutions on decolonisation the African countries put forward were almost automatically approved by the UN General Assembly.

We were never influenced or disappointed by the behaviour of the Western imperialist powers. Of course, we knew that their economic interest, their investment in South West Africa and South Africa was what they were concerned about, not about our people who were oppressed and denied their basic human rights. That we knew very well, and we decided we had to continue to struggle to achieve our freedom.

SWAPO strategy on three fronts

At the United Nations too, our position became much stronger. When I was first at the UN, SWAPO was not recognised. That came gradually, because of our activities. SWAPO designed a three-pronged strategy: the political front, the diplomatic front and the armed liberation struggle. We intensified all three fronts simultaneously. The political front meant working with the Organization of African Unity (OAU), the Non-Aligned Movement, the UN, and of course with our people back home. The diplomatic meant working with these and also the individual states, such as the Nordic countries, and countries like Belgium, France and Holland, and with supporters such as the Namibia Support Committee, Anti-Apartheid Movement in Britain, and in other countries.

Whenever there was an international conference we were there, and at all OAU liberation committee meetings. Eventually, in 1965 the OAU fully recognized SWAPO as the sole and authentic representative of the oppressed people of Namibia.

In 1962, I again went to petition at the United Nations, as in almost every subsequent year of our struggle, and also to several other conferences where our case could be heard. Most of 1962 was spent consolidating our work in Dar-es-Salaam and finding ways to absorb the growing numbers of SWAPO men and women finding their way to join us in exile.

The continent of Africa continued to awaken, which created a lot of activities for us. FRELIMO (Front for the Liberation of Mozambique) was just starting to fight in Mozambique, with the encouragement of President Nyerere, and of course MPLA was also fighting in Angola.

As more of our people arrived we sent them abroad for studies or military training, preparing them for the protracted struggle. Our committee in Dar-es-Salaam included people like Hifikepunye Lucas Pohamba (my first Minister of Home Affairs), Moses Tjitendero (the first Speaker of the National Assembly), Nickey Iyambo (first Minister of Health and Social Services), Nangolo Ithete, Simon Kaukungua-Mzee and his younger brother Shapua Kaukungua, Edwald Katjivena and others. Thus we mobilized the movement and started to set up offices in Cairo in 1962, in 1963 in Algeria (after it achieved independence at the end of 1962), and then throughout the continent.

Organization of African Unity (OAU) 1963

The overwhelmingly important development of 1963 in Africa was the formation, in Addis Ababa, of the Organization of African Unity (OAU), in which I and representatives of other African national liberation movements fully participated as observers. Our joint statement as representatives of national liberation movements was read by Oginga Odinga, the Vice President of KANU. The OAU brought together the 32 sovereign states of Africa on 25 May 1963, which we continue to honour as Africa Day.

Article 1 of the Charter of the OAU stated the purposes of the Organization, one of which was "to eradicate all forms of colonialism in Africa". Under Article 3, member states affirmed their "absolute dedication to the total emancipation of the African states which are still dependent".

At a later stage, President Nyerere insisted that the authentic liberation movements — FRELIMO, ANC and PAC, PAIGC, SWAPO, MPLA and others — be given observer status. He said, "We cannot talk about the situation in these countries in the absence of the national liberation movements who are directly involved. It would be meaningless for us to do so". Before that, we used to petition before the Liberation Committee and the Council of Ministers. Petitioners would enter the chamber, read their statements and then leave.

The OAU then set up the African Liberation Committee, the OAU's co-ordinating committee for the liberation of Africa, with headquarters in Dar-es-Salaam. Nine OAU members were appointed immediately — Algeria, Congo–Kinshasa (DRC), Egypt, Ethiopia, Ghana, Guinea–Conakry, Nigeria, Senegal and Tanganyika. President Nyerere gave them a building and in July 1963 they began their task of assisting the national liberation movements. Nyerere was the driving force behind these efforts. He again personally made an enormous contribution to the liberation of Africa. Tanganyika was not a rich country, but they shared with us every little they had. They had at that time only just overthrown British colonialism, and were no longer a supplier of raw materials. Yet Tanganyika (and later, Tanzania) would assist us as far as their resources would permit. The hosting of the African Liberation Committee was another example of their commitment to the liberation of Africa.

Nyerere was not alone in this, of course. The liberation of the continent was the priority of all OAU member states. It was their unanimous decision that the national liberation movements must be assisted bilaterally and collectively through the OAU Liberation Committee. We from the national liberation movements were encouraged to continue with the struggle in our own countries. In Dar-es-Salaam, approaches to embassies had been made for assistance, and at the conferences that I attended, and at the formation of the Non-Aligned Movement in Belgrade in 1961. When the OAU came into being and the Liberation Committee was given its task of rendering assistance to the national liberation movements, we began to get legitimate support. That helped us a lot. In due course other countries, such as India, China, the Soviet Union and the Nordic countries, as well as individuals and anti-apartheid movements in Europe and the Americas, especially the Caribbean countries, came to support those articles of the OAU Charter.

Recruits for military training — a typical experience

We needed to keep close to the people inside Namibia, to organize them and to recruit more young men and women into the military training. In May 1962, I called a meeting and told those present that I needed two volunteers to go on a mission to carry out political mass mobilisation inside Namibia. Comrades Lucas Hifikepunye Pohamba and Eliader Muatale, who later on sacrificed his life in the war, volunteered first. When Hidipo Hamutenya put up his hand I told him he was still young and I wanted him to go for study. Nyerere gave us £100 to give to those who volunteered to go back home. Kaunda agreed that they should travel with his delegation into Northern Rhodesia, where we met him after a PAFMECSA meeting, against Sir Wellsky's insistence on the continuation of the minority British settlers' rule in the Federation of Northern–Southern Rhodesia and Nyasaland, in Mbeya in July 1962.

Pohamba's return to Namibia with Eliander Muatale was difficult. After a fortnight in Lusaka he and Muatale travelled by train over the Victoria Falls only to be arrested at Plumtree, near the Botswana border. They were imprisoned there for a month and then held for another month in Bulawayo. SWAPO's protests to the British Government (Southern Rhodesia was still under the British Crown) eventually got them released, only to be handed over to the South African authorities. In August 1962 they were flown to Johannesburg, then ordered to be returned by train to South West Africa. They travelled from Johannesburg to Windhoek by train.

In Windhoek at last, they were welcomed by Aaron Hamutenya and his family in the Old Location, and quickly met with other SWAPO leaders. They had a confrontation with 'Native Commissioner' Blignaut in his office which nearly led to violence, and on leaving were arrested in Kaizer Street (now Independence Avenue). They were given six month sentences for having left the country illegally, but were released after three months and deported to their home areas — Pohamba to Uukuanjama and Muatale to Uukuambi.

Pohamba then spent the whole of 1963 in the north, working underground for SWAPO, and in February 1964 was present at a big meeting at Ohanguena called by South Africa's so-called Minister of Bantu Administration and Development, Nel de Wet. The story is well known to many since it was such a major public defiance of South African authority and had a widespread effect. The SWAPO members and supporters, led by Simon Kaukungua, had filled the meeting place early. However de Wet's pleasure at seeing such a large crowd soon disappeared when he heard Kaukungua, who stood up at the beginning and refused to be silenced. He then left, taking all the SWAPO crowd with him. Under some trees at a distance, Kaukungua spoke to the crowd, but some noticed that the puppets, in response to de Wet's anger, were loading their guns. Some of the crowd then surrounded them and told them, "If you shoot at us, you will die".

Kaukungua went into hiding when police reinforcements arrived and he was declared a 'wanted man', dead or alive. A few days later he and four others arrived at Pohamba's home, having decided to leave the country. Pohamba went with them, travelling on foot again up to Rundu, where, as he had done before, they posed as Angolans going to work in the South African mines. Much had happened since his first journey in 1961 and the year before, and by now we had Maxton Joseph Mutongolume, one of the Cape Town comrades, who was SWAPO

18   Jacob Kuhangua and Sam Nujoma (carrying a traditional walking stick) in conversation with a journalist, crossing the Zambezi River after they had been deported to Northern Rhodesia (Zambia) by the British colonials in Bechuanaland. 1964

representative in Francistown. They were detected by WENELA, but it so happened that I was in Francistown, with Appolus and Kuhangua. After a struggle they were released and given asylum. They had further trouble crossing at Kazungula and the British did not want them to enter into Northern Rhodesia. Simon Kapwepwe, Minister of Home Affairs, insisted that they be allowed to pass through and at last they made it back to Dar-es-Salaam.

Comrade Pohamba returned to Lusaka in September 1964, as SWAPO representative. Eliader Muatale carried on with political mass mobilization for a shorter time, but also had a hard journey to rejoin us in Dar-es-Salaam, in 1963.

More perilous journeys

I too had decided to travel to British Bechuanaland by train from Lusaka, to meet our people who were coming from South West Africa. I booked myself, as before, in a single first-class compartment and locked myself in. The then Southern Rhodesia security and immigration officials did not come into my first-class compartment which normally only whites occupied, while blacks travelled in the third class compartment. A problem arose when we arrived at Bulawayo and I had to change trains unexpectedly and wait on the platform for the next train. So I went to a book-shop and bought a book that looked like a Bible, sat on the platform and pretended to read. I was left alone by the British Rhodesian officials walking up and down along the platform. They thought I was a minister of a certain church. I sat there until my train was called and then ran to catch it just before it left. At Plumtree, the British Bechuanaland police and immigration officials were supposed to check through the train but there was no sign of any one of them, and I arrived in Francistown without any problems.

At Francistown train station I was met by Comrades Maxton Mutongolume (SWAPO representative) and others who had just arrived from South West Africa — Hifikepunye Pohamba, Simon Kuhangua and the others — and had a meeting with those already there. I was interviewed in Francistown by the District Commissioner, who wanted to know how I got there and why I had not been checked by the immigration officials. I simply told him I had come by train and none of the immigration officials were there, which he accepted.

An Oxfam representative named Cunningham travelled by car from Lusaka to Francistown and brought colleagues Jacob Kaukungua and Emil Appolus. He often travelled that road, and as he was a white man, already old, the immigration and police just took the two black men travelling with him to be his employees, and made no trouble for them.

We had a number of other SWAPO members in Francistown, with our representative, Maxton Joseph Mutongolume. Many colleagues who passed through where there were also refugees from South Africa. By this time the Bechuanaland People's Party was in existence, so they assisted members of SWAPO, ANC and PAC. Among the SWAPO members who came through were Peter Katjavivi and his colleagues, who were arrested in Southern Rhodesia and sent back to Bechuanaland and only released after we lodged a protest with the British government in London.

I stayed several weeks in Francistown, but eventually the British colonial authorities deported us to Zambia and I then went back to Tanganyika. Communication and movement of persons between South West Africa and SWAPO Provisional Headquarters in Tanganyika/Tanzania was very difficult until Zambia became independent in 1964, and then Botswana in 1966.

A difficult problem occurred in 1963 when Andreas Shipanga, Dr. Kenneth Abrahams, my brother Noah Nujoma and others were stranded in British Bechuanaland. I had to hire a 3-seater aircraft to fly from what was then Elisabethville (now Lubumbashi) in the former Zaire (now DRC) to Kasane to bring in the 27 men in a large number of shuttles. Since they could not pass through the Federation of Rhodesia and Nyasaland, the plane had to fly from Elisabethville to Kasane directly without touching down in Northern Rhodesia. Shipanga and a few others had first been kidnapped from Bechuanaland by the Boers and were later returned under strong pressure from the British government. I went personally with the plane to Elisabethville, but I was not allowed to fly to Kasane because of the need to over-fly the Federation. So the pilot went on alone to fetch two of them at a time, and had to make the round trip 14 times before all our stranded comrades were safely transported to Elizabethville. This airlift cost us about £4,000 sterling, which we were able to obtain from the OAU Liberation Committee Fund.

First acquisition of arms

Our preparations for the armed liberation struggle went on. We had men ready to enter the country, but we had no weapons. The first weapons which we used to launch the armed liberation struggle I obtained from Algeria after it achieved its independence in 1962. When the Algerians were in exile in Tunisia and Morocco fighting for the liberation of their country, we met, as we did later at several meetings of independent African states. We discussed the plans and strategies of waging the armed struggle. They had succeeded in overthrowing the French colonialists in Algeria, and we were encouraged by people who had successfully waged a war of liberation. We accepted their invitation, in 1963, to open an office in Algiers, with Solomon Mifima being our representative. I went to see Ahmed Ben Bella, the first Prime Minister of independent Algeria, and asked him if they could give us firearms. With authority from Ben Bella, they immediately gave us four weapons, and with these we were later able to launch the first action of the armed liberation struggle on 26 August 1966, at Omugulu-gOmbashe.

A senior official handed over to us two 'pepesha' sub-machine guns and two 'TT' pistols with spare magazines. In Algiers I bought four big black travelling bags and in each bag we put one sub-machine gun and a pistol, along with their magazines and ammunition. The big headache was how we were going to bring the weapons into Tanzania.

Luckily, during that time airports did not have modern electronic devices for detecting weapons and explosives. Mifima and I flew by Air Algerie to Cairo where we took a United Arab Airlines flight to Dar-es-Salaam. In Nairobi we were again in transit — so that part of the journey was easily managed. While in Algiers I had sent a telegram to SWAPO's chief representative in Dar-es-Salaam, Peter Nanyemba, instructing him to organize a press conference at the airport. This was planned so that we would not have to go through the customs and immigration with the concealed weapons, but through the VIP channel, as press conferences could be held only in the VIP lounge. Nanyemba went to the Foreign Office and tried to persuade them to allow the press conference, but they said, "No, if Sam Nujoma is coming here, where he is based, why should he hold a press conference at the airport?". My plans usually worked, but this one did not.

When we arrived in Dar-es-Salaam, we expected that Peter Nanyemba, along with somebody from protocol, would meet us and take us to the VIP lounge. But that failed to happen, and so we went on through immigration. My heart then started pounding. I was extremely worried that our weapons would be discovered and confiscated. At the customs office, an African official, very tall, in white shorts like those the British officials wore, stared at me and said, "What do you have in these bags?". I replied that I had second-hand clothes for the refugees. The bags were new, and he looked suspiciously at them. Then he looked at me four times, from head to foot. Then he took his white chalk and marked the bags, and we passed through! My heart was still pounding, but we had successfully brought through our sub-machine guns and pistols.

We hid the weapons in our cars and then started planning how to get them through Zambia, which had just achieved independence. However, the British were still in charge of security. We knew we had to smuggle them in through some people we knew in the border area who were UNIP members. We took them at night and went from there into Zambia. We had a friend, Mr Chikombe, from pre-Zambian independence days there, who was the Deputy Minister of Foreign Affairs (he unfortunately died accidentally in 1990). He had two wives and two houses in a suburb of Lusaka, but one house was more or less free, and nobody else went there, so we stored our weapons there.

When our first group of fighters were ready to cross into the Caprivi Strip, they carried the weapons we had brought from Algeria. They went through the Caprivi Strip and then Kavango Region before they finally arrived at the homestead of Eliaser Tuhadeleni Kaxumba Kandola in Uukuanjama district. There they were welcomed and clandestinely plans were worked out to find a suitable place in the northwestern region, where their first base was in the Ongandjera district. They then moved on, successfully recruiting and training many SWAPO activists who became part of the first groups of guerilla fighters.

By the end of 1964, SWAPO had freedom fighters in training in Egypt, Tanzania, the People's Republic of China and Algeria. Others started their university courses in such diverse countries as Finland, Nigeria, Poland, the United States, Yugoslavia and the Soviet Union, wherever we were offered scholarships for them. We had offices in Cairo and Algiers as well as our Provisional Headquarters in Dar-es-Salaam.

The threat of the Odendaal Report — 1964–1965

I continued to keep in close touch with events at home, where our SWAPO leaders continued to be arrested, oppressed and imprisoned by the South African security police in Windhoek and the other towns, as well as by the puppet chiefs in Ovamboland. The South Africans had set up a so-called Commission of Inquiry into South West African Affairs, under Professor Odendaal, which issued its report in 1964. The South African plan was to divide the country among nine separate ethnic groups, each of which would collaborate with South Africa, and thus put an end to the criticism of South Africa at the United Nations. SWAPO, the Boers thought, would become irrelevant. But South Africa announced that it was shelving the implementation of the Odendaal Report because the status of South West Africa was being considered by the International Court of Justice, and so the 'sub judice' rule applied.

As an observer, I attended the World Court proceedings at the Hague in March 1965 and, with Kuhangua, Secretary General of SWAPO, and Emil Appolus, Information and Publicity Secretary, presented a memorandum to the Court.

We denounced the "oppression and tyranny inflicted on our country, from the very day the mandate of South West Africa was entrusted to South Africa. We have been abandoned to live under the most obnoxious system ever devised to enslave man". We drew attention to the brutality inflicted under the Contract system, to South Africa's refusal to accept the jurisdiction of the International Court, to the building up of Walvis Bay as an important naval and military base (this had recently been fully reported by UPI) and the preparation for carrying out the recommendations of the Odendaal Report, despite South Africa's claim that it had been shelved:

> "We submit that the South African Government has systematically and deliberately built tension and hostility between people of different races in our country and the longer this state of affairs is allowed to continue the more formidable the task of repairing the terrible harm that has been done and restoring harmony and goodwill among the people of South West Africa, black or white, will become."

From our talks with Mr. Ernest Gross, a lawyer who represented Liberia and Ethiopia at the International Court of Justice, we were assured that the Court would find that apartheid was a violation of the mandate under which South Africa's obligation was to promote the welfare of the inhabitants, and that it was in conflict with UN principles which classed apartheid with piracy and slavery. South Africa presented apartheid as its fundamental philosophy, so we were certain that the Court would rule that apartheid must cease in South West Africa.

South Africa had 14 barristers in its defence team and were calling many witnesses — the first time witnesses had been called in a World Court case. Mr. Gross had only a few assistants and intended to call no witnesses. He was confident that the Court would support UN principles and would rule against apartheid.

Chief Hosea Kutako had written to the UN that year, warning them that if the UN failed us, the fight would go on. Our memorandum quoted this far-sighted paragraph from his letter:

> "Although certain powers within the United Nations [are] trying to delay this long-standing question of South West Africa, our confidence in the United Nations is not yet exhausted. Our wish is to continue fighting against oppression and brutality. We shall fight within the framework of the Charter of the United Nations and the Declaration of Human Rights. Yet it must be borne in mind that there is no human patience without limit. Hence any failure by the United Nations to settle this question may produce serious consequences."

We made our plea to the Court in these words:

> "In the light of all these, we hope that the International Court of Justice will return a judgement which will pave the way for the transfer of the Mandated Territory of South West Africa to the administration of the United Nations Trusteeship Commission. We feel that the time is long overdue for the Mandate to be revoked in keeping with the precedents of established territories."

Six years had passed since I had crossed the British Bechuanaland border. SWAPO now had a viable external provisional headquarters, with offices in a number of countries among governments in African and in the Non-Aligned world.

We had taken the first steps towards training men and women to fight if the peaceful solution we had long been demanding did not come about. Although the United Nations had failed for 15 years to impose its will on South Africa over its treatment of the people of South West Africa as a colony to be exploited and held back, it did seem that the imminent World Court judgement would pave the way for the revoking of the mandate and for the independence of our country.

9

Sixteen Hours in Windhoek

The South African apartheid regime attempted to create the impression that there were two SWAPO wings — 'External' and 'Internal' — and that the two were independent, not unified and not in communication. This was a deliberate lie. The truth of the matter is that there had been constant contact through our own clandestine channels between those of us who were in exile and the other members of SWAPO at home.

After the armed liberation struggle was launched, SWAPO had guerrilla fighters going in and out of the country who kept contact with those who were carrying out the political mass mobilization inside the country. We also sent in journalists to interview SWAPO leaders in the country. Of course, we could not tell the apartheid South African regime about this clandestine contact, but it was known by many people including journalists, lawyers, churchmen and other friends of ours who were able to visit South West Africa.

CANU join with SWAPO

Even during these early days of our struggle we were looking for ways of uniting with others in South West Africa who were dedicated to the struggle for the national liberation of our country. One such group was the Caprivi African National Union (CANU) which was formed in 1964, led by Comrade Bredan Simbwaye, a teacher in the Eastern Caprivi. He had been in close touch with UNIP in what was then Northern Rhodesia. The Caprivi Strip had been governed from Lusaka, Northern Rhodesia at one time, under an agreement between the British and the apartheid South Africa. It was closer to Barotseland, the Western province of what is today Zambia, than to the rest of South West Africa.

The rest of South West Africa was quite cut off from Caprivi in those days, as part of South Africa's policy of 'divide and rule'. Any Namibian who was not of the Mafwe or Masubia ethnic groupings was prevented from travelling to Caprivi Strip. The first Caprivian I met was Brendan Simbwaye. During our discussions in Lusaka in 1964, he informed me that he intended to launch the Caprivi African National Union and I suggested to him that we should merge in order not to have too many political parties. He went back to discuss my proposal with his colleagues and also to take with him the CANU constitution printed with the assistance of Munukayumbwa Sipalo, who was then UNIP Secretary General and who later became the Minister of Health in the first UNIP government and Nalumino Mundia, a former teacher in Caprivi together with Simbwaye, and later became the Zambian Prime Minister in Kaunda's government. The struggle in then Northern Rhodesia led by UNIP inspired the Caprivians to form their own party, since they had no contact with Windhoek.

After our meeting in Lusaka, Comrade Simbwaye went back to Caprivi Strip to launch CANU. At the launching in 1964, Comrade Simbwaye was elected as President, Albert Misheke Muyongo as Vice-President and Crispin Mulonda as Secretary General. Immediately after the launching, Comrade Simbwaye was arrested and Muyongo, Mulonda and Joseph Nawa escaped to Zambia where I had a meeting with them. In fact, I repeated my proposal for uniting the two parties, and we finally formalized the merger of SWAPO and CANU under the name of SWAPO. Muyongo became the acting Vice-President of SWAPO since Simbwaye was still under arrest inside the country.

According to scraps of information, Comrade Simbwaye was imprisoned, chained in a baobab tree-hole and tortured, then taken by the Boers from the Caprivi Strip to Outjo and thereafter to Warmbad area. We engaged lawyers to find out what happened to him, but to no avail. It was simply said that he had disappeared. During our struggle for independence, the same fate that befell Comrade Simbwaye befell hundreds of other Comrades such as John Nakawa, Johannes Kakuva, Toivo Shilongo, Sakeus Petrus Iita and many others who also disappeared without trace.

19 PLAN combatants crossing Cuando River from Zambia into the Caprivi part of Namibia, 1973

Since it was my aim to unite all Namibians against the common enemy — the colonial oppressors — my success in uniting CANU and SWAPO was an important achievement. The merger was followed by hundreds of CANU members, including my first Minister of Works, Transport and Communications, Richard Kapelwa Kabajani, joining us in exile in Zambia. Since many of these Comrades were living along the Zambezi river, they were especially skilled in rowing canoes. They made important contributions to the struggle by imparting their skills to their fellow freedom fighters. Thus SWAPO fighters were enabled to cross the Zambezi, Cuando and Kavango rivers into the interior of the country with their arms and ammunition.

Testing a challenge — the attempted return to Windhoek

In 1966, when I was at The Hague and the International Court of Justice was about to deliver its judgement on South West Africa, the leader of the South African legal team, Advocate de Villiers, claimed that I and my colleagues were self-exiled and could go back to South West Africa at any time and nothing would happen to us. I reported to the Central Committee of SWAPO in Dar-es-Salaam, and I and Mishake Muyongo, the acting Vice-President of SWAPO, were designated to challenge de Villiers' claim by returning to South West Africa. The South African regime was making much propaganda at The Hague. This was one untruth we would not allow to go without challenge.

With Muyongo, I flew from Dar-es-Salaam to Entebbe airport via Nairobi, to catch a British Caledonian Airways flight which normally flew to Lusaka. When we reached Nairobi we were told that this flight had been cancelled. So we flew back to Dar-es-Salaam and chartered a small plane, which took us eight hours from there to Mbeya, and then to Lusaka.

On our arrival at Lusaka International Airport, Muyongo suddenly developed sickness. This was a pretence: he was simply afraid, and I decided to continue alone on my challenging journey to Windhoek. However, our SWAPO representative in Lusaka, Comrade Hifikepunye Lucas Pohamba, would not allow me to travel to Windhoek alone and volunteered to go with me. This became his second re-entry into South West Africa from exile.

We took a truck, SWAPO's only transport in Lusaka, to Livingstone, which we reached at about 2 a.m. We slept for a few hours in a hotel and the next morning, 20 March 1966, we informed our people by telegram that we would arrive that day at Eros airport. We took a chartered plane belonging to then British Bechuanaland National Airline from Livingstone to Windhoek. We left Livingstone at about 10.15 a.m. and when we entered South West African air space the pilot started to announce: "This is pilot so-and-so, aircraft number such-and-such, carrying passengers Nujoma and Pohamba bound for Windhoek". We could hear the Boers telling him over the radio — we were only 3 in this small 4-seater aircraft — "Keep north-east! Keep north-east!".

We had no choice but to land at the new Ondekeremba International Airport, which was still under construction though the runway was complete. This was forced on the pilot by the Boers to prevent our landing at Eros airport, where thousands of SWAPO members and supporters — headed by the National Chairman of SWAPO, David Meroro, with SWAPO Secretary General John Ya Otto and other members of the national executive — were waiting to welcome us.

Immediately after the plane landed, the Boers tried to search us and insisted that we sign a document. We refused both of these, and told them, "This is our country and we have the right to return to our home country". A police sergeant put his hands on my shoulders and said I was under arrest, charged with leaving the country without a passport, and held also on suspicion of other offences. Pohamba was also charged with the same offences.

They took us from the airport to the city centre, driving through Klein Windhoek to the CID headquarters, off Leutwein Street. They clearly did not know quite how to treat us: we were taken to town in a very smart VIP vehicle.

Once at the police station we found the local police pretending to be very friendly. Pohamba, who was carrying SWAPO literature and badges, pinned a badge on one of the police, who said he really could not wear it because he was a civil servant. Another of the police, one Sergeant Burger, said "Tell me, Mr. Nujoma, how is Tanzania?". I told him, "Tanzania is a very tropical country with high humidity where they grow mangoes, pineapples and other tropical fruits. It has a variety of good climates, hot and tropical in Dar-es-Salaam and in Kilimanjaro, which is the highest mountain in Africa where they grow coffee and tea". He said "Oh yes, I remember it. During World War II, I flew from Abyssinia [now called Ethiopia] to Nairobi and then to Dar-es-Salaam, in a British plane". That was all he asked or informed me.

We insisted to be allowed to leave and go home and meet with comrades who we knew were anxious to know our whereabouts. I also demanded to see my wife and children, who were living in the Old Location, and for a time they said this was being arranged.

But in due course more high-powered police arrived at about 6 p.m., and the mood changed. They tried to question us, and to make us look at law books which they said proved that South Africa did not occupy 'South West Africa' illegally, but ruled it under the League of Nations mandate, which South Africa still upheld. These CID men had been flown in from Pretoria specially to deal with us.

We were able to respond with facts about their suppression of the people of South West Africa. In every argument, when they attempted to convince us that South Africa was ruling South West Africa under the League of Nations mandate, we countered them again with facts.

I threw all their books back which they earlier gave to us to read, saying: "No indigenous person in South West Africa participated in this agreement. It was all done without the consent of our people and was purely you white men's ideas of a different way of colonizing South West Africa. Take your books back".

We did not tell them that we had come back to challenge what South Africa had said at the World Court, but just that we had left the country and could come back to our country any time we wanted. One of them asked me, "And what happened to your uncle Nkrumah?". Ghanaian President Kwame Nkrumah had been overthrown on 24 February 1966, only a month earlier, and had gone into exile in Guinea. I quickly countered him with, "What happened to your uncle Verwoerd?". Verwoerd had survived an assassination attempt in April 1960 when he was shot twice in the head by David Platt, a white farmer. I added, "That too can happen in political life". I could see that the Boer had become angry, but then he remained silent. As it turned out, just a few months later on 6 September 1966, a second assassination attempt on Verwoerd was successful when he was stabbed to death in Cape Town by Dometrio Tjafenda, a parliamentary messenger.

When we were being interrogated at the police station, I had some South African rands and I sent one of the policemen to the Grand Hotel opposite the CID Headquarters to buy some soft drinks for us and bring them unopened, and some assorted biscuits. They said: "You don't trust us?". I replied, "How can I trust an oppressor? You are oppressing us. You are killing our people here". We drank the drinks and shared the biscuits with some of the policemen.

Later on, they realized we were not ready to co-operate and they took our belongings and locked us in a cell at the Windhoek police station. I was extremely tired. The previous day I had made the flight to Kenya to try and make the connection to Lusaka via Entebbe, then back to Dar-es-Salaam, and then the eight-hour flight to Lusaka, and then the truck journey to Livingstone. Finally, early on the morning of 20 March we had taken the flight to Windhoek. I slept deeply.

The Boers came back at 1 a.m. They had apparently been constantly in touch with then prime minister Verwoerd in Pretoria, telling him that I was not co-operating and that they considered me highly dangerous, and if allowed to go free in the country I could influence the population to rise in opposition against the minority white occupation of South West Africa, which would result in a pro-South West African indigenous decision in the International Court of Justice.

They told Pohamba, "Tomorrow you will have to go back where you came from". Pohamba tried to wake me to tell me what they had said, but I was still asleep. He told me later that they had tried to exhaust us by banging doors and turning the lights on and off, but I slept through it all. At 5 a.m. they came again, bringing our belongings, including my typewriter, and said, "Get dressed. You are going back where you came from". It appeared that the same evening they had been looking for the pilot. He had not taken off that same day and had spent the night in Windhoek. They found him and threatened to arrest him and impound the aircraft unless he agreed to take us back. He was technically under arrest, so he had to agree to fly us back to Zambia.

Eventually Pohamba woke me, saying, "It seems they are serious, they have brought our belongings". I got up and dressed but refused to leave willingly. We said "This is our country, we will not go". There were six policemen armed with sub-machine guns. They forced us into separate cars, each sitting in the back with an armed policeman on either side. We drove along Leutwein Street, passing the big German church and through Klein Windhoek on to the airport road. It is interesting to recall how, early in the morning of 21 March 1966, I was driven past the Administrator's house as a prisoner being deported from my own country. Now I live in that same house, the State House, as the first President of the Republic of Namibia. It was March 21 again, 24 years later in 1990, when we celebrated our independence, and declared March 21 our national day, Namibia Independence Day.

At the airport we sang some freedom songs. There were black workers around who observed closely what was happening. I refused to eat food that was offered by the pilot, though the drinks and biscuits the evening before were all the sustenance we had had while in Windhoek police station for those 16 hours.

At 6 a.m., the plane took off for Livingstone. The pilot was friendly, despite what he himself had gone through. We flew over Chobe and I sat with him, looking down at the thousands upon thousands of buffalo, wildebeest and other game. He was a South African working in Bechuanaland, which was only a few months away from its independence as the Republic of Botswana.

In Livingstone the next day, I held a press conference and told my story. It gave the lie to the South African claim that we were self-exiled and could return whenever we wished. In England, at Oxford University, an international conference had been organized to shed light on South African apartheid policies and to highlight the responsibility of the international community. This was timed with the closing months of the World Court hearings, and we were well represented at the Conference by Comrades Hage Geingob, Peter Nanyemba and others. The sponsors were the presidents or prime ministers of a number of African, Asian and Caribbean countries and the chairman was Olof Palme, who was at that time Minister of Communication in the Swedish Government. I flew on to London in time to make a statement, as the conference was closing, on my attempt to return home. That attempt and the Oxford Conference, on top of the sustained efforts of many people, all added to our expectations that the World Court would deliver a judgment that would make it possible to bring an end to South Africa's continued colonial administration of our country.

The World Court hearing had gone on since November 1960 and was the longest in its history. Many people and many governments were deeply concerned that it should deliver a judgement that would uphold the authority of the United Nations. For us it was a matter of getting our country back. We had seen enough of the United Nations to know that we could not depend on it alone to bring about our freedom. We knew we had to be ready to fight for our country's independence.

When I was at Windhoek police station in March 1966, the first group of our freedom fighters were already at Omugulu-gOmbashe in the Uukualuudhi district, preparing to mobilize and train people. Verwoerd and the CID no doubt knew this, but had not yet found them. Had they already done so when they held Comrade Pohamba and myself in the police cells, they would certainly not have sent us back to continue with the struggle abroad.

And when, during the hours of interrogation I was storming at the police, "You are killing our people!", a leading SWAPO activist, Leo Shoopala, had just been shot dead by Jack Ashipala, one of the Boer's puppets in Uukuambi, northern Namibia.

My flight to Windhoek had come just before we reached a turning point, which was to redirect the history of the struggle for the liberation of Namibia.

❖ ❖ ❖

10

The Hague Court — A 'Mockery of Justice'

Verwoerd was clearly afraid that my presence in the country might create unrest and even an uprising, and that in turn would have an effect on the World Court decision, which they desperately wanted to be in their favour. The final stage of this very long case had been carefully timed and the whole South African cabinet and many advisers planned every move.

There were supposed to be 15 judges at the International Court of Justice, including the judge president. Ethiopia and Liberia were jointly allowed to nominate one judge and South Africa could have theirs too, bringing the total number to 17. Nine of these we knew to be in our favour. But one of the judges, Judge Baddawi of Egypt, died in 1965; the judge from Peru was ill; and Sir Zafrullah Khan from Pakistan withdrew, because Ethiopia and Liberia had once nominated him (though he in fact had not sat as their judge). Zafrullah Khan happened also to be a great friend of South Africa and visited the country later.

When the final vote came, seven judges voted that Ethiopia and Liberia had a legal right and interest in condemning South Africa's violation of the mandate, and seven voted against. By means of the casting vote of the President of the Court, Percy C. Spencer of Australia, another friend of South Africa, the court did not make any judgement at all, but reversed their 1962 judgement.

There was a world outcry against the Court, and Verwoerd at once pretended that there had been a judgement in South Africa's favour.

It was a shock that the International Court of Justice, after sitting for six years, could do nothing more than reverse its own 1962 judgement, which had found that it indeed "had jurisdiction to adjudicate upon the merits of the dispute between South Africa and the two African members of the former League of Nations". At the end of its decision, or non-decision, the court now stated that:

> "99. In the light of these various considerations, the Court finds that the Applicants cannot be considered to have established any legal right or interest appertaining to them in the subject matter of the present claims, and that, accordingly, the Court must decline to give effect to them.
>
> 100. For these reasons, the Court, by the President's casting vote — the votes being equally divided — decides to reject the claims of the Empire of Ethiopia and the Republic of Liberia.
>
> (Signed) Percy C. Spencer, President"

On the day of the judgement SWAPO issued a long statement from Dar-es-Salaam, drafted by Comrade Peter Nanyemba, which ended by making it clear that we were now going to launch the armed liberation struggle:

> "Verwoerd must draw no comfort from this perfidious verdict of the International Court of Justice. The people of South West Africa together with their brothers in South Africa itself are braced for an onslaught on his criminal regime. Nothing can now make them change their course or allow a moment's retreat.
>
> As a matter of fact, this so-called judgement has brought Verwoerd's destruction nearer than before. For the effect it has on our people is that it relieves them once and for all of any illusions which they may have harboured about the United Nations as some kind of a saviour in their plight. It has now been brought down on us with devastating force how patently false such illusions can be.
>
> There can be no hesitation henceforth. The course has been set. We have no alternative but to rise in arms and bring about our own liberation. The supreme test must be faced and we must at once begin to cross the many rivers of blood on our march towards freedom. And as sure as night follows day, victory will be ours."

We sent a telegram at once to Diallo Telli, Secretary General of the OAU, urging him "to take immediate steps to assist materially the forceful liberation" of Namibia. Our telegram to U Thant, UN Secretary General, read:

> "Inherent right of self-determination of South West African people remains intact in spite of gross miscarriage of justice by International Court of Justice. SWAPO is determined to continue the struggle for the liberation of our country with arms in hand. World Court and United Nations with imperialist manoeuvres have betrayed interest of South West African people."

We had taken the case at The Hague very seriously and its failure to deliver a verdict shocked us deeply. Nevertheless, I knew that there were other roads to freedom and that we must now set out on one of them. I expressed my attitude to the struggle, now that it was entering its inevitable military phase, during a visit to London in 1966, with Solomon Mifima. I was scheduled to speak to Foreign Office, academic and business people at the Royal Institute of International Affairs, but before the meeting, Randolph Vigne, who had arranged it, and was later to set up the Namibia Support Committee, asked me to speak cautiously and moderately to the audience. He said they would be very sceptical about any talk of us winning an armed struggle against South Africa and would not react favourably to any suggestion that Britain should help us against South Africa. I told him that I had to say exactly the same things in London as I would in any other country. So I spoke very strongly about our determination to end South Africa's occupation of our country, by all other means, including armed struggle.

The organizer of the meeting later privately compared my position to that of De Gaulle in 1940 when France was conquered by Nazi Germany. He said that if I did not speak as if I believed in our ultimate victory, when we were still at an infant stage then, since South Africa was so strong, no one else would believe in it either. That was always my policy: to speak and act with complete confidence of our ultimate victory. It became all the more necessary now that we were confronting white South Africa militarily.

On that same visit to London my brief-case was stolen from my hotel room by a South African spy called Hans Lombard, who was pretending to be a revolutionary and a friend of the PAC, especially of its acting president, Leballo. The South Africans were desperate to know our next move.

By that time it was clear that South Africa was not prepared to give up South West Africa, and for us to go back to the World Court would be a waste of time. I returned to Dar-es-Salaam after my brief journey to South West Africa, and when the 'World Court fiasco', as we called it, was announced I flew directly to London to make a statement on the collapse of the case. I then flew straight back to Dar-es-Salaam, where the Central Committee of SWAPO sat and we decided to launch the armed liberation struggle. We were certainly not going to allow the 'World Court fiasco' to put a stop to the liberation of our country.

Our first groups of soldiers were already in the country, with the sub-machine guns and pistols I had brought from Algeria. I ordered that our men should be ready to go into action.

Verwoerd interpreted the Court's failure to deliver a judgement as a 'green light' to incorporate South West Africa into apartheid South Africa. This presented us with no other alternative but to take up arms, for which we had been preparing in case the Court action and other international pressures produced no favourable result. The launching of the armed liberation struggle instantly ended any ideas Verwoerd harboured of incorporating South West Africa as a fifth province.

There was already a climate of unrest and protest, with the killing of Shoopala and police searching for our fighters. The actual launching of military action at Omugulu-gOmbashe on 26 August 1966 was inevitable and was widely reported in the press in South West Africa and abroad. SWAPO was able to operate in the country, though our activities were always hampered by the Boers. The government was clever enough not to ban SWAPO inside South West Africa, because of its fear of the United Nations. Both inside and outside the country we kept the party united. However, a very unfortunate incident was a quarrel in Dar-es-Salaam in 1968 between Jacob Kuhangua, who had been a Secretary-General of SWAPO and with whom I had petitioned the United Nations, and Louis Nelengani who had been the Vice-President and had also been with us from the formation of SWAPO. This led to a fight between the two, leaving Kuhangua paralysed. We sent him to America for treatment, and he stayed on there to study. His sister, who became a member of the so-called parliament of the Ovamboland bantustan, ultimately fetched him and he returned to South West Africa, where, a sick man, he denounced SWAPO. Kuhangua died after

Independence. Nelengani returned to South West Africa, was arrested and broken by the South African police, and later died.

In the mid-1960s we came to realize that the armed liberation struggle would have to be given equal emphasis with the political mobilization inside the country and abroad, together with diplomatic and international political action. The UN was only a part of this scheme, though a very important one. We worked hard to co-ordinate action now that the World Court failed us and the armed struggle was to begin as the only effective way to liberate our country. The year before, we tried to prepare the General Assembly for the steps that would follow South Africa's defeat at The Hague. We had called for the termination of the mandate, which was inevitable after the World Court's non-decision, and an interim UN administration to prepare South West Africa for the establishment of its own administration. We urged, in petition, that a UN force should "be dispatched to the Territory immediately after the International Court of Justice gave its judgement in the case currently before it, in order to secure the removal of South African military and paramilitary personnel, to protect the lives of all the Territory's inhabitants and to maintain law and order". There was no hope of that now.

Two weeks after the 1966 World Court fiasco, the OAU sent a request to the UN that South West Africa be a priority topic at the forthcoming session. I gave evidence to the Special Committee of 24 (on decolonialization) and it recommended what we were urging — that the mandate be terminated and power be transferred to the UN.

The General Assembly debate, which ran for a full month, was made effective by the anger of most of Africa and the Third World, supported by the Nordic countries. The termination of the mandate was widely and fully supported, even by the Americans. Only the British, even though under the Labour government, were strongly opposed to it, but they were isolated. Later on, the British tried to interpret the new situation in South West Africa differently from other member states, using their own terminology to say that South Africa's continued occupation of South West Africa was not illegal but 'unlawful'.

We were well served in New York by our representative, Comrade Hage Geingob, who was still a student there, and had replaced Emil Appolus. Appolus had turned out to be a playboy and useless to us. He drifted away from SWAPO and years later came back to join the South African colonial administration of local bantustan political schemes.

20 SWAPO members in Dar-es-Salaam, 1964

Standing, left to right (this page): Lazarus Pohamba, Steven Shapua Kaukungua, Lucas Hifikepunye Pohamba, Edwald Katjivena
Seated, left to right (this page): Jackson Kashikuka, Simon S. Kaukungua, Sam Nujoma

Standing, left to right (this page): Epapharas Negongo,
  Josaphat Kahimise, Simeon Shihungileni
Seated, left to right (this page): Tobias Hainjeko,
  Thomas Nepaya

Resolution 2145, 27 October 1966

In New York, Comrade Geingob lobbied hard for Resolution 2145, and SWAPO was the driving force in getting it through, fully backed up by the OAU. We had first put our case strongly to the OAU Liberation Committee, from where it went to the Council of Ministers and finally to OAU Heads of State and Governments, where a resolution was passed and taken, via the Non-Aligned Movement Summit, to the General Assembly. We worked tirelessly. In fact, we always carried our important steps forward in the same way, first with the Heads of State of the OAU, then taking the resolution to the Non-Aligned Summit, where we lined up countries like India, Cuba, Yugoslavia, and other Latin American countries, and we could then go to the UN General Assembly satisfied that the resolution would be passed as we planned, and fully supported by the majority of UN member states. My colleagues and I had to work hard for the termination of the mandate by the UN with ceaseless petitioning, lobbying and press briefings.

I was present when, at last, on 27 October 1966, the UN General Assembly voted by 114 to 2 (South Africa and Portugal against) with three abstentions (France, Malawi and the United Kingdom) to terminate the mandate and place South West Africa under the direct responsibility of the UN.

UN General Assembly Resolution No. 2145 (1966) recalled that the World Court had earlier established the UN's supervisory powers, and then:

> "Reaffirmed that the people of South West Africa had the inalienable right to self-determination, freedom and independence;
>
> Declared that South Africa had failed to ensure the moral and material well-being and security of the indigenous inhabitants and had in fact disavowed the Mandate;
>
> Called on South Africa to refrain from any action tending to alter the Territory's international status;
>
> Resolved that the United Nations must discharge responsibilities with respect to South West Africa; and
>
> Established a 14-member Ad Hoc Committee for South West Africa to recommend practical means by which the Territory should be administered, so as to enable the people to achieve independence."

The termination of the mandate was a watershed decision in the history of the movement for the liberation of South West Africa led by SWAPO. I was conscious of a heavy new responsibility toward the people of South West Africa. Namibia was now 'international territory', but South Africa was still in control of the country illegally. We had no other option but to launch the war of liberation against them. If we seemed like David fighting Goliath, well and good, since we knew who had won *that* battle. This was a time to give credit to those who helped us to reach this new stage.

SWAPO's international supporters

With regard to the support we received on the African continent, I would like to acknowledge our gratitude to and appreciation of the late President, Dr. Kwame Nkrumah, for the inspiring stand he took. It was Ghana whose Permanent Representative proposed Resolution 2145. Ghana led by Nkrumah helped us with so many other services. One such service seemingly, perhaps, a small one, was that President Nkrumah saw to it that almost every colony was documented, and literature about it was printed and distributed throughout the world by Ghanaian embassies and High Commissions. We found this an inspiration. I recall how avidly we youngsters in Windhoek used to read *Ghana Today*, a high quality printed magazine. Such literature inspired us and also informed the rest of the world about the large areas of Africa that were still under colonialism.

Nkrumah's research team compiled information on every colony (which he also used in his book, *Neocolonialism, the Last Stage of Imperialism*). Ghana published pamphlets which were useful too, including one on South West Africa. They revealed how South Africa misused the mandate to achieve its colonial domination over our country. To give just one example, when we went to Japan in 1964 to attend the Hiroshima-Nagasaki protest, the Ghana Embassy displayed all these pamphlets — on Southern Rhodesia, South West Africa, Angola and other colonies. The Ghanaian Embassy gave a big reception for the African delegates and all the other delegations came too, bringing anti-colonial forces even more closely together.

We acknowledge other African leaders, like Patrice Lumumba, who took over in the Congo (DRC), after the uprisings that took place there in 1960. Many Belgians went through Angola to South West Africa, and blacks who were working in the municipality as drivers were kicked out to make room for these fleeing Belgians. Africans in Windhoek were beaten up and the name 'Lumumba' became a term of abuse against Africans. The power struggle and bloodshed in the Congo in 1960 and 1961 were a set-back, but honoured Lumumba as a symbol of African freedom and unity. He was murdered in January 1961 by Moice Tjombe of Katanga — inspired by the Belgians and the American CIA. The Third All-African People's Conference, which I attended in Cairo in March 1961, proclaimed Patrice Lumumba a 'hero of Africa'.

We honour also President Nyerere. It was he who received me in the then Tanganyika and assisted me to go through Sudan via Nairobi, Sudan to Accra, on to Monrovia and then to New York in 1960. He welcomed me back to Dar-es-Salaam in January 1961 when I opened the SWAPO office there. President Nyerere was a man who believed in our armed liberation struggle, although the independence of Tanganyika was not as a result of armed liberation struggle. Nevertheless he believed that where the colonialists did not want to negotiate the handing over of power to the majority by peaceful means, then armed struggle must be pursued. He maintained that philosophy until the day he died. He did a lot for us. He hosted and provided us with all the necessary means of livelihood throughout our liberation struggle, beginning with the first training camp at Kongwa, near Dondoma in central Tanzania. All the national liberation movements — ZAPU, and ZANU, ANC, PAC, FRELIMO, MPLA and SWAPO — were there and benefited from logistic facilities created by the Tanzania government.

At that time, Tanzania was the only independent state in East, Central and Southern Africa, having achieved independence at the end of 1961. On 25 May 1963, the OAU was founded in Addis Ababa, Ethiopia. The Liberation Committee was the first organ of the OAU to start operating, in July 1963, and President Nyerere provided the building in which the members of the OAU Liberation Committee worked. Tanzania was bombed by the Portuguese from Mozambique, for giving assistance to FRELIMO. President Nyerere made a great contribution to the total liberation of Africa, and he inspired all of us in the battle against the enemies of the African people.

After Zambia's independence, President Kaunda played a similar role, allowing SWAPO a military base in western Zambia. South Africa knew about this and bombed Lusaka on several occasions. Kaunda assisted the freedom fighters from Southern Rhodesia (Zimbabwe) when Ian Smith's planes destroyed the bridge and even attacked Lusaka itself. President Kaunda was very firm. I remember, during the Wilson administration when Smith launched Southern Rhodesia's UDI (Unilateral Declaration of Independence, a rebellion against the Crown) on 5 November 1965, Wilson sent forces there. Harrier jet fighters were based at Ndola, but they proved to be ineffective because Wilson refused to take any action against Smith. Wilson claimed that the white settlers were very strong. Yet he took military action against the Anguilla rebellion in the Caribbean Islands. When he met Smith on the *Tiger* and *Fearless* warships, Wilson referred to Smith as "Mr. Prime Minister". Wilson had a very strange colonial secretary, Arthur Bottomley, who was supposed to come from the left wing of the Labour Party, but who was quite ineffective in African politics. Under Wilson, the British Government never supported President Kenneth Kaunda's Government against Ian Smith and his UDI in Southern Rhodesia.

Together, Presidents Kaunda and Nyerere worked hard for the liberation of the sub-continent from colonial rule. A case in point was their co-operation, with the assistance of the government of the People's Republic of China, in the construction of a railway to connect the port of Dar-es-Salaam, Tanzania to Ndola, Zambia. Smith had launched an economic blockade to stop valuable materials getting through to Zambia from the Mozambican and South African ports, materials which Smith probably considered useful to Zambia because they stood in the way of his attacking Zambia. The existing route between Dar-es-Salaam and Ndola was a so-called 'hell-road' along which Zambian copper was transported from the copperbelt all the way to the port of Dar-es-Salaam. A lot of trucks overturned on the way as this road was not suitable for carrying heavy loads. So they decided to build the Tanzania-Zambia Railway line (TAZARA). The original intention was that the railway should be built by the British with the assistance of other Western countries, but those countries ended up claiming that it was too long and too expensive. So the Chinese took it on. All that cost Zambia a lot of money. Billions of dollars were spent on the TAZARA railway line. It took some years but the Chinese finished it on schedule, and the railway was properly constructed.

That strengthened Zambia's resistance against Ian Smith. They had, through their co-operation, successfully countered the white minority regimes in Angola and Mozambique under the Portuguese, Southern Rhodesia under British colonialists, and South West Africa under apartheid South African occupation.

I would like therefore to pay tribute to these two far-sighted leaders in the sub-continent, in east and central Africa, whose actions inspired us and enabled us to carry out the struggle against colonialism, and to reach the ultimate goal — complete liberation of the African continent — which was achieved at last on 10 May 1994.

This was an extremely difficult time for our national liberation movement. However, we were supported with arms from Cuba, and were also helped by the socialist countries and others in the international community, like India which played a very vital role, and by China, and by the anti-apartheid movements and support committees in Europe that helped the national liberation movement in Britain, Italy, France, Holland and Belgium, as well as smaller groups and individuals in many other countries. Their work was particularly valuable in helping to support the Namibian people led by SWAPO.

The Nordic countries gave us tremendous support. One might have expected this from Finland, since they had sent missionaries to Ovamboland from 1870 onwards. But the Finns were influenced by the Boers, though at a later stage the young missionaries came to see that the people were determined to free themselves so they also came to support us, particularly the youth. The Swedes were always progressive, not only with regard to Namibia, but whenever oppression was going on Sweden was always supportive. Even when the Vietnam war was on, Sweden stood up for its principles. The US government went as far as to withdraw its ambassador from Sweden after the Swedish Prime Minister, the late Olaf Palme, took part in a demonstration outside the American embassy in Stockholm. Sweden started to assist us in the mid-1960s through their embassy in Tanzania, and in due course we opened an office in Stockholm and were on close terms with their government, which gave us a lot of invaluable material aid. The Norwegians were generous too, both at government and grassroots level, and assisted SWAPO to build a modern Technical Secondary School at Loudima Congo-Brazzaville.

Much has changed since we were only a handful of Namibians in Dar-es-Salaam. Over the years, of course, thousands more Namibians joined us. When, in 1963, the first group went for military training in Cairo, this was possible because President Gamal Abdel Nasser of Egypt had offered me training and tickets. Nasser was a dedicated supporter of African liberation. The Chinese government always took SWAPO seriously, not only by training our first groups of soldiers but also providing us with weapons, after we had reached the stage that Tanzania would accept our arms. Military training was also undertaken by Algeria, Cuba, Ghana, Nigeria, the Soviet Union and Yugoslavia, and, of course, Tanzania whose government had provided us with the first training base.

While I was moving about from Africa to Europe to the United Nations, mobilizing support for the armed liberation struggle, the first group of our cadres to return to Namibia were establishing their military training camp at Omugulu-gOmbashe in the Uukualuudhi district in north western Namibia (now Omusati Region).

❖ ❖ ❖

11

From Caprivi to Omugulu-gOmbashe

Our experience of the Windhoek uprising on 10 December 1959 taught us a lesson: that to be an effective force against brutal apartheid South Africa, we must not only be able to defend ourselves against these barbaric attacks, but we should also be in position to retaliate against the enemy. It was against this background that the SWAPO Central Committee decided to pursue simultaneously its three-pronged strategy, namely:

1. to carry out an effective mass political mobilisation inside the country,
2. to carry out an effective international political and diplomatic campaign, including petitioning the UN, aimed at isolating apartheid South Africa, and,
3. to carry out military training of SWAPO cadres to effectively engage the enemy on all fronts, while simultaneously sending some of the cadres for further education.

The decision to complement the political mass mobilisation and diplomatic campaign with armed liberation struggle was, as I have related already, inevitable. It was supported internationally, and also strongly supported by our people back home. Our SWAPO leaders — such as Comrades Eliaser Tuhadeleni (Kaxumba Kandola), Reverend Hendrik Witbooi, David Meroro, Andimba Toivo Ya Toivo, John Ya Otto, Nathaniel Maxuilili, Dr Thomas Iihuhua, Simon Kaukungua, Aaron Mushimba, Jerry Ekandjo, Aaron Hamutenya, and Gabriel Mbidi, to mention but a few — played a vital role, particularly in politically mobilizing the people inside the country to join the armed liberation struggle. In this regard, they were also assisted and encouraged by the return of Comrades Lukas Hifikepunye Pohamba and Eliader Muatale to South West Africa in 1962, who carried out an effective mass political campaign until they returned to exile in 1963 and 1964 respectively, taking many cadres with them. At this stage, there was no chance of working underground at home, like Lukas Hifikepunye Pohamba or, in 1964, Eliader Muatale, who later sacrificed his life in the battle.

The South African plan which had been laid out in the Odendaal Commission's Report — the implementation of which would have fragmented the country into tribal homelands to be run by hand-picked puppet chiefs — was supposed to be shelved, or so the South Africans claimed, until the verdict of the International Court of Justice (ICJ) at The Hague was announced in 1966. The ICJ verdict, which was effectively in favour of Pretoria, turned even more people to SWAPO and to joining the armed liberation struggle.

On the one hand, it would have been unwise not to prepare our people for waging the armed liberation struggle against apartheid South Africa, because we knew that the Western powers — particularly Britain and West Germany — had vast investments in both South Africa and South West Africa. Due to that unholy alliance, they would unashamedly side with the minority white oppressors against the African majority. West Germany had also supplied apartheid South Africa with blueprints for the manufacture of military combat armoured vehicles to be deployed against SWAPO. This trend was further demonstrated by the Australian Judge Spencer at the International Court of Justice, who also voted in favour of South Africa. On the other hand, as I have related, we were encouraged by Mwalimu Julius Nyerere, President of the United Republic of Tanzania (formerly Tanganyika), who provided SWAPO and other liberation movements with logistics and a military training camp at Kongwa, near Dodoma, about 300 miles inland from Dar-es-Salaam.

In July 1962 for the first time, SWAPO sent seven men to Egypt for military training. These were Tobias Hainjeko, John Otto Nankudhu, Vilho Haitembu, Titus Muailepeni Shitilifa, Patrick Israel Iyambo (Lungada), Petrus Hambija and Lazarus Sakaria. They were trained in guerrilla warfare tactics and given regular army training with small weapons and heavy weapons, as well as marine training, parachuting, hand-to-hand combat and military topography. They were also trained as company commanders with the purpose of themselves training new recruits on their return to South West Africa.

In January 1963, Comrades Tobias Hainjeko and Titus Muailepeni were joined by four cadres including Eliader Muatale, while some of them proceeded to the Nanking Military Academy in the People's Republic of China where they were trained until April 1964. On 27 May 1963, we opened our military camp at Kongwa in Tanzania, with those Comrades who had received military training from Egypt, Algeria, Ghana, China, the Soviet Union and North Korea. Comrade Tobias Hainjeko thus became the first Commander of the South West Africa Liberation Army (SWALA), with Comrade Petrus Hambija as Military Secretary and Titus Mwailepeni as Deputy Military Secretary of SWALA.

Two weeks later, in June 1963, a group led by Comrade Dimo Hamaambo, now Chief of Defence Force in the Namibia Defence Force, arrived from Algeria. Comrade Hamaambo was, incidentally, one of the very few Namibians who had been to Europe at that time. He had been a stowaway on a merchant ship in the early 1950s, and had served a short sentence in Brixton prison in London before he was sent back by plane to South West Africa.

As time went by, we were joined at Kongwa by more SWAPO members from inside the country via British Bechuanaland. We trained them, together with recruits from Mozambique, led by the late Eduardo Mondlane, the first President of the FRELIMO Party of Mozambique, and the MPLA led by the late Dr. Antonio Augustino Neto, first President of the People's Republic of Angola, and by ZANU and ZAPU of Zimbabwe, as well as the ANC and PAC of South Africa.

I was in constant contact with Commander Tobias Hainjeko and the Military Council, and I regularly visited the training camp at Kongwa, but the day-to-day decisions regarding training and tactics were carried out by the Military Council of which I was the Chairman. The decision had been taken, even before the International Court of Justice fiasco, to send the first group of 10 guerrilla fighters inside the country, despite the fact that the men were poorly equipped. The first task of these commandos was to recruit and train the SWAPO members, as well as to deploy guerrilla tactics and capture weapons from the enemy.

The first group

The first group, known as "G1", was armed only with the two PPSH sub-machine guns and two TT-pistols I had obtained in 1963 from the Algerian Government, and with hunting knives. This group was led by John Otto Nankudhu (Koshiuanda), Commander of the Commandos, and consisted of Simeon Linekela Shixungileni (Kambo), deputy; Patrick Israel Iyambo (Lungada), reconnoitre and secretary; Messah Victory Namuandi (Shiuajanga), Chief of the Reconnaissance; James Hamukuaja Angula (Shoonjeka); and Nelson Kavela (Sadrag).

On 4 March 1965, G1 left on their first mission, accompanied by Comrades Tobias Hainjeko and Peter Nanyemba (who was then SWAPO Representative in Tanzania). From the Kongwa training base they travelled nearly 1000 km to Mbeya (Tanzania) at the borders with Zambia, where they stored their weapons.

From Mbeya, Comrades Hainjeko and Nankudhu then proceeded alone, crossing the border 30 kilometers into Zambia, to the village of Nakonde. There they contacted Mr. Shikombe, a member of the UNIP and Deputy Minister of Foreign Affairs, who was also known to them from their first journey from South West Africa to Tanganyika. Mr Shikombe extended a warm welcome, and later transported their weapons from Nankonde to Lusaka (1100 kilometres), and then to the border between Zambia and South West Africa in the Caprivi Strip region.
Meanwhile, G1 travelled from Mbeya to Lusaka and on to the border with Zambia and South West Africa. At the border they were given the two PPSH sub-machine guns and two 7.6 mm TT pistols by Comrade Peter Nanyemba. Nanyemba and Hainjeko remained behind.

After G1 received their weapons at the borders, they proceeded to Sesheke (Zambia) and crossed, at great risk, into Katima Mulilo in the far eastern Caprivi Strip. They then travelled back into Zambia to cross the Cuando River into Angola, and made their way into the north western corner of South West Africa into the Mbukushu area. They went to the house of a certain SWAPO member who wholeheartedly welcomed them. The next day, he took some of them to Andara Roman Catholic Mission where they bought three bicycles.

While G1 were in the Mbukushu area, they split up into two subgroups. The reconnaissance sub-group, consisting of Messah Victory Shiuajanga, Patrick Iyambo (Lungada) and Nelson Kavela Sadrag, together proceeded to cross the Kavango River into Kavango district heading west for Rundu, and then further north-west towards Ovamboland. They headed to the homestead of Comrade Eliaser Tuhadeleni (Kaxumba ka Ndola) at Endola in Uukuanjama district, which was their assembling point. On their way to the assembling point, their weapons were concealed in suitcases at the backs of their bicycles.

The next day, the second section which had remained behind in Mbukushu area, armed only with pistols, followed on foot. They spent

21 Tobias Hainjeko (L), first Commander of South West Africa Liberation Army (SWALA); Peter Nanyemba (R), first SWAPO Secretary for Defence. Mbeya, Tanzania, 16 April 1965

four weeks on the journey before they arrived at the homestead of Comrade Eliaser Tuhadeleni Kaxumba, where they found their fellow combatants waiting for them. They had fruitful discussions with Comrade Kaxumba, who in turn informed other SWAPO leaders such as Comrades Herman Toivo Ya Toivo, Josef Matheus (Jo'burg), Erastus Mbumba, Lot Homateni, Lamek Iithete and many others, of their presence in the country. All of them paid them a visit, including Comrade Ben Amathila from Walvis Bay.

After their consultations with SWAPO leadership, the group then split up again for political mobilization. Patrick Iyambo (Lungada) and Simeon Shixungileni were assigned to go to Okalongo district and work with Comrade Natanael Lot Homateni, while Nelson Kavela went to work with Comrade Jonas Nashivela at Onakaolo in Ongenga district. Messah Victory Namuandi (Shiuajanga) went to work with Naftali Iyambo Lungada [not related to Patrick Iyambo Lungada] at Ukualumbe in Ongandjera district. Later on, James Hamukuaja went to Festus Heita at Omundudu, while John Nankudhu stayed at Eliaser

Tuhadeleni Kaxumba's house as a group commander, with Comrade Kaxumba as a political mobiliser.

In January 1966, Comrade John Nankudhu called a reconnaissance meeting at Ontamanzi in Ongandjera district with Comrades Simeon Shixungileni, Victory Namuandi, Patrick Iyambo, Nelson Kavela and James Hamukuaja to inform them that the next phase would be the military training of young local activists.

In March 1966, these men established their first military training camp, known as 'Ondaadhi', meaning reconnaissance, at Ontamanzi. Among the first trainees were Comrades Eliaser Tuhadeleni Kaxumba, Immanuel Shifidi, Festus Heita, Johannes Musheko, Paulus Shikolalje, Simeon Namuganga, Henok Jacob 'Malila', Festus Nanjolo, Kornelius Shelungu, Thomas Haimbodi, Isak Shoome and Festus Muaala. Due to the movements of enemy agents in the area, they decided to shift from Ondaadhi, and established a new military training base called Oondjokwe, at Uuvudhija between Uukuambi and Ongandjera districts. At the same time, they continued to recruit and train local activists. However, the enemy also came to establish a base within this area under the pretext of being road constructors.

As part of the military strategy, Comrade Patrick Lungada spied on these so-called road constructors. Later on, Comrade Rehabeam Nambinga was assigned a reconnaissance mission, under the pretext of searching for employment at such construction sites. Mr. Swanepoel, the so-called owner of the road construction company, refused to employ him. In fact, Swanepoel was a captain in the South African Security Police who was used as a State witness against those who were later on detained (captured) and imprisoned in Pretoria.

Omugulu-gOmbashe base, June 1966

In June 1966, this group went to Omugulu-gOmbashe, aiming to reach the Oshiwandu mountain which is situated between Kaokoveld and Uukualuudhi. However, due to the road construction, they decided to remain there and establish a military base in Omugulu-gOmbashe. They settled at Otunganga in the Omugulu-gOmbashe area. At that stage, Commander Nakundhu's group had trained between 80 and 90 SWAPO activists. At the same time, they also started to dig dungeons and trenches for defensive purposes and for storing their ammunition.

While at Omugulu-gOmbashe, they also made contact with the local people. They sent Mr. Shikalepo Iileka, one of the local activists, to

Kaokoveld to mobilise the masses in support of SWAPO. After Iileka returned from Kaokoveld, he informed them that the people in the area were ready to join the SWAPO guerillas — 'Eendume Domomufitu', as they were popularly called at that time.

They received a message from Comrade Ya Toivo informing them that one of the members of G2, Leonard Phillemon Shuuya ('Castro'), had arrived there. Comrades Nankudhu and Tuhadeleni went to meet Castro at Comrade Isak Shoome's house, located a few miles from Omugulu-gOmbashe. They interrogated Castro as to whether he had been detained by the South African Security Police, which he denied completely. After questioning him, they took him to the base where he was further interrogated for the whole day by members of the reconnaissance. During the second interrogation, Castro again denied having been captured and recruited by the enemy. However, he mentioned that the SWAPO leadership in exile had sent money through Comrade Ya Toivo's postal address. Commander Nankudhu then decided to accompany Castro to Comrade Ya Toivo in order to collect the said money. Comrade Ya Toivo was unaware of any such money and cautioned Commander Nankudhu to be extra-vigilant with Castro.

Commander Nankudhu headed back to base, but fell ill while in Ongandjera district. Castro, who failed to turn up at the assembling point he had agreed with Nankudhu, found him later on in Ongandjera district in Comrade Lamek Iithete's house. Commander Nankudhu was still under treatment, so he ordered Castro to return to Omugulu-gOmbashe and stay there until his return. Castro proceeded to Omugulu-gOmbashe as instructed. However, he left the base before Commander Nankudhu's arrival there, under the pretext of going to find whether the money was available at Ya Toivo in Ondonga district. On 25 August 1966, due to reports of movements of strangers in the Omugulu-gOmbashe area and the disappearance of Castro from the base, Commander Nankudhu decided to return to Omugulu-gOmbashe.

26 August 1966, attack at Omugulu-gOmbashe

The following day, 26 August 1966, at about 5 a.m, the South African Security Police led by Captain Swanepoel, and guided by Castro, attacked the military base at Omugulu-gOmbashe. During this surprise attack, the South Africans used eight helicopter gunships, accompanied by personnel carriers. Commander Nakundhu ordered his fellow combatants to return fire. After a brief exchange, Commander Nankudhu realised they could not continue to counter the enemy fire power, and ordered his unit to retreat. But Comrades Lungada, Rehabeam Nambinga and Jonas Nakale insisted on fighting. Two Comrades, Akapeke Hipangelua and Jonas Nakale, sacrificed their lives in this battle. Later that day, Comrades Lungada and Nambinga also retreated and went to inform Mr. Shipaleko Iileka about the attack.

Shikalepo then went on horseback to the area where the battle had taken place, under the pretext of searching for his cattle. At the scene, he was summarily arrested by the South Africa Security Police. Mr. Iileka was released, and he returned to inform Comrades Lungada and Nambinga of those who had been either captured or injured or had died during the attack.

The names of the freedom fighters who were captured during the Omugulu-gOmbashe battle are as follows:
1. Julius Shilongo 'Kashuku'
2. Phillemon Shitilifa
3. Shinima Niilenge 'Harakatyi'
4. Ndjaula Shaningua 'Mankono' (died after Independence)
5. Sakeus Philipus Itika (died after his release from Pretoria prison)
6. Petrus Simon Niilenge (died in detention at Robben Island prison)
7. James Amukuaja (died in Pretoria prison under suspicious circumstances), and
8. Thomas Haimbodi.

The next day, 27 August 1966, Comrade Nankudhu went back to the spot to find comrades who were injured during the battle. After Commander Nankudhu inspected the area, he went to the house of Mr. Kamanja, who had supported them some time before when they met with Comrades Lungada and Nambinga. The three guerrillas then proceeded to Uukualuudhi, and then later on to Ongandjera. They arrived at Comrade Lamek Iithete's house, and were informed that Castro had just left there.

Retaliation — 27 September 1966

Those who fought at Omugulu-gOmbashe on 26 August 1966 numbered many more than the early group of 10 which had spearheaded the re-entry of our guerrilla fighters in 1965 and 1966. At this stage, many more SWAPO activists had been recruited and trained, and had scattered into

22 Above: Veterans of the 26 August 1966 attack at Omugulu-gOmbashe, gathered at commemorative ceremony, Omugulu-gOmbashe, 26 August, 1990

23 Right: Monument at the site, dedicated to victims and survivors.
Inscribed:
"26 August, 1966.
The torch of the armed struggle was lit and the path to freedom was illuminated.
Independence was their aim"

the countryside around Ovamboland area before the South African security police launched the 26 August attack at Omugulu-gOmbashe. However, the political mass mobilisation was completed.

Through an underground network, the SWAPO guerilla fighters communicated with one another and assembled at Iiti jee Holo area, north-east of Oshakati, to devise a new military strategy, particularly identifying the South African military bases as their prime targets. The reconnaissance group was then sent to Oshakati, Ondagwa and Oshikango to reconnoitre the South African Security Police stations.

After they returned and submitted their findings, they decided to carry out a retaliatory action, and on 27 September 1966, they attacked and burnt down Oshikango police station and the government administrative building. During the same attack on that evening, the Portuguese army post on the Angolan side, north of Oshikango, was also targeted. This attack was successful because the enemy, on both sides of the borders, had run away, leaving the whole area ablaze. The Portuguese army post was complemented by a fuelling station, which also was burnt down. No casualties were suffered on our side, but three Portuguese soldiers were killed and a number of South African security police were injured. After they attacked Oshikango, the group then returned to their base at Iiti jee Holo, and later on moved to Okalonga ka Nepaya, south of Onguediva.

On 16 November 1966, Comrade John Nankudhu was captured at Ohakueenjanga area while on a mission to re-group his unit to attack Ondangua police station. He was taken to Oshakati Security Police Station, and later on transferred to Pretoria Central Prison. In the absence of Comrade Nankudhu, Comrade Simeon Shixungileni (Kambo) was appointed as the Commander of their Group. Comrade Simeon Shixungeleni was also wounded and then captured during a battle which took place north of the Okatana Roman Catholic Church.

Commander Patrick Iyambo (Lungada)

At this stage, Comrade Lungada was the only commander among Group 1 who survived to return to SWAPO. He evaded capture at every turn, taunting the enemy and successfully carrying out raids, while he also continued with political mass mobilisation work. Despite the enormous monetary reward of R1000 (one thousand rand) promised to anyone who captured him or revealed information leading to his capture — whether dead or alive — he was never betrayed to the enemy.

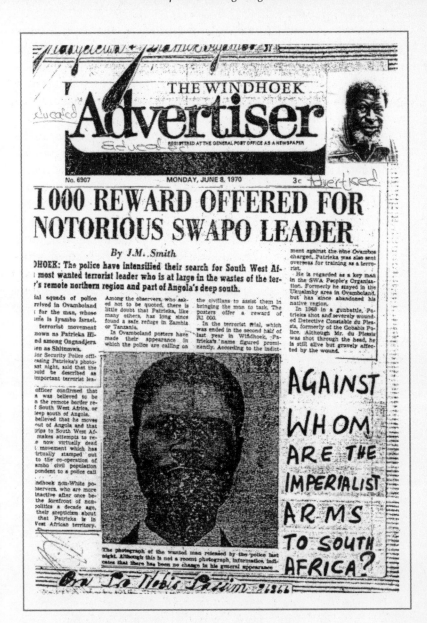

24 "R1000 reward offered for notorious SWAPO leader" — Windhoek Advertiser, Monday 8 June, 1970

After they encountered Commander Lungada, the superstitious belief became entrenched among the South African security police that the SWAPO guerrillas (Eendume Domomfitu) had super-human powers. Such characteristics were attributed to Commander Lungada, who was also described by the Boers as 'unique' and 'sophisticated'. There was a fast-spreading legend among the local population and South African police forces that, as part of their training, the SWAPO guerrillas were cooked to render them bullet-proof! The Boers became so paranoid in their search for Commander Lungada that ant-hills or lizards or even a donkey could be shot at if found in the direction they thought Commander Lungada had headed. The story of how he out-manoeuvred the enemy was fascinating. The Boers made fools of themselves during their so-called hot pursuits after the Commander, to the extent that on a number of occasions they even asked the Commander himself whether he had seen 'Lungada'! Comrade Lungada, true to his determination and bravery as a well-trained combatant, continued with his underground operations. After the Omugulu-gOmbashe battle, a certain warrant officer at Ondangua Police Station got wind of the fact that one of our commandos was still in the Ongandjera district (near Okahao, where I was born). At about 8 p.m. one evening, the warrant officer and some of his men went and surrounded the house of Patrick Lungada's brother, where the Commander was staying. The police warrant officer was in front, leading his armed men. Patrick Lungada had taken cover in one of the stockade passages characteristic of Ovambo homesteads, and shot the warrant officer in the head when they suddenly confronted each other. The Boer soldier fell down and died on the spot while his men ran away. His body remained there until the next day, when the local people removed it and took it to the Okahao clinic.

The following day, a Sunday, the Boers came by helicopter during midday and took away the corpse from the clinic, in full view of the members of the congregation. Typical of the Boers' cruelties, they then went straight to the house and beat Patrick Lungada's brother to death and seriously injured his wife. She was taken, unconscious, to Onandjokwe hospital, but she eventually recovered after hospitalisation.

These atrocities and acts of repression did not deter the people from supporting SWAPO — instead it made SWAPO even more popular. In fact, this was the first time a Boer police warrant officer had been seen killed by a SWAPO guerrilla fighter. People began to lose any fear of the white oppressors and to see that they were neither superior nor untouchable.

25 Patrick Iyambo (Lungada), at ceremony held on 26 August 1990 to commemorate the 26 August 1966 attack on Omugulu-gOmbashe

Comrade Patrick Iyambo Lungada was one of the most heroic fighters SWAPO ever produced. He was a great sharp-shooter, fast as lightning in action (his Egyptian training officers compared his running speed to that of an ostrich), and fearless as a commander. He continued to operate clandestinely inside the country for the next 9 years, until 1974. In that year he returned to exile in Zambia via Angola, leading one of the largest groups to join SWAPO in exile — this was after the overthrow of the fascist regime of Marcello Caetano in Portugal, by young army officers who then allowed SWAPO members to pass through Angola to Zambia to join SWAPO in exile.

Commander Lungada proudly reported himself to the PLAN Military Headquarters in Zambia. He presented his 7.6 mm TT pistol to his superior, and pronounced that he had accomplished his mission. Lungada was the only one of the first group who survived to return to SWAPO in exile, and gave a full account of the launching of the armed liberation struggle on 26 August 1966, and the political mass mobilization of the Namibian people. He had bravely carried out the task when many of his colleagues had been captured or killed by enemy forces.

After Commander Lungada reported himself to the PLAN Headquarters, he was sent for further military training to the Soviet Union. After he returned, he went back to the battle front and resumed his combat duties, but he was later on wounded and sent to the German Democratic Republic (GDR) for medical treatment. After recovering, he returned to Zambia at the PLAN Military Headquarters. Next, Commander Lungada was assigned to operate from Angola, first at Lumbango and, later, on the battle field. He again engaged with the South African occupation forces at a number of battles on the North Eastern Front. Then, soon before the UN repatriation, he worked in a new role, still as one of the senior PLAN Commanders, in the SWAPO transit camps both in Luanda and Kwanza-Sul, Angola.

During the implementation of UN Resolution 435, Comrade Lungada returned with other SWAPO members and was again engaged in mass political mobilisation which paved the way for SWAPO's victory. At independence, Commander Patrick Lungada joined the Namibian Police in 1990 and assumed the Rank of Inspector — which he retained until his death from natural illness on 25 July 1991.

I was honoured to inaugurate the Police College named after Israel Patrick Iyambo (Lungada) on 29 May 1998.

Group 2

The three groups which followed G1 were called G2, G3 and G4, and consisted of 10 trained guerrillas each. G1 had already established itself inside the country. The second group, G2, consisted of Leonard Phillemon Shuuya ('Castro'), second-in-command of SWALA; Lazarus Haiduua Zachariah (Shakala), Chief of SWALA Military Police; Helao Shityuwete, Secretary; Elia Ndume, Medical Assistant; Julius Shilongo, Reconnoitre; Eino Kamati Ekandjo, Demolition Squad; and Jonas Shimueefeleni, Festus Nehale, Nghidipo Jesaja Haufiku and David

Hamunime. Though Castro was the second-in-command of SWALA, he was not trusted with the responsibility of leading the group, and this task was given to Lazarus Zachariah (Shakala).

In February 1966, G2 left Kongwa Training Camp for South West Africa. They set off by land-rover and headed west to the Tanzania-Zambian border. Like G1, this group was also to pick up their weapons and ammunition at Mbeya, and then enter South West Africa through the Caprivi Strip. They undertook their long journey via Lusaka and Livingstone and then to Mambova, a village in the swamps of the Zambezi River. They spent two days in Mambova waiting for the Zambezi Transport riverboat to arrive. Together with their land-rover on the riverboat — which could be seen from miles away — they cruised up the Zambezi and docked at Mwandi. Mwandi is a half-way station on the Zambian side, while on the other bank of the river is the Caprivi Strip, part of South West Africa. G2 then left their land-rover at Mwandi and proceeded on the river, with weapons and equipment concealed in their baggage.

The Zambezi boat was scheduled to dock at Sesheke in Zambia, where they intended to disembark and cross secretly into South West Africa through Katima-Mulilo. But unexpectedly, the boat changed course and moved directly towards the South West African side, where it docked at Katima-Mulilo in broad daylight. They were expecting an attack by the South African colonial police stationed at Katima-Mulilo, but their guerrilla training enabled them to mix with other passengers on the boat before they stepped ashore. They went and sat under trees some 100m from the river, with other local passengers. After a long wait, they caught a bus from Katima-Mulilo where the Zambezi River cuts north, and then crossed the River back into Zambia at Sesheke. They secretly stayed at Sesheke for some time, and made the necessary preparations before proceeding along the Zambezi River again to cross the Cuando River at Kaunga Mashi into Angola. Eventually they crossed the Kavango River again into South West Africa.

While in Kavango district, they had a direct engagement with the South African occupation forces near the Kavango River, west of Rundu. They suffered no casualties, but they believed that during the battle some enemy soldiers were killed and some were injured because the enemy soldiers were not able to take immediate follow-up action. However, disaster struck after the enemy sent troop reinforcements and eight of them were captured. Comrade Julius Shilongo managed to evade capture that day, but he was later captured at Omugulu-gOmbashe, on 26 August 1966.

The damage caused by 'Castro'

One member of their group, Leonard Phillemon Shuuya 'Castro', was among the eight G2 captured. Castro was later on released from detention in Pretoria and sent into exile. But he had been recruited by the South African security police in return for a large bribe — they promised to pay him half in advance and the remaining half upon the completion of his mission. He betrayed groups that were to follow later; some of them were eventually rounded up by waiting Boer security men at Katima-Mulilo, and only Castro proceeded to Uukualuudhi district, where Commander John Otto Nankudhu and his group, G1, were now located. Castro never informed them that he had been captured by the enemy, and he deliberately fed a lot of disinformation to the guerrillas as well as to the SWAPO leadership, both in and outside the country.

The damage caused by Castro to our liberation struggle was great since he was also responsible for the arrests of Comrades Ya Toivo and Nathanael Homateni and many others in the north. Castro was sent by the South African security police to approach Comrade Ya Toivo for the procurement of dynamite to be used by SWAPO freedom fighters against the enemy targets. Comrade Ya Toivo had himself already warned Commander Nankudhu to be extra-vigilant with Castro. Unfortunately ignoring his own advice, he reluctantly approached a worker at Tsumeb Corporation Limited to provide him with substances for explosives. This action led to Comrade Herman Toivo Ya Toivo being arrested, tried, convicted and imprisoned for 20 years on Robben Island.

Castro's mission did not end with the arrest of SWAPO leaders inside the country. He also succeeded in bringing about the deaths of many combatants, including Comrade Tobias Hainjeko, Head-in-Command of SWALA. He lured Tobias Hainjeko to his death by misinforming him to travel from Zambia in May 1967. Castro gave Hainjeko a map to follow and put him on the Zambezi Transport riverboat from Mambova in Zambia to Katima-Mulilo on the Namibian side. The South African police then intercepted and boarded the boat before it docked at Sesheke on the Zambian side. Commander Hainjeko was a brave son and fearless freedom fighter, and he died in action on the Zambezi River. Before he died, he shot dead a South African police warrant officer named Grobler, who was the commanding officer at Katima-Mulilo, and wounded another who later died from the injuries. This event took place on 18 May 1967, the day which is today popularly commemorated as Namibian Heroes' Day.

Group 3

In June 1966, G3 left Tanzania. This group consisted of Commander Kaleb Tjipahura; Deputy Rudolph Kadhikua; and S. Kakuambi, J. Haiduua, B. Naunjango, Thomas Haimbodi, A. Aluteni, P. Hamalua Ndadi, I. Ipinge and Eliader Muatale. Eliader Muatale was later killed by combined Portuguese and South African forces. Hamalua Ndadi died as they were crossing the Cuando River, while Ipinge was sent back to Zambia due to exhaustion. In other words, there were only seven who survived the perilous crossing of the Cuando River.

After crossing the Cuando River, the seven G3 proceeded in the direction of western Caprivi on the way to Botswana, and then crossed the Kavango River between Maun and Shakawe. After crossing the borders into Botswana, they thought they were lucky to get a ride to Oshakawe. Unfortunately, the driver of the truck took them straight to a police station! They were briefly arrested, but succeeded in convincing the police that they were on their way to the South African mines in search of employment. They were eventually allowed to proceed to their destination.

Ready for armed struggle

In November 1966, the first five groups were deployed in three regions of our country — Eastern Caprivi, Kavango and Ovamboland. At the time when I returned to Windhoek with Comrade Hifikepunye Pohamba on 20 March 1966, putting the lie to the Boers' claim at The Hague (International Court of Justice) that SWAPO leaders were 'self-exiled' and free to return home without being arrested by South African police, our combatants were already inside the country setting up what we called 'roving military training camps'. In fact, their task was not only to establish bases and undertake the military training of local individuals and groups to prepare them for the inevitable armed liberation struggle, but also to recruit new cadres and send them back to their homes where they would be ready when called to fight the enemy.

I later learned how some had fared. For example, one of them, Comrade Isak Shoome Elago, evaded capture by staying away from his home in the Uukualuudhi district for three years before he was finally captured and taken together with others to Pretoria. Until 1972, he was held in detention along with the eight survivors of Omugulu-gOmbashe and a number of other Comrades from Caprivi, without charge or trial, while their families thought that they were dead.

Also taken to prison in Pretoria with Comrade Isak Shoome Elago was my father Daniel Utoni Nujoma, who at the time was already over 70 years old, and whose sole 'crime' was being my father. He was in fact arrested while he was in Okahao hospital receiving treatment. He was first taken to Ondangua, then to Kavango before he was sent to Pretoria prison. There he was imprisoned in a small cell where he could not move, with ice cold water dripping on his head. As a result he developed TB from which he later died.

Trial of the Omugulu-gOmbashe fighters and others, August 1967

In August 1967, the Omugulu-gOmbashe captives and those betrayed by "Castro" in the Caprivi district were put on trial. The trial charge sheets included a list of attacks on the homesteads of bodyguards of the most notorious puppet chiefs, an armed raid (to obtain weapons) on a white settler farm at Kalahari Kroon in the Grootfontein district, and the destruction of the police stations and government compound at Oshikango on 27 September 1966, when the offices and the house of the 'Acting Bantu Commissioner' had been reduced to ashes by our guerrilla fighters.

After prolonged solitary confinement and torture, the captured guerrillas were brought to trial in Pretoria. They stood in the dock, with 10 SWAPO leaders: Comrades Herman Toivo Ya Toivo, Eliaser Tuhadeleni, Nathaniel Maxuilili among them. There were 81 names on the charge sheet. Among the first 10 on the list were the names of Comrades Hifikepunye Pohamba, Maxton Joseph Mutongolume (now senior SWAPO official), Katjivena (now Head of Public Affairs at the NBC) and Peter Mueshihange — with mine (Sam Nujoma), as 'Accused Number One'. The other four have since then either sacrificed their lives or retired from the political scene.

Among the hundreds detained by the police in 1967 were Comrade Aaron Hamutenya and Gabriel Mbidi who had been my good friends in Windhoek and had both remained committed SWAPO leaders. They had been seized in their homes in Windhoek Old Location.

On 21 June 1967, less than two months before the trial began, the South African Terrorism Act was gazetted, having been rushed through parliament in the first week of June. The Act — which was made retrospective to 1962 — would have enabled the South African courts to sentence our freedom fighters and SWAPO civilian leaders to death for actions committed many years before its enactment. This retrospective clause — extreme by any standards — and the fact that the prisoners were taken out of South West Africa and put on trial in a foreign country, South Africa itself, gave us a great opportunity to convince the world of the criminal wickedness of the Verwoerd regime, and of the urgent need for something to be done in defence not only of the SWAPO freedom fighters facing death in the dock in Pretoria, but also of the SWAPO leaders and activists who had neither been in exile nor received any military training.

The General Assembly of the UN met at a special session from April to June 1967, and produced a resolution which set up the United Nations Council for South West Africa under United Nations Trusteeship. These were intended to be instruments of the 'de jure' Government of Namibia, which was the UN itself. The Western powers abstained when the resolution was put to the vote, though one by one they came to accept both the Council and the Trusteeship. In fact, all Western powers came to accept, except Britain, which took nearly 20 years even to accept General Assembly Resolution 2145 (passed on 27 October 1966), which terminated the mandate to administer South West Africa which was given to South Africa by the League of Nations in 1922.

SWAPO carried out effective campaigns to rally international solidarity. Groups and states, mainly OAU Member States, movements of Non-Aligned countries, anti-apartheid movements of Nordic countries, Holland, the United Kingdom, Australia, Belgium, Canada, France, the United States of America — to mention but a few — intensified their campaigns in defence of those on trial in Pretoria, many of whom were faced with a very real threat of the death penalty.

The defendants were also aided by Comrade Herman Toivo ya Toivo (Andimba), who made a historic statement from the dock on behalf of all the defendants. This statement was published in many countries, adding to support on our side. His statement read (in part):

> "I speak of *we* because I am trying to speak not only for myself but also for others as well, and especially for those of my fellow accused who have not had the benefit of any education."

He continued:

> "My Lord, we find ourselves here in a foreign country, convicted under laws made by people who we have always considered as foreigners. We find ourselves tried by a judge who is not our countryman and who has not shared our background."

26 *Andimba Toivo Herman Ya Toivo, one of the founder members of SWAPO (pictured in May 1984). He was sentenced in January 1968, with 36 other Namibians, on charges of inciting revolution and armed resistance against the racist apartheid South African government and its colonial administration of Namibia.*

His statement went on:

> "We are Namibians and not South Africans. We do not now, and will not in the future, recognise your right to govern us; to make laws for us, in which we had no say; to treat our country as if it were your property and us as if you were our masters. We have

always regarded South Africa as an intruder in our country. This is how we have always felt and this is how we feel now and it is on this basis that we have faced this trial.

...I am a loyal Namibian and I could not betray my people to their enemies. I admit that I decided to assist those who had taken up arms; I know that the struggle will be long and bitter. I also know that my people will wage that struggle whatever the cost.

...We believe that South Africa has a choice — either to live at peace with us or to subdue us by force. If you choose to crush us and impose your will on us, then you not only betray your trust but you will live in security for only so long as your power is greater than ours.

My Lord, you found it necessary to brand me as a coward. During the Second World War, when it became evident that both my country and your country were threatened by the dark clouds of Nazism, I risked my life to defend both of them, wearing a uniform with an orange band on it. But some of your countrymen, when called to battle to defend civilisation, resorted to sabotage against their own fatherland. I volunteered to face German bullets, and as a guard of military installations both in 'South West Africa' and the Republic was prepared to be the victim of their sabotage. Today they are our masters sitting in judgement and are considered the heroes, and I am called the coward. When I considered my country, I am proud that my countrymen have taken up arms for their people and I believe that anyone who calls himself a man would not despise them."

We were strongly disturbed, having been insulted by the racist Judge Ludorf, who earlier on had stated that we were merely innocent children misled by communists. However, he later fumed with anger during and after Ya Toivo's statement and was very much embarrassed because the court was full of diplomats who had come to hear the verdict, and some cheered Ya Toivo on when he read his statement. Prosecutor Oosthuizen was also visibly uneasy in his chair, as were many white senior policemen in court who favoured the imposition of the death penalty.

When the prosecutor argued against mitigation, he stressed the 'defiant' character of Ya Toivo's statement, which he described as displaying no proper sense of 'remorse' and as maintaining a spirit of opposition to the existing arrangements for governing South West Africa.

Brave men and traitors

The case was "The state v. Tuhadeleni and 36 Others". The Judge began by reading out the names of those on trial, the charges and the so-called "terroristic" activities each defendant had allegedly committed. The list of the accused was as follows (names in brackets are combat names):

Accused No 1	Eliaser Tuhadeleni (Kaxumba Kandola)
Accused No 2	John Otto Nankudhu (Koshiuanda)
Accused No 3	Simeon Shihungileni (Kambo)
Accused No 4	Julius Shilongo (Kashuku)
Accused No 5	Lazarus Zachariah (Shakala)
Accused No 6	David Hamunime (Keenongoja)
Accused No 7	Helao Joseph Shityuwete (Kandindima)
Accused No 8	Eino Kamati Ekandjo (Ma-questions)
Accused No 9	Festus Nehale (Ndengu)
Accused No 10	Nghidipo Jesaja Haufiku (Kambua)
Accused No 11	Immanuel August Shifidi
Accused No 12	Kaleb Hanganee Tjipahura (Day by Day)
Accused No 13	Rudolph Kadhikwa
Accused No 14	Abel Shuudeni Aluteni (The Great)
Accused No 15	Bethuel Nuunjango
Accused No 16	Michael Nghifingila Moses
Accused No 17	Mathias Elia Kanjeule (Shimbungu)
Accused No 18	Malakia Shivute Uushona
Accused No 19	John Shiponeni
Accused No 20	Petrus Kamati
Accused No 21	Herman Toivo ya Toivo Andimba
Accused No 22	John Ya Otto Waniipupu
Accused No 23	Jason Mutumbulua
Accused No 24	Nathaniel Gottlieb Maxuilili (Kayula)
Accused No 25	Matthew Joseph (Jo'burg)
Accused No 26	Jonas Nashivela
Accused No 27	Nathanael Lot Homateni
Accused No 28	Phillemon Kakwalindishishi Shitilifa
Accused No 29	Simeon Namunganga Hamulemo
Accused No 30	Shinima Niilenge (Harakatji)
Accused No 31	Ndjaula Shaningua (Mankono)
Accused No 32	Sakeus Philipus Itika (Oshivela)
Accused No 33	Efraim Kapolo

Accused No 34   Simeon Iitula
Accused No 35   Naftalie Amungulu (Kombandjele)
Accused No 36   Petrus Simon Niilenge
Accused No 37   Rehabeam Olavi Nambinga

With others unknown by the state, they were charged with conspiring to overthrow the white South African Government and the South West African administration by violence to replace it with a SWAPO government. They were charged under the Terrorism Act, as well as other legislation such as the Suppression of Communism Act.

The proceedings were conducted in Afrikaans and did not make any sense to those who could not understand Afrikaans, and no efforts were made to either switch to English or to allow the proceedings to be interpreted into Namibian local languages.

During the trial, one of the accused, Efraim Kapolo, died in the Pretoria jail from torture. Three others, Comrades Festus Nehale, Petrus Niilenge and Jonas Shimueefeleni, died of negligence and mistreatment on Robben Island. From 1966 to 1967, two more — one an Omugulu-gOmbashe prisoner — were released but later died as a result of torture and beatings during their imprisonment.

Of course, we knew precisely what we were fighting for and did not need anyone to tell us how we were going to achieve our independence. We, in fact, intensified the armed liberation struggle after the trial, and our campaign was well supported by many countries. Ludorf, after all, did not impose the death sentence as he had been threatening the defendants. Some of our men got life sentences while some were sentenced to 10 years imprisonment, to be served in the South African prison on Robben Island.

As in any war situation, we experienced some painful setbacks. The killing in action of the Head-in-Command of South West Africa Liberation Army (SWALA), Tobias Hainjeko, near Katima-Mulilo in 1967, was a severe setback, but his brave actions — shooting the warrant officer and continuing to fire while his men got away — inspired our people. For the second time a Boer warrant-officer, Grobler, had fallen to our firearms, and this was a great encouragement to our combatants to intensify the war of national liberation to its final victory.

We learnt that Grobler was replaced by a son of Mr. Jansen, a senate member of Prime Minister Balthazar Johannes Vorster's government in Cape Town. Before he left, he told his father to tell Prime Minister Vorster that he would not even use his pistol and waste the government's bullets. He would catch the 'terrorists' with his dog! He thought he was going to be chasing 'tsotsis'. He was totally unaware that SWAPO guerrilla fighters were well-trained in guerrilla tactics. The very morning he landed at Katima-Mulilo Air Strip, he demanded to go straight on patrol. Our guerrilla fighters had planted a double-tank land mine and, fortunately for us and unfortunately for him, he and his dog were blown up, blasted to pieces within a second. There was no body to be recovered, only pieces of flesh on the branches of the trees. He had not even eaten lunch there. He was given a 'hero's funeral' by the South African Prime Minister Vorster, who also invited black South Africans to the funeral. But they did not attend, saying that he went to fight against the Namibians who were fighting to free and regain their country.

The bravery of commanders such as Patrick Iyambo Lungada at Okahao and Tobias Hainjeko at Katima-Mulilo really gave the people confidence. They saw that we had firepower similar to that the white man possessed, and that led them to join the armed liberation struggle, though they had been afraid before.

Of course, there were informers and traitors, and we were to suffer even more, later on, for the actions of spies who infiltrated our forces outside the country. As mentioned already, Leonard Phillemon Shuuya ('Castro') was the first of these after the war of liberation was launched. Eventually we traced the source of the betrayal, apprehended him and handed him over to the Tanzanian authorities who kept him away while the struggle continued. Eventually, President Nyerere released him, along with others who had been held, and he was resettled in Norway. It is believed that after independence he returned to a free Namibia.

After Omugulu-gOmbashe and the death of Commander Tobias Hainjeko, we fully realized the enormity of our losses, and recognised the need to re-organize our military strategies. SWAPO Central Committee and PLAN Military Council saw that Omugulu-gOmbashe had been too large a concentration of guerrilla fighters. For future military operations we decided to change tactics and to deploy our fighters in smaller, more mobile groups from sections, platoons and companies — not only in Ovamboland, Caprivi and Kavango, but also in the so-called Police Zone (white areas) like Tsumeb, Otavi, Grootfontein and Otjiwarongo districts. These small groups of guerrilla fighters were well-trained and well-equipped with modern weapons, including land mines which we used effectively against enemy armoured cars. This strategy enabled us to minimise losses on our side while ensuring that heavy casualties were inflicted on the enemy.

The support of the people was indispensable. They fed and sheltered the freedom fighters, who were indeed their own sons, daughters, brothers and sisters. Our fighters were never 'terrorists'. If the meaning of 'terrorist' is to trample innocent people into political subjugation, then it was the minority white South Africans who were the terrorists — a foreign army and security force determined to crush the spirit of resistance of the Namibians, to oppress and deny them their inalienable rights to self-determination and independence in the land of their birth.

Continuation on the political and diplomatic fronts

I spoke at a meeting in London on 26 August 1968, during the second anniversary of the launching of the armed liberation struggle, and tried to put into perspective our struggle and our hopes for the future. I was anxious also to counteract the barrage of propaganda which South Africa had kept up ever since the World Court fiasco two years before.

"As it is usual with any group which is denied its political rights, we in Namibia started to form political movements to fight for political freedom and political rights through democratic methods. SWAPO is an organization open to all the people of my country regardless of race or creed. Namibia is a big country and we have room for all Namibians.

The Namibian question has been discussed, as you probably all know, in the debates of the United Nations for more than 20 years without tangible results, at least positive ones. From the UN chambers the ball game reached the International Court of Justice. The decision — or should I say indecision? — of the court is well known to you all.

In the history of any oppressed people there comes a time when a change is forcing itself forward, and a new stand has to be taken. The problems facing the people will have to be re-examined and a new strategy solution has to be put into practice. Until the judgement of the ICJ at The Hague, we did not wish to venture into a change, because change was to depend upon the outcome of our case. It must be said again — as it has been said many times before — that we had at least a hope for a positive outcome of the case. The final judgement was therefore a letdown and disappointment which snatched all those hopes away and left us alone. What could we do? We could not let our grief overpower us — now it was up to us to overpower our grief, up to us to make a new decision, and to put that decision into action. Non-violence had led us nowhere; if anything, it has only worsened our plight. The only alternative left was to take up arms into our hands and use them like arms that had been used against us as long as an oppressor has been in our country. The launching of the armed liberation struggle — it was the new solution we should put into practice to dislodge the oppressor and achieve freedom.

It would be very wrong of Britain or the USA, and all Western countries, to believe that we are just 'frustrated terrorists'. There is a struggle for liberation in the whole of southern Africa which is fought by the indigenous peoples for their human dignity and equality, and it is not communist-inspired, as the white minority regimes of southern Africa use as an argument in order to ingratiate the Western countries."

I appealed to the Western countries:

"...to come on to the side of Africa ... and to start giving moral and material support to the just struggle. One of the most important things is to isolate apartheid South Africa from the rest of the world in all respects — rendering her without communication in any form.

We from SWAPO can only look ahead to a greater and more intensive battle. The solidarity and support from all over the world is a major factor, contributing to the positive outcome of this battle — which is the inevitable end to the oppressors' losing battle.

I pay tribute to all those gallant sons and daughters of Namibia who sacrificed their lives in the struggle for freedom. I, especially, think of our freedom fighters — such as those led by Comrade Tobias Hainjeko, our people in prison on Robben Island, and I also pay tribute to all those who were cold-bloodedly murdered in Windhoek Old Location in 1959."

Twenty-five years later, as President of the Republic of Namibia, it was an historic and personally moving moment for me to meet with the Comrades who participated in the battle of Omugulu-gOmbashe and commemorate the launching of the armed liberation struggle.

The following names are those of the comrades who died:

— in detention at Robben Island:
1. Festus Nehale, 4 March 1971
2. Petrus Simon Niilenge, 8 March 1974
3. Jonas Shimueefeleni, 18 August 1974

— during interrogation in Pretoria Central Prison:
4. James Amukuaja, 15 September 1966
5. Efraim Kapolo, September 1967

— after they were released from Robben Island:
6. Immanuel Shifidi (assassinated) 11 November 1986
7. Kaleb Hanganee Tjipahura (natural causes) 1985
8. Israel Nashilongo Taapopi (died in Cassinga Massacre) 4 May 1978
9. David Shikomba (natural causes) September 1990
10. Philipus Itika

My final appeal, spoken at the meeting in London on 26 August 1968, was:

> "Help SWAPO and support our liberation struggle, so that we can soon come to play our part in a totally liberated Africa!"

Winning such support now became a major assignment for me.

12

The Struggle Intensifies on All Fronts

From 1966 when we launched the armed liberation struggle we also expanded our diplomatic establishment and representation, at the UN in New York and in many other places outside Africa. By 1970 we had SWAPO offices in Stockholm, London, Belgrade, Moscow, Bucharest, Paris and Helsinki. This was to help mobilize the international community. SWAPO intensified the political mobilisation too, inside the country, and of course the armed liberation struggle, which was the most effective against the enemy.

The decision to go to war, coming so soon after the International Court of Justice fiasco, followed by the Pretoria trial of SWAPO members in 1968, brought SWAPO much more into the limelight. These developments also established more clearly the existence of our country as more than just an appendage to South Africa called South West Africa.

The UN was determined, after the ICJ fiasco, to support the people of South West Africa in their just struggle for freedom and independence. This determination facilitated the setting up, in 1967 under General Assembly Resolution 2248, of the UN Council for South West Africa, as the 'de jure' government of the country. The intention was that the Council would administer the country until it achieved its independence. South Africa refused to co-operate, of course, and the Council was unable to enter South West Africa. Like the Special Committee before it, its members could visit only countries like Botswana, Zambia and Tanzania, and then return to report to the UN General Assembly.

27 On one of many hundreds of diplomatic journeys, Sam Nujoma at Rome Airport, in transit to Dar-es-Salaam, 24 July 1968

When the UN Council for South West Africa came to Dar-es-Salaam in April 1968, I put to them SWAPO's decision, which was fully supported within the country, that the name which we in SWAPO had come to use for our country — Namibia — should be officially adopted by the UN. I made a strong statement, highlighting the treatment of our guerrillas and political leaders on trial in Pretoria, and the second group awaiting trial, as well as the reign of terror that the apartheid South African white minority regime had launched on the country since Omugulu-gOmbashe. We demanded that the Council enter Namibia (I used the new name throughout my statement) "with or without the co-operation of the white South African government" to carry out General Assembly Resolution 2145 (XXI) of 29 October 1966. I ended:

"SWAPO's fight in Namibia is not against whites but against the system which subjugates the Africans. This fight will go on until victory is attained. Victory may be attained without the unnecessary loss of human life; on the other hand, there may be much bloodshed before the final goal is achieved. The United Nations must act to avoid this last alternative and this consideration must be the guiding line of the Council as it prepares to enter Namibia."

The name Namibia had been carefully thought out. Kerina had been promoting the name Namib, but Namibia was finally named by SWAPO. The Council said in its report to the UN Secretary General, U Thant:

> "The representatives of the South West African people informed the Council that they wish their country to be called Namibia. The Council supports this request and considers that the name Namibia should be used in all formal references to the Territory."

The proposal was made by the Council as a whole but it was Mustafa Rateb Abdel-Wahab, the Egyptian delegate, then President of the Council, who was instrumental in achieving this. He accepted it in Dar-es-Salaam, the UN Council adopted it, and took it to the UN General Assembly, who formally inaugurated the new name. So it went through. Abdel-Wahab was a skilled and effective chairman, and when you have such a chairman you can really get things done. You can explain precisely what you want to be done beforehand so that when you appear before him and his colleagues, he will already know what your objective is, will support you, and see that it is adopted.

Abdel-Wahab, who later became an Ambassador, was at this time dealing with the affairs of the Fourth Committee. He was a career diplomat, going back to the early days of King Farouk. I have seldom worked with so skilful a diplomat. Others like him, especially those skilled in drafting resolutions, were Ambassador Clark of Nigeria, Tanzania's Permanent Representative at the UN, John Malecela (who later became his country's Prime Minister) and Vernon Mwaanga of Zambia, who was very dynamic. At that time the continent was very united as far as the decolonization issue was concerned, so that we were able to push through some of these far-reaching resolutions.

The name Namibia was adopted by the United Nations, but some newspapers and governments, particularly the British Government, were against it. Their UN delegates accused us of imposing the name on the people. We did our best to explain the reason we had chosen the name Namibia, and the people at home had supported that choice.

The Namib Desert had always been our 'shield', keeping colonizers out and the slave traders at bay for many centuries. It also ran down to the coast, which teemed with fish and which contained our two ports, Walvis Bay and Lüderitz. It was the source also of our rich diamond deposits. All these things, we wrote in *Namibia Today* (January 1969):

> "... constitute such a vivid versatility of the Namib, unknown of any other desert in the world. Conceived from these perspectives, the Namib, we believe, is not just a wasted land of dunes, but a resourceful region. The natural defence shield, the rich fishing ground, uranium, and the diamond fields of the Namib are valuable attributes of our national territory. This is the reason why we have chosen to call our country Namibia — the land of the brave.
>
> The United Nations and the Organization of African Unity have both embraced Namibia as the genuine name of that nation. The adoption of this name by the African nations and the UN is in conformity with the principles of self-determination. For, it is we, the people of Namibia, who must ultimately shape our own destiny and identity, and we call it Namibia."

We had come a long way since I had set up our first small office in Dar-es-Salaam which we shared with our PAFMECSA colleagues. The Council's report to the Secretary-General was a good summary of our status at this stage. The "Working Group on Political Questions" stated:

> "It would appear that SWAPO is the best organized group among the various South West African political movements. The other groups are SWANU and NUDO-SWANUF. SWAPO operates entirely from its provisional headquarters in Dar-es-Salaam where the National Executive Committee is based. The provisional headquarters organization of SWAPO in Dar-es-Salaam is divided into various functional departments corresponding to normal departmental and agency organizations of national governments. In addition, SWAPO also maintains branch offices in various capitals. At the moment there are branches of SWAPO in Lusaka, Algiers, Cairo, London, Helsinki and New York. These branches are entirely responsible to the provisional headquarters in Dar-es-Salaam and they also act as diplomatic outposts for SWAPO.

From the testimony of SWAPO leaders it was clear that the SWAPO organization is maintained as the nucleus of a government. On the other hand, there was no evidence available regarding a similar structure and organization for the other two political groups with which meetings were held."

In the main body of the report there was an endorsement of the armed liberation struggle, in so many words:

"The Council has been greatly impressed by the courage of the people of South West Africa and their determination to attain the independence of their Territory and is convinced that their efforts will lead to the achievement of this objective with the necessary and active support of the international community."

Tanga Consultative Congress

Though the Council praised our organization there was still much to do. We had representatives in many countries, and more and more member states were coming to recognize that only SWAPO was fighting to free their country from foreign domination, and that only SWAPO could really speak for the people of Namibia. We had to put the organization on the best possible footing.

SWAPO held, from 26 December 1969 to 2 January 1970, a consultative congress at Tanga in Tanzania. The war, from its small beginnings, had been going on for three years, but was not, until Tanga, given its central position in our strategy. The congress was attended by observers from countries which were able to supply us with arms and ammunition, and with military training beyond the level of what we ourselves undertook at Kongwa: Algeria, Czechoslovakia, Cuba, China, Egypt, Rumania, USSR and Yugoslavia gave us support in ways that Western countries, to whom we had put our case for assistance against apartheid South Africa, would not. The Congress thanked them and other countries, both of the Non-Aligned Movement and the socialist countries. It also expressed appreciation for "material humanitarian assistance and moral support given to SWAPO by progressive organizations and people in Britain, Belgium, Denmark, Finland, France, Holland, Norway, Portugal, Sweden, Switzerland, Australia and the US, to mention but a few".

28 Attendees of the Tanga Consultative Congress in Tanzania, 1969–1970
Seated (L to R): Mishake Muyongo (Acting Vice President of SWAPO),
Nickey Iyambo, Sam Nujoma (President of SWAPO)
Middle, standing (L to R): Solomon Mifima, Ngarikutuke Tjiriange,
Richard Kapelwa (Kabajani), Maxton Joseph Mutongolume,
Johannes Kahana, Paul Helmut
Back, standing (L to R): Dr. Iyambo Indongo, Vinia Ndadi,
Homateni Kaluenja, Lazarus Pohamba, Lucas Pohamba,
Peter Nanyemba, Mzee Simon Kaukungua, Ewald Kavitjena,
Moses Garoeb, Jekonia Ndafenongo.
Photograph in frame: Comrade Tobias Hainjeko (First Commander)
Photo taken by Ben Amathila

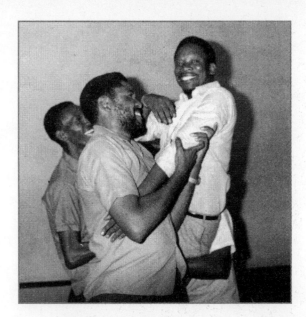

29 Comrade Moses Garoeb, after being elected as a member of SWAPO Central Committee, being held shoulder high by Comrade Peter Nanyemba, with Mishake Muyongo looking on. Tanga, Tanzania, December 1970

We supported the Palestinians, Vietnamese, Cubans and other Latin Americans, "our black American brothers and sisters", and we condemned the governments of France, West Germany, the United States and Britain for their open assistance to apartheid South Africa in Namibia, and in particular Britain, France and the United States "for their diplomatic manoeuvres at the United Nations for the purpose of sabotaging the Namibian question, thus prolonging the illegal occupation of Namibia by the Pretoria racists."

This brought us much criticism in the West, as we had not before expressed these views so strongly and publicly. But it was also noticed by observers — as in the American publication *Africa Report* — that "there were no genuflexions towards Soviet and Chinese ideologies".

We reorganized the leadership, electing Bredan Simbwaye, formerly President of CANU, as Vice-President, with Mishake Muyongo acting for this unaccounted-for prisoner of the apartheid South Africa. Moses Garoeb, back from his studies in the United States, became Administrative Secretary; and Nelengani, formerly Vice President, was expelled. Kuhangua, now an invalid, was replaced by Garoeb. We also elected a National Executive of ten members plus two co-options, and a Central Committee of thirty. It was decided that the National Executive committee members would be based at our Provisional Headquarters instead of being scattered as before.

Tanga was decisive, in that we re-restructured the party very effectively by electing Secretaries for many new departments, and formalizing the activities of the existing ones. They were given specific tasks: the Secretary for Education to seek scholarships for our growing numbers of students; the Secretary for Information to inform and influence world public opinion; the Secretary for Defence to acquire weapons, uniforms, boots and all necessary materials needed for us to continue to wage the war. SWAPO became much more effective after Tanga. It was there that we developed the three-pronged strategy of political, diplomatic and military action, and where a much clearer structure was established within which the departmental secretaries could carry out their work. The salient point of the Congress, however, was its reaffirmation:

> "That the armed liberation struggle is the only effective strategy to bring about the liberation of Namibia.
>
> "That the Namibian people have already accepted the armed liberation struggle as an inevitability in our struggle for self-determination and national independence.
>
> "That SWAPO shall leave no stone unturned, give up no ground gained and shall spare no life when called for, to make Namibia free and independent within the shortest possible time."

The South West Africa Liberation Army (SWALA) was renamed People's Liberation Army of Namibia (PLAN) and the Chairmanship of the Military Council as well as the post of Supreme Commander was given to me as President, with Peter Nanyemba as Secretary for Defence and Transport.

Tanga had done much to raise the profile of SWAPO in the armed liberation struggle. The endorsement we had received from the UN Council for Namibia, as it was now formally titled, did not stop us from making demands of the UN while at the same time deploring its having "done nothing in these [24] years to live up to its obligations with respect to the people of Namibia." It in fact encouraged us to demand:

> "That the United Nations must carry out, to the letters of Resolution 2145 XXI (of 1966) which terminated the South African mandate and administration over Namibia.

> "That the United Nations recognize SWAPO as the only true representative movement in Namibia, and must give direct material and moral support to SWAPO to carry out the armed liberation struggle in Namibia."

To carry out the war against South Africa we had not only to ensure the continued supply of arms and support from our allies and to be internationally recognized as representing the people of Namibia: we needed to be able to carry out the war both from within Namibia and from across its borders. At that time the only point where Namibia touched an independent African country capable of supporting us was the eastern end of the Caprivi Strip — and that country was Zambia. Botswana on our eastern border was infested with South African agents and under extreme pressure from Pretoria: they could do little to assist us at that stage. One of the achievements of Tanga was the behind-the-scenes talks with Zambia which prepared the way for the moving of our Provisional Headquarters in Tanzania, which was so distant from Namibia, into the territory of our Zambian neighbour.

In July and September 1970 we lost two key figures in our history, both of whom I personally mourned. They were Chief Hosea Kutako, the father of our freedom struggle, and President Gamal Abdel Nasser of the United Arab Republic, a firm friend who was committed to our cause and was able to assist us in the outside world. He had shown confidence in SWAPO from an early stage. I cabled the United Arab Republic government:

> "The world has lost a great man and all those who fight for freedom and human dignity have lost a brother in the struggle. The people of Namibia join you in mourning President Nasser's tragic death."

I also attended President Nasser's funeral in Cairo. It was well attended by statesmen from all over the world. These included the British Foreign Secretary, Sir Alec Douglas Home, despite the bitterness that had once existed. Home had visited Namibia briefly in 1969 and expressed himself as satisfied with the apartheid South African administration, despite the UN position and the human rights issues involved. Any bitterness we may have felt towards Britain over this has similarly passed away.

Nasser had inspired us in Namibia as far back as 1956 when he fought against the British, French and Israelis after he had taken over the Suez Canal. When we read about the fighting, in the newspapers in then South West Africa, we were firmly on the Egyptian side. The Suez war united and mobilized the Egyptian people. North African leaders like Nasser, and others in Asia, politically inspired those of us in the colonised and occupied parts of Africa.

Chief Kutako's instructions to me to get the apartheid South Africa out of our country were not in any way cancelled by his death. I felt my responsibility was made even greater by it. We held memorial services and meetings to honour Chief Hosea Kutako in many places. In the United Nations building in New York, in due course, a very impressive sculpture of Chief Hosea Kutako was put on permanent display. The driving force in getting this done was the Reverend Michael Scott, who won the support of the Fourth Committee for the presentation of the bust. Money was raised to offer it to the UN, as numerous countries have done with other gifts.

Our strength outside the country was matched internally. PLAN had improved weapons. 'Bazookas', rocket launchers and land mines were playing their part as groups of trained guerrillas entered the country. The work that had gone into the organization of OPO and the continued work of SWAPO in the face of growing Boer oppression bore fruit in the response to the Contract Workers' strike call that went out on 13 December 1971.

We had planted the seeds in fertile ground, which had already been prepared by workers fighting for their rights against employees who treated them like slaves, or worse. When I first gave evidence to the Fourth Committee at the UN, in 1960, I told them about the fish-canning workers of Lüderitz, whose action had been forcibly broken by the authorities. I paid specific tribute to one of them, who had lost his life in the clash. Many more had suffered and died, their deaths often unrecorded, and the 1971–2 Contract strike was the outcome of all their effort and suffering.

Over a two-month period the strike brought out 20,000 workers in all types of employment. The Contract strike was partly organized underground by our members and we sent funds to strikers from outside, though the name of SWAPO was kept out of the strike, by our decision. The demand was for an end to the SWANLA semi-slave Contract system, and though this was not achieved, the Government had to agree, through SWANLA, to some improvements in pay and conditions of work.

The strike had other results which far surpassed these improvements (which still left the workers united in their hatred of the Contract slavery system). Out of Tanga had arisen new structures: such as the Women's

Council and the Elder's Council which brought together and gave recognition to these members, always highly respected in our society; and the Youth League, which like them was a self-governing organ to Central Committee approval. The Youth League both helped to launch the strike and was itself made a local reality by its role in organizing it. While internal leaders like Maxuilili, Meroro and Ya Otto were banned or in prison, a new generation of students and workers took over much of their duties. Their dedication was needed in the face of increasing government oppression, particularly in the State of Emergency declared in Ovamboland in February 1972. Meetings were banned, as was the free movement in and out, and indefinite detention without a warrant of arrest was legalized. The Emergency also gave greater authority to the puppets, whose role had been increased with the implementation of the Odendaal Commission's plan, despite strong opposition from the United Nations. These apartheid South African manoeuvres strengthened support for SWAPO and increased the number of people who came to join SWAPO to wage the armed liberation struggle.

The imposing of bantustans, and the ending of the strike, made people realize that no change could come except through the armed liberation struggle. That was the only hope of the people as a whole. There were a few individuals who benefited from the deceptive bantustan scheme. They were paid a lot of money, like the chiefs in the Caprivi Strip who were getting about R3,000 a month, and some Herero chiefs who were paid R2,000 a month. But other chiefs who were not supportive of the bantustans, like the Nama chiefs, including Comrade Hendrik Witbooi, were paid nothing at all.

The local chiefs in the Kaokoveld were divided in such a way that within each 30 square km there was a chief and sub-chief who were put on the apartheid South African payroll to report constantly on the movements of SWAPO guerrilla fighters. The South African troops were there and they recruited the local people, the Ovahimba and Ovatjimba, but the guerrillas were still very effective there and the South African troops were often routed.

The actions of the puppet bantustan chiefs, like Kambonde and Uushona Shiimi, also brought attention to what South Africa was guilty of — for example, the flogging of SWAPO members by the chiefs' courts, which was brought to the world attention by the Anglican church in 1973. But it was the armed liberation struggle that was always the most effective: it brought people to SWAPO and created hope for a better future for all oppressed Namibian people.

Outside the country, however, it was the Contract strike which focused attention on Namibia in quite a new way. Our campaign had grown from petitioning the United Nations and the World Court to come to our rescue to world-wide anti-colonial lobbying in support of our guerrilla campaign. Both of these had to be organized outside Namibia.

The strike represented an important stage in our struggle and was immediately recognized as such by the worldwide trade union movements. It brought great sympathy to our cause in many countries. A huge new constituency now saw SWAPO as a grassroots party made up of the people of Namibia and not, as South Africa lied about us, just as exiled politicians claiming to speak for them. It was a vital factor in preparing SWAPO to enter the world stage, with a renewed confidence and determination to fight, and with the international community on our side.

13

Workers' Struggle and Diplomatic Advance

The Contract strike had major effects within the country and brought much attention to our cause beyond the UN and the OAU Member States, NGOs and individuals. As South Africa's bantustan policy was enforced and its security forces were increased to suppress PLAN activities, SWAPO became more and more the focus of the people's hopes. But South Africa, since the World Court fiasco in 1966, was even more scornful of the UN and world opinion than before. Malan's slogan about the Boer Government's attitude to Namibia had been *"ons sal nie buk nie!"* (We will not bow). And Verwoerd and Vorster kept up the same arrogance.

They told their fellow whites and puppet-chiefs that they had wiped out PLAN, the SWAPO military wing, and that they had full control in Namibia. They claimed that the Odendaal Plan was being carried out successfully and that the people of Namibia would soon be separated in nine ethnic bantustans, ruled by their own people though under Pretoria's control, leaving no room for SWAPO to succeed.

We knew that only military force and mass political mobilization backed by the support of the people would force South Africa out of Namibia. This would not come about through pitched battles and the gaining of territory by conquest alone. We were prepared to use guerrilla tactics which in the end could be so effective that South Africa would realize that it had more to gain by getting out than by remaining, spending huge sums of money, and losing the lives of their young men in defending the possession of a country which they knew was not theirs.

Our mission in many countries, our constant presence at international conferences, and the annual series of meetings at the OAU, the Movement of Non-Aligned Countries and the UN General Assembly, increased worldwide support to our cause. The Contract strike had drawn the support of the trade unions and brought world wide support from non-governmental organizations which also rendered financial and material support to the striking workers in Namibia.

My colleagues and I travelled worldwide in campaigning and organizing support for Namibian self-determination. In addition to the time spent with my Comrades in SWAPO Health and Education Centres and with PLAN combatants at the battlefields, I spent a large part of each year in the air, in hotel rooms and conference halls. I found this routine of constant travel exhausting, until I had taught myself how to diet and relax to the best advantage. We worked to ensure that in every conference there was a resolution passed in support of the struggle of the Namibian people.

South Africa, with the support of Britain and France, did not recognize the UN Council for Namibia, and many Western countries continued to trade with South Africa and Namibia in violation of UN resolutions. We realized that the UN's reputation was at risk, but we considered our own military and political campaign to liberate Namibia to be far more effective. We kept up our three-pronged strategy, combining political mass mobilisation in Namibia, work on the diplomatic front to isolate the apartheid white minority regime at international level, and the armed liberation struggle as the only effective way to defeat the enemy.

When in 1971 it was put to me that the case against South Africa should be brought back to the International Court of Justice, we were not at all in favour of this. Only five years before we had experienced the utter failure of the World Court not only to give a judgement in favour, but to deliver a judgement at all — after five years of hearings. Now to go back for an Advisory Opinion, when in 1966 the Court had reversed its own Opinion of 1962, seemed not only pointless but also a distraction from the real battle that had to be fought. The application to the World Court was made nevertheless by the Security Council, which put the question: "What are the legal consequences for states of the continued presence of South Africa in Namibia notwithstanding the Security Council Resolution 276 (1970)?". This seemed to us an anticlimax after the progress the UN had made since the General Assembly terminated the mandate in 1966 under Resolution 2145.

In 1968 the Security Council had called on South Africa to end the illegal trial of our 37 guerrillas and SWAPO leaders in Pretoria and condemned its flagrant defiance of UN authority over Namibia. The General Assembly had also then proclaimed that "in accordance with the desires of its people, South West Africa will henceforth be known as Namibia".

The following year, South Africa's only response having been to push through the Odendaal Plan, the Security Council at last recognized the termination of the mandate by the General Assembly and the illegality of all South Africa's actions since General Assembly Resolution 2145. The same year it called on member states to refrain from dealing with South Africa acting in the name of Namibia, and demanded South Africa's withdrawal. In 1970 this resolution — No 276 — was strengthened and made even more specific. Resolution 276 also set up an ad-hoc committee which recommended that the question be taken back to the World Court.

We had supported and lobbied hard for all of these resolutions, and Britain and France had abstained in the vote on all of them, with the United States and Finland also abstaining on the 1969 'withdrawal' resolution. It was in fact the Finnish ambassador to the UN, Jacobsen, and Vernon Mwaanga, the Zambian Ambassador, who told us that they had done much research and were sure that the judgement was going to be in our favour because of the composition of the bench. Still, we opposed the making of the application because of the previous injustice of the World Court in 1966 and we really did not want to have anything to do with it. There had been political pressure throughout the world after what I called the "mockery of justice" of the ICJ in 1966. Nobody trusted the Court after that. We made a tremendous lot of propaganda against it and against the plan of going back to it for an opinion in 1970. But the composition of the judges had indeed changed, and there was not the manoeuvring among South Africa's friends at the Court that there had been previously.

On 27 January 1971, South Africa told the Court that it was willing to hold a plebiscite to determine "whether it was the will of the inhabitants that the Territory should continue to be administered by South Africa or should henceforth be administered by the United Nations". They proposed that this plebiscite be jointly supervised by themselves and the Court, represented by a committee of independent experts.

We still very much doubted the capacity of the Court to hand down an opinion in our favour. Nevertheless, we responded in favour of the plebiscite, though not of South Africa's joint supervision of it. I called a press conference in my office in Dar-es-Salaam two days later and announced our acceptance of the idea, pointing out that:

> "The proposed 'plebiscite' can be genuine only if carried out under the following conditions:
>
> 1. A general climate of peace, harmony and free political activity must prevail throughout the country to ensure the participation of all Namibians irrespective of race, creed or colour, in a 'plebiscite'.
>
> 2. Noting that Namibia is presently under South African military occupation, a genuine 'plebiscite' can only be carried out if all the South African troops and police are withdrawn from Namibian territory.
>
> 3. The unconditional release of all Namibian political prisoners currently imprisoned on Robben Island in South Africa as well as those now being held in Namibia. All must be returned to their country as well as all Namibians currently in exile without risk of arrest, detention, intimidation or imprisonment.
>
> 4. The dismantling of all bantustans which aim at dividing the people on an ethnic basis; and that such a 'plebiscite' be conducted on the principle 'one man, one vote'.
>
> 5. That such a 'plebiscite' be conducted under the supervision of the United Nations and the Organization of African Unity."

The UN could mobilize over a hundred member states, including super powers, to force South Africa from Namibia in so many ways, if it had only the will to do so. But we had only one way forward, and I ended by putting it as strongly as I could, in these words:

> "In conclusion, I would like to reiterate that as long as South Africa remains in Namibia, SWAPO will continue to wage the armed liberation struggle — indeed to intensify it until Namibia is free and independent."

Negotiation might have been possible on some of these conditions. We were confident that, given what we later called a "free and fair" plebiscite, South Africa's rule would have been overwhelmingly condemned by the voters. The South Africans were deceived by their own bantustan propaganda, and by the attitude of their puppets, to think they could win such a plebiscite.

They managed to convince many journalists that even if there was opposition from the Hereros and the others in the south, the Ovambos would vote solidly for South African rule. After five years, SWAPO was known by everybody in Namibia, from the very old down to young children. The SWAPO challenge by armed liberation struggle aroused the people, especially in the north, to the awareness of the goals we were fighting to achieve.

In the first week of February 1971, all the judges expressed themselves against the plebiscite, and a possible turning point was passed. But we reached another one on 21 June 1971, when the Court gave its Advisory Opinion as to the legal consequences of South Africa's continued presence in Namibia:

> "The Court is of the opinion: (1) that the continued presence of South Africa in Namibia being illegal, South Africa is under obligation to withdraw its administration from Namibia immediately and end its occupation of the Territory."

Thirteen judges were in favour but the British and French judges voted against this first clause. The Court was further of the opinion, but with Sweden and Nigeria also voting against, as they disagreed on the strength of the obligations of member states:

> "(2) that Member states of the United Nations are under obligation to recognize the illegality of South Africa's presence in Namibia and the invalidity of its acts on behalf of or concerning Namibia, and to refrain from any acts and in particular any dealings with the Government of South Africa implying recognition of the legality of, or lending support or assistance to such presence or administration;

> (3) that it is incumbent upon States which are not members of the United Nations to give assistance within the scope of the United Nations to give assistance within the scope of paragraph (2) above, in accordance with United Nations decisions regarding Namibia."

The 20,000-word opinion cleared up many matters. The two that were most important were that the Security Council, unlike the General Assembly, had the power to enforce the withdrawal of South Africa from Namibia, and that UN member states had to comply with UN Security Council resolutions even if they had voted against them and even if they were not members of the Security Council.

Though we had opposed a court action, the Advisory Opinion was a victory for our cause. South Africa bitterly attacked the Court, with wild accusations that the Court had been 'packed' against South Africa, and declared that they rejected the ruling 'in toto'. Among the judges who had voted for all three parts of the Opinion were those from the United States and Spain as well as the President of the Court, Sir Zafrullah Khan of Pakistan, who had stood down in 1966 and had thus helped to bring about the deplorable non-decision of 1966.

Some of our advisers pointed out that the claims South Africa and the British and French judges made for the wrongness of the Opinion were based on an idea of international law which was going out of date and did not take into account the new international structures.

I gave an immediate response to the ruling:

"We welcome the ruling of the World Court. The question of the legality of South Africa's presence in Namibia can no longer be used as a political tool in the United Nations or any other international forum. Moreover, the Opinion gives moral support to the struggle of the Namibian people."

I quoted the Vice-President of the Court, Judge Ammoun of Lebanon, who said in his separate opinion:

"The struggle continues for the purpose of asserting, yet once more, the right of self-determination, more particularly in southern Africa and, specifically, Namibia. Indeed one has to recognize that the right of peoples to self-determination, before being written in letters that were not granted but won in bitter struggle, had first been written down with the blood of the peoples, in the finally awakened conscience of humanity."

SWAPO National Chairman David Meroro said, on the same day in Windhoek, that:

"The solution to the Namibian problem remains primarily with the dedicated efforts of SWAPO and secondly with those of the international community."

One of the new developments that followed the Opinion inside Namibia was the setting up in November 1971 of the Namibia National Convention (NNC), consisting of SWAPO and eight smaller parties, dedicated to working for independence and against the South African bantustan policy.

The judgement was also very soon followed by an important move by the black Lutheran churches in Namibia, which had the full approval of SWAPO and helped to bury forever the idea that South Africa was ruling us with our consent. This took the form of an Open Letter to B. J. Vorster, the South African Prime Minister. It was prompted by the World Court decision.

The letter dealt with South Africa's assault on human rights in Namibia, on the race policy which slighted and intimidated 'the non white population', with the Group Areas Act and bantustans which denied freedom of movement, with the lack of freedom of speech, the denial of the vote, so-called "job reservation" (colour bar) and with the slave Contract system. The church leaders called for co-operation with UN to "seek a peaceful solution to the problems of our land and see to it that Human Rights be put into operation and that South West Africa may become a self-sufficient and independent state".

Bishop Auala of the Ovambo-Kavango Church and Pastor Gowaseb of the Rhenish Mission Church in the south then met Prime Minister Vorster in Windhoek in August, with other church leaders. Despite Vorster's verbal attacks on them, they did not alter their position. This confrontation between the black churches and the South African government greatly reduced the authorities' credibility and greatly strengthened our case internationally.

Even though the Court application came out in our favour, and strengthened our position at international level, the British Government again did not want to accept the Advisory Opinion. They said that South Africa's occupation of Namibia was not illegal, again using another word 'unlawful', which means the same. But even Britain could not vote against the Security Council Resolution No. 310 that followed the 1971 Advisory Opinion and, with France, Britain abstained again.

For SWAPO, that meeting with the Security Council added a new dimension to the diplomatic front, and also was soon to provide me with the most important platform I had ever occupied.

◆ ◆ ◆

14

Worldwide Recognition

What made the turning point of 1971 most real for SWAPO in a political sense was when I was invited to address the United Nations Security Council on 5 October 1971. This was also a historic moment, since I was the first African liberation movement representative to be so invited, and then only after all the African members of the Council had made application in the correct way, as there were very strict rules governing procedure in the Security Council.

The South Africans were opposed to my being invited and were angry when the invitation was issued. They wanted to speak themselves too, but they were called upon only to petition, like anyone else. We sat in our seats despite the South African protests, since, along with the UN Council for Namibia, we were the main participants at the meeting. We were supported also by the UN Committee Against Apartheid and the Committee on Decolonisation (popularly known as the 'Committee of 24'). The Security Council members were overwhelmed by this and South Africa had to give way. After they had read their petition, they were told to withdraw, while we remained seated. They then had to occupy seats at the side of the council chamber. This was a major tactical victory for SWAPO in the eyes of Security Council members, and the South Africans sank even lower because of the status granted to SWAPO. South African Foreign Minister Hilgard Muller was less aggressive than his predecessor Eric Louw, and made fewer enemies, but he had a hopeless task in trying to defend a case for which there was no defence. The whole world was against apartheid yet he had to go on defending it.

30   Sam Nujoma, seated as a speaker at UN Security Council session, New York, 5 October 1971

The South Africans had almost no friends. Even the British did not want to be seen talking to them and anyone who wished to deal with them made sure they did so in dark corners, unobserved. By contrast, our reputation stood high. It was a real achievement at the diplomatic level for us to address the Security Council and did much to foster the cause of Namibia's independence.

Address to the United Nations Security Council, 5 October 1971

Remembering my first appearance as a petitioner to the Fourth Committee of the General Assembly in 1960, when my colleagues and I were very much subordinate to the delegates of this Committee of the General Assembly, I had good reason to begin my speech by referring to "privileges in life that should be accompanied by particular solemnity. The privilege that this august body has bestowed upon me as the first freedom-fighter to be accorded this opportunity is indeed one of such privileges".

The session had been called to look at ways of enforcing the many General Assembly and Security Council resolutions in the light of the ICJ Advisory Opinion, which had unequivocally stated that "the continued presence of South Africa in Namibia being illegal, South Africa is under the obligation to withdraw its administration from Namibia immediately and thus put an end to its occupation of the Territory".

It is interesting to look at the speech again today, as a statement of SWAPO's position on many issues at that early stage of our full emergence on to the world stage. I quoted the *New York Times* to introduce the main point of my address, to which all else was subsidiary. It had said:

> "With this historic 13 to 2 verdict, the Court has cleared away the legal and political fog that for years obscured the status of the former German colony."

It must be recalled that from the early days of petitioning, Chief Hosea Kutako, his representative Michael Scott and those who followed later had invoked Article 39 of the UN Charter, under Chapter VII ("Action with respect to threats to the peace, breaches of the peace and acts of aggression"). This empowered the Security Council to "determine the existence of any threat to the peace, breach of the peace, or act of aggression" and to decide on the use of Articles 41 (sanctions, diplomatic boycott) or 42 (action by forces of member states) "to maintain or restore international peace and security".

Now at last, in the wording of a UN Resolution, it was declared that:

> "South Africa's continued illegal presence in Namibia constitutes an internationally wrongful act and a breach of international obligations and that South Africa remains accountable to the international community for any violations of its international obligations or the rights of the people of Namibia,"

and secondly, that:

> "any refusal of the South African Government to withdraw from Namibia would create conditions detrimental to the maintenance of peace and security in the region."

I therefore put a strong emphasis on Chapter VII in my main appeal as I went on:

> "Thus, the Namibian people and the peace-loving people of the world have won the legal contest. Now it is up to the Security

Council to live up to its responsibility. The United Nations is confronted with the most determined and most serious onslaught on its principles since the Organization was set up. Therefore the Security Council, as an organ which has been conferred with the primary responsibility for the maintenance of international peace and security, should and must not fail to take authoritative and decisive action.

This time, we are not asking for declaratory statements which have no effect on the illegal occupation forces. On the contrary, we are imploring this august body to take concrete and immediate action under Chapter VII. In that Chapter, Article 39 enjoins upon the Security Council the duty to determine the existence of any threat to peace, breach of peace, or act of aggression, and to take appropriate action."

I had to say that the only people who doubted whether conditions for invoking Chapter VII existed were the major Western powers, though the 'legal fog' had cleared for them, too:

"They do so not because the situation in Namibia does not threaten international peace and security but because they want their agents in South Africa to continue to provide them with cheap labour, which results in enormous profits for their investors."

I went on to point to South Africa's aggressive stance and the threat it posed in respect for international law:

"How can the situation in Namibia be described as peaceful when South Africa is arming itself to the teeth with the most advanced weapons of destruction? How does one explain the fact that today the South African army is fighting in Angola, Mozambique, Namibia and Zimbabwe? How does one explain the constant threats made against independent African states? For instance, Vorster threatened President Kaunda in the following terms: 'We will hit you so hard that you will not forget it.' Lastly, what is to become of international law if the countries represented here can ignore with impunity any interpretation of law that is not in their favour? Where are the advocates of 'law and order'?"

I welcomed the stand taken by the Government of the United States in accepting the ICJ Advisory Opinion as stated by Secretary of State William Rogers in the General Assembly, adding:

"We hope the United States will follow up this responsibility with appropriate measures to end South Africa's illegal occupation of Namibia."

Much of the speech was refutation of the claims made by the South African Foreign Minister, Hilgard Muller. I showed that his economic facts and figures "had no bearing on the lives of the Africans; that, as in South Africa, everything in Namibia was geared towards benefiting the whites at the expense of the Africans; that, in any event, it was independence we wanted; and that

"we will never be wooed by roads, hospitals, schools and so forth, as long as South Africa remains on Namibian soil."

To rebut Muller's arguments that his Government was "making determined efforts to bring the peoples of South West Africa towards self-government", I called these efforts " a gross abuse of the noble concept of self-determination and a euphemism for apartheid".

Quotations from the Open Letter of Bishop Auala and Pastor Gowaseb on the subject proved my point, and, after their eloquent words, the simple scorn of a group of students at Ondangua was extra ammunition. They had said, as reported in the Namibian press: "Ovambos would rather suggest to Vorster and company to create 'Whitestans' for Germans, Afrikaners and English, elsewhere but not in Namibia".

I attacked Muller's claims on wages, his comparisons between Namibia and other African countries, and on education (on which my quotations from Verwoerd, who had created 'Bantu Education', spoke volumes). On education, in particular, I was able to strike a positive note, which was much quoted later. Published versions of the speech headlined the positive part of the education argument: "SWAPO EDUCATED MORE NAMIBIANS THAN SOUTH AFRICA IN 50 YEARS":

"Mr Muller conveniently omitted to mention the system of Bantu Education .... for very obvious reasons. The fact is that education for whites is free and compulsory, whereas the same cannot be said of the education of the Africans. In more than 40 years of its maladministration of Namibia the white Government of South Africa dismally failed to prepare our people by not providing them with meaningful education which would enable them to run a modern government when Namibia becomes independent. Bantu education certainly cannot prepare us to handle the complexities of modern establishments.

That does not mean that we ourselves have been idle. I am pleased to state here that SWAPO has educated more Namibians than South Africa has done over the past 50 years. Through our initiatives I am proud and happy to announce that in the past 10 years we have educated 25 engineers, four medical doctors, including the first Namibian woman doctor, seven lawyers and more than 35 holders of university degrees in various fields. To some those figures may appear modest and insignificant. To us, who have been denied so much for so long, it is a record of which we are justly proud and which we are determined to improve upon. Our sincere thanks must go to all those countries — both members and non-members of this organization — which generously gave scholarships for our people to undertake further studies. It is our hope that they will continue doing so in the future."

On the subject of our demand for independence and for human rights, I again referred to the Open Letter, telling the Security Council that:

"the impact that Open Letter had on the white population of Namibia was as traumatic as it was hysterical. The same impact was felt in South Africa. The Prime Minister of White South Africa, John [Johannes] Vorster, flew to Windhoek and had a four-hour confrontation with a delegation of eight led by the two courageous spiritual leaders. They were threatened and intimidated but they firmly stood by the Open Letter they had sent to the Prime Minister. They also reiterated their stand in rejecting the condemnation of the local whites, who could not understand their Government's failure to silence these spiritual leaders once and for all."

Mr Muller had cited the Onguediva Training Institute in Ovamboland as an "impressive complex" of high school, teacher training and trades centre. I countered that Onguediva was a perpetual source of trouble for the South African occupation authorities, and that the biggest of its many anti-Government demonstrations took place after the ICJ Advisory Opinion. This demonstration forced the South African authorities to close down the institution, expelling hundreds of students. Onguediva, which I called "a symbol of the new nationalism" had also suffered from the expulsion of many students for refusing to accept Afrikaans as their medium of instruction, which "came as a profound shock to the South African authorities. Similar demonstrations have taken place at the Augustineum High School in Windhoek, where 70 students were expelled only last week". This was nearly five years before the Soweto uprising on the same issue.

My colleagues and I had agreed that my speech should be hard hitting and should deal with the South African claims that we were "better off under the South Africans", that chaos would follow when they left and that the economic structure would collapse. In dealing with these claims, I made very specific references to the whites, as on many other occasions:

> "SWAPO of Namibia therefore wishes to reiterate that we recognize the contribution that all people in Namibia, including those who came as settlers from Europe, must make for the general well-being and prosperity of our country. The white people have nothing to fear as long as they play a constructive role in the reconstruction of the country."

Before ending my speech I made a declaration,

> "in the name of the people of Namibia, that unless this august body acts decisively to secure the withdrawal of South Africa from the international territory of Namibia, we shall have no alternative but to continue the armed liberation struggle with greater intensity. We do not love bloodshed, but when we are dealing with a Government like that of South Africa which believes in violence and bloodshed we must be prepared to meet it on its own terms. Our struggle may be long and protracted, our struggle may be bloody and costly in terms of human life; it is a price we are prepared to pay for our independence."

We had much to thank the OAU for, and I concluded by expressing our gratitude to the President of Mauritania, who had spoken on behalf of the entire OAU member states, and the five foreign ministers with him, and "through them to the entire OAU member states".

Despite the intensity of the armed struggle going on in Southern Rhodesia and over the Portuguese counter-insurgency attacks in Angola, Mozambique and Guinea-Bissao, the speech drew much attention to our cause among governments such as those of the Western countries, especially the Nordic countries, which had been uncertain in their attitude to us. Within two or three months, what I had said about the Namibian people's economic sufferings and the new spirit of resistance in the country was borne out by the great Contract strike, which though not organized in the name of SWAPO, we had helped to organize underground. The strike further aroused world opinion in our favour and helped us to mobilize support in many countries so that we were able to hold the first international conference on Namibia, in Brussels in May 1972.

Brussels Conference, May 1972

We had continued always to attend conferences relevant to our cause, however much travelling this entailed. If Namibia could be on the agenda, we would make certain to attend. We would always prepare a resolution in advance, having found out the nature of the conference and judged what aspects of our struggle it could accommodate. Sometimes we would have to accept that we could not call for support for the armed liberation struggle, so we would seek to make other political or diplomatic gains. There was a growing list of Security Council and General Assembly resolutions and it was always a task to work for their implementation through gaining support at international meetings.

The major conferences I would attend myself, sometimes perhaps for only part of the time, to add strength to our delegation at a particular point. As the leader, what I had to say would get more of a hearing than the words of other representatives of SWAPO, and, however exhausting the ceaseless travel this involved, I would be there. Namibia was still surprisingly unknown and it was very important to lose no chance of getting our cause supported in whatever part of the world this could be done.

We had made real progress, however, and it became clear that we were in a position to convene our own international gathering. The effect of the Contract strike had been to cause many socialist and labour parties to become interested. We received tremendous international support in Brussels, and for the first time in Western Europe. There were many international figures there, such as the former Indian Foreign Minister, Krishna Menon, who had supported Namibia at the United Nations from the beginning, and Lord Caradon, who had been Britain's Permanent Representative at the UN, to mention only two.

Much of the work for the Brussels conference was done by a Belgian National Committee in which a lawyer friend to SWAPO, Paulette

Pierson-Mathy, played a leading part. But the actual initiation of the conference was our work, as was the raising of the necessary funds. I travelled to many countries to get this support — sometimes coming away with only $500US, but sometimes with $10,000. And so we succeeded in getting the conference funded and organized.

We saw Brussels as a centre of Western Europe activities where we felt it was essential for us to make a greater impact, since, as I put it at the preparatory meeting held in Brussels in February, it was necessary to "build up public opinion in countries like Great Britain, France, West Germany, whose governments are assisting — through financial, economic, political and military aid — the racist regime of South Africa, in suppressing the aspirations of the African people in Namibia to self-determination".

We had the support at that early stage, not only of Belgian committees representing political parties, chiefly the Socialist Party, trade unions, churches, and lawyers but also the patronage of the heads of state of Egypt, Senegal and Mauritania, Yugoslavia and Romania, and Guyana. By the time the conference opened in May, six more African heads of state had become patrons, including our oldest supporters in Africa, Tanzania and Zambia.

Brussels was a very valuable meeting, coming as it did after the Advisory Opinion and the Contract strike. In addition to government representatives and those of the UN and OAU, it collected in one place, for the first time, many who had never had such an opportunity to concentrate on the objectives before us and to share ideas and plans of speeding up the implementation of UN Security Council and General Assembly Resolutions on the decolonisation of Namibia.

It also brought together many of our leading SWAPO members, including some who had not previously experienced international arenas. As at all successful conferences, much was achieved outside the main chamber, though the standard of the main address was very high and the resolutions effectively made the points we wanted emphasised. It also brought together supporters from non-governmental organizations — established ones such as the Namibia Support Committee and Anti-Apartheid Movement of Britain, but also new ones from other European countries and America, who had been alerted to the situation in our country by the Contract strike. The liberation movements of South Africa, Zimbabwe, Angola, Mozambique and even from Asia and Latin America were present. The Afro-Asian People's Solidarity Organization did good work in mobilizing many groups to which it was affiliated.

We had become skilled in managing such conferences. We ensured that the resolutions we drafted were put beforehand to the heads of delegations. They were given their own copies, so that when the resolutions came up the delegations would be well aware of them and give them their support. Brussels went entirely to our satisfaction. It had been our own initiative, we had raised the money and had worked well with the Belgians and others who had done the local organizational work.

I closed the conference on 28 May by re-emphasizing its four basic aims, which were achieved in varying degrees. Even the second of these had some success, if only with the smaller countries:

"(1) To internationalize the case of Namibia and remind the world, the Western world in particular, that the question of Namibia is an international responsibility and to remind them of the support this involves towards the Namibian people.

(2) To encourage Western European countries to rethink their present relations — political, economic, military etc. — with apartheid South Africa as regards the international territory of Namibia.

(3) To gain support — political, moral and financial — for SWAPO and the struggling people of Namibia.

(4) To formulate resolutions which will help in finding ways and means of gaining independence and freedom for Namibia."

I came away from Brussels with a strong impression that our profile had been greatly raised by the conference.

The 1971 Advisory Opinion, the Contract strike and the growing strength of our guerrilla forces gave us a new claim on the international community to join with us in the struggle for national independence. At Brussels we had taken a major step to mobilise public opinion against South Africa's illegal occupation and towards decisive action by the international community.

❖ ❖ ❖

15

Waldheim Initiatives

SWAPO kept the success of the Brussels Conference and our heightened profile at the United Nations in perspective. We remained masters of our own destiny. We knew that we had to keep up the struggle militarily, politically and diplomatically or the world would leave us to some sort of accommodation with South Africa. Up to the mid-1960s this could have happened within the terms of the mandate, or some bastardised form of it, had not South Africa under Verwoerd been so provocative and hostile, even to its friends at the UN.

In the early 1970s events took a new turn with the demise of Verwoerd, knifed to death by a parliamentary attendant in 1966. His successor B. J. Vorster, a very different character, set out to fool the world into thinking that South Africa meant to give Namibia its freedom. We had seen enough of the UN, and the influence of South Africa's trading partners there, to know that he could be successful there if we and our friends in the OAU and the Non-Aligned Movement did not fight back.

At the same time, the struggle for majority rule in Zimbabwe was going on, and in that instance the Africans had the former colonial power, Britain, to take their part, however reluctantly in the case of some British politicians, against the Ian Smith regime which had made a Unilateral Declaration of Independence (UDI) for Southern Rhodesia in November 1965. British public opinion was very strongly against UDI and would not allow Smith to get away with an "internal settlement" using Bishop Muzorewa and other political stooges in Southern Rhodesia.

By contrast to Zimbabwe, Namibia had no world power like Britain to contend on our behalf directly with South Africa, but we were fortunate that the Secretary-Generalship of the United Nations had come into the hands of Dr. Kurt Waldheim, with whom I had a very good understanding.

In February 1972, Secretary-General Waldheim was invited by the Security Council to "initiate as soon as possible contacts with all the parties concerned". Their objective was to seek ways of compelling South Africa to comply with UN resolutions on Namibia. Not only was Vorster's government arrogantly flouting UN resolutions, but they were also hastening the process of setting up bantustans in Namibia, and also repressing SWAPO opposition with detentions and harsh treatment. The so-called 'Proclamation R17' was issued in February 1972, putting Ovamboland into a state of emergency. Many of our people were savagely treated by the police, the puppet chiefs and their bodyguards.

The only factor capable of keeping up the political morale of the people at this time was the impact of our PLAN fighters, who attacked police and puppet installations and personnel across northern Namibia, showing that, despite the ending of the Contract strike, the fight was being intensified.

I met Kurt Waldheim in Geneva on 29 February 1972 and had a long talk with him at the Inter-Continental Hotel. Besides describing the worsening situation in Namibia, I highlighted the positive signs on our side — the Open Letter from the church leaders and the workers' solidarity in the Contract strike. The reality of South African rule was made crystal clear by the expulsion of the Anglican Bishop Winter and two assistants, which was timed "so that they are conveniently out of the way for your [Waldheim's] visit". Most of Namibia's Anglicans were in Ovamboland and Bishop Winter had been able to penetrate the news black-out while on his pastoral visits there. First his permit to go to Ovamboland was withdrawn and then his residence permit. I was also able to show the Secretary-General the letter smuggled out of Robben Island prison, cataloguing the cruelties and hardships inflicted on the SWAPO prisoners illegally held there by the apartheid South African regime.

I urged him not to allow his visit to be interpreted as a softening of UN attitudes towards South Africa and to meet Namibians, however much the South Africans tried to stop him, including those on Robben Island and in Ovamboland. I told him he must meet not only government-paid chiefs and headmen but also "workers who are on strike, missionaries and ordinary citizens, who are not hand-picked by the South African illegal administration".

Our position with regard to the UN was quite unequivocal. I said:

> "We can only accept full and total independence for Namibia now. Our resolve to take up arms in 1966 came after the let-down by the international community through the International Court of Justice. We want to emphasize that we will continue to fight for our freedom where international action leads to no result until we have achieved our independence."

The South Africans did not get the better of Waldheim as they had with Carpio and De Alva ten years before. He was of a different calibre altogether. Although he was with the South African foreign minister Muller during the three days he spent in Namibia in March, and with Vorster and others in Cape Town, he never lost sight of our point of view and did not allow himself to be tricked by the South Africans.

In his memoires, *In the Eye of the Storm* (London, 1985) Waldheim recalls Vorster's words in the South African parliament that "if he [Waldheim] wishes to come to South Africa to act as a mouthpiece for the extremists of the OAU and others ... he will be wasting his time." Waldheim goes on:

> "The talks proved fruitless. I had insisted that I should visit Namibia, and my hosts fulfilled that commitment in minimum fashion. I was flown to the northern province of the territory, adjacent to the border with Angola, where I met representatives of the Ovambo, the largest single tribal grouping. They complained of frequent incidents involving South African troops, to which the government rejoinder was that its military operations were necessary because of the terrorist activities of SWAPO. I found the atmosphere extremely tense ... The authorities were reluctant to take me to Windhoek, because as my other contacts told me, they feared that local groups would stage demonstrations against the government and its policies. I insisted that I could not return to New York without interviewing their representatives. The facilities provided were minimal. My visit was not announced in advance and I was put up in a small, almost unknown hotel. Meetings were arranged with the local groups in a room at the airport shortly before my departure. I was far from happy about such treatment ... Many had travelled from distant parts of the

territory to see me. In the limited time available I could do little more than listen. I was sufficiently encouraged to recommend on my return the appointment of a United Nations representative to Namibia to explore the possibilities of a peaceful solution."

Waldheim later told me that when he left Cape Town after attempting to negotiate with the South Africans, something like a communiqué was issued. On returning to New York he found that the South Africans had changed the wording — it was different from the text that had been agreed. He called his colleagues and pointed this out to them. But it had already been issued. This was one of the many ways in which the South Africans tried to frustrate the UN. They were very clever at this though it made them deeply distrusted and disliked there. On this occasion no real damage was done, except to anything that might have been left of the South Africans' reputation for straight dealing.

Waldheim and I met again on 22 May 1972 in New York, where I was visiting at the invitation of the Security Council's Ad Hoc sub committee on Namibia. He reported to the Security Council:

"I informed Mr. Nujoma of the results of my contacts with the Government of South Africa and of my visit to Namibia. Mr. Nujoma subsequently conveyed to me the views of SWAPO, which were that a peaceful solution of the problem of Namibia could be found only on the basis of total withdrawal of South Africa's administration from the territory and acceptance of Namibia's right to independence and national sovereignty as one entity."

In July 1972 the Security Council endorsed his recommendation that contact with South Africa be continued since Vorster's government seemed to be willing at least to discuss our independence, which no South African government had ever done before. But what Waldheim meant and what Vorster meant by "self-determination" differed totally, as Waldheim quickly found out.

A Special Representative, Dr. Alfred Escher, a career diplomat from Switzerland with no UN experience, was appointed to negotiate on Waldheim's behalf, after South Africa had objected to many others proposed for the task. When I met Alfred Escher in Cairo I knew at once that this UN initiative was doomed. I found him typically conservative in his views and realized that he was useless to our cause. He spent nearly a month in South Africa, and a week in Namibia where he had talks with some of our leaders such as Ya Otto, Meroro and Maxuilili. In spite of this he allowed himself to be deceived by the South Africans, who talked about independence "after experience of self-government" without making it clear that this 'self-government' would be regional, i.e. in the bantustans. They even appeared to entertain the idea of "one-man-one-vote", but again this would apply only to the bantustans elections. Escher was particularly unsuited to his task as, in our talks with him, he appeared to accept South African views of Namibian "tribes", characterizing some as more "advanced" (and worthy of self government) than others. The Ovambos would, in his view, be best off under European "tutelage".

Waldheim wrote that Escher "fell into a South African trap". When Escher told Vorster that he believed that the majority of Namibians wanted "a united independent Namibian to be established with United Nations assistance", they induced him to initial a document recording his talks with the South African point of view. Specifically, he approved the idea that the inhabitants of Namibia should gain experience in 'self-government', on a regional basis, before self-determination could be exercised. This was the thin end of the wedge for introducing the 'homelands' (bantustan) policy while retaining restrictive legislation, particularly on freedom of movement, in order to check the infiltration of SWAPO personnel from neighbouring Angola and Zambia. Escher's action was construed as nothing less than a United Nations endorsement of the policy of "separate development" — that is, apartheid.

Sadly, Dr. Escher made a mess of things. We had to denounce him, once we discovered that he was trusted by the South Africans and that they knew he was sympathetic to them.

Any doubts as to South Africa's real attitudes were dispelled in February 1973 when the South African parliament debated the "Development of Self-Government for Native Nations in South West Africa Bill". It was now obvious to all that "self-government on a regional basis" meant dividing the country into bantustans, with an economically and politically dominant white so-called "homeland" and thus keeping South African control. We learned later that Vorster was even offering the whites in Namibia some form of annexation of their "homeland" (which, as defined by the Odendaal Report, was larger in area than all the other "homelands" put together).

We had succeeded in making it an absolutely fixed principle in negotiations that Namibia should retain complete territorial integrity, and it was as much on this issue as on any other that the Security Council unanimously agreed to end Waldheim's negotiation at the end of 1973. The General Assembly and the UN Council for Namibia had already both called for them to be ended. South Africa was protected at this time only by the intervention of the United States, Britain and France, who stopped their expulsion from the UN by exercising a triple veto in the Security Council.

The scrapping of the negotiations meant that Vorster had now succeeded in turning even his friends in the UN against him. It was also a diplomatic victory for SWAPO, but one that we regretted because of the role that Waldheim had played, in good faith. He not only worked hard for Namibian independence, but we also found him very sincere. Whenever I intended to see Waldheim, whether in New York at the headquarters of the UN or elsewhere, he would give preference to my appointment and I would spend more than an hour with him. He genuinely had Namibia's interests at heart. We never found him arrogant or unhelpful. His appointment as Secretary-General had indeed been backed up by African delegates, who made up a big number. If you have the African countries' support, then you have to pay attention to the African issues. We had campaigned for Waldheim when he was Austrian permanent representative at the UN. We talked to the other African delegates and we became a close friend of his. He never let us down.

The Waldheim years at the UN were good for us in other ways and bad for South Africa. The day after the Security Council ended Waldheim's negotiations, the General Assembly voted to recognize SWAPO as the "authentic representative of the Namibian people". This had already been done by the OAU and was a logical step as South Africa began scheming to develop ways of imposing its bantustan puppets as spokesmen for Namibia.

That same week the first appointment of a UN Commissioner for Namibia was made. There had been several "acting" commissioners since the post was created in 1967, along with the UN Council for Namibia, but they could not perform effectively without full powers. The choice, which we heartily endorsed, was Sean MacBride. He was a very brilliant lawyer, with experience as a former Foreign Minister of Ireland. He knew what he was doing and was extremely good at it. He was the type of man who, if he believed in something, could not be deflected and would pursue his course. So far we were concerned, he always took the right course. He had been involved in international politics, he was a member of the International Commission of Jurists and had been head of Amnesty International.

31 Sam Nujoma with first UN Commissioner for Namibia, Sean MacBride, pictured on the front cover of an issue of the official SWAPO organ, "Namibia Today". Lusaka, September/October 1974

The profile of the UN Council for Namibia had been raised during the negotiations and it became even more prominent with MacBride as Commissioner. He did not find it easy to work with the Council members, however, and was sometimes openly critical of them, such as of what he called their "going on safari" when they travelled as a body to collect evidence, at great expense.

His energy brought quick results, and we went along with his ideas since he was clearly far more effective than the usual slow-moving UN committees we had worked with for so long. He set up the UN Institute for Namibia, in Lusaka, and the Nationhood Training Programme in New York to produce the essential personnel to administer the future independent Namibia, where the education of black Namibians had for so long been shamefully neglected.

Through his legal background he was able to organize lawyers to work out the terms of decree — called 'UN Decree No. 1 on the Natural Resources of Namibia' — to protect the country's natural wealth by requiring exporters to be licensed by the UN Council for Namibia. This provided a lever for member states on the Council and others to bring companies contravening the decree to court in their countries. The main target was the Rössing Uranium mine, against which action was initiated after the decree was endorsed by the General Assembly. It was not thought that a British court would enforce the decree. One reason was that Britain did not recognize the authority of the Council for Namibia as the *de jure* government of Namibia — a status MacBride more than anybody had achieved for the Council. Britain did not in fact accept the termination of the mandate under General Assembly Resolution 2145 (1966) until 1974 when Prime Minister Callaghan at last agreed that the mandate was no longer in force, and then because South Africa itself had repudiated it.

We made further progress in our international standing through the goodwill of Kurt Waldheim and the energy of Sean MacBride. UN radio transmitters carried broadcasts into Namibia reporting on the progress towards the liberation of our country. Namibia was admitted, through the Council, to the World Health Organization (WHO) and was invited to sessions of the International Labour Organization and International Civil Aviation Authority. In these various bodies our SWAPO members played key roles in Namibian delegations which accompanied the UN Council for Namibia.

Inside Namibia, SWAPO participated in the National Convention, created in 1972 out of the parties opposed to the South African apartheid regime. We were always in favour of unity, and supported the National Convention until it became inactive. Some elements wanted only the limelight, so we left. The freedom struggle was really carried out single-handed by SWAPO, inside the country as well as internationally.

Throughout these Waldheim years we stuck close to our old friends and supporters in the OAU and I was able to show them at the Addis Ababa summit in April 1973, which Waldheim also attended, a large amount of South African war materials which our forces had recently captured, some of the materials being of NATO (North Atlantic Treaty Origanization) origin, despite the arms embargo imposed by the UN. I quoted a PLAN war communiqué of 23 April 1973:

> "The SWAPO freedom fighters captured the following war items — Belgian-made FAL 308 and light machine guns of the same origin; British-made Bren light machine guns and ammunition; radio transmitter Serial No 3537, Model TR 28-A2; First Aid bags containing anti-snakebite serum, aromatic chalk with opium, bandages, syringes, military uniforms and many other materials."

32   *PLAN combatants inspecting captured enemy weapons and supplies*

Other events that I reported there, and at the UN Council for Namibia meeting in Lusaka in 13 June that year, included South African cross-border raids into Zambia, the blowing up of the ELOK church printing press at Oniipa in northern Namibia, the arrest of Comrade John Ya Otto and eight SWAPO members who were leading a demonstration against the Ovamboland bantustan proclamation, and the conditions in which our prisoners on Robben Island were being illegally held.

But it was not all a story of our sufferings. I was also able to tell the OAU and the Council of our victories on the battlefield in the five regions in which we were operating; of SWAPO combat actions far south of the war zone, such as, in March 1973, the attack on the government administration building in Katutura township outside Windhoek and the cutting of its communications with the city of Windhoek. The growth of militancy in the church communities had also added a new dimension. I told the Council:

> "The entire religious community, as it were, rallied behind the national cause. This in turn gave a moral and political inspiration and impetus to the students' and youths' resistance against the occupying colonial regime."

The new element in the struggle did not yet involve Namibians, as I put it:

> "Because of the heavy losses sustained by the enemy at the hands of SWAPO freedom fighters, the Pretoria regime was forced to recruit black South Africans into its armed forces. Mr. President, I would like to stress that this is the first time in the history of the white racist South Africa of this new element of forcing blacks to kill blacks [which] will undoubtedly result in serious consequences in southern Africa."

A time would come when Namibians would be drawn in too, first through so-called counter-insurgency forces, like Koevoet ('crowbar'), and later, through conscription into the South West African Territorial Force (SWATF). It is one of the victories of peace that the warlike killing of Africans by other Africans ended, in Namibia, at independence. But it continued in South Africa, with the evil influence of Vorster's action in 1973 being felt in the undercover operations of former Koevoet, 101 Battalion and other such personnel, in promoting the internecine slaughter which has so tragically, and intentionally, hindered progress towards non-racial democracy in South Africa.

Waldheim, speaking in Zambia at this time, had said that "The frontiers of freedom and the spirit of the brotherhood of man end at the Zambezi river". Though hopes had been raised by these first serious, direct negotiations between the UN and South Africa, we knew that much suffering lay ahead of us before that frontier was to reach the Orange River, but that unforeseen events lay ahead too, such as one of great importance which was to occur in Angola the following year.

16

The Collapse of The Portuguese Empire in Africa

Dr Kurt Waldheim had done his best for Namibia, using the full authority of his office as UN Secretary-General to negotiate as instructed by the UN Security Council with the South African regime on the question of the Namibian peace settlement. However, the South African negotiating team were devious and dishonest, as he soon learned, and he also lacked the support of the United States, Britain and France to enforce his demands. South Africa knew that the UN would stop short of mandatory sanctions, for fear of damaging the Western economies — especially those of Britain, Canada, West Germany, France, Switzerland, the USA, and other NATO (North Atlantic Treaty Organization) member states whose citizens had heavy investments in Namibia and in South Africa itself.

Our military efforts had increased and the South Africans' military presence was growing, particularly in the Eastern Caprivi, which was still a vital point of entry for PLAN fighters. SWAPO's popularity had grown, both at home and in the international scene. Even Britain, which had always kept SWAPO at arm's length, made a friendly approach to us, donating funds to the UN Institute for Namibia and encouraging contact, through their Lusaka High Commission as well as in London.

South Africa was conscious of a real threat of complete isolation if UN demands were completely ignored and started to step up the bantustan programmes. The fragmenting of Namibia had been totally unacceptable since the UN had thrown out the 'Good Offices' Commission's report, and hostility to South Africa was much greater in the 1970s than it had been in 1958.

The real attitude of the Boers was made clear by their response to a world outcry in 1973 at the imposition, by the chiefs' courts in the north, of floggings of political activists. Women were flogged as well as men, and they suffered terrible pain. The Minister of Bantu Administration and Development (as 'Native Affairs' was renamed by Verwoerd) said that these floggings were "an old custom of the tribe and the Minister wants to have nothing to do with it". Flogging of that kind was in fact introduced by Native Commissioner Major Hahn 'Shongola' (who himself habitually carried a whip) in the 1930s. The administration was forced by the bad publicity to put a stop to the floggings, which were in fact carried out on the orders of the South African police.

In spite of much that had gone our way, I still felt that we were fighting an enemy of great power and that, despite the friends and allies we had attracted, we were still at a great disadvantage. Our people could enter the country as guerrillas or on political missions, but only with very great difficulty, and our members outside remained few. The geographical isolation of Namibia remained almost complete: South Africa to the south; the so-called 'Skeleton Coast' (the Namib Desert) and the great Atlantic Ocean to the west; to the east the Kalahari Desert and Botswana, whose Government dared not to provoke South Africa by letting us through; and to the north, the Portuguese colony of Angola.

Then, quite out of the blue, on 25 April 1974, a group of army officers seized power in Lisbon, overthrowing the Caetano regime and announcing that all Portuguese colonies in Africa would be given their independence. This was a complete break with Portugal's past. At a single stroke its 500-year imperial exploitation of Africa was over. The young officers of the Armed forces Movement had seen the waste and destruction of the past 13 years of war in Angola, Mozambique and Guinea-Bissao, and their disillusion with Portuguese posturing as an imperial power quickly spread to the ordinary Portuguese soldiers.

It was also a complete break with our own more recent history. Now we had an open frontier — 800 km long — to the north. Our geographical isolation was over. It was as if a locked door had suddenly swung open.

I realized instantly that the struggle was in a new phase — as did our enemy Prime Minister Balthazar Johannes Vorster and the main operator for Western interests at the time, Dr. Henry Kissinger. For us the new phase meant that, given a harmonious relationship with the new Government of an independent Angola, we could at last make direct attacks across our northern frontier and send in our forces and weapons on a large scale. The simultaneous collapse of Portuguese rule in Mozambique opened another front which South Africa would have to defend on its eastern flank. Already the war of liberation was raging in Zimbabwe, and the Limpopo River was no longer the secure frontier it had been for so many years. South Africa would be weakened by being so over-stretched, while we would be greatly strengthened by the proximity our forces would soon have to recruit Namibians wanting to take up arms to fight against the foreign racist forces occupying our motherland.

First across the border

The first group to cross the border, at Oshikango in May 1974, was led by John Ya Otto and included my three sons, Utoni, Ndeshipanda and Nefungo, along with 12 others, most of them also from Windhoek. They were guided by the legendary PLAN fighter Patrick Iyambo Lungada.

Our men were all amazed at the welcome they received in Angola from the Portuguese soldiers, whose leaders sent us messages through them. It was Portuguese soldiers who had rebelled against the regime, and they received our SWAPO members, so recently their enemies, with open arms. The South Africans telephoned to tell the Portuguese to try to kidnap those crossing the border, but instead the Portuguese protected them. Our men were surprised when the Portuguese offered them food and invited them to eat in restaurants where whites had prepared food for them. Some of our men were straight from the war zone and knew that the Portuguese had been collaborating with the Boers. It was all very strange.

Crossing the border was a very tough journey nevertheless, on foot at first, then by bus to Huila and on to Sa de Bandeira (later Lubango) from where they took a train to Vila Luso. Here their troubles began again. They were detained there while more parties arrived and were held with them by the Portuguese authorities. Eventually, John Ya Otto managed to negotiate with the Portuguese to allow them to proceed by truck to Zambia. They were by then about 300 strong. They were held up at Musuma while clashes between the forces of MPLA (National Front for the Liberation of Angola) and UNITA (National Union for the Total Independence of Angola) went on about them, and landmines threatened to blow them to pieces.

Their funds ran out and they had to sell their clothes to buy food. At last they travelled the final 100 km to Kalabo where the Zambian Government proposed to treat them as ordinary refugees and to keep them at Maheba, under the control of the UNHCR (United Nations High Commissioner for Refugees) and the Zambian Ministry of Home Affairs. Fortunately, their whereabouts became known to the SWAPO Provincial Headquarters in Lusaka. I protested at once to President Kaunda, making it clear that these were not refugees but were recognized by the OAU as members of SWAPO, fighting for the liberation of their country. Dr. Iyambo Indongo travelled to the camp and arranged for the Namibians to be moved to Lusaka, after a four month stay. I met my sons and the rest of the group at last, and scholarships or military training were organized for all of them.

These early groups were followed by a constant stream. They were mostly from Ovamboland, it being more difficult for those from Windhoek and the central and southern regions of the country to get past the South African security at Tsumeb and Oshivelo. Oshivelo had been created to prevent people from travelling to the border areas from the rest of the country. South Africa tried to stop this exodus from the country because they knew that all taking part were on their way to join SWAPO. Soon their numbers ran into thousands. We had to open a temporary office in Katanga province, with Peter Tsheehama as our representative, to assist those who came through Angola and Zaire (DRC) by rail.

Militarily we quickly took advantage of the open frontier and moved small groups from Zambia to carry out attacks into Ovamboland. In January 1975, Angola's three rival movements signed an accord by which, among other provisions, MPLA, to which we stood closest, opened an office at Ondjiva (formerly known as Pereira d'Eca), only 30 miles north of the frontier, and through which Namibian groups travelled. By July 1975 we were attacking SADF (South African Defence Force) convoys on the Namibian side of the frontier and making our first strikes against the Calueque Dam on the Kunene River, inside Angola. This led to South African raids on MPLA and the permanent guarding of the dam by the SADF. The Angolan war was under way, with MPLA, aided by its Cuban allies from October 1975, under threat from South African forces and what was left of FNLA (National Front for the Liberation of Angola), with UNITA armed and aided by the South Africans and the American CIA (Central Intelligence Agency).

The 'Chipenda Column' meets MPLA/Cuban firepower

The so-called 'Operation Zulu' of the South African army column, with FNLA and UNITA units, moved into Angola, taking Benguela, Lobito and Novo Redondo. The 2000-strong force, known as the 'Chipenda Column' after its FNLA commander, was in a strong position when, in November, the Portuguese authorities simply abandoned their former colony. The High Commissioner and all their military personnel left, announcing the ultimate transfer of sovereignty to the people of Angola.

Cuban reinforcements arrived in the nick of time, and early in December 1975 the South African/FNLA/UNITA forces were stopped at the Queve River, two hours' drive from Luanda, after a part of the column was ambushed with the loss of at least 200 troops and many armed vehicles were destroyed and captured. For the first time the Boers and their surrogates tasted the firepower of the 122-mm rocket-launchers from MPLA and Cuban allied forces. PLAN was only marginally involved but we learned that the South African troops, FNLA and UNITA surrogates were rooted out up to Kunene Province as they could not face the MPLA/Cuban firepower.

By 26 March 1976, MPLA and Cuban international forces had driven all South African forces and UNITA/FNLA out of Angola. They blamed the Americans for not honouring their promise to support them, and Holden Roberto of FNLA for his unreliability before the final encounter in which they were militarily humiliated and suffered heavy casualties.

Meanwhile the so-called Chipenda Column, together with Mobuto-Zaire troops led by the CIA, reached Caxito River which is only 30 km from the centre of the city of Luanda. Their purpose was to capture Luanda in order to install Holden Roberto as the first President of Angola. However, the CIA-led Zaire and FNLA troops were attacked while crossing the Caxito bridge, and some panicked and fell into the river. Holden Roberto was present at this battle, and it was reported by one of the journalists also present — and who had actually been issued an invitation card to attend the inauguration of Holden Roberto — that one of the rocket-shells fell close to Roberto's feet. This frightened Roberto so much that he retreated all the way from Caxito River to Kinshasa, Zaire.

Angola — an independent sovereign state

At the time the Portuguese High Commissioner departed Angola unceremoniously for Portugal, the MPLA armed forces seized power and President of MPLA Dr. Antonio Agostinho Neto proclaimed Angola an

Independent Sovereign State on 11 November 1975. He became the first President of the People's Republic of Angola.

We could see the South Africans' lack of both political will and military power, and the morale of our PLAN forces rose to new heights, just when we needed as many recruits as possible from the thousands of Namibians entering Angola to join SWAPO.

The Americans turned against Vorster's government at this time, and the US Senate passed the so-called Clark Amendment in November 1975, forbidding US military support for any of the rival parties in Angola. The CIA had kept its aid to FNLA and UNITA very quiet. John Stockwell, head of the CIA operation in Angola at the time, later wrote that the CIA had seen their involvement as a means not only of keeping MPLA out of power but of keeping SWAPO bases out of southern Angola.

We could see that though the West did not want to see Soviet interests advanced, as they perceived it, by MPLA in power, they would not come out in support of the apartheid regime in South Africa.

President Dr. Neto was very helpful indeed. I was already in Luanda on 26 March 1976, attending the ongoing Afro-Asian People's Organization Solidarity Conference, when the last of the South African troops had pulled back over the Namibian border. I started to organize the transfer to Angola of some of our forces. We already had a few there — over 200 volunteers, who were given crash military training in Zambia — whom General Dimo Hamaambo had brought over the Zambian border during the transitional period when there was nobody in control in Angola.

Now the Portuguese officers who had overthrown the Caetano regime in Portugal were no longer interested in maintaining the colony. But by the middle of May 1976, PLAN combatants were in full force to ensure the maintenance of a safe route for the new recruits entering Angola from Namibia. They were not 'officially' there, but their presence was now in order. The rest came by plane and in trucks from Zambia to Luanda and then south to their new bases.

We had to maintain a route also for the Namibians who continued to pour into Angola to join the struggle, and to care for the refugees from both sides of the frontier. Our main transit centre was at Cassinga, 200 km inside Angola, which was given to us by President Neto because there was an old iron mine there and the necessary infrastructure for a new settlement. It was used to receive the refugees who were then moved on to Lubango, which was to become and remain SWAPO's military operational headquarters in southern Angola.

33 (Above)
Sam Nujoma, with
President Neto,
addressing Afro-Asian
People's Solidarity
Organization,
4 February 1976,
Luanda

34 (Left)
Dr. Antonio
Agostinho Neto,
First President of
the People's Republic
of Angola

Vantage points in Angola

Thus, the Angolan Government under the dynamic leadership of Dr. Antonio Agostinho Neto gave us the opportunities to establish PLAN Military Headquarters at Lubango in southern Angola and relocate SWAPO Provisional Headquarters from Lusaka to Luanda.

By the end of 1976, PLAN had, under General Dimo Hamaambo, established forward operational bases which put PLAN combatants in place to strike at any South African military base inside Namibia, from the Atlantic Ocean all the way to the Caprivi Strip along the Zambian frontier: Eastern region covering Caprivi Strip; North-Eastern region covering Kavango region; Northern and North-Western regions covering Ovambo and Kaokoland regions; with the Commanding Headquarters at Villa da Ponte.

In May 1976 President Neto invited me to accompany him on a tour of the south and we travelled together to Manonge (formerly Silva Porto), Lubango and Namibe. He had seen none of these places himself, having been barred from them on tribal grounds by Portuguese laws similar to those we had in Namibia. We got on well with the local people— Muila, Kipungus, Tjokues and Himbas — who were related ethnically to the Kavango people and others in eastern and Northern Namibia. I was able to meet many new arrivals from Namibia and to recruit them into PLAN.

I knew President Neto well and our relationship was very cordial. We had discussed the transfer of SWAPO Provincial Headquarters from Lusaka to Luanda at an early stage and he was supportive when we made the move. SWAPO had previously had difficulties in establishing ourselves in Angola due to the lack of materials and food, and the disruption caused by the war going on in Angola. Politically we always had the support of the Angolan government. The Soviet Union was there supporting the MPLA, as were all the socialist countries, and Cuba with its armed forces. We too benefited from the practical support of the Soviet Union and its allies, such as the German Democratic Republic (East Germany) and Czechoslovakia, in terms of weapons and ammunition. We had to fight powerful South African troops which had already been in Angola and thus knew the terrain well. We had to build up our armed forces too, and during that time were able to draw on the thousands of young SWAPO members who daily crossed the border into Angola to reinforce PLAN to intensify the armed liberation struggle.

35 Strategic planning over a map

A lot of training had to be done, much of it in Angola, and some platoons and even companies were sent abroad for specialized training in the usage of anti-air weapons of various types, and artillery pieces.

Even after the defeat of the South Africans by Cuban and FAPLA (Angolan Army) forces, the South Africans remained in control of the air space and could come in at any time. They were thus able to install UNITA at Jamba, close to the Caprivi Strip, in order to intercept PLAN combatants. UNITA surrogates served the South Africans well and (like Koevoet, which was nominally a police unit) were in reality part of the South African Defence Force, in whose camps they were trained and by whose commanders they were led when they fought against PLAN combatants.

Some myths, and a traitor

There is a story that we were on bad terms with MPLA at this time, but this was certainly not true. As power in Angola was seized by MPLA, our opportunities of setting up our military headquarters and main bases inside Angola were stalled. In 1975, PLAN under Comrade Dimo Hamaambo, had established positions inside southern Angola. To enable our forces to move into these new areas from Zambia we preserved corridors, on the basis of strict neutrality in the internal political and military conflicts between the three rival movements in Angola.

Those who spread false stories that SWAPO and UNITA were allies did not know of the connections between SWAPO and MPLA — and especially the relationship between me personally and President Neto — which had begun long before in Dar-es-Salaam. PLAN and FAPLA worked and fought together against the Portuguese and South African troops when we both had forward camps at Kaunga Mashi, in Western province of Zambia, before the April 1974 coup occurred in Portugal. FAPLA had a military base at Shangombo, and we always shared military intelligence, and our soldiers worked together against the common enemy.

It also became part of the mythology that the Ovambos and Ovimbundu were closely related tribally, which is also untrue. The Ovimbundu were known to us in early days as a trading people, middlemen between the Portuguese and the old Ovambo kingdoms, with whom they traded tobacco, liquor, firearms and even slaves. Their home area was north of that of Ovambo-speaking people. The latter were quite numerous in Angola, of course, as the frontier was drawn by an Anglo-Portuguese commission right through the Kwanyama kingdom of Ovamboland.

As MPLA duly won its way to power, our hopes of transferring the centre of our operation to Angola were fulfilled. FNLA was corrupt and ineffective, with its external Zairean influence. Their leader, Jonas Savimbi, was known to work for PEDE (Policia International Defence d'Estate), the Portuguese Secret Police, and UNITA was by now fully in the pay of the South Africans. We knew that Savimbi had flown to Pretoria to beg the South Africans to stay on in Angola after the collapse of their 'Operation Zulu'. How could SWAPO collaborate with such a traitor?

Such friendship as we had with UNITA had existed long before Angolan independence and was no more than with all other liberation movements, such as those from the Seychelles, Comoros and elsewhere. The Seychelles, for example, shared our Dar-es-Salaam office, after the Tanzanian government had asked us to assist them. They remain our friends to this day, and when their President, after winning the election in Seychelles, made a state visit to Tanzania, he came directly to the SWAPO office. We were on good terms with all the national liberation movements, even those who were really nothing at that time. After Savimbi broke away from FNLA, where he was so-called Foreign Minister of GRAE (Government of Angola in Exile), based in Kinshasa and supported by CIA Mobuto (which had merged with FNLA), he amounted to nothing at all. That was why he had been picked up by the South Africans, who fed his personal ambitions.

What was immediately important to us, and indeed very historic, in the fall of the Portuguese and the independence of Angola, was that early in 1976 we were at last able to take full advantage of the long border with Namibia. Logistic bases in our operation against South Africa were provided to us by the Angolan government. This put us in a strong position militarily, enabling SWAPO to strike at the South Africans right from the Atlantic Ocean all the way to the Caprivi Strip along the Zambian frontier.

◆ ◆ ◆

17

SWAPO — Home and Exile

The departure of SWAPO leaders and activists from the north, and also many of our members from Windhoek and other parts of the country, had its effects on the Party at home. The South Africans were determined to make good of the heavy blow they suffered in the first bantustan elections in Ovamboland in August 1973, in which fewer than 2.5% voted: that means that the majority of the people in Ovamboland had boycotted the elections very successfully.

A second poll was held to elect more puppet councillors in August 1976, and SWAPO again boycotted these bogus elections. This time the South Africans used every possible means of coercion: a show of force; threatened denial of pensions, work permits, job recruitment and cultivation of land rights; and coercion at the polls by tribal police, who were also deployed. Foreign correspondents who were flown in to see the long queues at the polling station knew nothing of the coercion, nor of the widespread public flogging of SWAPO members and supporters. These newsmen were the 'observers' who the South African claimed verified the 72.8% turn-out. It is a fact that the figure was concocted without reference to the actual votes cast.

The sustained and concerted attempt to discredit SWAPO and build up the pretence that South Africa was offering Namibia genuine self-government was carried out through the western media by an outpouring of official propaganda. In October 1974 the diplomatic correspondents were invited to hear Vorster tell the South African Senate that his country was "at crossroads ... and the choice lies between peace on the one hand and an escalation of strife on the other. The people of South West Africa [Namibia] should be allowed to decide their own future without being hampered or disturbed", he said. What he meant was that the 'native nations' or 'bantustans' — which had been promoted ever since the Odendaal Commission's Report, to divide our country into ethnic groupings in order to facilitate South African control — must not be hampered or disturbed by SWAPO.

The vicious repression of SWAPO members was stepped up accordingly. The South African Appeal Court stopped the floggings in February 1975, but detention and torture of SWAPO members and activists in police cells and prisons went on. Many more fled the country, and the number of SWAPO members in exile increased. In 1975 I was joined in Lusaka by David Meroro, SWAPO National Chairman, with whom I had worked since the formation of SWAPO in Windhoek. He had been a victim of police brutality, and was held in solitary confinement for five months under the so-called Terrorism Act.

A letter sent for a very high price

SWAPO Youth League leaders carried on the fight with great courage, while most senior SWAPO members were imprisoned on Robben Island and others jailed in Namibia or South Africa, and others left the country to join the armed liberation struggle.

In 1973 the Youth League leaders wrote a letter to me which showed that the Central Committee in exile and the Youth League at home were in complete agreement, but that the Youth League had no idea of the difficulties that confronted us in the outside world. They wrote:

"The Honourable President Sam Nujoma,

We must know or bear in mind that the Struggle for our Freedom is a matter that needs seriousness and therefore we must not play with it.

1974 must be a year of sacrifice for Freedom and a year of the realisation of the power of SWAPO, not only abroad, but also inside Namibia. We must not wait on the UNO to bring us Freedom on a silver plate. We must rely on the power we wield in Solidarity with our Brothers of Independent African States.

The Youth League would like to send a delegation to the meeting during May this year, but the problem is money. We are going to publish a monthly newspaper inside Namibia and we shall welcome information from the SWAPO offices abroad.

Our Comrades, Jerry Ekandjo, Jacob Shidika and Martin Kapeuasha are kept in jail for fun and we would like to suggest that you must use your influence abroad so that these Comrades can be released because S. A.'s Mandate over Namibia is already terminated and she has thus no right to prosecute any politician in Namibia.

We hope and trust that you will do this immediately. S.A. is now jailing innocent people since 1974 because we mentioned at our last meeting that this year we are to bring the Boers' regime to a fall. Bring this to the attention of the United Nations and Organization of African Unity.

We are pleased because our Arab Brothers had boycotted S.A. with oil. We, the Namibians are not suffering because of the embargo and therefore we call for total oil boycott against S.A. The Boers are feeling the Oil Boycott, it is why they are propagating that it is the blacks who are suffering, Arabia must not waste his oil by giving it to S.A.

We must now awake out of our sleep and free Namibia in 5 months' time. We must pull up our socks before it is too late.

June, this year must be the month of Namibia's freedom. Until when are you waiting for somebody to free us. SWAPO's liberation Army must now fight the Boers and free Namibia before June [1974]. We promised the people that Namibia is to be free this year and now they are waiting for this freedom to come. Don't make us liars all in any possible way. Yours faithfully,

1. Nashilongo E. Taapopi (Chairman)
2. Joseph Kashea (Acting Secretary)
3. Shihepo Iimbili (Treasurer)"

The letter was addressed to the Administrative Secretary of SWAPO in Dar-es-Salaam. However, it was intercepted by the postal services of Klein Windhoek which alerted the Security Branch of the South African Police the same day. Within that week, Taaipopi, Kashea and Iimbili — young men passionate for their country's freedom — were arrested and indicted for incitement to murder, public violence, and arson. They were sentenced to ten years imprisonment on Robben Island.

The propaganda campaign against SWAPO

It was a tragedy that some of the Youth Leaguers, when they joined us in exile in Zambia, were led astray by one group of dissidents led by Andreas Shipanga. He had been bribed by pro-South African financiers in West Germany. When the struggle demanded bloodshed and sacrifices, Shipanga turned traitor and went back to Namibia to join other South African surrogates in the service of the Boers.

The propaganda campaign to destroy SWAPO as a whole, as well as individuals, also increased. Vorster decided that the only way to deal with my effectiveness as President of SWAPO from its inception 15 years before was to attack me personally, and this he did on numerous occasions. A typical example was his speech in the South African Parliament in April 1975, in which he slandered both SWAPO and me with words that were widely quoted. He said: "If someone wants to have talks with me on South West Africa on the basis that SWAPO is South West Africa and Sam Nujoma is the leader of South West Africa, then I say 'Forget it!'".

In the late 1950s in Cape Town, Comrade Herman Ya Toivo had been friendly with Professor Jack Simons of Cape Town University and his wife, the trade unionist Ray Alexander. This must have been the Special Branch file source Vorster used in his speech. He went on: "SWAPO was conceived and born in sin. It was born in Cape Town as the child of the four communists in 1957. These four communists made Sam Nujoma, who was an Ovambo, the leader of the Ovamboland People's Organization, or the OPO". He then quoted what he said were the three aims of SWAPO as laid down in its constitution. He claimed, without foundation, that one of these called for "the confiscation of land of all whites and non-whites who do not support the organization". He went on: "Does anyone in his right mind expect me to negotiate with such a person? I want to make it clear now that I do not even want to be seen with the fellow. I told the leaders of Africa 'You must not even try to sell Sam Nujoma to me because I am not buying him under any circumstances!'".

The Press seized on the word 'adventurer' from another part of the speech, when Vorster said: "I do not care who recognizes Sam Nujoma, the adventurer, the child of Ben Turok and others. South Africa does not recognize him". In the following month, he told the Press: "With regard to Sam Nujoma, time was when he was the big mogul. That attitude has changed very much".

I do not believe I have met Mr. Ben Turok, though I did meet Brian Bunting after the massacre in Windhoek, and later Professor Simons and Ray Alexander when they were in exile in Zambia. As a matter of fact, the ANC leaders and the Liberal Party, in particular the late Patrick Duncan and his immediate colleagues, were closer to OPO and SWAPO in its early days in Cape Town.

The South African government, under both Vorster and P. W. Botha, tried hard to associate SWAPO with communists, regardless of the truth. They also tried to capture SWAPO Soviet instructors at our military academy in Angola, without any success. We guarded them jealously. However, in 1981 when the South African troops invaded Angola and occupied the Cunene Province they captured some Soviet military instructors who were advisors to the Angolan Army (FAPLA) at Ongiva. They were paraded as SWAPO military advisors, which was simply a lie. The South Africans did this in an attempt to prove to the western powers that SWAPO was really a communist agent.

These attacks were necessary for Vorster to oppose SWAPO's status as "sole authentic representative of the Namibian people", conferred first by the OAU and in 1977 by the UN General Assembly. The recognition of SWAPO and its established status was the result of my long association with African leaders and other anti-apartheid forces from many parts of the world.

My former colleague at the UN, first President of SWANU, Advocate Fanuel Jariretundu Kozonguizi, wrote in 1975 about my contribution to SWAPO and the struggle:

> "Their single advantage has been in the single-mindedness and presence in their lobby of the person of their President. It is not an exaggeration to say that during the last 15 years he had hardly spent a month in one place. While he himself travelled throughout the world, Sam Nujoma had made effective appointments at strategic places throughout the world and especially in Africa."

Kozonguizi, who had returned to Namibia and was involved in local politics, claimed also that "SWAPO's single asset in this battle for sole recognition was their declaration of an armed liberation struggle in 1966".

It was never the case that we claimed to be the sole political group in the country. It was, however, correct that we were the only political party that carried out effective political mass mobilization and the armed liberation struggle against the continued illegal occupation of

Namibia by apartheid South Africa. It is the fact that both the OAU and the UN recognized SWAPO as the "sole authentic representative" of the Namibian people. Had this not been so, South Africa would not have tried to set up puppets and infiltrate agents to speak in favour of the continuation of the South African apartheid rule in Namibia, to create confusion among genuine supporters to the cause of Namibia's freedom and independence. Despite personal political attacks on me, as well as blackmail on SWAPO, Vorster and his minority white-clique dismally failed to convince the Western powers that SWAPO was "conceived in sin" as a "child of communists".

In the meantime, Vorster and his pro-Nazi Broederbond (Afrikaner secret society) forgot that history has revealed that he, Malan, Verwoerd and Strijdom trained Boer commandos and clandestinely sent them to Germany to fight on the side of Nazi Hitler against the Allies. We in Namibia are proud that some of our citizens actively participated on the side of the British under the United Party, led by General Jan Smuts of South Africa, during World War II.

SWAPO withdrew from the Namibia National Convention (NNC) at the end of 1975. We realized that some of the elements within it had been infiltrated by the police and that others were dealing direct with the authorities. We had to realize that this was a useless front. We were always ready for unity, from the days when we joined with the Caprivi African National Union (CANU). But after getting out of the NNC it became clear that we could carry out a much more effective political campaign on our own, among the workers. There were strikes and much other activity which mobilized and united the people against the common enemy.

The collapse of the Portuguese empire in Africa in April 1974 sent shock waves through the South African racist regime, which caused them, among many other responses, to embark upon an exercise of deception, telling the world that they did not believe in discrimination and apartheid. They tried to create the impression, even in some African countries, that their 'natives' were not yet ready for self-rule: they had to be brought to that stage and it would take years. That was, of course, an insult to the intelligence of any self-respecting black person.

The minority white South Africans also realized that they had to increase greatly their military strength, and stretch their troops from Mozambique all the way to Southern Rhodesia, and then along the Angola-Namibia border. They realized that they were fighting a losing battle. In an attempt to maintain white domination, Vorster sent troops to Southern Rhodesia to reinforce Ian Smith, who could have collapsed earlier in his rebellion against the British Crown in Zimbabwe. The propaganda against UDI labelled Ian Smith an outcast, yet he survived for 15 years with Vorster's support, militarily and economically.

A new strategy of deception

The white South Africans had come to realize that they could no longer do as they wanted by oppressing the indigenous people and continuing to defy the world's rejection of apartheid. They had to pretend to be sympathetic to black rights. They even tried to put together a 'non-alliance' in Africa. They would be part of it, provided they were allowed to continue their racist policies. They wanted to use these tactics to disarm the African countries and to eliminate support of the national liberation movements, particularly SWAPO, Zimbabwe African National Union — Patriotic Front (ZANU-PF) and the African National Congress (ANC) of South Africa.

To respond to the new situation, a new strategy of deception was worked out by Vorster and Ian Smith: in Southern Rhodesia to create puppet regimes led by Muzorewa; and in Namibia to establish the 'Democratic Turnhalle Alliance' (DTA). The strategy included the creation of new names: Southern Rhodesia became 'Rhodesia/Zimbabwe' and Namibia became, in their new terminology, 'South West Africa/Namibia'. Up until then Vorster had become angry whenever he heard the word Namibia.

The 'Turnhalle' strategy implemented in 1975 was bound to fail because none of those who were involved had support among the Namibian people. Our political campaign inside the country was effective, backed up by the armed liberation struggle, and the diplomatic isolation of South Africa which had also become effective. We had exposed the South Africans at every international conference so effectively that South Africa was finally expelled from the UN General Assembly session in 1972.

The ruse of name-changing to 'South West Africa/Namibia' did not alter the repressive laws in Namibia, and that demonstrated to the Namibian people that the DTA quislings were on the enemy payroll and were not working in their interest. Genuine change could only be achieved through intensification of the armed liberation struggle waged by SWAPO.

The apartheid South African regime also made great efforts to weaken SWAPO outside Namibia by infiltrating spies into our movement. The first attempt was in 1976 when Andreas Shipanga and six others attempted to split SWAPO through the support of West Germany. Hans-Dietrich Genscher, the West German Foreign Minister, paid a visit to Lusaka, Zambia and invited the SWAPO leadership for lunch. We refused his invitation with our demand that the FRG government close down its Consulate in Windhoek and stop financing German-only white schools, which was contrary to the Security Council resolutions. But Shipanga and the six others went for lunch with the FRG Foreign Minister, against the SWAPO leadership decision.

In West Germany there were, of course, both the anti-apartheid movement and individual SWAPO supporters. But the West German government was narrow-minded and had negative attitudes towards SWAPO. They were working hand in hand with apartheid South Africa, for fear that Germans in Namibia were going to lose their property, and also for fear that if a lot of Germans returned to Germany from Namibia it would increase the problem of unemployment in Germany.

Vorster also attempted to create the impression that the leadership of SWAPO was being challenged by members of SWAPO Youth League who came to Zambia through Angola after the Portuguese coup, behind leaders like Shipanga. We had the Youth League in exile, as we had the other wings of the party — the SWAPO Women's Council, Elders' Council and the People's Liberation Army of Namibia (PLAN). We also had democratic elections every 5 years for the leadership of the Party. There were elements sent by the South Africans to spy on SWAPO, without doubt, and those were the ones that followed the reactionary Shipanga, who was supported by West Germany. The South African military intelligence and the Special Branch must have spent millions of rand in bribing such people. They were well-dressed and some arrived with brand new cars. Even if some succeeded in misleading people, the national liberation war was increasingly effective. Every year we made more progress until 21 March 1990 when genuine freedom and independence were achieved.

I believe that it is in the nature of any war like ours for the enemy to infiltrate the national liberation movement. We knew very well who these infiltrators were in many cases. We were in touch with the people inside the country, and they told us who were recruited by the enemy. So we knew who they were and we organized foreign journeys, sometimes even scholarships, to get them out of the way. In the case of Shipanga and the others, we simply asked them to leave because they were interfering with the real struggle. They were going round the Embassies saying that they were being denied this and that. So I told President Kaunda that we wanted to concentrate on the real enemy, and that these people were making disturbances and hindering the struggle against the enemy. The Zambians knew this too, so they just flew them to Tanzania, where they were held in detention. Much was made of this by our enemies, but the numbers were very small. Fewer than a hundred were involved, and the stories spread by some of Shipanga's friends that hundreds and even thousands were being detained were simply lies. There was really no uproar at all. The matter did not affect the front area, which was more important, and the armed liberation struggle continued with intensity.

Consultative Congress July 1976, Nampundwe, Zambia; false allegations of SWAPO 'Communism'; and the Church in the Liberation Struggle

The month after the trouble with Shipanga and his few followers in Lusaka, SWAPO held a national congress in Walvis Bay (29 to 31 May 1976). This congress totally rejected the Turnhalle Conference and endorsed the leadership of SWAPO, with myself as President.

The following July we held a Consultative Congress at Nampundwe in Zambia, the first since the Tanga Consultative Congress in December 1969/January 1970. The delegates agreed to amend the Constitution and political programme. Among the modifications to our structure, we created a direct link between PLAN and the Secretary for Defence, Peter Nanyemba, who reported to me as President and Commander-in-Chief. We also set up the Central Committee for the first time and an Executive Committee to formulate policy as a 'Political Bureau'. At the Nampundwe Congress we also reviewed the Shipanga incident and sought ways of avoiding a similar occurrence in the future.

Party structures like 'central committee' and 'politburo' and a new commitment to a 'classless society in a free Namibia' also came out of the Nampundwe Consultative Congress.

Because of our adoption of these structures and because of the increased arms and technical aid we had begun to receive from the socialist countries — above all from the Soviet Union — it was often falsely claimed by our opponents that we were a Marxist-Leninist organization, and that if we came into power "the hammer and sickle would fly over the Tintenpalast". The South Africans believed, or pretended to believe, that if they left Namibia the Cubans, backed by the Soviet Union, would pour into Namibia from Angola, and there would be a war and consequences "too ghastly to contemplate", as Vorster said. But these claims disregarded the fact that SWAPO had also received humanitarian support from the Nordic countries, particularly Sweden, and in addition we were funded by the World Council of Churches in Geneva, as well as having close links with the Commonwealth and with anti-apartheid groups of supporters in many western and non-aligned countries.

The World Council of Churches played a very effective role too, even influencing the churches here in Namibia. The Lutherans, Catholics and Anglicans all supported us, though the Anglicans had been vocal from the early 1970s when three of their bishops — Mize, Winter and Woods, and another leading clergyman Canon Ed Morrow — were deported, as was David de Beers.

However, after the verdict of the International Council of Justice in The Hague that the presence of the South African apartheid regime in Namibia was illegal, the two black Lutheran Churches came into head-on collision with that regime in the publication of their Open Letter in July 1971. In this letter, the black churches stated clearly their demand that the United Nations must supervise the elections.

The Deutsche Evangelische Kirche in Südwest Afrika (German Lutheran Church) distanced itself from the Open Letter. This church was never prepared to question the legality of the apartheid regime and the racist laws imposed by it. They declared their readiness to always "work for the people" and to conduct their activities in accordance with the constitution of the Southwest African Administration. Their leader Landesprepst Kurt Kirschnereit stated in January 1973 that: "In order to fulfil our Christian responsibility in a multiracial country, we have to be subject to the recognised principles of the country. Any faction which has as its aim the overthrowing of this constitution must be blamed. A church which pursues these goals must take to the catacombs" (*Namibia Woche: 'Menschenrechte Mussel Kraft* by P. Leifeld).

This statement by the leader of the German Lutheran Church also called for the banning of SWAPO and the persecution of the two black Lutheran Churches.

The white apartheid regime welcomed this support from the white Lutherans. In a letter in 1975 to the Lutheran World Federation, racist Prime Minister B. J. Vorster explained: "South Africa is a Christian country with complete freedom of religion. Our policies, therefore, are built on and rely on the teaching of Luther" (*Namibia — Old and New*, G. Totemeyer, pp. 20–30).

The Lutheran World Federation condemned this stand of its member, the German Lutheran Church. On several occasions the Lutheran World Federation intervened in order to bring its white member church in Namibia theologically into line with its two black member churches. Instead, in line with its own position of so-called neutrality, the German Lutheran Church made itself an accomplice in the suppression of the black population. This stand of the German Lutheran Church led to its suspension in the early 1980s from the Lutheran World Federation. (I must point out too, more than 20 years later, that there is a local church in Namibia still supported by the German Lutheran Church which is very much anti-SWAPO Government, continuing in the opposition that originated long before the independence of Namibia was achieved.)

In spite of all the evidence to the contrary, many of the whites in Namibia believed the South African propaganda about SWAPO being communist. This was an isolated country, with many neo-Nazis in our commercial life then, as there still are now. There are very few among the Germans today who are really progressive. We have some of them in our government, as we also have some of Afrikaner stock.

But most of the whites in Namibia simply never knew SWAPO. They mistook our decision to confront the South African administration to mean that SWAPO was a communist-inspired organization. We were not. We were fighting for our rights and for the freedom and independence of our own country. We had no other alternative. The South Africans were pursuing a policy of annexation of Namibia to South Africa, and they pursued that up to the last moment. That is why they had a huge army, which was intended to occupy our country forever. This also raises another question.

Why did South Africa spend so much to keep Namibia?

The fact is that the Afrikaners — particularly the poor Boers who had been the underdogs among the whites, after they had won the election in South Africa in 1948 — thought of 'South West Africa' as their own country. Of course, South Africa was their country too, but they had to share it with well over a million Britons and other whites in South Africa who participated in the Second World War equally with them.

And therefore Namibia was the only place where these white people, even if they were illiterate, could be employed in the municipalities, in the railways, in government departments and parastatals, where they were paid a salary a hundred times higher than the pay of the African worker who actually did the work.

Also, they had to defend this country because it was the only one where the Afrikaner could dominate. That was the real, underlying reason they tried to keep Namibia. They were joined by German fascists, neo-Nazis who still continued to celebrate Hitler's birthday in this country until 1990 when we achieved independence. They were in league together.

There were strategic motives too. They wanted to keep the Kunene River as their frontier rather than the Orange River. For a similar reason, Vorster made an alliance with Ian Smith, when Smith launched his 'Unilateral Declaration of Independence' in 1965. He even built a railway line over Beit Bridge to connect Southern Rhodesia to South Africa, in order to maintain the so-called 'border of freedom' at the Zambezi River.

The price that the Afrikaner Nationalists made South Africa pay so that they could hold on to Namibia was out of all proportion to its actual value to South Africa. The people who made money out of it were shareholders in the big mining and fishing enterprises — some of them South Africans, but most of them in Europe and America. The price that was paid was enormous and may have permanently weakened South Africa. The money spent on running Namibia and fighting PLAN from 1966 onwards could have been spent to develop South Africa, and Namibia as a colony, in many ways. That money, along with thousands of lives lost, achieved nothing.

The Western governments that continued to support South Africa, with their exercise of vetoes at the UN Security Council, their 'constructive engagement', 'linkage' and clandestine arms supplies, were the losers too. The trading partner they were supporting for purely mercenary reasons has now much less to offer than it would have had if they had compelled South Africa to withdraw in favour of the UN-controlled free and fair, genuine elections, before we were obliged to take up arms and fight for our rights, our freedom, our sovereignty and our independence.

❖ ❖ ❖

18

Resolution 385 and the Kissinger 'Shuttle'

The years of our move to Angola, the events leading up to the Nampundwe Consultative Congress in Zambia and the elimination of some puppets like Chief Elifas in the country, were also years of progress at the United Nations.

In 1974, South Africa's intransigent show of contempt for the United Nations continued their inexorable progress toward being barred from the General Assembly. Demands for the expulsion of South Africa from the UN because of its continual defiance of Security Council Resolutions followed, but were stopped — the first two times — by a triple veto exercised by the US, Britain and France.

Frustration at the UN was reaching breaking point, particularly among certain African member states, with whom we were at all times closely working together. The Western Security Council members realized that they were getting nowhere with the Vorster regime, so they collaborated in the passing of Security Council Resolution 385 in January 1976.

This was the strongest resolution yet marshalled against South Africa's illegal occupation of our country. Its key paragraphs were the reiterated demand for South Africa's withdrawal from Namibia and that:

"free elections under the supervision and control of the United Nations be held for the whole of Namibia as one entity."

36 Sam Nujoma (seated at table, far right), President of SWAPO, addressing the UN Security Council (other members of the SWAPO delegation seated behind). New York, 30 May 1975

To make it clear that the UN were prepared to be thwarted no longer, Paragraph 9 demanded:

"that South Africa urgently make a solemn declaration accepting the foregoing provision for the holding of free elections in Namibia under UN supervision and control, undertaking to comply with the resolutions and decisions of the United Nations and with the advisory opinion of the International Court of Justice of 21 June 1971 in regard to Namibia and recognizing the territorial integrity and unity of Namibia as a nation."

The final clause, Paragraph 12, declared 31 August 1976 as the deadline for:

"reviewing South Africa's compliance with the terms of present resolution and, in the event of non compliance by South Africa, for the purpose of considering the appropriate measures to be taken under the Charter of the United Nations."

Here at last was the commitment that the first Namibian petitioners, the Reverend Michael Scott and my colleagues and I in SWAPO and the smaller parties, had been working towards in the days of Chief

Hosea Kutako. It now became the great objective of the major Western powers to induce South Africa to meet the terms of Resolution 385 without invoking the UN Charter, with its implied threat of armed intervention under Chapter 39.

South Africa's attempts to weaken and isolate SWAPO by getting African countries on their side failed, and South Africa produced nothing to give even an appearance of conceding to Resolution 385. The American administration under Richard Nixon then started their own process by sending Secretary of State Henry Kissinger on his so-called 'peace shuttle', to give at least the appearance that something was being done to solve the problem of Namibia, and to redeem the honour of the United Nations before the 31 August deadline.

Kissinger started his 'shuttle' in April 1976 and had some success in getting Ian Smith, who was also under pressure from Vorster, to agree to 'majority rule' after a two-year period. He made no progress with Vorster over Namibia, and when he spoke at the UN General Assembly in September 1976 he had only his success with Ian Smith to take credit for. This was itself brought about with the help of Vorster.

Kissinger tried to set up a conference at Geneva to settle the question of Namibian independence but Vorster would not agree to South African participation. Their only answer to Resolution 385 was to set up their conference at the Turnhalle in Windhoek, to which they summoned white politicians from their own side and their black puppets. The South African government were determined to keep up the pretence that such people really represented the Namibian people, and were not controlled from Pretoria. The Turnhalle was a total failure as a means of buying-off the United Nations, largely thanks to the OAU and our own determined lobbying. Kissinger's Namibian 'shuttle' could not claim this to its credit. It was in fact an embarrassment to him.

Kissinger's policy had originally been the so-called 'Tar Baby option' during the Nixon administration. A State Department memorandum had proposed that the white-governed regions of Southern Africa were there to stay and, while not approving of them in public, the US would be better served by doing business with them than by disrupting them. It even advised a partial relaxing of the arms embargo against South Africa. The State Department would also avoid the issue of South Africa's illegal occupation of Namibia — at least bilaterally. All this was to be done quietly, with increased aid to the African states to placate them.

Kissinger could very rarely get away from this earlier policy background. It stuck to him, one might say, like tar. Yet he was clearly in favour of both Southern Rhodesian and Namibian independence. South Africa, too, favoured Southern Rhodesian independence, provided the whites could keep control through quislings like Bishop Muzorewa. South Africa was determined not to allow the UN to 'control and supervise' the independence process for Namibia — they knew that, if fairly done, this would inevitably lead to a SWAPO government. The Ford administration and Henry Kissinger were not prepared to put any real pressure on Vorster, so their Namibian policy had no chance of success.

SWAPO always held the view that we would co-operate with any genuine diplomatic moves towards our goals. I therefore indicated my intention to meet Kissinger, and was able to do so during the UN General Assembly session in 1976.

Comrade Theo-Ben Gurirab, my Foreign Minister of Namibia who at that time was our representative in New York, arranged an appointment and we met Kissinger in his 35th floor suite in the Waldorf Astoria Tower Hotel in New York, on 29 September 1976. We told him our position: as far as we were concerned, South Africa's occupation of our country was illegal and we wanted the United States to support us politically and diplomatically in order to bring about the implementation of the resolutions of the General Assembly and the Security Council. Kissinger said "Yes, the United States will give you its support". We said we would not meet the puppet groups in Windhoek to play Vorster's game by talking about future constitutions. We would consider a conference direct with South Africa — provided it was under UN sponsorship, and provided our other conditions, which were set out in Resolution 385, were met (such as the release of all political prisoners).

The DTA elements, including Clemens Kapuuo, were in New York as part of South Africa's attempt to 'sell' the Turnhalle quislings to the international community. Kissinger made a point of saying "I know these people are here but I shall not see them. The United States government considers you to be much more important than they are".

When we finished, after an hour, he said rather hastily and, for such a sophisticated man, naively: "The press is out there — what we have been talking about here is not what you must say to them!". Kissinger always travelled with a huge number of press men, waiting to pick up whatever news they could, so he was nervous, quite unnecessarily, that we would commit him publicly.

37 With Henry Kissinger, pictured in The New York Times, the photo accompanying a feature on Sam Nujoma as "Man in the News". 29 September 1976

All I said to the press was that I still hoped the United States would exert pressure on South Africa "to talk to SWAPO and find a peaceful solution and eventually to transfer power to the Namibian people through SWAPO". I said I had dismissed the proposed Windhoek talks totally, but that we were willing to talk to the South Africans at another conference, perhaps in Geneva, though I had not in any event committed SWAPO. I insisted, "Our talks must be a completely new arrangement, a new venture: they must not be extensions of the tribal constitutional talks in Windhoek". I said the next move was up to Vorster.

Kissinger told the journalists: "I think already there has been considerable progress and we are operating on the assumption that the meeting in Geneva will eventually emerge". 'Eventually' turned out to be four years later — but it took the Administration of President Carter to get South Africa to face us in Geneva, at a meeting that was doomed from the start, as we shall see.

American press reports are always colourful and I was amused at the *New York Daily News* description of me as "a handsome, stocky man with a grey streaked Van Dyck beard". This was very unlike the monster I was represented as in South African newspaper cartoons (see Chapter 21) and in Vorster's verbal abuse. The press reports were on the whole very fair towards SWAPO's aims and objectives of holding free and fair elections under the supervision and control of the United Nations.

It had not all been plain sailing with Kissinger. Earlier in the year, in Lusaka, he had talked about South Africa committing itself to a timetable for Namibian 'self-determination' as if it was up to South Africa to decide our future. President Nyerere had made it very clear to him that no decision would be accepted in Africa, or internationally, without SWAPO and the UN both being involved in the process. I had also issued a statement from Luanda reacting to information we had received that Kissinger had put pressure on South Africa to agree to Namibian independence "on condition that military bases at Walvis Bay were given to the United States".

A few days after my meeting with Kissinger, I visited President Fidel Castro in Havana, which led to press speculation that we were planning to launch "a full scale human-led offensive in southern Africa against South West Africa", as the *Daily News* put it. The South Africans and their surrogates in Namibia did a lot of talking about this threatened invasion, which must have made Kissinger's job more difficult still. He was also under pressure from the Soviet Union and his 'shuttle' had been attacked in a tough statement shortly before.

He entertained Andrei Gromyko, the Soviet Foreign Minister, to dinner the night after our talk. Next day he met Secretary General Waldheim and told him that his southern Africa meeting was "very friendly, very fruitful".

For a moment it looked as if Kissinger's international stature and negotiating skill were going to move things on. Even if Resolution 385 were side-tracked, South Africa might be compelled at last to get out, on terms acceptable to the UN. South Africa, as so often before, knew that the US and its Western allies would not go the whole way to force them to implement Resolution 385. Sure enough, in October 1976 the US, Britain and France combined in yet another triple veto of a Security Council resolution which this time called for sanctions against South Africa because of its refusal to comply with Resolution 385. The failure of the Kissinger 'peace shuttle' led, therefore, only to more frustration internationally.

In 1974 the OAU had given SWAPO observer status, and with that went the title "sole authentic Representative of the people of Namibia". Then in December 1976 the UN General Assembly accorded us the same recognition. This boosted the morale of SWAPO freedom fighters and the people of Namibia in general, and raised the status of Namibian representatives at every international conference as well as at national level. It enabled us also to campaign for humanitarian assistance which came to us from many countries, of which Sweden, which had long been rendering such assistance to SWAPO, was pre-eminent.

Even Britain gave us some help, sending teachers to Zambia and Angola to work with our people in the SWAPO Health and Education Centres. We knew the British government did not like SWAPO and it took many years for them to accept that they had to recognize the struggle of the Namibian people led by SWAPO. They could no longer avoid us, despite Vorster's ceaseless verbal attacks on SWAPO and on me personally, as the US government had reverted to some of the friendliness of earlier days. At least the Kissinger 'shuttle' had raised our profile among the few countries that objected to our being "sole and authentic representative of the people of Namibia".

Sean MacBride's energy and resourcefulness had also helped to advance SWAPO and the cause of Namibian independence. He had been an extremely hard worker but he was getting old and his health had deteriorated. He resigned as UN Commissioner for Namibia in September 1976. The appointment of Martti Ahtisaari as UN Commissioner for Namibia in succession to Sean McBride was supported by us.

38   Sam Nujoma, President of SWAPO, addressing the UN Security Council. New York, 28 September 1976

Ahtisaari had been friendly when he was the Finnish Ambassador to Tanzania and we had known him through his membership of the Finnish Social Democratic Party. He was to play an important role for years to come, though not always as our ally.

MacBride had established the legality of the UN Council for Namibia and with it the principle that the UN Council for Namibia was the only body in the UN that had been given the mandate to administer the country. He was a brilliant lawyer who always did his level best for Namibia, and he was a fighter too. He also won the Nobel Peace Prize when he was UN Commission for Namibia. He had been detained at the age of 10 with his father, in the course of the Irish independence struggle. His father had been executed by the British — I visited his grave in Dublin in 1987. We were sorry to see Sean McBride go but welcomed Ahtisaari.

The Kissinger shuttle had been instructive. Our belief was that Western initiatives would never, on their own, contain the element of real

39 In discussion outside the UN Security Council Chamber.
(L to R) Sean MacBride, Commissioner for Namibia;
Sam Nujoma, President of SWAPO; Theo-Ben Gurirab, Representative
of SWAPO in New York. New York, 28 September 1976

pressure that would be needed to force South African withdrawal from Namibia. As the Western objective was to protect their interests in Southern Africa and they seemed incapable of looking at these other than in the short term, we realized there was little hope of their going all the way, and demanding the imposition of sanctions.

Even less likely, as I knew from approaches I had made to Western governments in the early 1960s, would they be prepared to get involved in an armed struggle on our side. We would have to continue to conduct the armed liberation struggle on our own, with arms and aid from outside the ranks of the Western permanent members of the Security Council. Above all we would need the support of the mass of our people inside occupied Namibia.

The Western powers did not want the apartheid South African colonial regime to be overthrown as Portugal had lost its colonies. Portuguese troops had been made to fight in foreign, tropical conditions, faced with extreme humidity, mosquitoes and with very poor pay. The West had invested so much in South Africa and Namibia that they did not want to see the same disruption there that had occurred in Mozambique and Angola. They thought that as Namibia was a direct responsibility of the United Nations, they could use their influence to prevent the nationalist liberation movement from taking over in Namibia.

They knew that the Soviet Union was helping MPLA to consolidate its power in Angola, and they did not want to see this happen, with a possible threat to their investment, in Namibia. They thought there should be some kind of orderly hand-over. They rightly judged the ultimate defeat of apartheid South Africa by SWAPO to be inevitable, and that is what motivated them to intervene as they did, to save their economic interests in the region, above all in South Africa itself.

Our diplomatic campaign, as ever, carried on and we were soon caught up in another Western move to try and redeem the failures of both the Waldheim and Kissinger initiatives.

The Central Committee of SWAPO, in the face of Western Power reluctance to invoke Chapter 7 of the Charter of the United Nations and impose comprehensive mandatory sanctions against the South African apartheid regime's illegal occupation of Namibia, because of their economic and strategic interests, decided to intensify the armed popular resistance throughout Namibia, as the only effective way to liberate our country. We resolved to rely on our own initiative politically, diplomatically and militarily. SWAPO pursued this policy with vigour and determination until the final victory.

◆ ◆ ◆

19

The Western Contact Group

The United Nations had tried, through Kurt Waldheim and Alfred Escher, to commit the apartheid South African regime to Namibia's independence. This initiative had been followed by Kissinger's efforts on behalf of the United States and its allies. The initiative remained with the West when the Carter administration took office and a group of Western member states — Britain, Canada, France, the United States and West Germany, all with strong southern African connections and all at that time Security Council members — made an approach to Vorster and his cabinet. Their objective was to get them to agree to UN-supervised and controlled free elections, as laid down by the UN Security Council Resolution 385 of January 1976.

The South Africans appeared to listen, and we went along with the draft proposals which Secretary General Waldheim presented to the UN in June 1977. We had serious concerns, and I had issued a statement the month before from Luanda saying that SWAPO did not approve of such initiatives from the Western Contact Group, since it was SWAPO which had been recognized by the UN "as the sole and authentic representative of the Namibian people", and therefore only we and the UN council for Namibia should deal directly with South Africa. For member states to do so outside the UN framework was in defiance of the International Court of Justice Opinion of 1971.

Furthermore, the Western Contact Group seemed willing to accept some of South Africa's arguments at face value, such as the appointment in July 1977 of Judge Martinus Theuns Steyn as Administrator General in charge of the

40   SWAPO President Sam Nujoma (front), Hidipo Hamutenya (L, second row), Theo-Ben Gurirab, Representative of SWAPO in New York (R, second row), and other members of SWAPO delegation: Kapuka Nauyala (L third row) and Anna Mupetami (R third row), 18 October 1977

transition to elections under the UN. This new post was meant to take the place of the interim Turnhalle government which South Africa had wanted to impose on the Namibian people without democratic elections held under UN supervision and control. I had argued that the appointment should be made by the UN Council for Namibia, but the Western Contact Group supported South Africa's position. We knew that Steyn and his successors such as Gerrit Viljoen, who was also chairman of the Afrikaner secret society, the Broederbond, were there purely to implement the Vorster policy of white domination which certainly offered no genuine independence for Namibia.

The appointment of Judge Steyn was thought to be a gesture towards the Western Contact Group, as Steyn was presented by South Africa as the man to create peace and improve race relations in Namibia. He was actually given instructions to try to gain confidence from the black majority in the country to join the bogus DTA (Democratic Turnhalle

Alliance) Interim Government. He hand-picked so-called ministers, and frequently gave big parties as part of his attempt to get support from the Africans, but he did not get any such support, except among the puppets who were already on Pretoria's minority white payroll.

When South Africa annexed Walvis Bay the same month (July 1977), we protested strongly and had to work hard to make the Contact Group (as the Western Contact Group foreign ministers and their ambassadors were also known) accept that there must be undertakings that Walvis Bay would be re-integrated into Namibia after independence. The Boers tried hard to sell to the Western Contact Group the Turnhalle as the interim government, but gave up and dissolved it in November 1977. They would not abandon their position that SWAPO must be on an equal footing with their stooges and under their control, and they planned to hand over power to DTA, whose members had collaborated with South Africa.

It seems strange that I was so often accused of being "intransigent" when the basic stumbling block for years to come was South Africa's refusal either to meet direct with SWAPO or to give up the idea that they could manipulate local politicians and puppets in order to hold on to their power. They rejected the Western Contact Group's original proposals, which were revised in October 1977, and they rejected them again. At the so-called 'Proximity Talks' in New York in February 1978, they clearly meant to show SWAPO up as the party that would not compromise in the interests of peace and progress, but in fact made fools of themselves. 'Pik' Botha's outbursts about not allowing Namibia to be "overrun and governed by Marxist terrorists" did not impress anybody, including South Africa's Western trade partners.

A week after the final proposals (which, with small changes, later became UN Security Council Resolution 435) had been put to the Security Council, the South Africa government, through the Administrator General, issued Proclamation AG26 to give them the excuse to harass and repress SWAPO leaders and activists in Namibia. But worse happened, hardly a fortnight after that.

Cassinga massacre, 4 May 1978

While we were negotiating with the Western Contact Group in New York, the South African army launched a barbaric attack on the SWAPO refugee transit centre at Cassinga, about 200km from the Namibian border in Angola.

41   SWAPO Secretary for Health and Social Welfare Dr. Iyambo Indongo addressing the Assembly of the World Health Organization (WHO) on 4th May 1978 in Geneva, Switzerland. At the moment this photograph was taken, Dr. Indongo (presently Advisor to the Minister of Health and Social Services and personal physician to the President) was as yet unaware of the atrocity which had taken place that same day at Cassinga.

On 4 May 1978, at 7 a.m. when the camp residents were gathered at the morning assembly to be assigned to their daily duties, South African Buccaneer jet bombers dropped poison gas, causing the assembled refugees to drop unconscious. Then waves of mirage jet fighters strafed and dropped bombs, setting the whole refugee centre ablaze. A third attack wave dropped paratroopers who shot and bayoneted those of our comrades who were already seriously injured. The result of this dastardly military attack on the Namibian refugee centre inside Angola was a massacre of about 1,000 dead and wounded. Many were missing, and many others were captured and taken to the concentration camp at Kaiganachab, 11 km west of the town of Mariental. Others disappeared, possibly taken to South Africa, and were never seen again. To bear witness to the sacrifice so many undertook that day, we remember Cassinga Day — 4 May 1978 — and the hundreds of innocent civilians who were wounded, disabled, captured and killed.

On 5 May 1978, the so-called South African Defence issued a statement, aimed at listeners in the Western world, claiming that Cassinga

42   Victims of the Cassinga Massacre, 4 May 1978: one of two mass graves

was a communist-type military training camp. But Cassinga was never a military camp where soldiers were based. The South Africans were lucky, however — there had been a PLAN company in transit which had left Cassinga the previous night — and the South Africans would have had heavy casualties if they had met them there.

The South Africans further claimed that they had attacked and humiliated SWAPO, that SWAPO's backbone was broken and it would never be able to recover. These false claims were part of their psychological warfare, aiming ultimately to force SWAPO to join its puppet government in Namibia. The clear intention of the Pretoria regime was to torpedo the negotiations over the implementation of Resolution 385 of January 1976 — between the Western Contact Group and SWAPO, as well as between the apartheid regime itself and the Western Contact Group.

Of course, I had to break off negotiations at once, and I left New York and flew to Angola "to bury our dead Comrades", as my statement said.

After Cassinga

I met the Front Line Heads of State — our neighbours Mozambique, Zimbabwe, Botswana, Zambia, Angola, plus Nigeria — in Luanda on 16 June, and announced that we would resume talks, after two months suspension in protest against the Cassinga massacre. Shortly thereafter, we also, albeit reluctantly, agreed to the terms of UN Security Council Resolution 432, which effectively put off the question of re-integration of Walvis Bay until the earliest possible date after independence.

It was widely held that SWAPO was constantly pressured by the Front Line States to endorse what the Western Contact Group and South Africa had planned. At another meeting in December 1977 in Lagos the whole matter was thrashed out, with full understanding by Angola and Zambia, whose people both made immense sacrifices in supporting SWAPO. Their countries were frequently bombed and parts of their countries were occupied, along with the killing and maiming of their innocent civilians. However, the Governments of Angola and Zambia were always willing to see our points of view. I recall only once having to speak in disagreement and 'agree to disagree' when one of the other heads of state urged us to fall in with the wishes of the apartheid white South Africa and the Western Contact Group.

The Western Contact Group and some UN officials had been quite confident that independence would come soon, when Martti Ahtisaari, who had been appointed Special Representative for Namibia by the UN Secretary-General, and 50 officials spent 16 days in August 1977 in Windhoek planning the activity of the UN Transition Assistance Group (UNTAG). We heard that the US government was already renting a building for its embassy. But we knew the South Africans better than they did, and though on 8 September 1978 we had agreed to the Secretary General's proposal of a cease-fire, we were still prepared for a long and bitter struggle for Namibia to gain genuine independence rather than become a glorified 'bantustan'.

Visit of the Western Contact Group to Pretoria

Vorster was ill, and P. W. Botha, then acting Prime Minister, rejected the figure of 7,500 UN troops to form part of the United Nations Transitional Assistance Group (UNTAG). The South Africans were very obviously looking for ways of blocking Resolution 435, enacted 29 September 1978, which in Paragraph 3 established UNTAG and in Paragraph 6 declared:

> ... all unilateral measures taken by the illegal administration in Namibia in relation to the electoral process, including unilateral registration of voters, or transfer of power, in contravention of resolutions 385 (1976), 431 (1978) and the present resolution, are null and void.

A fortnight later, as a result of a financial scandal, Vorster was replaced by P. W. Botha, and the foreign ministers of the Western Contact Group flew to Pretoria early in October to try to get their plan back on course. They were humiliated by P. W. Botha, who refused to depart from his decision to hold internal elections. This refusal flew fully in the face of the mandatory "supervised and controlled free elections in an integrated united Namibia", which was the key point of UN Resolution 385, now 435.

SWAPO's objectives always included the encouragement of negotiations, direct with South Africa if possible. Mediators such as the Western Contact Group had supported many resolutions of the UN General Assembly and Security Council. It would have been foolish not to participate or encourage them. What they were doing coincided with our strategy on the diplomatic front. We saw that this would widen the diplomatic front, make it more effective, and further isolate the apartheid regime. It would involve all the Western countries, particularly Britain, whose government, whether Labour or Conservative, was reluctant to recognize the illegality of the South African occupation of Namibia, calling it "unlawful".

Our willingness to work with the Western Contact Group was also increased by our awareness that the Carter administration was much more favourably disposed towards the liberation movements than its predecessors. They recognized SWAPO as the only effective liberation movement in Namibia. When I went to Washington during the Carter administration, I was for the first time provided with a government vehicle and with full security. I was surprised by the positive policy adopted by the Carter administration towards Namibia's struggle.

Andrew Young, the US Permanent Representative at the UN, was the driving force at the beginning, but later the Secretary of State, Cyrus Vance, was the chief negotiator for the Americans among the Western Contact Group, aided by a flexible and skilful official, Donald McHenry. We did not find the British Foreign Secretary David Owen helpful, however. On one occasion, he told the other foreign ministers of the Western Contact Group that he had no sympathy with me as I was an "uncompromising politician".

Nevertheless we got along. During the negotiations, the most striking thing, and very shameful, was the October 1978 meeting of all the foreign ministers of the Western Contact Group with P. W. Botha in Pretoria, from which they came back empty-handed. Botha told them that they were selling out to terrorists, and they achieved absolutely nothing. They never explained what their purpose had been or why they failed. Cyrus Vance could find very little to say about it in his book, except, like David Owen, to claim that at the very last minute P. W. Botha had agreed, contradicting South African Foreign Minister 'Pik' Botha's position, that the bogus elections they were to hold did not mean that the UN supervised elections would follow. It was indeed a disgraceful affair for the Western Contact Group. Even if Vance and Owen were right, P. W. Botha later back-tracked on this last-minute concession.

We did not want the Western Contact Group to come to Namibia because their presence created the impression that they recognized South Africa's illegal occupation of Namibia, and we issued a statement saying so. They made the mistake also of talking to the Turnhalle puppets, who were indeed no more than stooges appointed by the apartheid South African regime with the aim of maintaining its illegal occupation. The South African Government's appointment of the Turnhalle, and of the DTA 'Interim Government' that succeeded it, had been effected in order to defeat the resolutions of the General Assembly and Security Council, and in fact to incorporate Namibia physically into South Africa.

South Africa intensified its acts of aggression against the Front Line States, particularly occupying southern Angola. The Contact Group lacked the political will to impose economic sanctions upon the South African regime, so we had to depend on support from the Organization of African Unity, the Movement of Non-aligned, Nordic and Socialist countries, and other progressive UN member states, to constantly insist on the implementation of the General Assembly and Security Council resolutions on Namibia, in particular Resolution 435.

We were aware of the failure of the Western Contact Group to put pressure on South Africa and of South Africa's continuing military occupation of Namibia, so we intensified the armed liberation struggle. We continued carrying out our three-pronged strategies: the political mass mobilization inside Namibia, the intensification of the diplomatic offensive, and the armed liberation struggle inside the country. It was the armed liberation struggle that more than anything else motivated the Namibian people to support the struggle waged by SWAPO against apartheid South Africa's illegal occupation.

Negotiating with the Western Contact Group

The actions of the 'Gang of Five', as the Western Contact Group were referred to, were based on the resolutions of the General Assembly and Security Council. Whenever a resolution on Namibia was passed by the Security Council, it would recall the key resolutions of the General Assembly in 1966: Resolution 2145 which terminated South Africa's mandate over South West Africa; and Resolution 2248 which established the UN Council for South West Africa as the legal authority in the country, until independence. We did not therefore expect the OAU members, non-aligned countries or socialist countries to intervene against the Western Contact Group. The resolutions were supported by the majority member states of the UN, and as such they strengthened SWAPO's position in demanding the immediate implementation of the UN resolutions on Namibia.

43   *Western Contact Group members: (far L) Paul Andre la Pointe (Canada); David Owen (UK); Louis de Guiringaud (France); Cyrus Vance (USA); Hans-Dietrich Genscher (Federal Republic of Germany), prior to the Security Council meeting which adopted Resolution 431 (requesting the appointment of a Special Representative for Namibia to "ensure the early independence of Namibia through free elections under the supervision and control of the United Nations") and Resolution 432 (declaring that "the territorial integrity and unity of Namibia must be assured through the reintegration of Walvis Bay within the territory"). New York, 27 July, 1978*

We ourselves did not oppose the Western Contact Group, even though we could never believe that they held Namibian interests quite as close to their hearts as they held other concerns, primarily Western economic ones. We differed on implementation, and I was accused of being 'intransigent' or 'uncompromising' because I would not agree to any plan or principle that would obstruct Namibia's progress towards full and genuine independence.

The Western Contact Group wanted SWAPO to join the DTA puppet-show in Namibia, because they were fully aware, as were the South African minority white settlers, that the South African quislings would certainly lose in free and fair elections. But holding of free and fair elections in Namibia, controlled and supervised by the UN, and based on the principle of 'one man, one vote', was the 'bottom line' for SWAPO. It was out of the question that SWAPO should join South Africa's DTA puppet interim government, with its aim of setting up the divisive 'bantustans' and the partitioning of our country. We rejected that, totally. I was not going to compromise. That was always the decision of the central committee and the politburo of SWAPO, supported by the majority of the Namibian people.

The Western Contact Group also pressed us hard to withdraw from the armed liberation struggle — as they put it, to "abandon violence". Again our reply was unequivocal: we had no alternative while the apartheid South African regime had more than 100,000 troops in Namibia alone, in clear violation of the UN resolutions. SWAPO insisted that we would only sign the cease-fire with South Africa on the implementation of Resolution 435.

During the negotiations in 1977, when we first began meeting the Western Contact Group in New York, they put forward the idea that some officials could observe the elections. But we insisted that, since there was ongoing war, there was a need for a UN peace-keeping force in Namibia. That was our terminology. They had at first thought that we would just agree with the plans they had worked out together with the minority white South African regime, but we insisted that:

> "SWAPO's position is that there must be a UN peace-keeping force for Namibia to ensure that South African troops are withdrawn, otherwise the war will continue, which will defeat the aims of the United Nations to assist the Namibian people to exercise their inalienable right to self-determination and national independence through democratic elections."

They disagreed, and we almost had to walk out of the meeting. It went on and on, however, difficult though it was, and UN Security Council Resolution 435 was finally passed at the end of 1978.

At that first New York meeting in 1977, we travelled first class, even our secretaries, paid for by the Western Contact Group, and were put up in an expensive hotel, the UN Plaza, right opposite the UN building. When we would not agree with the proposals they put forward to my delegation, their attitudes changed: for the next round of talks we travelled on economy class tickets and stayed in the tiny Roosevelt Hotel on 3rd Avenue.

South African military build-up in Namibia — an explanation?

After the first meeting, the Western Contact Group always expected SWAPO to reject everything that was being proposed. But of course we had to weigh each of the proposals in the balance, bearing in mind always the diplomatic and political situation. In the 'Proximity Talk' in New York in February 1978, as I have said, the South African Foreign Minister 'Pik' Botha expected us to oppose outright the retention of South African troops in Namibia. But we said, "Yes, if the South African troops are confined to their bases in Oshivelo, Grootfontein or Mpacha, SWAPO guerrilla forces will also be confined to their bases". Botha put on a show of anger over some minor points and flew back to Pretoria 'to seek for new instruction and advice'.

The South Africans would never recognize this paragraph. They claimed that we were crossing the border all the time from Angola. This was an obvious lie. Why should they have had more than 100,000 armed forces in Namibia, and constructed those huge military bases, just to catch little bands of three or four guerrillas jumping over the border and back to Angola, as they claimed? Massive infantry, military and air bases, communication control centres like that at Grootfontein, Rundu, Ondangua and Oshakati — all that was meant for a handful of guerrillas crossing the border and running back again? The fact of the matter was that our PLAN combatants were effective and permanently fighting in all the regions inside Namibia at all times.

South Africa meant to show that, in spite of the negotiations and the UN's adoption of Resolution 435, they would crush SWAPO militarily. P. W. Botha was convinced he could eliminate SWAPO and show the international community how strong South Africa was militarily. They thought they would create the same impression with us. Their greatest crime, the Cassinga massacre of 4 May 1978, was aimed to show their military superiority, as well as to stop the negotiations initiated by the Western Contact Group.

Our only meeting with the South Africans was with three generals (van Tonder, van Westhuizen and Herman), led by van Tonder. This was arranged by President Kaunda who was always in contact with them. Their task was to assess our political stand and attitudes. They knew that, in spite of the massacre of our guerrilla forces in Shatotwa, Zambia in 1976 and the attack on our transit camp in Cassinga in 1978, there was no way they could militarily defeat SWAPO. They were also supporting UNITA (National Union for the Total Independence of Angola), which was by that time part of the South African army and being used to intercept and block SWAPO and PLAN combatants on their way to fight inside Namibia. They wanted UNITA to take over Angola completely so that SWAPO would have no base to operate from militarily. I and my colleagues who talked with these generals found them naïve and unsophisticated. They attempted to convince us to return to Namibia and join the DTA puppet Interim Government. We rejected their ideas and proposals *in toto*, and their mission failed completely.

More reflections on a difficult relationship

When we commenced the talks in 1977, my delegation consisted of Theo-Ben Gurirab, Hidipo Hamutenya, Ngarikutuke Tjiriange, Kapuka Nauyala, Anna Mupetami (Secretary) and we were joined by the delegation from inside Namibia led by SWAPO Vice President Hendrik Witbooi, Festus Naholo, Martha Ford, Daniel Tjongarero and Mokganedi Tlhabanello. I led SWAPO delegates to all the meetings during the negotiations with the Western Contact Group in 1977 and 1978, up to the adoption of Resolution 435 by the Security Council.

The Western Contact Group would meet the South Africans inside the UN building and then meet us outside; the South Africans in the morning and SWAPO in the afternoon, or vice versa. The South Africans remained arrogant throughout. It was always they who refused to talk to us, not SWAPO who refused to talk to them. Yet the Western Contact Group were clearly sympathetic to the apartheid South African regime.

The role of the Western Contact Group was supposed to be that of mediator and carrier of messages between the parties — to take from us what we proposed and convey it to the South African regime. But how they operated in this role demonstrated their lack of dedication to this role. At one time, they were on their way to South Africa, with Donald McHenry as US spokesman in the group. They got as far as Lusaka where they spoke to President Nyerere, then the Chairman of the Front Line States, and to President Kaunda. They decided they had done enough — that, having spoken to Presidents Nyerere and Kaunda, there was no longer any need for them to go on to South Africa to convey our message to the Botha Pretoria regime.

When we met them in the British High Commission in Lusaka and they told us this, I just gathered my delegation and we walked out, leaving them there. We said: "You are not serious; you are just messengers of the Boers. Why do you bring the messages of the Boers to us and when we ask you to respond on our behalf you do not want to go — yet you are supposed to be mediators". After that they went on to Pretoria, to keep the negotiations going, but what they really wanted to do was to pressure us to come and join the so-called Interim Government. When they realized we were serious and would not agree, they had to try another tactic. On our part, we saw the importance of intensifying the armed liberation struggle and increased our diplomatic campaign. In spite of their negative attitudes towards SWAPO, the negotiations had continued as part of the diplomatic campaigns against the enemy.

After Resolution 435

The South Africans were strongly opposed to the UN having any power in deciding the future of Namibia. South Africa, for example, complained that she would not entertain the idea of UN control and supervision of the elections, and the British supported them all the time in this. Similarly the British would not agree to there being a UN peace-keeping force and certainly not under that name. They wanted some officers, some in uniform and some observers. We repeatedly said no, there must be a full-scale peace-keeping force because there was war in Namibia and there could be no free and fair elections while fighting continued in the country.

The Western Contact Group eventually came to realize how strong SWAPO was. When the Americans sent their officials to observe the withdrawal of South African troops from southern Angola in 1981, they saw how South Africa was spending so much money and had so many soldiers, and could judge that a war was being fought against a formidable opponent. Then, when two of their officials who were observing the withdrawal of South African troops from Angola, died in a bomb explosion at a petrol station inside the South African military base at Oshakati, they withdrew that observer group.

I had dealt earlier with Kissinger who was a diplomat and a manipulator, and we played our diplomatic card well when dealing with the Western Contact Group. We did not believe in violence for its own sake. But, I said, "You, the US, Britain and France, as permanent members of the Security Council, are supposed to ensure the maintenance of world peace and security. How could your countries support the apartheid South Africa's illegal occupation of Namibia!".

The passing of the Resolution 435 in September 1978 was the second major step after Resolution 385 nearly three years earlier, but we were conscious that the implementation of the Resolution would demand great efforts from us. My mind had always been clearly fixed and inflexible on one point: we must concede nothing in the negotiations which would put SWAPO and the people of Namibia at the mercy of the minority white South Africans when preparations for genuine elections really got under way. It would not be enough for the Western Contact Group, and even the UN negotiators, to agree to plans acceptable to South Africa without signing the cease-fire between SWAPO and apartheid South Africa — parties to the conflict in Namibia. Even if I was to be blamed for being uncompromising and intransigent, we had to maintain our stance on the implementation of Resolution 435.

A very senior UN official, Brian Urquhart, Waldheim's deputy for peace-keeping, has written that "SWAPO kept the Namibian issue alive by desultory guerrilla activities, which would then trigger reprisals by South Africa". He used belittling words like 'desultory' when in fact our operations were unceasing — but he was right in one regard, that without the war and the sacrifice of life and limb by so many of our fighters, there would have been no further progress.

Urquhart also wrote of Vorster's and P. W. Botha's Namibian policy:

"Nowhere has the South African talent for delay and obfuscation been deployed with such skill."

With Resolution 435 achieved, the South Africans went into a long period of "delay and obfuscation" which called on greater than ever military activities on our part. Only by our guerrilla war could we hope to wear down the South Africans, keep up the morale of the people, and force the United Nations, through the good offices of our friends in the OAU and the Non-Aligned Movement, to keep up the pressure for apartheid South Africa to be compelled to implement UN Security Council Resolution 435.

At the end of the day, Resolution 435 was acceptable to us, though we had had to make concessions, in particular again allowing the deferment of the Walvis Bay issue until after independence. We still had the gravest doubts that the South Africans would "play the game" and that the Western countries would have the will to force them to honour their commitments regarding the holding of UN-supervised and controlled elections. Ten years of bloodshed were to follow as we greatly increased our military attacks on South African military bases inside Namibia.

I was interested to read David Owen's comments, in his autobiography, on the negotiations of the Western Contact Group. He gave credit to Andrew Young and Donald McHenry for taking the lead in the negotiations, though he clearly felt that their final successful outcome 10 years later was to his credit as well. He wrote:

> "I have rarely felt such pleasure as when I returned to Windhoek in 1990 on the eve of independence and saw Sam Nujoma just before his inauguration as President. The new constitution for Namibia is a model for the rest of Africa — there has been a marvellous spirit of reconciliation and co-operation between South Africa and the new Namibian government. There are excellent prospects that Walvis Bay will be returned to Namibia."

Once again, I felt that we knew our old colonial oppressors better than he did and, indeed, the issue of the port of Walvis Bay remained unresolved almost a further twenty years, until 1 March 1994 when it was finally integrated into the Republic of Namibia.

Lord Owen probably thought in September 1978 that the prospects were excellent for the implementation of Resolution 435, but the difficult part was only just beginning.

The whole process had started in June 1975 with a draft resolution put before the Security Council by five OAU member states calling, on our behalf, for sanctions against South Africa as a "threat to international peace and security". We had promoted this all the way to the UN — only to see it stopped by the triple veto of Britain, France and the United States. This threat of sanctions was undoubtedly a factor in sending Kissinger on his shuttle diplomacy, which ultimately failed because of South Africa's refusal to deal with SWAPO as its excuse for non-compliance.

There were benefits from renewed activity, such as Resolutions 387 and 393 in March and August 1976 respectively, condemning South Africa's attacks on Zambia and Angola, and, in December 1976, the General Assembly's recognition of SWAPO as "sole authentic representative" of the Namibian people. The latter came after another triple veto of a draft resolution invoking Chapter VII of the UN Charter, and merely endorsed the state of affairs already recognized by both UN Secretary-General Kurt Waldheim in 1975 and the US Secretary of State Henry Kissinger only three months before our meeting in New York.

The successful negotiations among the Western Contact Group, SWAPO and South Africa had been completed in less than 18 months from the first meeting in New York of the Western Contact Group with South Africa's UN Ambassador Brand Fourie in April 1977, to the unanimous adoption of Resolution 435 by the Security Council on 29 September 1978.

Having achieved Resolution 435, the so-called 'Western plan' for South Africa's withdrawal from Namibia, the Western Contact Group then found that its implementation was a much more difficult process, mainly because South Africa's word could not be relied on.

As the end of the Carter administration's four-year term came into view, South Africa's motive for delay and deceit increased and the hopes that Resolution 435 had aroused — more in the Front Line States than in SWAPO as we knew the South Africans better — began to disappear. SWAPO had to intensify the armed liberation struggle in the country in the knowledge that international diplomacy by itself would not immediately bring Namibia's freedom and genuine independence.

As history shows, due to the Reagan administration's pro-South Africa policy of so-called 'constructive engagement', the implementation of Resolution 435 was delayed for the next 10 years.

◆ ◆ ◆

20

US Policy towards Namibia in the 1970s and 1980s

In the mid-1970s, the United States' pursuit of its strategic interests and foreign policy objectives in Africa went through rethinking and remodelling, particularly with regard to southern Africa. Henry Kissinger was on the African political scene in a big way by this time. He had a background in military counter-intelligence for the US during World War II, and had been appointed Assistant for National Security Affairs under Richard Nixon in 1969. He was then appointed Secretary of State by Gerald Ford in 1973. In that capacity he was intimately involved in the political picture on the African continent.

Dr. Kissinger's mindset was fixed on the Cold War. In the wake of the seizure of power in Mozambique by FRELIMO and in Angola by MPLA, he saw danger coming that could undermine US and other Western interests in Africa. In May of 1976, Kissinger delivered a major US foreign policy speech in Lusaka, Zambia.

It was assumed that the Front Line States had direct influence on the national liberation movements of Zimbabwe, South Africa and Namibia, in addition to also having their own economic and security interests. In those three countries, the ZANU Patriotic Front, the ANC and SWAPO renewed their resolve to intensify the armed liberation struggle to end colonialism, apartheid and oppression in their countries. For its part, the apartheid regime in Pretoria had unleashed a total military onslaught and other acts of aggression and destabilisation against the Front Line and other African states.

44   Henry Kissinger, 1973

While there was 'sanctions-busting' concerning Rhodesia, the progressive and peace-loving forces were intensifying punitive sanctions against Pretoria to end apartheid and its illegal occupation of Namibia. Saving the whites and ensuring unhindered and continued access to raw materials, strategic minerals and sea lanes was clearly the rescue mission that brought Henry Kissinger to southern Africa, not self-determination, independence and human rights of the black majority. All that and the US obsession with the presence of Cuban troops in Angola, not forgetting its support for Jonas Savimbi and UNITA, influenced Dr. Kissinger's manoeuvrings in the region.

In 1976, in keeping with this cunning gameplan, two of the nine State Department senior officials were sent to southern Africa. They were William D. Rogers, US Under-Secretary, and William Schaufele, the Head of the Africa Bureau. I met them in Lusaka in 1976. What they put on the table was the stillborn idea of a Namibian Conference, either in Windhoek or in Geneva, where, they suggested, SWAPO and the internal puppet political groupings would meet to sort out their differences and agree on the future of Namibia. I rejected the idea with the contempt it deserved. By then SWAPO had already declared its willingness for a face-to-face meeting with the occupationist regime for the sole purpose of discussing the practical modalities of transferring power to the Namibian people, under the leadership of SWAPO, with the assistance of the United Nations. We had put the onus on the shoulders of Pretoria and given the international community a plan of action to deal with.

Dr. Kissinger actually wanted to turn the Namibian struggle against colonialism into a mere local tribal conflict in which Pretoria would act as a disinterested bystander with limited concern only, at the envisaged Namibian Conference. Some leaders of the Front Line States were being drawn into this dubious scheme. The aim was to deliver SWAPO into the hands of the enemy on the basis of John Vorster's deceitful promise to leave Namibia once the Namibians had agreed among themselves on the future of their country. I clearly told Messrs. Rogers and Schaufele that SWAPO would not yield in its opposition to such a futile conference.

Later, in September 1976, my colleagues and I met with Henry Kissinger in New York, at the Waldorf Astoria Towers, the official residence of the US Ambassador to the United Nations, to further discuss the idea of a so-called Namibian All-Parties Conference which his two top aides had earlier raised with me in Lusaka. It was a frank and useful meeting. Dr. Kissinger shared with us his encounters with John Vorster in Zurich and a number of African leaders, as well as his own assessments of their respective views on Namibia's decolonisation, and about SWAPO.

On 30 September 1976, Dr. Kissinger presented, in his speech before the UN General Assembly, the objective of the proposed conference and the UN's role in it. This idea had earlier been hatched with Vorster in Zurich. According to this plan, 31 December 1978 was fixed as a target date for Namibia's independence. Dr. Kissinger rather misleadingly implied in his speech before the General Assembly that I had endorsed the plan, which I did not do and could not have done. Mwalimu Julius Nyerere also expressed his opposition to the idea. His strong stance saved SWAPO, not least by preserving the integrity of the sacred cause of the Namibian people. Had it not been for his behind-the-scenes vigilance and firmness in his dealings with Dr. Kissinger, quite a lot would have been sacrificed. For example, South Africa's polecat status in the community of nations would have been removed.

Dr. Kissinger's agenda was really not about independence, or the eradication of apartheid in Zimbabwe, Namibia and South Africa. Nor was it about the prevention of military aggression against and destabilisation of the Front Line States. Rather, the objective was to further US aims and interests in the region, driven by Cold War priorities. President Ford's Administration, and Dr. Kissinger in particular, inevitably failed to realise their objectives in Southern Africa, except for giving regrettable legitimacy and prestige to the racist Pretoria regime, which caused painful frustrations to the world community and also, ironically, embarrassments to Dr. Kissinger and his collaborators.

That marked Dr. Kissinger's exit and paved the way for the next US Administration.

The Carter Administration

When President Jimmy Carter and his team came to power in January 1977, they inherited Kissinger's legacy and his Cold War game plan for Southern Africa. The Carter Administration also had to contend with the right-wing Republican leadership in Congress, who were friends of the apartheid regime, supporters of Jonas Savimbi as well as the various puppet groups in Namibia.

During the transition period from one administration to the next, much of what Dr. Kissinger had been doing in 1976 was still on the cards. The Cold War was alive and the Security Council was used as an arena of ideological confrontation and abuse of the veto power was common. Both the Soviet Union and China were suspicious of the Western Contact Group, due to the extensive economic and strategic ties between their governments and corporations and apartheid South Africa. Initially, the Western Contact Group skirted the Security Council and operated parallel with and not through it.

45   *Western Contact Group members: (L to R) Cyrus Vance (USA); Louis de Guiringaud (France); David Owen (UK); Hans-Dietrich Genscher (Federal Republic of Germany). New York, 27 July 1978*

Mr. Cyrus Vance, the new US Secretary of State, recruited able and dedicated assistants: Andrew Young, Richard Morse and Donald McHenry, amongst others. Don McHenry became the principal negotiator, policy strategist and the undisputed leader of the Western Contact Group. It was left to Ambassador Andrew Young to initiate political contacts on possible "exploratory talks" by contacting all the relevant African interlocutors at the UN and in the various capitals. SWAPO office in New York was one of them.

The underlying rationale of the Western Contact Group in the Security Council was summarised by Ambassador Don McHenry as follows:

a) The UN inherited a legal responsibility for the territory from the League of Nations;

b) The UN provided the channel to those who had the best chance of communicating with the South Africans;

c) It was believed that if at any time it would be necessary to 'invoke measures', it would be important that at least three permanent members of the Security Council were involved in some way from the beginning, so as to avoid any splits in the Contact Group at the end of the line;

d) By making the negotiations a multilateral effort at the UN, the possibility of deadlock because of any one party's bilateral policies would be reduced.

The basis of their approach towards Namibia was Security Council Resolution 385 of January 1976. The UN Commissioner for Namibia, Dr. Sean McBride, and SWAPO had formulated the ideas that went into that resolution at the International Conference for Human Rights in Namibia, held in 1975 in Dakar. SWAPO was prepared to take a chance in the proposed negotiations because of our confidence in the support of the Namibian people, in the event of any free and fair elections, and our favourable position to resort to the General Assembly, through the UN Council for Namibia, if a sell-out deal became apparent.

I must say, SWAPO did not really trust anybody at the outset — the Western Contact Group, the Front Line States and Nigeria, the UN bureaucrats, and naturally racist South Africa. For, at the outset, what the Carter aides were selling us was Kissinger's old wine in a new bottle. At the same time, we could not really altogether reject a negotiated settlement. I put the case to the SWAPO Central Committee and, after an in-depth discussion of the costs and benefits, we agreed to diplomatic negotiations initiated under the leadership of the Carter

Administration. We were ready for "exploratory talks" anywhere — except as guests of the Boers or their payroll puppets in Namibia or South Africa.

We constituted a SWAPO negotiating team of experienced comrades, under my chairmanship. The Central Committee took a position that we must negotiate, while at the same time intensifying the armed liberation struggle, until the conditions for the cessation of hostilities were created and a cease-fire signed between the warring parties i.e., SWAPO and the illegal occupying regime of racist South Africa.

On this basis, we decided to pursue political and diplomatic actions and the armed liberation struggle concurrently. As I have emphasised many times already in this text, we saw them as complementary and not contradictory. Pretoria kept on denying the fighting capacity of the People's Liberation Army of Namibia (PLAN), SWAPO's military wing, while at the same time it continued steadily building up its massive troop strength in Namibia to fight PLAN. Pretoria's lies were, however, constantly exposed to the world by its own endless communications to the UN Secretary-General, complaining about SWAPO's military operations at different times and places right inside Namibia. All those letters and cables are on file at the UN.

Among the major African policy issues that the Carter Administration had to confront at the start were the Namibian and Rhodesian colonial situations. Mr. Vance, unlike his predecessor, Dr. Kissinger, was more businesslike and reassuring. He was not a Cold War 'hawk'. For example, he indicated that he did not perceive the Soviet Union's relations with certain African countries as being a part of its broad strategic design. While he saw this as a disturbing challenge in Africa, and mostly in southern Africa, he was not unduly alarmed. It was this new approach which made us to open up and welcome the Western initiative which Ambassador Young and his colleagues were pushing in the UN circles and beyond in Africa. Vance recalled the initial phase of the Carter Administration's diplomacy in the following words:

> "As had been true during the Nixon and Ford Administrations, our ability and determination to pursue a balanced policy towards the Soviet Union was most severely tested in the Third World ... What we did in Africa in the early months of 1977 would have a major effect on Third World perceptions of our policy towards the developing nations..."

I welcomed this constructive attitude.

The Carter Administration came in with a firm conviction that Namibia's independence was achievable. They also believed that a success here would guarantee an end to the colonial oppression and bring about democracy, political pluralism and reconciliation between the black and the white communities in the country. This view further held that Namibia's peaceful transition to self-determination and independence, with international assistance, would augur well for those desperate whites in South Africa itself to accept the ANC and majority rule, democracy and a new, non-racial dispensation in that country.

On the other hand, even though the concept of 'linkage' later grew most notorious and actually destructive under the Reagan Administration, the Carter Administration too had, surprisingly, promoted linkage as a viable negotiating device. The idea was broached with President Agostinho Neto of Angola. They thought Namibia's independence could result in a speedy withdrawal of Cuban troops from Angola, because South African military would be out of Namibia.

Of course, Dr. Chester Crocker later transformed this strategy into an ideology rooted in the ruthless 'constructive engagement' policy with the racist regime of Pretoria. This diabolical scheme was sugar-coated and sold to some African leaders who bought it, lock, stock and barrel. Mwalimu Nyerere, for one, understood the whole plot for what it really was. But others were not so insightful and almost handed over SWAPO leadership to a certain death at the hands of the fascist Boers.

After some delay, the Western Contact Group resumed its interaction with SWAPO. I received an invitation for 'proximity talks' in February 1978. South Africa too was invited; the Namibian puppets were not. This time, the Contact Group's five Foreign Ministers played a direct role in the goings-on by meeting separately with the two belligerents. I carefully explained SWAPO's position to them. At this stage, the Contact Group's settlement proposal was being constructed in a working form for serious discussions.

This was a critical phase, both within SWAPO itself and between us, the Pretoria regime, the UN and the Western Contact Group. Earlier, I had informed the Front Line States that SWAPO could be flexible in the discussions, provided that South Africa would accept certain critical conditions, and provided that the question of Walvis Bay and the Offshore Islands was resolved.

Other thorny issues included the confinement to base both of South African and SWAPO troops inside Namibia during the transition period, under the UN surveillance. I also insisted that UNTAG's strength should be, at least, 7,500 troops and 1,000 observers. If these conditions were accepted, SWAPO would tolerate the presence of a South African token force of 1,500 troops during the elections period, but that this military contingent should be confined to a single base in the southern part of the country, namely at Karasburg. SWAPO's position was communicated in an official letter dated 8 September 1978, addressed to Dr. Kurt Waldheim, UN Secretary-General.

No sooner had the "proximity talks" begun than South African Minister of Foreign Affairs 'Pik' Botha — who earlier had boasted of having a full mandate from his government to discuss any matter and take any decision — withdrew from the talks after American press reports that South African military bases had been attacked by SWAPO military forces. Botha ran away from New York unceremoniously and returned to Pretoria, ostensibly to obtain more signing power. SWAPO had once again outmanoeuvred the enemy, this time, on the political and diplomatic front. Following Botha's hasty departure, a meeting was held at the US-UN Mission to reflect on the situation and a way forward.

After that meeting, the Front Line States, SWAPO and other close friends met at Ambassador Salim Ahmed Salim's residence, outside New York City, for a post mortem and to plan ahead for the next round of the 'proximity talks'. We agreed to build on our achievement and put further pressure on the enemy. True to type, the racist regime had decided on a new war-path.

During the months of April and May 1978, the Western Contact Group carried out active shuttle diplomacy to restart the talks and obtain reactions to their settlement proposal. In mid-April, Pretoria had for purely tactical reasons indicated acceptance. SWAPO, while maintaining flexibility, insisted on the inclusion of Walvis Bay in the Western independence plan. It was at this stage of the most delicate negotiations, in New York and Washington, when the South African military perpetrated the Cassinga massacre on 4 May 1978, more than 150 miles deep inside Angola, killing and maiming many hundreds of defenceless civilian refugees.

I cut short my stay in New York and immediately returned to Angola to deal with that barbaric human carnage. In a letter I sent to Ambassador Andrew Young, before I departed, I firmly stated that for SWAPO the negotiations had to be deferred indefinitely in light of the Cassinga massacre. Clearly, racist South Africa's lack of sincerity about the negotiations was exposed. It was obvious that the large-scale military invasion and attack inside Angola and the massacre of innocent Namibian refugees must have been planned a long time in advance. I challenged the Western Contact Group over their commitment to Namibia's independence and demonstrate their bona fides in the face of Pretoria's hostile and dastardly act.

After an extended break, another meeting was convened in June 1979 in Luanda. There SWAPO was expected to indicate its acceptance of the Western Contact Group's settlement proposal, and also there the question of Walvis Bay would be resolved. In Luanda, SWAPO had to confront not only the Contact Group but also the Front Line States in rather heated exchanges. Eventually, as regards Walvis Bay, a breakthrough came from SWAPO for a separate resolution of the Security Council specifically on Walvis Bay and the Off-Shore Islands as well as for their reintegration into the rest of Namibia. Before this, the Contact Group had stood firm that this question should be shelved for post-independence negotiations. SWAPO was equally adamant that, without agreement on this fundamental issue, we would not accept the Western settlement plan. Now, the way forward was clear.

In 1977, Vorster's regime had, by an act of the all-white, racist South African Parliament, annexed Walvis Bay. In the face of this challenge, SWAPO's response was quick. We requested the UN Council for Namibia to urge the General Assembly, as a matter of utmost urgency, to adopt a strong resolution condemning Pretoria and declaring Walvis Bay and the Off-Shore Islands as inviolable and integral parts of Namibia. This was done promptly. SWAPO, moreover, demanded in Luanda that the Western Contact Group had to undertake to ensure the adoption of an identical resolution by the Security Council as a condition for me and my SWAPO colleagues to accept the settlement plan, which we were not, to begin with, entirely happy about. When the time came, the Security Council did adopt Resolution 432 (1978) on Walvis Bay and the Off-Shore Islands, and thus the 'Western Proposal' was endorsed by the Council on 27 July 1978.

Shortly thereafter, in September 1978, P. W. Botha succeeded Vorster as Prime Minister of South Africa, and later became its State President. Not only was he a die-hard racist and militarist, but he was also a particularly vicious foe against SWAPO and against myself personally.

Around the same time, the Security Council adopted Resolution 435 (29 September 1978). It endorsed the Secretary-General's decolonisation plan and authorised the creation and deployment of UNTAG in Namibia. In spite of this apparent progress, the negotiating atmosphere was still very much tense and divisive, in light of Pretoria's negative position. The apartheid regime insisted that the Western Contact Group should instead deal with the bogus Turnhalle Alliance in Windhoek about Namibia's future. Again, SWAPO urged the Front Line States, the OAU and the Non-Aligned Movement to demand comprehensive and mandatory sanctions against the illegal regime for its defiance and tactics of delay.

In October 1978, the five Foreign Ministers of the Western Contact Group went to South Africa to stop Pretoria from proceeding with its plan to hold unilateral elections in December 1978 in Namibia for an internal settlement. To my utter dismay, this strong team of five Foreign Ministers, representing the most powerful nations on earth, left South Africa virtually empty-handed, after meeting P. W. Botha on 16–18 October. In view of this despicable failure, SWAPO's demand, joined by those of the African States and the Third World, for mandatory sanctions against Pretoria was further intensified.

The farcical elections went ahead in Namibia in 1978. The DTA was declared the 'winner', but it was a meaningless victory. The world at large did not recognise the outcome, and Pretoria had to face wrath expressed around the globe, including verbal condemnations by its Western friends. "Isolate racist South Africa!" became the international community's loud and united battle cry.

The best way to achieve this had to be the imposition of mandatory sanctions. At the same time, all-round solidarity with and support for SWAPO, as the sole and authentic representative of the oppressed Namibian people, was declared by the United Nations. This represented the full diplomatic recognition of SWAPO, as well as a vote of confidence in us by the international community.

In the meantime, the Western Contact Group transferred the task of establishing UNTAG to the UN Secretariat. As the future would tragically show, both the Western Contact Group and the UN itself mishandled the question of confining both the South African and SWAPO troops to designated bases inside Namibia, as contained in UN Security Council Resolution 435. This neglect eventually proved fatal, more than 10 years later, when on 1 April 1989 — the same day as the commencement of the UN Security Council Resolution 435 — South Africa's fascist army violated the cease-fire and attacked SWAPO forces inside Namibia.

The UN could have prevented that tragedy by acting differently at the end of the 1970s. But South Africa lied, and the UN accepted the distortion of the real military situation on the ground in Namibia. Pretoria had repeatedly refused to acknowledge the physical presence of our armed guerrilla units inside the country. Both Pretoria and the UN knew the true facts, but the latter preferred to pretend otherwise.

By 1979, Mrs. Margaret Thatcher became Britain's powerful and blindly conservative Prime Minister. Mrs. Margaret Thatcher's sympathy for whites in Southern Africa was publicly declared. 'UN-bashing' was made an official policy. The 1979 Camp David accords on the Middle East were hailed as the best way to solve difficult political problems from outside the United Nations. Dr. Crocker would build on this later in dealing with Namibia. The previous Anglo-American proposal on Rhodesia was cast aside in favour of the Lancaster House negotiations on the independence of Zimbabwe. And Prime Minister Thatcher would in a few years time find a mentor and friend in President Ronald Reagan of the United States of America.

The Reagan years

Slowly but surely, the Western Contact Group shifted away from its focus on Namibia to other national, regional and international priorities. International politics and strategic realignments entered a new confrontational phase.

By the time 1979 came around, many far-reaching changes had occurred on the world scene, some good but most of them bad for Namibia's independence. That year, Ambassador Martti Ahtisaari of Finland became the UN Commissioner for Namibia, thus strengthening the ranks of the UN Council for Namibia in its activities around the world towards the rapid decolonisation of our country. Earlier in 1979, a major international conference held in Maputo, Mozambique, in support of and solidarity with the struggling peoples of Namibia and Zimbabwe and their national liberation movements, namely SWAPO of Namibia and the Patriotic Front of Zimbabwe. By then SWAPO's diplomatic status had already been enhanced in the UN to that of Permanent Observer. Furthermore, in 1979, SWAPO was duly admitted as a full member of the Movement of Non-Aligned Countries at its summit held in Havana, Cuba. All this constituted good news for the struggling people of Namibia.

Bad news for our struggle came in different forms, both inside Africa and elsewhere. In 1979, two great sons of Africa and SWAPO's reliable allies, Presidents Agostinho Neto of Angola and Murtala Muhamed of

Nigeria, passed away at the worst possible time for the Namibian cause. At the same time, a certain brand of doctrinaire conservatism embraced by various Western governments, and exemplified by the political ideology of President Ronald Reagan, grew stronger. By the time the Commonwealth Summit convened in Lusaka, Zambia, in 1979, it was very clear to me that the struggle would be long and bitter. But we were not intimidated by all this. Meanwhile in the USA, the political temperature was rising steeply against the Carter Administration.

The 1979 Iranian Islamic Revolution created dramatic events that culminated in the American hostage crisis. The handling of the hostage crisis in Tehran, and the related military fiasco created by a bungled helicopter rescue operation, politically buried President Carter. His Secretary of State Cyrus Vance resigned in protest.

US national priorities had to be reconsidered carefully and Africa, particularly the work of the Western Contact Group, had to be shelved indefinitely. Governor of California Ronald Reagan had emerged as the strongest Republican challenger against the Democratic incumbent Jimmy Carter, and Reagan successfully capitalised on the hostage issue. By now, to all intents and purposes, the 1980 American election campaign had started in earnest. Consequently, by the time of the visit of yet another UN working team to South Africa, led by Mr. Brian Urquhart and including Mr. Martti Ahtisaari and General Prem Chand, the negotiating game concerning Namibia was practically up. The Pretoria regime was in no mood to do anything of substance to break the impasse.

The fiercely confrontational politics of Prime Minister Thatcher and the Cold War ideology of Ronald Reagan were welcome news to racist South Africa. P. W. Botha and his clique remained intransigent and defiant. This was happening at the time when the ZANU-PF victory was announced, which was a severe shock to Botha's regime. I received Urquhart's team in Luanda and expressed to them my dismay that they had been duped by the Boers and the puppets they met in Windhoek, en route to Luanda.

From then on, the UN was just trying to appear busy with the DMZ and other mundane matters in hopes of keeping the Western Contact Group's spirit alive. The Boers had a big deception working, as the Pre-Implementation Meeting (PIM) on Namibia, held in Geneva in early January 1981, clearly confirmed. They were just buying time until the situation changed in Washington. Nothing of importance did in fact happen in the negotiations until the Reagan Administration came to power in late January in 1981. With immediate effect, the Reagan

Administration set out to change the political, economic security and strategic map of the world.

This arrogance of power earned the title of the "Reagan Doctrine". It was the reactionary platform of a cruel enterprise capitalism; of renewed East-West showdown; of UN-bashing; and of the victimisation of the Third World. For example, Jonas Savimbi and UNITA and various other selected bandit groups in the world were embraced as 'freedom fighters' and given military and political support. SWAPO and the other legitimate national liberation movements of Africa and elsewhere were branded as terrorist groups and blacklisted.

For southern Africa, a notorious policy of so-called 'constructive engagement' was put in place. Dr. Chester Crocker, an old Kissinger-hand, became its implementor. And so, a dramatic and vicious process of confrontation was unleashed in southern Africa, and Namibia came out the worst of it. Resolution 435 was first declared "dead in the water" and thereafter taken up only to be mutilated into something ineffectual.

Similarly, the UN was initially ignored but later infiltrated and turned into an ally. What the Western Contact Group and the UN had been doing all along ended abruptly. Dr. Crocker launched his own series of subversive meetings with the Front Line States and SWAPO, under the pretext of creating better conditions for expediting the implementation of Resolution 435. In actual fact, he was destroying Resolution 435 by indirectly rewriting its salient provisions and adding his own crooked ideas. One such terrible effort was the introduction of the so-called "impartiality package" to deny SWAPO the internationally accepted UN support. Crocker and the Reagan Administration were fully aware that Pretoria had created a substantial "slush fund" to help the treacherous internal parties to strengthen their collective position against SWAPO. These were some of Dr. Crocker's sinister doings.

Of course, none of this came as a surprise to me because Crocker's approach was consistent with the political-military nuclear-intelligence alliance that Washington had forged with P. W. Botha's regime, right from the word go. The truth finally came out about the "slush fund", and the development of nuclear weapons in South Africa with the support of the Reagan Administration was publicly exposed.

For the next 10 years, Namibia's independence was delayed, and Savimbi was given stinger missiles, increased military support and well-coordinated political exposure in the USA to influence the American media and the general public in his favour.

Both Washington and Pretoria stood firmly behind Savimbi and UNITA in their common opposition against the Angolan government. Mikhail Gorbachev of the USSR succumbed under government pressure, joined the anti-progressive cause and abandoned the old friends. Gorbachev himself died a political death as a quisling and traitor in the eyes of his own people and the progressive world. So did his doomed ideals of glasnost and perestroika. He is now a haunted man. It was President François Mitterand of France who rejected linkage as a totally extraneous issue, either to Namibia's independence or the work of the Western Contact Group, refused any association of France with it, and suspended France's further participation in the work of the Western Contact Group with regard to Namibia.

Reagan's moderate Secretary of State George Shultz might have been unsure, at the beginning, about the US–Namibia–Angola policy; but the CIA and the Pentagon gained the upper hand, particularly in respect of support for apartheid South Africa and the UNITA bandits.

The 1975 Clark Amendment barring military aid to UNITA was repealed, and military-intelligence specialists were installed in Jamba to co-ordinate military operations with the South African forces occupying Namibia and with UNITA. The war expanded in several dimensions in the south-western region of Africa, while the quadripartite negotiations on the linkage issue continued in many places, such as Brazzaville, Cairo, London, Geneva and New York.

The final agreement on linkage was signed by those parties on 22 December 1988 in New York. In the wake of this, 1 April 1989 was set by the Security Council as the starting date for the implementation of UN Security Council Resolution 435 and the deployment of UNTAG in Namibia.

◆ ◆ ◆

21

Geneva and the Reagan Years

In the US elections in November 1980, the Democratic Party administration under Jimmy Carter was replaced by that of the Republican Party with Ronald Reagan as President. Ronald Reagan, sworn in January 1981, adopted a policy of 'constructive engagement' (which we called *destructive* engagement). The Reagan Administration (January 1981–January 1989) embraced the apartheid South African policy and, effectively, publicly supported the South African minority white government's suppression of the nationalist movements, which the Reagan Administration considered to be 'communist inspired'. The Reagan Administration went to the extent of attempting to destroy Resolution 435 and replace it with decisions taken outside the UN framework to support South Africa's policy of dividing Namibia into ethnic groupings, under the DTA puppet Interim Turnhalle, controlled by the South African regime.

Security Council Resolution 435 was for us merely the mechanism for implementing Resolution 385. It had been brought about despite our distrust of the Western Contact Group, whose five countries — Canada, Great Britain, France, West Germany and USA — were the main trading partners with South Africa. They had weakened Resolution 385 — no longer was it accepted that the illegality of South Africa's occupation meant that South Africa must withdraw from Namibia. They attempted to defuse the condemnation against apartheid South Africa, and exercised their vetoes in the UN Security Council to prevent South Africa from being expelled from the UN because of its non-compliance with the UN resolutions on Namibia. The apartheid South African government that had oppressed us for so long and defied the United Nations by ignoring its resolutions would itself be part of the process of handing over Namibia to its rightful owners, the Namibians. It was for this reason that we had fought so long and hard both for a UN peacekeeping force, and to have PLAN combatants confined to bases inside Namibia, when the implementation of Resolution 435 was to take place.

Though the Western Contact Group countries were South Africa's trading partners, they had shown themselves capable of resisting South African pressure and conceding some of our essential demands. Resolution 432, for the early reintegration of Walvis Bay into Namibia, was another case in point. The Western Contact Group had learned for themselves that South Africa was not to be trusted. In Cyrus Vance's account of the negotiations, he states that he never knew, even after he had ceased to be Secretary of State, whether or not South Africa was negotiating in good faith.

The parties who negotiated Resolution 435 were: the Namibian people (represented by SWAPO); the UN (represented by the United Nations Council for Namibia on one hand and South Africa on the other); and the Western Contact Group as mediators. SWAPO, the Front Line States and Nigeria, backed up by the UN General Assembly member states, all insisted on the speedy implementation of UN Security Council Resolution 435. The UN view was reflected by the Front Line States with the added factor of the UN's own honour and credibility being at stake. South Africa's acceptance of Resolution 435 was never more than a pretence; Namibian independence to them meant rule by their own puppets and without SWAPO, in another form of bantustan.

The South African regime was determined to crush SWAPO and its military wing, PLAN, and to suppress the struggle of the Namibian people. However, as the history has shown, the united Namibian people under the leadership of SWAPO remained determined and dedicated to defeating the enemy militarily. Even though in numbers and materials, and logistically, South African were so much larger than we were, our soldiers were well-trained, courageous and resolute.

As more white South African soldiers died on the battle fronts, the apartheid regime went to the extent of recruiting foreign mercenaries from all over the world to fight for the continuation of its illegal occupation. However, the Namibian people had the motivation to fight for their country which the white South Africans and mercenaries lacked, since few were prepared to die in a foreign country to which they did not belong. PLAN was also the inspiration of SWAPO leaders and activists inside the country and of ordinary Namibians who rejoiced in their victories and were encouraged by every shot that was fired to keep up the struggle against racist South African rule. So the war went on, with even more fury than before.

P. W. Botha, who had been Vorster's Minister of Defence for a number of years before succeeding him as State President, let it be known that South Africa would retain its forces in Namibia "for as long as there is no visible and actual peace in the territory". His threat to increase their numbers was carried out, and a whole new military phase began with preparation for the recruitment of black Namibians into SWATF (South West Africa Territorial Force) and Koevoet (meaning 'crowbar') Units, who were brought in two years later. General Magnus Malan, who was the overall commander of the South Africa Defence (SAD) Force in Namibia, was the mastermind of the Koevoet units, which included 32 Battalion (originally known as Bushmen Battalion, Ezuwa and Etango). Their role was to deceive people by distributing Bibles and teaching in schools during the day, while at night conducting a reign of terror.

We had to contend also with a build-up of the puppet regime inside Namibia. In December 1978, bogus elections were held for the Constituent Assembly, the so-called 'Third Tier' of bantustan government. These elections were yet another humiliation for the Western Contact Group, whose Foreign Ministers had been told by P. W. Botha that, though he would go ahead with the elections against their will, he would still recognize the UN plan to hold "free and fair" UN-supervised and controlled elections in the future. The Constituent Assembly were given to understand that they were there to stay, and they did in fact become a National Assembly not very long after. All this despite UN Security Council Resolution 439 which declared these elections and the resulting Constituent Assembly "null and void". SWAPO refused to take part in the bogus elections, and also campaigned strongly at international level to ensure that no UN member states recognised P. W. Botha's puppet Constituent Assembly in Namibia.

UNTAG had nevertheless begun its work, under Martti Ahtisaari, early in 1979. I met his party, led by Brian Urquhart, the Deputy Secretary-General, in Luanda in February 1979. It was clear to me that they did not represent the UN members who had supported us in our struggle, but rather the element that wanted to settle the Namibian question once and for all, whatever the concessions to South Africa that might be necessary, against the interests of the Namibian people.

South Africa was still on its course of delaying implementation of Resolution 435 by raising objections, pretending sincerity on one hand, and putting obstacles in the way on the other. The size of the military component of UNTAG was the most serious of these obstacles and I knew that we would not be supported in our demand for a genuine peace-keeping force with a real military capability when the Western Contact Group, after their failure to stop the bogus December elections, announced that the size of the force would be agreed between the UN Special Representative Ahtisaari and the Administrator-General in the "light of the prevailing circumstances".

Ahtisaari was also to work out the modalities of the elections to be held under UN supervision and control, though the Western Contact Group continued to omit the words "and control" in their statements, and the date of the poll. South African repression, the reign of terror against the civilian population by Koevoet and the military conscription into the enemy army greatly increased the flow of our people into exile, and thus the numbers we had to first care for in our new reception centre at Viana outside Luanda, and then settle in the Health and Education Centre further south in Kwanza Sul, if they were not to go for military training or scholarships. Our weapons were constantly improving, with 122 mm rockets, SAM-7 ground-to-air missile launchers, and more vehicles to transport our fighters from our main base at Lubango into Cunene Province. And at the same time, our friends at the UN, and non-governmental organizations in many countries, mounted a major campaign for sanctions against South Africa, to compel P. W. Botha to accept the implementation of Resolution 435.

Waldheim announced 15 March 1979 as the date for the cease-fire, with "free and fair" elections to follow by 30 September of the same year. As the war entered its most serious phase yet, the South Africans defied sanctions by converting the 'Constituent' into the 'National' Assembly, and by committing further acts of repression against many SWAPO activists, churchmen and even businessmen who were thought to be secretly aiding our guerrilla forces in the war zone.

Gradually the Western Contact Group's move to implement Resolution 385 by means of 435, and so take the heat off South Africa, began to lose momentum. Though the British had not been helpful in the negotiations, the replacement of Prime Minister Callaghan by Prime Minister Margaret Thatcher in 1979 was bad news. Thatcher came into office denouncing economic sanctions against the Ian Smith regime in Zimbabwe. But when the Nigerian delegation at the Commonwealth

Summit in Lusaka announced the taking over the Shell oil Company in Nigeria, she quickly reversed her position, calling a meeting at the UK Foreign office in Lancaster House with the leaders of the national liberation movements of Zimbabwe and Ian Smith of the white minority regime. The election which resulted saw a sweeping victory for ZANU(PF) led by Prime Minister Robert Mugabe. The eclipse of Smith's puppet Bishop Abel Muzorewa seemed to foreshadow that of his colleague Dirk Mudge in Namibia, but there was yet to be a ten-year long struggle in Namibia before genuine elections under UN supervision and control by UNTAG could take place. However, far worse than the advent of Thatcher was the loss of the Presidential election by Jimmy Carter in November 1980 and the completely new atmosphere with the Reagan Administration due to take office in January 1981.

Destructive engagement

The Reagan team downgraded the Namibian issue, placing it in the hands of Dr. Chester Crocker, Assistant Secretary of State for African Affairs, an academician married to a white Rhodesian, whose view we already knew to be hostile to SWAPO. We also knew him to be prowhite South African, having described them as "proud Afrikaners". "Constructive engagement" was championed and pursued by Crocker and became the cornerstone of the Reagan Administration policy towards South Africa when this was made known in March 1981. To the astonishment of everyone the Reagan Administration offered military training to white South Africans in techniques of counter-insurgency and intelligence. I was shown a copy of the influential American journal *Foreign Affairs* in which Crocker wrote, late in 1989, an article setting out his views on what American policy in southern Africa should be.

He addressed those "in the international community who might be tempted to follow the disastrous Namibian precedent of turning the United Nations into a propaganda agent for their favourite nationalist group before the Namibians themselves have even voted". The article also made the case for "constructive engagement". At the time we saw that Crocker's views were hostile both to SWAPO and the UN, and so doubtless did the South Africans, who continued their delaying tactics and double-talk on implementation of the Resolution 435 until the new US pro-South African policy became fully and officially known.

The true nature of the new US position was certainly made clear by Crocker when he wrote:

"The real choice we will face in Southern Africa in the 1980s concerns our readiness to compete with our global adversary in the politics of a changing region whose future depends on those who participate in changing it".

Before this, the USA's policy had always been moderate, even friendly towards us, despite US economic involvement with white South Africa — from the days of Mennen Williams, Crocker's predecessor under President Kennedy, whose phrase "Africa for the Africans" so shocked the colonialists in 1959, to Cyrus Vance, a decent, fair man, and Andrew Young, whose background was in the black liberation movement in Atlanta, Georgia. Now came the greatest single change in the forces committed to democracy in Southern Africa, and above all in Namibia. The new Reagan policy, as championed by Chester Crocker, had drawn the Namibian struggle for liberation and independence into East-West Cold War ideological conflicts. Crocker wrote:

"Constructive engagement in the region as a whole is the only basis for Western credibility in Salisbury and Maputo. Our credibility in Moscow and Havana depends on adopting a strong line against the principle of introducing external combat forces into the region ... there can be no presumed Communist right to exploit and militarize external tensions, particularly in this region where important Western economic resources and strategic interests are exposed."

Cuban internationalist forces had been in Angola since 1975 at the invitation of the legitimate government of MPLA, led by President Antonio Augustinho Neto, because of the South African military invasion of Angola in 1975/6. The Reagan Administration now saw Cuba as "exploiting and militarizing regional tensions" in Angola and putting "Western economic resources and strategic interests" at risk. The nearest of such resources and interests were in Namibia. It would be only a matter of time before the withdrawal of the Cubans would be demanded, since Western interests would be thought safest in the white South African hands. The apartheid South African regime's proposed "demilitarized zone" thus had a clear purpose, to stop our guerrilla reinforcements from entering Namibia from Angola.

When Deputy Secretary-General Urquhart left in October 1980 to report to Secretary-General Waldheim in New York, he had to deal with a new South African complaint, namely that the UN would not act impartially but would favour SWAPO in the implementation process.

It seems that, after a farewell barbecue, Urquhart suggested "a meeting of all parties to prepare for implementation". President Botha subsequently agreed to this, and even to an independence date of 1 March 1981. Urquhart wrote in his memoirs:

> "I have no means of knowing whether in October 1980 the South African government had any real intention of going ahead with a Namibian settlement. Certainly everyone else had, and it was generally held that we had pushed the matter further forward than ever before. On 4 November however, with Ronald Reagan's victory over Jimmy Carter, the pressure went out of the enterprise."

Geneva Conference, January 1981

The UN Secretary General Kurt Waldheim initiated the so-called 'confidence building' or 'pre-implentation' meeting in Geneva in early January 1981. SWAPO agreed to participate in this meeting, despite the fact that the puppet parties would be present, as it had the blessing of the Secretary-General, who attended the opening session. The puppet parties were represented by 29 delegates, who sat together, with Dirk Mudge their main spokesman; Danie Hough, the Administrator-General in their midst; Brand Fourie, the Permanent Secretary for Foreign Affairs; Van Zyl; P. Nienhaus (formerly Minister of Community Development under Vorster); and other officials hovering about behind them, altogether making a very clear picture of puppets and puppet masters.

During the bilateral talks in Geneva with the American delegations and South Africans over a dinner, the Americans were believed to have told the white South African officials to be extra vigilant with the Namibian nationalist movement, that one day they would be overthrown by them and America would not send troops to rescue them. Nienhaus, after hearing this, collapsed at the table and was rushed to hospital. When he later returned to South Africa he retired from active politics.

It was clear to all that these representatives of many small splinter parties had no real mandate from the people and were simply there to speak for the white apartheid South African policy. I instructed that our delegation — dressed in their best suits and contrasting smartly with the unimpressive looking puppet delegation — would rise in unison when introduced by the Chairman, Brian Urquhart, and give the clenched-fist "Africa!" salute, to demonstrate our unity.

We acted throughout in a disciplined and well-organized manner, but the blocking tactics of Mudge and his colleagues made all progress impossible. While we patiently put the case for a realistic cease-fire date, the puppets kept up a ceaseless barrage of unspecific accusations against UN impartiality. I hit back with a press statement:

"The concern of the international community and of those who have helped in drawing up the UN plan for Namibian independence was to ensure that South Africa does not use its administrative machinery, police force and various other armed security agencies to intimidate the Namibian people and therefore prevent them from exercising their democratic rights in electing leaders of their choice. It is absurd that the colonial power, which in actual fact is responsible for organizing the elections, should be the one to demand 'impartiality' from the United Nations. It is rather that the UN and the international community should require assurances from South Africa."

(Above and facing page) SWAPO delegation at the United Nations "confidence building" session, opened by Secretary General Kurt Waldheim. Geneva, 7 January, 1981

Urquhart described us as a "model of civility and common sense", in contrast with "the deplorable exhibition put on by the representatives of the internal parties". It was clear to everyone that South Africa wanted the conference to fail, so that they could stay in power and prepare themselves over a long period, in a changed climate with Reagan in power in the US, to fight an election against SWAPO, if it were ever to come to that. The London Times called the Geneva Conference

"...an unmitigated disaster for the Western powers, who have invested immense diplomatic effort ... their credibility is in tatters and they are now confronted with renewed calls at the UN for sanctions — which was just what the settlement was designed to prevent".

With the knowledge that the UN plan had come to a full stop and that under Reagan, due to take office a week after the conference ended, the US might well lead the Contact Group in a very different direction from

47 Above (L to R, seated at table): Axel Johannes; Peter Nanyemba; Kapuka Nauyala (in white suit); Netumbo Nandi-Ndaitwah; Nahas Angula; Shapua Kaukungua

46 Left facing page (L to R, seated at table): Richard Kabadjani-Kapelua; Theo-Ben Gurirab, permanent Observer to the UN; Sam Nujoma, President of SWAPO; Hidipo Hamutenya. (Seated second row): Hadino Hishongua; Usko Nambinga

that taken by President Carter's team, I told the delegates at a working session that "South Africa's manifest interference and prevarications" meant that:

> "Like all the previous efforts of the international community to find a peaceful solution to the Namibian problem, the conference had failed in this noble objective.
>
> Consequently the oppressed people of Namibia are left with no other alternative but to continue with the armed liberation struggle until the final victory. The responsibility for the continued loss of lives and suffering lies with the Pretoria regime. We are certain of one thing: SWAPO enjoys the overwhelming support of the oppressed people of Namibia, whose yearning for freedom will continue to inspire the combatants of the People's Liberation Army of Namibia (PLAN) to persevere in the armed liberation struggle until the final victory."

Apartheid regime vs one man, his family and friends

My own situation continued to be one of constant travel and diplomatic campaign among our friends in the OAU and a growing number of nations round the world who recognized SWAPO as the sole representatives of the Namibian people and heeded the call I made at the January 1981 Geneva Conference "to render all-round support and assistance to the Namibian patriots who are resisting the illegal occupation and colonial oppression by the white minority South African regime in Namibia".

My other immediate and major diplomatic task was to achieve the imposition of "comprehensive and mandatory sanctions including an oil embargo ... to compel the Pretoria regime to relinquish its illegal occupation and oppression of the Namibian people".

This period had seen my dear wife's escape from Namibia through Botswana in December 1977, and our meeting again after a separation of 18 years, and the death of my father, Utoni Daniel Nujoma, in Okahao the following year, his health having never recovered from his long detention, when already ill, in Pretoria. There was a military camp near my parents' home and South African soldiers were stationed right next to our homestead in the belief that they would ambush me when I came home to mourn with my people at my father's funeral. My mother and others at home were much harassed by them, and by the puppet authorities.

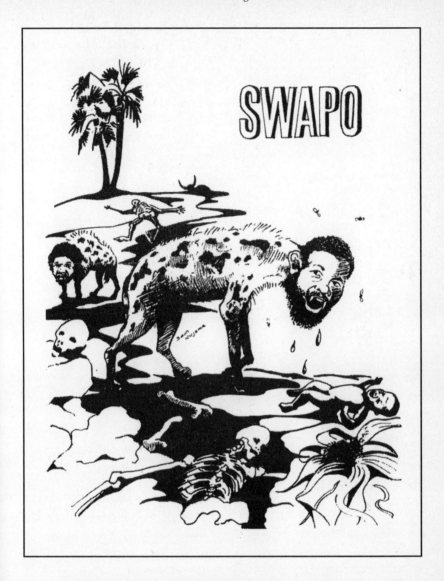

48   Typical anti-Nujoma propaganda leaflet distributed by South African military intelligence in Namibia during the 1980s

49 Anti-SWAPO, pro-Turnhalle propaganda cartoon, circulated by the apartheid regime in Namibia, mid 1980s.

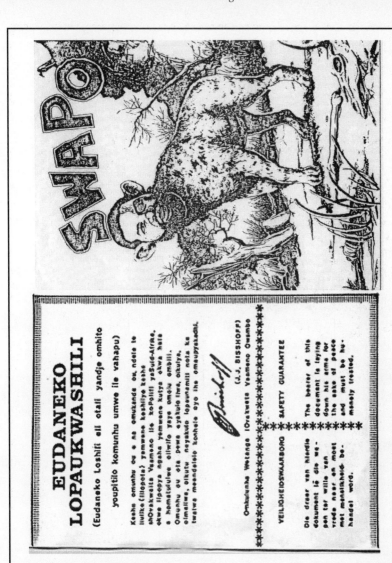

50 Propaganda leaflet (3) The item shown incorporates a so-called "safety guarantee" to lure Namibian freedom fighters to surrender their arms with a promise of immunity — "The bearer of this document is laying down his arms for the sake of peace and must be treated humanely".

The puppet authorities constantly searched for my brother Stephen Nujoma, a teacher, who had stayed to care for our parents at Etunda. Though ambushed several times and almost killed, he was clever enough to escape them, and went into a hiding in Kavango. When he came back to Etunda and found they were still looking for him, my brother travelled secretly to Windhoek, where we found him in hiding on our return from exile.

One of my cousins, the son of my mother's elder sister, Johannes Akaupa Kasino, was in fact killed. The South African army took his body, and my mother and the other women from the community followed it to Oshakati. She and the others sat down and cried until a Boer officer came out and asked: "Why are all these old ladies crying here?". He was told: "We have the body here of their son who was killed". So they were allowed to take the body home for burial. My mother was frequently terrorized and interrogated with questions about me, over many years. Such actions were part of the South African army and Koevoet practices of terrorizing the people in the war zone, and very many families suffered the same way.

The South African regime sent over many spies and tried to spread propaganda about my private life. They said that I lived in a big hotel with a swimming pool on the roof, and I was said to be surrounded by white women. At one time a spy was sent to Lusaka to take photos of me in the "hotel". When he arrived in Lusaka, I was living at Kamwala House No. 7, in the old African township of Lusaka, Zambia. He failed completely to get any picture of me at all because it was difficult for a white person to find his way about undetected in an African township, especially at night because there were no lights. The South African military intelligence did not stop at slander, but also included violent tactics in their personal campaign against me. They sent many parcel bombs and letters containing explosives, addressed to me personally and also to other SWAPO leaders. But we had special units who were specially trained in the detection of such materials, and parcel and letter bombs were always defused and destroyed before any harm was done.

A lot of the South African propaganda against me failed totally. Leaflets were even thrown from aircraft showing me as a monster, eating babies and urinating on a church. The people of this country are very Christian and such pictures were calculated to destroy SWAPO completely. But the people never believed this propaganda. The main aim for Vorster's regime was to discredit me as a person in the eyes of the Namibian people and eventually to destroy SWAPO's popularity.

My task as President of SWAPO was made easier by the fact that we had always been working as a team. Decisions were taken collectively and responsibilities were shared by the SWAPO Central Committee which met twice a year, the Political Bureau of the Central Committee which met four times a year or could be convened any time once the situation dictated, and the Military Council which met four times a year and sometimes more depending, again, on the situation.

"Constitutional Principles"

Though I had made clear in Geneva and in many speeches and statements our democratic principles and pragmatic view of future economic policy, the Western Contact Group found it necessary to bind us to a set of "Constitutional Principles" early in 1982.

Much was later made of the fact that the constitution could be adopted only by a two-thirds majority of a constituent assembly, but we had no objection to that. More serious was the proviso that set up a system designed to reduce SWAPO's power in favour of the white minority. Also in their favour were clauses that meant we could not dispense with the very large civil service — 47,000 strong — which the South Africans had built up to run the country on bantustan lines (nine separate administrations, each with its own overstaffed departments), and the 'Third Tier' central government around the National Assembly, controlled by the white administration.

We realized that perpetuating such a large bureaucracy would take up huge sums of money from our national budget that would better be put to combating the extreme poverty we have inherited from the apartheid colonial administration. But we would accept this burden in the interests of stopping a stampede of whites out of the country. This was the tactical policy adopted by SWAPO — that there would be no white exodus from Namibia to South Africa to reinforce white extremists and delay the progress of South Africa to achieving a non-racial and democratic government.

Although Reagan's policies were so harmful to our prospects of early independence, they did have the effect of increasing enormously the humanitarian support we received such as foodstuffs, medical equipment, clothing and other basic human needs from the Nordic countries, Holland, Belgium, the World Council of Churches, the Lutheran World Federation, the Namibia Support Committee, and anti-apartheid movements from Europe, America, Australia and Canada.

And most importantly the increase of military hardware for PLAN from the Soviet Union and other socialist countries.

After Geneva — the consequences of linkage

The months after the Geneva conference confirmed all our worst predictions of the Reagan Administration's South Africa policy with 'constructive engagement' as the framework. We had already seen it in place in the visit of South African generals for talks in Washington with Mrs. Jeanne Kirkpatrick, Andrew Young's successor at the UN; in a leaked report revealing the new relationship, with 'Pik' Botha demanding increased US support for South African policies; in the visit by Dirk Mudge and a DTA delegation to the UN; and in the announcement by President Reagan of so-called 'covert aid' to UNITA.

We worked hard with our friends all over the world to counter this new strengthening of South Africa's position. In April 1981 the Non-Aligned Summit in Algiers called for mandatory sanctions against South Africa. The resolution that was adopted was duly introduced at a meeting of the Security Council, specially requested by the African members of the Council in April, and only defeated by the triple-veto of the US, Britain and France. With Reagan and Thatcher in office, the Western members showed how wide the gap was growing by urging, although to no avail, that puppet Peter Kalangula of Ovamboland bantustan be invited to address the Security Council.

There were already signs that the Western Contact Group were beginning to move away from Resolution 435. At the end of June 1981, I expressed dismay to the Liberation Committee of the OAU at Arusha, in Tanzania, that the US, "one of the authors of the resolution and a permanent member of the Security Council, is now trying to sabotage Resolution 435".

The most serious cause for delay appeared in June 1981 during a high-level US mission to South Africa and Namibia led by Reagan's Under Deputy Secretary of State, William Clark, with Chester Crocker, Assistant Secretary of State for African Affairs. Clark made it clear that the US was not committed to UN Security Council Resolution 435, and also met the DTA puppet leaders in Windhoek. He later recognized their standing in the negotiations for the first time, and, most seriously, let it be known that the withdrawal of Cuban troops from Angola was now a quid pro quo (pre-condition) for the withdrawal from Namibia of the South African colonial administration.

By September 1981, the concept of 'linkage' of these two matters having become established US policy, Reagan sent a letter to the heads of the Front Line States requiring their agreement, and Crocker announced that Resolution 435 would have to be "supplemented by additional measures" and was also conditional upon 'linkage'. In November, Vice-President George Bush, at the start of a seven-nation African tour, released a major policy statement in Nairobi. Called "A New Partnership with Africa", it offered help to African nations to restructure their economies, as well as in security, peace-making and human rights advancement. But what affected us most was at the core of the statement:

> "My Government is not ashamed to state the US interest in seeing an end to the presence of Cuban forces in Angola. Their introduction seven years ago tore the fabric of reciprocal restraint between the US and the Soviet Union in the developing world".

South African troops would withdraw from Namibia only when the Cubans had gone.

The South Africans had already taken up 'linkage' and this became for the next seven years the greatest obstacle in the way of freedom and independence for Namibia. We had no option but to struggle on to remove that obstacle by mounting political pressure inside the country and by maintaining diplomatic contacts with the West, despite the reversal of policy brought about by the US Reagan Administration.

The response of the other members of the Western Contact Group varied. As it became clear that changing Resolution 435 was part of the Reagan policy of distancing the US from the United Nations, they found it difficult to fall in with Crocker's moves. The French were the most critical of linkage, followed by the Canadians.

The French Foreign Minister Claude Cheysson, spoke against it in Dar-es-Salaam in October 1982, saying "Everything is ready. One could simply push a button", but for the "stagnation" caused by the US and South African insistence that the Cubans vacate Angola as part of the Namibian settlement. The Western Contact Group, he said:

> "never accepted that there should be such a link and we will never accept it. We see no justification for any request being put to the Government of Angola. Of course, we know that the Americans do not feel that way. They have entered into a kind of negotiation with the apartheid South African regime but that is their business."

51 *(L to R) Chairman of PLO, Yasser Arafat; Prime Minister of India, Indira Gandhi; Deputy Chairperson, Upper House of Parliament of India, Dr. Najma Heptulla; President of SWAPO, Sam Nujoma. At Seventh Non-Aligned Summit, New Delhi, India, March 1983*

At the end of 1983, Monsieur Cheysson announced that France would suspend its participation in the Western Contact Group because of the Reagan Administration's insistence on the linkage of Resolution 435 to the withdrawal of Cuban internationalist forces from Angola. He said that the Western Contact Group should now be "dormant, in the absence of any ability to exercise honestly the mandate confided in it". Britain was equivocal, denying any commitment to linkage, yet agreeing with it as a general principle. SWAPO, despite an early distrust of the Western Contact Group and hostility towards us from the Reagan Administration, co-operated as best we could with the Western Contact Group up to this point, even in spite of 'linkage'.

Summit of the Non-Aligned Countries, March 1983

I attacked 'linkage' strongly at the Seventh Summit of the Non-Aligned Countries, chaired by my good friend, the late Mrs. Indira Gandhi at New Delhi in March 1983: "The issue of linkage," I said, "is a nefarious exercise of unbridled blackmail which has now come to characterize the whole process of the so-called 'constructive engagement', a policy

52 At the Seventh Non-Aligned Summit, (L to R) Prime Minister of India, Indira Gandhi; President of Cuba, Fidel Castro; Secretary-General of the Non-Aligned Movement Natvar Singh, paying respect to the National Anthem of India. New Delhi, India, 7 March 1983

whereby the Reagan Administration has publicly and unmistakably embraced apartheid South Africa as a friend and an ally". I went on to deplore "the attempts being made to undermine the United Nations' responsibility for Namibia", and urged the Summit to designate some of the Foreign Ministers of member states to participate in a meeting of the Security Council which they must request. This had effectively been done in 1981 after the Algiers Summit, when the Security Council had debated a sanctions motion which was defeated by a shameful triple veto by the US, France and Britain.

The call I made in New Delhi was repeated at a major solidarity conference held at UNESCO in Paris, and in May 1983 the Security Council duly met, as we had planned. This time the outcome was Security Council Resolution 532, which condemned South Africa's continued presence in Namibia. The US cast the only dissenting vote. Resolution

53 (L to R) SWAPO President Sam Nujoma and UN Secretary-General Javier Pérez de Cuéllar. Luanda, Angola, 26 August 1983

532 was a victory for SWAPO and the Namibian people, and we were further strengthened and encouraged by the commitment to our cause of the new Secretary-General, Javier Pérez de Cuéllar.

But 1983 brought setbacks, too. A very unfortunate one was the loss of Peter Nanyemba, who died after his car collided with a petrol tanker in Lubango. He had been our representative in Botswana in 1962 and Tanzania from 1963 until becoming Secretary for Defence in 1970. Comrade Peter Nanyemba served his Party and country with commitment and dedication. He left a widow and four young children.

An obituary for Comrade Peter Nanyemba, published in the *London Times* and written by Peter Katjavivi, read in part:

> "At first the People's Liberation Army of Namibia (PLAN) consisted of small groups of fighters equipped with light arms, who penetrated north-eastern Namibia through the Caprivi Strip. With time, however, and helped by Nanyemba ... PLAN grew in strength and experience. By the late 1970s groups of PLAN fighters were operating sophisticated weaponry from roving bases inside Namibia and reaching the capital Windhoek in their attacks on South African military installations."

54   Comrade Peter Nanyemba, SWAPO Secretary for Defence, 1970–1983

This intense phase of the war in Angola and northern Namibia coincided with a critical chapter in the international diplomatic campaign and will be recorded in the history of our national liberation struggle. More generally, we suffered from the increasingly Cold War-oriented policies of the US government under Reagan, with UK Prime Minister Thatcher in close support, and from a massive South African propaganda and blackmail attack against SWAPO both inside Namibia and worldwide.

On 1 January 1984, my New Year message to the Namibian people (which had become an annual tradition), dealt with this attack. It makes interesting reading today, as evidence of SWAPO's commitment to national reconciliation and democracy so many years before we were able to put it into practice:

> "Over the years the racist rulers of South Africa have been carrying out a propaganda campaign aimed at creating suspicion or frightening the Namibian people, especially the white community, not to join or support SWAPO.
>
> Our struggle has never been and will never be a struggle against an individual or against whites as a community. We cannot commit the crime of practising racial discrimination which we are opposed to and fighting bitterly against.
>
> Another hysterical propaganda is that we are 'communist robbers', who will rob the people of their property rights. On the contrary, SWAPO is fighting for the protection of each and every Namibian citizen and his or her property. We are fighting for the reinstatement of the rights of the majority in our country.
>
> Concerning foreign companies in Namibia, SWAPO will have no objection to such companies operating in Namibia but under a new agreement, or within the guidelines of the policy laid down by the new Namibian government, based on just mutual interests and co-operation.
>
> SWAPO has time and again said, and I repeat it here, that all law-abiding Namibians — whites, blacks, coloureds — will be entitled to equal social facilities and their human rights will be protected before the law. We want to create a new democratic society in which the freedom of the people will be guaranteed."

South Africa's aggression in Angola, its repression of our people, the destabilizing attacks on its neighbours and continued internal constitutional ploys — from Turnhalle to National Assembly and now Multi-Party Conference — to justify its presence in our country, made even its US ally lose patience. In October 1983, the Security Council passed Resolution 539, condemning South Africa yet again for its continuing presence in Namibia, and rejecting 'linkage'. The US did not this time exercise its veto, nor did it vote against the resolution. It merely abstained.

So we entered 1984, the centenary of the German colonial occupation of Namibia, aware of changing diplomatic and political climate, but knowing that nothing must deflect us from our determination to continue the armed liberation struggle until South Africa accepted the cease-fire we had so long offered. This would be the prelude to the final agreement for the implementation of the UN Security Council Resolution 435 and our return to play our part in a new, independent and democratic Namibia.

◆ ◆ ◆

22

At the Height of the War, 1980–1985

As early as 1978 the first missionaries of what was to be called the UN Transitional Assistance Group (UNTAG) were in the country and an atmosphere began to build up, especially in Windhoek and the main centres, that there was going to be a new dispensation, though not the genuine independence which was our goal. I emphasized repeatedly at press conferences in African capitals and elsewhere that we would not rely solely on the implementation of Resolution 435 to bring us our freedom, but on the struggle of our people, spearheaded by our guerrilla army, PLAN.

Heavy PLAN operations at the end of 1978 and in the early months of 1979 took place because we had to react to the 1978 Cassinga massacre, to ensure that our people would know that SWAPO and its military wing PLAN were stronger and more effective than ever before, especially after the Cassinga massacre. Our forces attacked Katima Mulilo in August 1978 with 122mm rockets, and we struck deeper into Ovamboland sector in repeated attacks in October 1979, against South African installations at Kongo and against so-called homeguards, which were armed units enforcing bantustan rule on behalf of puppet chiefs.

We created the eastern Front, covering eastern Caprivi and Kavango; the north-eastern Front of eastern Ovamboland; and the north-western Front of western Ovamboland and the Kaokoveld. All of these Fronts had their own sectors, deep inside the country, within which PLAN combatants operated effectively.

55 Closing of military session at PLAN Headquarters in Lubango, Angola. (L to R) PLAN Army Commander Dimo Hamaambo; SWAPO National Chairman David Meroro; President Sam Nujoma; Administrative Secretary Moses Garoeb; Secretary for Defence Peter Nanyemba. 1981

In the six months after the Cassinga massacre, PLAN combatants were militarily active on all the Fronts. It was part of our strategy, under Comrade Peter (Ndilimani) Nanyemba as Defence Secretary, to carry out military offensives on all these Fronts at the same time, to confuse and over-stretch the enemy's military power which would result in heavy enemy casualties and expenditure.

PLAN combatants scored many successes on the battlefields: these included the shooting down of South African air force planes, and the destruction of combat vehicles, among them Casspirs and wolf wares anti-mine combat vehicles. A number of armoured vehicles and a Casspir were actually captured by PLAN fighters, which was most spectacular. The South Africans admitted to three destroyed, captured and others damaged, which means, without doubt, that the real figure was much higher.

One example of these successes occurred in February 1978. Under Commanders Kakuwa Kembale and Immanuel Noshingulu, and armed with AK47 assault rifles, 122 Grand P and artillery, PLAN combatants launched a surprise attack against the South African Defence Force (SADF) base at Elundu. The enemy base was destroyed, but the

56   *South African soldier Johan van der Mescht, captured when SA base was overrun by PLAN combatants. February, 1978*

PLAN cadres suffered no casualties. When silence had fallen, PLAN combatants overran the base and captured numerous arms and other weapons. While they were searching the base, Commanders Danger Ashipala and Communication Officer Malakia Eilo (well-known as Kamati-ka-Eilo) captured Johan van der Mescht, a white soldier who was in a state of shock and confusion, it apparently being the first time he had experienced battle with PLAN combatants.

When captured, van der Mescht refused to talk and also refused to walk. It was necessary for the combatants to carry him in order to fulfil their task, which was to safely transport their prisoner to the PLAN Regional Headquarters at Haipeto. South African Airforce and infantry battalions were by now in pursuit, and so the PLAN combatants broke into two groups to distract the attention of the enemy. While those under Commanders Danger Ashipala and Kamati-ka-Eilo were moving the prisoner towards the Namibia-Angola border, the other group under Commander Haufiku engaged with the enemy. This fierce battle continued for an hour and a half, during which six PLAN combatants gave their lives. The enemy casualties, though, were far more numerous, with 75 dead and wounded during the battle.

When Commanders Ashipala and Kamati reached the Namibia-Angola border with the prisoner, they met with Deputy Commander of PLAN Jonas Haiduwa, and together proceeded to the Regional Headquarters at Haipeto where the prisoner received medical treatment for slight injuries. Their arrival was observed by senior PLAN Commanders Charles Philip Dixon Namholo, Martin Shalli and Shindjuusha Nangula, to mention but a few. Always, such successes further boosted the morale of the PLAN combatants, and served to undermine the military supremacy of the South African troops.

The South African army had no morale to fight and the loss of a single white soldier gave them problems at home, where the dead man's family and friends would ask why their son had died in Namibia, which was not their country. The outcry was even greater when white soldiers lost their lives in Angola. By way of justification, whites were told that the war was necessary to stop the Cubans and communism coming close to South Africa, and that it was necessary to destroy SWAPO to prevent communism — which would jeopardise western economic interests, western family values and bring anarchy into Namibia. In South Africa, due to the intensification of the war in Namibia, many white South Africans at the universities, especially at the University of Cape Town, boycotted and refused to be recruited into the South African Defence Force.

The scale of South Africa's military presence in Namibia certainly revealed the real nature of what the western press described as 'bush war'. How could anyone believe that the war of liberation waged by SWAPO was insignificant when the South African regime had built such enormous infantry and air bases? The air base at Grootfontein could simultaneously handle two aeroplanes, taking off and landing; Ondangua air base kept a permanent squadron of jet fighters, British-made Buccaneer jet bombers, French-made Mirage -1, 2 and 3, British Hawker fighters (the latest was the Cheetah jointly produced by South Africa and Israel and British Canberra), and French-made Allouettes and Super Felon Puma helicopters.

On the ground, the South African infantry was equipped with Casspirs, wolfwares and the latest "red-cat" G3, G5 and G6 artillery which the South African regime modernised from what was originally an American 155mm artillery rocket launcher. This the Americans had developed during the Vietnam war and it was believed to have the capacity of carrying nuclear warheads. The US 155mm artillery rocket launcher had been smuggled in from the island of Antigua via Spain

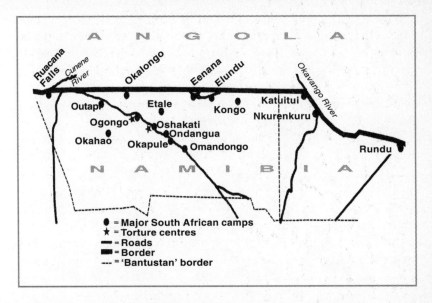

57   South Africa's military buildup in the north by the end of the 1970s

and then Israel, avoiding the UN arms embargo against South Africa. The 155mm G5 artillery system was claimed to be an entirely South African-developed system, and Pretoria had announced it as such. However, there had been earlier announcements made by Taiwan and Israel that they had developed their own 155mm artillery systems. The World Campaign Against Military and Nuclear Collaboration with South Africa disclosed that the three systems were in fact the same, and it had been developed by the Space Research Corporation based in Vermont, Canada. The system could launch missiles with a range of up to 40km, and provided the SADF with a formidable weapon in the war against Angola because of its long range. The weapons reached South Africa via New York and Antigua, where trade union leaders helped to expose the deal with South Africa. The G6, a mobile version of the G5, was developed to enable rapid retreat from the scene of attack. The supply of the G6 system was arranged soon after the South African–CIA invasion of Angola in 1975. When subsequent developments led to the withdrawal of the US from involvement, this resulted in the G6 being provided to South Africa.

58 Plan combatants together with Cuban military advisers in the bush close to the Angola-Namibia border, 17 August 1982

59 Wreckage of South African aircraft brought down by PLAN anti-aircraft guns, in southern Angola, 1982

Aided by such long-range weapons, the South African 32 Battalion tried to create a 'buffer zone' to stop our units from crossing from southern Angola to reinforce those already in the war zone. We were able to hit back, and in June 1980 they admitted to having lost 90 men in action against PLAN and FAPLA forces. They already had five so-called 'ethnic units' in the field — black soldiers under the command of a white officer — whose losses they could conceal. But for the most part, the morale and fighting power of their forces was lower, and we dealt with them quite easily when we ambushed them, destroyed their armed cars with anti-tank land mines, and attacked their military camps.

As far back as 1972 we had encountered black South African troops in the Caprivi Strip. On one occasion we wiped out a platoon by surrounding their military camp and then drawing them out by laying false tracks to deceive them. These troops had as little stomach for the fight as the young white National Servicemen who were brought in later and were not trained to face PLAN fire-power. This battle was commanded by Peter Tshirumbu Theeshama who opened fire on the enemy with a DP heavy machine gun (*Omuandi gua Shikoko*). PLAN fighters then captured the enemy's FN rifles and radio communications equipment after having over-run their military observation post.

From there the Boers did not trust these black South Africans to fight the war for them and so started recruiting the locals. The first ones they used as informers, because they knew the language and could go among the people and ask them for information. Sometimes they pretended to be PLAN freedom fighters, but that did not work because their attitude towards the people was not the same as ours. These imposters would go to the local people and say, "We are freedom fighters; you must prepare food for us, we are hungry". But genuine PLAN fighters would come and talk to the people, who would then voluntarily bring them food. The local population knew also that if they fed those false guerrillas, they would reveal themselves as supporters of the armed liberation struggle, and white troops would come and beat them up or they would be subjected to retribution by the Koevoet, SADF or South West Africa Territorial Force (SWATF), as for example happened at Oshikuku, an event which I will recount later. So they always took care to recognise the enemy false guerrillas apart from the real PLAN combatants.

Special units like SWATF, 32 Battalion, and later 101 and 102 Battalions, and the most brutal, Koevoet, were trained as killer units and had loyalty only to their white officers. For instance, these killer units would murder civilians in villages and cut off their heads. These would be presented to their white officers as the heads of PLAN fighters for a reward of "kopgeld" — literally, head money. This was how the South African General Magnus Malan had encouraged blacks to kill blacks.

Our victories against the enemy patrols, bases and their puppet home-guards scared off white farmers from the lands they intended to occupy in the Mangetti triangle and sent shock waves among the white population and soldiers in particular. The encouragement of the Reagan administration with its policy of "constructive engagement" made P. W. Botha's regime believe that they had the support of major Western powers, and thus they launched a second invasion into Angola.

South Africa crosses through Namibia into Angola

General Geldenhuys, then their Military Intelligence Chief, Foreign Minister Botha and even the UNITA leader Jonas Savimbi had been received at the White House by the time the South Africans crossed again into Angola. Dirk Mudge had led a DTA delegation to Washington, whereas we were feeling the effects of State Department enmity. In August 1982 the South Africans covered almost as much territory as they had done in 1975. FAPLA (Angolan Army) was now a better trained, armed and led force than it had been before, and the South African columns met with much resistance. Nevertheless they were able to occupy the whole of Cunene province of Angola, entering from the far northwest of Namibia. In defiance of world outrage, but with the connivance of the US Reagan administration, they stayed there for two years or more.

A Security Council resolution condemning their presence in Angola was in fact vetoed by the US in 1982. Britain abstained, on the grounds that the draft resolution described the South Africans as "racist"!

P. W. Botha and his military chiefs still believed they could destroy PLAN and SWAPO. Backed up and supported by the people, PLAN kept up the struggle in such a way that, wherever they operated, the South Africans could never claim to have defeated us, to have stopped our attacks and prevented our guerrillas from attacking them on all fronts.

A *New York Times* correspondent, Joseph Lelyveld, wrote in August 1982 that we had no need to be "a match for the South African military machine" in the type of war that was being fought. "In the kind of anti-colonial struggle they have been waging", he wrote, "survival and victory are virtually synonymous. And SWAPO has survived".

Not only did we survive but, in spite of the South African occupation of southern Angola, their huge military expenditure, aircraft, tanks, bases and manpower — which at peak exceeded 100,000 men under arms in Namibia — we grew in strength as the years passed. In fact, as time went on, in spite of our losses, our lack of field hospitals and medical supplies, and the cruelty of many of the South Africans who captured our men and treated them harshly in the extreme, we got stronger. They in due course fell behind our FAPLA and Cuban allies in the technology that had given them essential air dominance in the earlier years. Our strength was fundamentally in our soldiers' belief in our cause for freedom and independence. This made our soldiers courageous, enduring and resourceful. They would fight to the last bullet or to the last man. They would cover enormous distances on foot and at speed — for which they were trained. They never gave up in pursuit of the enemy, and one would always find them disciplined and with high morale. The high morale and fighting spirit among PLAN combatants was apparent from their freedom songs, and other revolutionary songs known as *"Omayimbilo go mokahonde"* (literally meaning songs that PLAN fighters sing having engaged with the enemy and caused enemy blood to flow).

Furthermore, we never lacked new recruits, though for most young people, to join PLAN meant a long and dangerous journey, much of it on foot, through southern Angola, first to go through tough training. Even after the final cease-fire on 1 April 1989, young people were still crossing the border and travelling as far as Lubango to join PLAN.

The years that followed have been much written about. One book stated that "1983 to 1987 were dark, frustrating years, yet the combined might of the strongest military powers of two continents failed to break the will of the Namibian and Angolan people" [Denis Herbstein and John Evenson, *The Devils are Amongst Us: The War for Namibia*: London, 1989]. We suffered severe blows during the long years of the struggle — the 'mockery of justice' at the World Court in 1966, the 1976 Shatotwa (Zambia) raid and the 1978 Cassinga massacre, the so-called 'pre-implementation' talks in Geneva in 1981, and others — but we were always ready with alternatives. The armed liberation struggle was inevitable after The Hague fiasco in 1966, and we had already planned for that eventuality.

Similarly, when the Geneva Conference was wrecked by the South Africans, we knew that we must now intensify the armed liberation struggle and we did so. At Geneva, Dirk Mudge said: "SWAPO will be defeated militarily!", and we knew that they had already worked out

60   PLAN combatants fire anti-tank gun at the shooting range in Lubango, Angola, 1982

with General Geldenhuys a plan to launch an attack in southern Angola so as to occupy it and prevent the SWAPO fighters from reaching Namibia. But we had already worked out our own contingency plans, so that when they tried to convince the Angolan government to prevent SWAPO from operating any more south of the Angolan 16th parallel, we had our routes prepared and could continue to inflict heavy casualties on the enemy occupation forces inside Namibia. This was one of our greatest achievements — to keep the war going, sending in fresh forces on missions deep inside Namibia when the 16th parallel was, in theory, a barrier.

South Africa combined their air force, infantry, artillery, and even cavalry and motorcycles against PLAN combatants. We mowed down the troopers and captured their horses and machine guns. The air force could not see our scattered groups of guerrillas, but we could always see their land forces and shoot them down before they knew they had been observed. Many South African soldiers became terribly frightened and as a result they started to recruit more blacks. We would find units of 100 men with only two Boers among them. In their Casspir combat vehicles there would be one Boer manning the radio, and one driver, who might himself be black. The single Boer's job was to see that the blacks did not run away.

We saw lots of signs showing how scared they were. The houses they built round Ondangua, Grootfontein, Oshivelo, Rundu, Kongo, Ruacana, Karibibi, Keetmanshoop, Katima Mulilo, Opuwo and Oshakati — to mention but a few — were fortified with bunkers and air raid shelters. The headquarters of Brigadier Hans Dreyer ("Sterk Hans"), who set up and commanded Koevoet, had an extra large fortified bunker in Oshakati (presently, a Government Guest House). The South African army was further strengthened by their naval base at Walvis Bay which was strategically placed for communication purposes, monitoring the whole southern African Atlantic coastal region.

Having occupied Cunene province in southern Angola, the South African regime now insisted on a new pre-condition to Resolution 435: that this area should be cut off by a demilitarized zone (DMZ) south of the 16th parallel so that SWAPO combatants would be unable to reach the Namibian border from inside Angola. Their aim as always, and as Dirk Mudge had boasted in Geneva, was to stop PLAN fighters from entering Namibia.

While negotiations proceeded over the DMZ and other preconditions introduced by the South African regime with the Reagan Administration's active support, SWAPO intensified the armed liberation struggle. As I have mentioned, PLAN captured South African weapons in large quantities, among them Casspirs. These were made in West Germany and showed details of the date of export to South Africa. We condemned the West Germans: "While we are negotiating you are supplying weapons to the South African racist regime, to suppress our rights to self-determination and independence. It is our right to fight for our freedom and independence". This was a serious embarrassment to the West Germans, as it was to the South Africans, that they allowed these and other sophisticated weapons to fall into what they considered terrorist hands.

The South African occupation of Cunene province enabled them to build up UNITA together with SWATF and Koevoet elements, which were very weak militarily. They supplied military materials and arms to UNITA at Jamba which they established as Jonas Savimbi's headquarters in Cuando Cubango province, near the Caprivi Strip, on the Angolan side of Cuando River. The South African army trained Savimbi's elements there as well as inside Namibia. Savimbi himself was flown to Cape Town for secret talks with the South African government in March 1982, followed by more secret talks in South Africa and in Namibia. He was also helped by a big public relations firm which convinced many Americans that UNITA was a major political and military force in Angola. The truth was that Savimbi never controlled a single town of any importance in Angola, and UNITA existed only as another so-called 'ethnic unit' under the South African Defence Force. Their role was to assist in intercepting PLAN combatants with the purpose of cutting them off from entering Namibia.

The South African propaganda continued to belittle SWAPO's successes. But this did not affect the morale of PLAN fighters, and our friends in the socialist countries continued to supply us with the firearms and war materials we needed. Our forces benefited also from specialist training given in the Soviet Union, and from Cuba's input of military advisers at our military academy in Lubango.

To keep the West Germans firmly on their side, the South Africans repeatedly claimed that East German military advisers and even combat troops were assisting PLAN. This was a lie. The German Democratic Republic (East Germany) did, of course, train some PLAN fighters in military intelligence and information gathering in East Germany, and indeed sent us doctors and teachers to work in SWAPO Health and Education Centres, but no East German military personnel of any kind were sent to PLAN's military academy or to the battle field. The GDR also played a major role in providing scholarships to our young children. Today there are hundreds of Namibian graduates from the former GDR universities, and other institutions of higher learning and technical colleges who are today contributing to the re-construction of the Namibian economy.

Massacre at Oshikuku, 10 March 1982

At the same time that Savimbi of UNITA and the South African government were engaging in secret talks, another murderous incident was perpetrated against innocent Namibian civilians by Koevoet elements in the north. During the struggle of liberation many other such dreadful incidents, though not related in this book, nevertheless took place. The story of Oshikuku is representative of those.

On 10 March 1982, a few hours after midnight, a Koevoet hit squad forcibly entered the homestead of Gisela Uupindi, in Oshipanda village in the Uukuambi district. Five armed Koevoet ejected the eleven residents of the homestead, and grilled them for information about

61   Men, women and children victims of Oshikuku massacre, northern Namibia

62   Preparation of a mass grave, March, 1982

Ms. Uupindi's son, Mr. Mateus Akumbe, who was an employee of the Consolidated Diamond Mines at Oranjemund, and who was not present in the homestead. The residents repeatedly denied knowledge of the whereabouts of Mr. Akumbe. They were then held by the Koevoet at gunpoint while the homestead was ransacked for money, clothing and other valuables. Finally, the victims, including two young children, were lined up and shot. The Koevoet killers left eleven people for dead, and then continued to fire rounds into the air and at a parked vehicle as they departed the area. Miraculously, one of the eleven, Mr. Yoliindje Nuuyoma, survived unwounded, and was able later to give his eye-witness account of the massacre.

Another one of the eleven, Ms. Penehafo Angula, sustained severe bullet wounds and fractured legs, but also lived. Those two were the only survivors.

Eight victims who were killed on the spot were Gisela Uupindi, aged 58; Bernadete Tobias, aged 30; Benedicts Tobias, aged 20; Abiatar Augustinas, 19; Johannes Silas, 10; Gisela Nepolo, 8; Celine Erasmus and Frans Herbert (ages not recorded).

A ninth victim, 8 year-old Erastus Nepolo, who had been shot in the stomach, was fatally wounded and died a few days later at St. Martin Roman Catholic Hospital, Oshikuku. Mrs. Ruth Emvula, a nurse who tended the dying child, related that he had been barely able to speak, but uttered the few words, "Oh! Omakakunya", an Owambo derogatory for the notorious Koevoet, SADF and SWATF colonial forces.

On the day, Mr. Nuuyoma and Mr. Akumbe reported the slaughter to police at the Oshakati police station. The police response was that no vehicles were available, and so no police were sent to investigate. Before sunset, the eight corpses were removed and transported by the members of the community to the Oshikuku hospital mortuary. They were buried in a mass grave in a cemetery close to the hospital. When the little boy Erastus Nepolo died a few days later, he was buried in another grave close to the mass grave of his relatives.

The residents of Oshipanda and neighbouring villages gathered to mourn the dead. Among them was Father Gerard Heimerikx, known as "Pata Kayishala ka Nangombe", of the Roman Catholic Church. Father Heimerikx, who originally came from Holland, condemned the brutal murder of the innocent civilians in the strongest possible terms. This eventually landed him in trouble with the racist South African authorities. Because of his condemnation of the atrocity, Father Heimerikx himself was placed on the Koevoet 'death list'. He was forced to flee the country, but while in exile he worked in SWAPO Health and Education Centres on many occasions, where he rendered spiritual services to the exiled Namibians.

As I have said, the terrible event described here was only one of many such that occurred during the armed liberation struggle. As in so many other cases, it was clear that Ms. Uupindi's household members were targeted and victimised because of their support of members of PLAN. In spite of such tragedies, the people steadfastly continued in their determination to support the PLAN freedom fighters, even as the dangers increased, particularly in areas near the Angola-Namibia borders during this intense phase of the struggle.

Lusaka Accord and Joint Monitoring Commission (JMC)

As 1983 ended, the South Africans at last agreed to withdraw from southern Angola — but it was more than a year before the last of their forces returned to Namibia. The so-called Lusaka Accord was brokered by the Americans, and the South Africans and Angolans set up a Joint Monitoring Commission (JMC) charged with patrolling the frontier to prevent PLAN fighters from crossing either side of the borders.

The cease-fire they had agreed was in force in the triangle contained by the Cunene and Cuando Cubango rivers and a 300-mile border strip. It was not observed by UNITA, against whom engagements were fought during this period. The major battle took place just before the Lusaka meeting, when FAPLA tanks inflicted heavy losses on the South Africans when they intercepted a South African attack planned against a PLAN base north of Cuvelai. The Cuban internationalist forces and Soviet military aid had also greatly strengthened FAPLA at this time, but the South Africans still had air superiority, which gave them a considerable advantage strategically.

For our part, the war in Namibia was not halted. The Lusaka Accord had followed cease-fire negotiations in which SWAPO had also been involved. I had tried hard to get the South Africans into direct talks with us over this, by offering a 30-day 'disengagement of forces' followed by face-to-face talks aimed at agreeing on a cease-fire. As usual, the apartheid South African regime refused to sit down with SWAPO, thus prolonging the war.

The Joint Monitoring Commission did not work. The Angolans were our allies, and the South Africans the enemies of both of us, with UNITA fighting against both of us under South African control. The South African regime even brought their latest puppet grouping, the Multi-Party Conference (MPC), and lined them up with its UNITA surrogate, which confused matters still further. We repeatedly tried to cut through this muddle of negotiating parties by seeking direct cease-fire talks with the South African Government. In May 1984 I had a telephone interview with the South African Press Association in Windhoek. I called on the South African Government to meet us for urgent peace talks. They made no response.

World outrage at the South African take-over of southern Angola had the effect of increasing both our diplomatic and military support. With new ground-to-air missiles we were able to bring down South African helicopters, and jet-fighters. In September 1983, we inflicted

63 Weapons used by PLAN combatants during the armed liberation struggle (above L), T-35 Soviet-made tank; (above R) Strella C-2m); (below) Indian Mahindra-Mahindra mounted with 106mm ATK anti-tank rocket launcher. Six PLAN members were trained to operate the 106mm recoil gun in India in 1986. They returned to the Angola operational area to train others, and the battery was first used in a major counter-offensive in 1987, south of Cubango–Cuando Province in Angola. The battery remained with Operational HQ until 1989 when the cease-fire agreement came into force.

heavy causalities on the South Africans, especially in the Kavango sector of the north-eastern Front. This operation was part of a major thrust into Namibia. Willem Steenkamp, a South African writer, has quoted one of their officers saying of this campaign that, "at one stage we thought we'd lost the war" (in *South Africa's Border War, 1966–89*: Gibraltar, 1989).

Our military operations increased and we brought men and women into all our war Fronts, even reactivating the eastern Front by bringing in cadres clandestinely over the Botswana border, at Rietfontein near Gobabis in October 1983. I made a solemn pledge in Lusaka on 7 March 1984 that SWAPO would "continue to intensify the war against South African occupation forces inside Namibia regardless of the disengagement of troops in southern Angola". This was the one course of action to which there was no alternative: either the Boers must meet us for peace talks or the war would continue with intensity.

We increased the pressure after the JMC came to an end in May 1985. There were a few South African troops guarding Caluegue Dam which used UNITA elements as informers to monitor PLAN combatants' movements, and they eventually followed their masters to Namibia. We still had to take extreme care in crossing Cunene province to the border. We had many vehicles which carried men, women and materials, and the South African aircraft searched for them. Our men and women travelled by night, without lights, and became very skilled at this. There were inevitably some accidents but they continued to bring supplies to the frontier.

Our great success in keeping up the war inside Namibia in the face of the much larger South African army, their technology and air cover, and the terror that units like Koevoet inflicted on the people, was due to the mobility of our fighters who could cover great distances rapidly on foot, and in their capacity to be unseen. Wherever they were in place for more than a day or two they dug trenches and slept in dug-outs where, should the enemy attack, bullets would not find them; and while travelling they would keep under cover of the natural terrain. We dealt with the South African planes with our anti-air defences. Our guerrillas would watch the South African planes, deliberately starting fires to bring them near. It was part of our strategy to cause them considerable problems on the border while our guerrillas were penetrating deep into the country, demoralizing their forces with surprise attacks.

By this time all the South African and Namibian economies were geared towards sustaining the war to destroy SWAPO. The thousands of lives of soldiers and civilians that were lost, the destruction of towns and villages and the devastation of the countryside of southern Angola, the repression of Namibian civilians, the billions of rand taken out of the South African and Namibian economies to pay for the war and mercenaries — all these were the cost of the Boers' determination to stop SWAPO from liberating Namibia. We had known from the start that we would have to fight to liberate ourselves. We remembered the words of Eric Louw aimed at Chief Hosea Kutako in the 1950s, which were, in effect: "We fought for this country. We conquered this country. If you want to take it from us you will have to take up arms". So, SWAPO nobly took up this challenge and intensified the armed liberation struggle to its logical conclusion.

As from the beginning of the struggle, we continued to be supported in this effort, materially and otherwise, by other countries. The military arms and ammunition we received from the Soviet Union (USSR) were modern and effective. Without them we could not have defeated the South African regime which was militarily supported by the Reagan administration and its NATO allies.

It was the General-Secretary of the Communist Party and President of the USSR Leonid Brezhnev who gave us anti-aircraft missiles. At the height of the war, Brezhnev sent us two shiploads of weaponry, vehicles, ammunition, mines, explosives, oil, lubricants, medical equipment, combat food stuffs, combat shoes and the famous T-35 World War II tanks. We were in a full-scale war, better prepared and equipped to the teeth, and PLAN fighters were able to inflict heavy casualties on the SADF, SWATF, Koevoet and its Southern Rhodesia Selous Scouts and UNITA surrogates.

Other socialist countries rendered SWAPO military assistance, of course, such as the People's Republic of China and the Democratic People's Republic of Korea. The German Democratic Republic supplied us with AK47 rifles as well as taking a large number of our war refugees, including children made orphans by the war or wounded during the massacre at Cassinga. We will recall with pride that East Germany sent an aeroplane to fly the Cassinga war victims back to their country for medical treatment. Children who were orphaned by war were enrolled in kindergartens and then primary and secondary schools.

Other support continued as well. The Republic of Cuba offered scholarships to thousands of Namibian children, of whom some were war orphans in SWAPO's care in Angola. The Cuban government flew a thousand children to Cuba where two secondary schools had been

64 President Nujoma meeting with Hu Yaobang, General Secretary of the Communist Party of China, attended by interpreters. Beijing, 16 March 1985

65 Being greeted by President Fidel Castro. Havana, Cuba, 1977

built for them on the Island of Youth. The secondary schools were named after our Namibian heroes Hendrik Witbooi and Hosea Kutako, and they also employed Namibian teachers. These two secondary schools alone cost the Cuban government the equivalent of millions of American dollars.

Political battles continue

We knew South Africa's refusal to meet SWAPO was politically based. They wanted peace but feared that they would lose authority with their own followers and with the DTA black puppets in Namibia, and their white supporters in South Africa itself. Because of this fear, they did not want to end the war as long as SWAPO was undefeated. The apartheid regime also refused to admit that there was military conflict going on at all, so there could not therefore be a cease-fire. If we were just a handful of terrorists, as they claimed SWAPO to be, why was it that photographs from a US satellite showed the war zone, both sides of the border, to be the most heavily militarized areas in the world, as the press reported?

The South African Nationalist Party and its inner ruling Broederbonder and extremists had to go along with their refusal to meet SWAPO and do all they could to build up the MPC puppets as a more credible alternative than their Turnhalle predecessors had been. They imposed a DTA puppet interim government in Namibia that they thought would lead it to the so-called independence without elections been held in the country.

Politically, the bantustan concept was built up with its infrastructure of capitals like Oshakati and Katima Mulilo, parliaments, bureaucracies, and the deceptive Turnhalle political machinery. The bantustans were created in attempt to deceive the people into believing they were governing themselves, and to persuade the Western countries that South Africa was in the process of creating a democratic structure in Namibia. Their idea was that the West would then persuade SWAPO to abandon the armed liberation struggle and participate in the Boers' deceitful elections exercise.

When the South African Defence Force invaded Angola and occupied Cunene province in 1981, the UN Security Council passed Resolution 532 (May 1983) which called upon South Africa to withdraw, and the US sent observers to monitor the South African withdrawal. They were again cheated by the usual South African propaganda that we were a few terrorists in Angola who crossed the border occasionally and quickly jumped back again and that we were in no way significant. The monitoring team went to Oshakati where two of them were killed by a bomb as they were filling up their car at a petrol station inside the South African Defence Force Military headquarters. If today you enter the State Department building in Washington you will see engraved on a column the names of Americans who met their deaths in the service throughout the world. They include these two, who died in Namibia in an honourable cause.

Nevertheless, this was held against us instead of the South African regime — as I discovered when, in 1988, I called on the Under Secretary, Sam Armacost, Chester Crocker's superior at the State Department, and asked why the US had stopped the UN's annual US$ 500,000 grant to the UN Institute for Namibia in Lusaka. I protested that this was humanitarian assistance, given to Namibians for the education they had been denied in their own country. He replied that they were under pressure from the US citizens who claimed that SWAPO had killed their fellow Americans in the Oshakati petrol filling station. I pointed out that those deaths had occurred in the middle of a major South African military base: it was the South Africans who were answerable for that incident.

Despite the fact that South Africa had agreed to the withdrawal of its troops from Angola, it continued to carry out economic sabotage against the People's Republic of Angola. Such sabotage was exposed by the capture of an officer and the killing of two NCOs in the Cabinda enclave beyond the far northern border of Angola. The South Africans first denied the report that, when intercepted, their men had been on a sabotage mission to the oil installations in Cabinda. But they had to eat their words when the captured South African officer, Captain du Toit, confessed everything on television, even stating that he and his men had carried UNITA leaflets to leave behind and thus give the impression that their sabotage mission was carried out by UNITA.

Katutura

The Americans continued to work for a settlement in South Africa's favour by trying to manoeuvre SWAPO into line with the puppets and by arming UNITA. Such aid had been forbidden by the Clark Amendment, passed during the Carter Administration. It was repealed in July 1985. All they got for their trouble was the Cabinda scandal, and the setting up of the so-called Interim Government in Windhoek on 16 July 1985. This 'Transitional Government of National Unity' was condemned by 4,000 Namibians at a rally in Katutura Stadium followed by a peaceful march into the streets, with 1,500 people chanting "Resolution 435 now!". Koevoet men attacked the crowd, in full view of observers. This incident showed up the rotten nature of South African rule through puppets backed by killer squads who were trained to brutalise our people.

The Koevoet attack on peaceful civilians coincided with the final day of the UN Security Council meeting which passed Resolution 566, the US and Britain abstaining.

I spoke very critically of these powers, whose "abstention means a polite 'no'". They had, I said,

> "sent a clear message to our people that human liberty and justice are meaningless when it comes to protecting the economic, strategic and ideological interests of these recalcitrant states."

The US had, in fact, already recalled its ambassador from South Africa in protest at the Cabinda incident and the repressive behaviour of the South African police repression in response to the protests and civil uprisings in the South African black townships that were going on at the time.

Our view of the war at this stage is well illustrated by the statement we circulated during the meeting of the Security Council in June 1985. The South African General George Meiring had boasted that "SWAPO are losing and we are winning ... We must put all our efforts into the last stretch". However, SWAPO's statement read:

> "After 19 years of futile efforts to stem the tide of the armed liberation struggle in Namibia, the South African army of occupation in Namibia has, contrary to Meiring's claim, lost hope of ever being able to win that war."

I referred to the drain of young white South Africans who were refusing to "serve in Namibia in a war which every sane person knows South Africa cannot win". I continued:

> "Furthermore George Meiring's admission that some 40,000 South African soldiers are deployed in the northern sector of the

war zone in Namibia is but an interesting sign that the South African army is being deployed on an over-stretched military line, when one takes into account the fact that a good proportion of that army is being deployed to deal with popular uprisings within the South African apartheid republic.

The 'success' perception of the South African Army is different from ours. When, for instance, Meiring talks of the possibility of the apartheid state to end the war in Namibia within the next two years, he is indulging in fantasy and thus perceiving victory from some kind of conventional warfare perspective, something which is certainly not available to the South African Army in Namibia.

We are prepared, as Meiring and others are bound to realize, for a long-drawn-out struggle. For SWAPO the struggle will go on as long as apartheid South Africa refuses to accept the demand of the Namibian people to determine their own future destiny through free, fair and democratic elections under the supervision and control of the United Nations.

The Namibian people want genuine independence and are prepared to fight and, if necessary, die for it. SWAPO is not only here to stay, but will continue also to organize, mobilize and indeed lead the Namibian people in their just and heroic struggle in order to ensure that sooner or later the price in blood and treasure for South Africa's occupation of our country will exceed not only the benefit of Pretoria but also Pretoria's willingness and ability to continue to pay. This is for us the main strategic objective and we will do everything in our power to realize it. The struggle continues! Victory is certain!"

PLAN activities on several fronts reached a new height from June to August 1985. Bridges were blown, telegraph pylons and power lines were brought down, the Eenhana military base badly damaged in a mortar attack and the Onguediva Training College, much used as a propaganda showpiece by the South Africans, was bombed. Our sabotage activities were widespread and mines were laid to do maximum damage to South African patrols. The South African military leaders began to panic when their intelligence brought them reports that we were in a position to strike with force in Tsumeb and Windhoek.

Perhaps in response to these reports, on 14 September 1985, on the pretext of following up a PLAN unit, South African 101 Battalion crossed the border into Angola.

This brought the war to the start of its final phase, which was to be fought out in Angola, involving the forces of MPLA, SWAPO and Cuban internationalist forces on one hand, South Africa and UNITA on the other, in the final showdown which brought the Namibian people the victory SWAPO had fought and died for through the past 23 years of the heroic armed liberation struggle.

◆ ◆ ◆

23

From Strength to Strength, 1985–1989

My New Year's message on 1 January 1984 spoke of the situation of repression, poverty and economic decline in Namibia, the obstacles raised in the way of freedom by the Interim Government and the extraneous "linkage" issue imposed by the Reagan Administration on the long-drawn-out process of righting the wrongs done to us through 100 years of colonial and foreign rule, and the subjugation of our people.

I was able to offset these serious ills with an account of our successes on the diplomatic and political fronts, such as the French rejection of linkage, the British and Canadian vote in favour of Resolution 539 which, *inter alia*, rejected linkage and the US abstention "instead of voting against the Resolution as was expected".

The Non-Aligned Summit in New Delhi and the UN General Assembly meeting in 1983 had led the world community in supporting our position and rejecting linkage. "In short," I said, "the overwhelming majority of the world community is with us demanding independence now!".

The military front had seen victories for PLAN:

"to such an extent that the enemy was forced to admit and even announce many of our actions ... admitting that 1983 was the most active and successful year of operations by PLAN combatants. South Africa was being forced to spend between 3 and 4 million US dollars per day in its war of aggression against the Namibian people."

I ended by proclaiming our willingness to negotiate with anyone "genuinely interested in the decolonization of our country" and challenging South Africa to agree in 1984 to free and fair elections, as set out in Resolution 435. "He or she will clearly see that SWAPO is incontestably the sole and authentic representative of the Namibian people".

I quote the above at length to show the strength of our position internationally and to underline our commitment to Resolution 435 and democratic elections. First, however, the war would have to end and I responded positively, on 5 January 1984, to President Dos Santos's letter of 31 December 1983 calling for consultations between SWAPO and South Africa, "to agree the exact date for a cease-fire." We, I said, had:

> "always been agreeable to the immediate signing of a cease-fire, as provided for in Resolution 435, which must be implemented forthwith without interference of extraneous and irrelevant issues such as linkage, parallelism or reciprocity."

South Africa would not meet us directly but did not want to be found guilty of wrecking seven years of negotiations by the Western Contact Group. We agreed to meet a South African delegation in Lusaka. It would, we also accepted, include representatives of the Multi-Party Conference (MPC). Instead, we found ourselves confronting a large group of representatives of the puppet parties, and some others who fully accepted 435, and sitting under the joint chairmanship of President Kaunda and the Administrator-General of Namibia, Dr. Willie Van Niekerk. The meeting was a typical example of South Africa's muddled policy, due to the stupidity and arrogance of its leaders at that time. P. W. Botha, I learned, had gone to some trouble to effect the meeting, even going secretly to Lusaka to arrange it with President Kaunda. We were given to understand that the South African delegation would have full powers and that any agreement reached would be honoured in Pretoria, even including the dropping of linkage. Instead of working towards this, most of the three days were wasted in the quarrels of the MPC delegates, some of whom — with church, trades union and student leaders — wanted to join our delegation. We conceded that they would sit with the MPC delegation, in the interest of making progress. The only SWANU official of any importance who had not come over to us, Moses Katjiuongua, repeated Mudge's performance at Geneva in 1981 by demanding that the UN cancel SWAPO's "sole and authentic representative" status. We had long before agreed that this would take place as soon as the cease-fire was in force and implementation of 435 under way. We could obviously not put ourselves on the same footing as the puppet parties earlier than that, in case they and their South African masters then backed away from Resolution 435, as they so often had done before.

The contrast between their side and ours was very marked. President Kaunda had provided a bar at the Mlungushi Hall where we met, and some of the puppets could not resist the gin-and-tonic and brandy provided, got drunk and were even seen lying on the floor. It was a shameful thing, and deeply embarrassing to Dirk Mudge. Some of the puppets were not sober during the whole meeting and we gathered that they were used to being given a lot of alcohol so that they would not be fully aware of what was being said and done in their names.

We had insisted, as a condition of our attending, that a large party of SWAPO members (led by the Acting President Nathaniel Maxuilili, who had been under house arrest in Walvis Bay for the past 16 years) as well as church, trade unions, student and other leaders, be brought from Namibia to Lusaka, and they were a great advantage of the meeting for us. I told them: "We are attending a serious conference to talk about the future of our country. Nobody should drink anything except soft drinks, tea or coffee". None of them, or of our delegation from exile, touched any liquor during the meeting.

I tried to push the conference to the conclusion the world was waiting for. In my main speech, on 11 May 1984, I appealed to Dr. Van Niekerk, whom I had welcomed warmly, shaking his hand when we met, to "go down in history as the man who, at last, contributed through fair and decisive leadership at this meeting to the independence of Namibia." This assumed that he had come with "full authority and a clear mandate" to do so. I said,

> "I now wish to inform the Administrator-General and, through him, his government that I have been fully mandated by the Central Committee of SWAPO to sign a cease-fire with South Africa at this meeting and to proceed with the overall implementation of Security Council Resolution 435 in order to bring about the independence of Namibia."

I concluded,

> "I therefore strongly propose that the delegation of South Africa and SWAPO gathered here resolve to ask the South African government to initiate, as a matter of the utmost urgency, the implementation of Resolution 435, starting with the cease-fire arrangements."

My words were, of course, wasted. South Africa had no such intentions and the puppets continued to play for time. Van Niekerk emphasized from the chair that the Cuban forces must leave Angola, and the DTA delegates and others shouted "Cuban troops out!". Apart from that, he tried to appear neutral. I requested President Kaunda to arrange private talks with Van Niekerk and I confronted him with the question: "Why are you here, and yet you are not seriously negotiating?". He replied, "But I have no power to do so: power lies with Pretoria. I am just here to accompany these people." The whole idea seems to have been to get SWAPO to talk to the MPC, whom we did not recognize, and who were afraid that we would take over from them (as we later did, after the implementation of Resolution 435), and not to the South African government, who had all the power.

Clumsiness and duplicity

We had benefited by meeting with our SWAPO comrades and other friends and allies from inside Namibia, and we had shown up yet again the hollowness of South Africa's claims that they were seeking a peaceful solution. We had nevertheless to continue with other tactics and actions against the South Africans, though never closing the door on fresh South African approaches. Two of these followed, which should be recorded to show the clumsiness and duplicity of Botha's government in trying to settle the question of Namibia's independence. These two attempts were aimed at both continuing South Africa's rule through puppets, in which category we were to be included, and at achieving this without the involvement of the United Nations.

In May 1984, President Kaunda, whose guest I was at State House in Lusaka, asked me if I would meet three South African generals who could speak for the South African government. When I showed interest, he said: "Well, they are here in State House at this moment, waiting to see you". So I went to meet them, accompanied by SWAPO's Secretary for Foreign Affairs, Theo-Ben Gurirab, and Hidipo Hamutenya, Kapuka Nauyala and other SWAPO senior officials. Their spokesman was General Van der Westhuizen, head of their military counter-intelligence (the other two were Van Tonder and Herman). Their purpose was to get us to return to Namibia and prepare to take part, with the puppets, in a new "government of national unity". I realized that they were simply asking us to surrender, lay down our arms and come back to act as yet another internal party, entirely at their mercy.

We spoke very politely and diplomatically with them but found them untrained in this field and rather crude in handling their case. Above all, we felt ourselves to be talking from a position of strength. We countered them with the request that their government agree to a cease-fire date and proceed with implementation of Resolution 435.

In July 1984, they tried yet again to forestall our taking power as a national liberation movement, backed by the world community, as had happened with the respective liberation movements in the former Portuguese colonies and in the British colony of Southern Rhodesia. But the Boers could not face this in their colony of "Suidwes Afrika". This time we went to meet them in the Cape Verde Islands, where I was greeted at the airport by the Foreign Minister of Cape Verde. He showed me a telegram he had received from Pretoria which said that the Administrator-General would talk with us on condition we agreed to lay down our arms and return to Namibia to take part in their idea of the "democratic process".

I ignored the telegram and awaited Dr. Van Niekerk, who duly arrived with his security men but no puppets. It was extremely hot and humid and, in contrast with the cool safari suits or shirts we were wearing, Van Niekerk arrived in a thick suit with what looked like a bullet-proof waistcoat. He was sweating profusely. When the Cape Verde Foreign Minister, after greeting us and wishing our negotiations well, left the room I immediately took the chair. We did not want a repetition of Lusaka where we had to endure South Africa's co-chairmanship with our host. I started: "Since you find us here, I welcome your delegation. Let us start by examining how these talks should proceed". After some general remarks, I began to read a statement but Van Niekerk interrupted me, saying, "I have come here to discuss, but, as the Cape Verde Foreign Minister has told you, only on condition that you lay down your arms and agree that your members will return to Namibia to participate in the democratic process".

I replied: "SWAPO certainly does not work on the basis of your instructions. If you have come here to negotiate seriously, let us sit down together and make a start". He became angry and said: "I didn't come here for that", and walked out.

The whole meeting had taken only about 10 minutes. It was plain that he was not serious, and his tactic had failed. Chester Crocker was dismayed when I told him later that the Boers had walked out because we would not share power with the DTA under South African control. Our position never shifted. We would come back only to democratic elections, supervised and controlled by the United Nations, with a peace-keeping force in place, all as clearly spelt out in Resolution 435.

The South Africans could not understand that we had responded to pressure by intensifying the armed liberation struggle and that we were militarily very strong at that point. They believed their own propaganda about destroying PLAN and winning the war. Above all, they could not stomach the arguments of people like General Geldenhuys who told P. W. Botha that the struggle was 80 per cent political and only 20 per cent military. We were confident that the political battle had already been won by SWAPO and that we would dominate when genuine elections took place, in which we were not at the mercy of the white South African regime. More than once we had been told of plans to get us back and lock us up — once when one of the Front Line States leaders was secretly asked by Vorster to hand us over to prevent a situation "too ghastly to contemplate"; and once in 1978 when our return to Windhoek was being discussed between UN officials and the South Africans, who let this slip.

Successes on the diplomatic front

In March 1984 the Botha regime made a very grave error in releasing the founder member of the Ovamboland People's Congress, Andimba Herman Toivo ya Toivo, who had been on Robben Island since 1968 and was a symbol world-wide of Namibian defiance of South Africa's illegal occupation of our country. Believing their own untrue stories that SWAPO was internally divided, they calculated that Comrade Ya Toivo would lead a split in SWAPO. Andreas Shipanga was sent to meet him in Windhoek gaol, to which he had been brought by the Boers, so that he could persuade Ya Toivo to join what we called "the circus", i.e. the Multi-Party Conference. Ya Toivo's reaction on seeing Shipanga before him as he was about to leave the gaol was simply to turn his back on him and walk away.

Within days he was on his way to join us. Having mistakenly released such a key figure, who was in the world limelight, the South Africans had to make the best of a bad job and allow him a 30-day permit to leave the country. With Comrades Witbooi, Tjongarero, Bessinger and Crispin Matongo, Andimba Toivo ya Toivo flew to Lusaka where he and I met for the first time. We had a long and intimate talk about the years when we had been building up what became SWAPO, recalling how our trains had passed each other near Tsumeb in December 1958, and going over all that had happened since.

66 (L to R) Hendrik Witbooi, Sam Nujoma and Toivo ya Toivo who had just been released after 18 years as a political prisoner on Robben Island in South Africa. Lusaka, April 1984

Ya Toivo's release, followed by that of many of his fellow SWAPO prisoners, looked like a climb-down by South Africa and was widely hailed as a victory for SWAPO and our allies world-wide. He was elected to the Secretary-Generalship, vacant since Jacob Kuhangua's resignation from SWAPO, years before, and travelled widely to meet our friends and allies in both East and West. In 1984 he led a delegation to a special UN conference to commemorate 100 years since German colonialism was imposed on Namibia, and was enthusiastically applauded at the concluding plenary. His liberty was correctly proclaimed a victory for SWAPO and the Namibian people.

I travelled a great deal too in 1984 and the next two years, keeping up the pressure internationally and meeting with many governments, attending a major world conference on Namibia in Paris, talks with Pope John Paul II in the Vatican, with the Italian government in Rome, and the General Assembly where the US permanent representative Jeanne Kirkpatrick continued to defend "constructive engagement" and the defunct Western Contact Group.

67   Meeting with Indian Premier Rajiv Gandhi during the 8th Non-Aligned Summit. Harare, Zimbabwe, August 1986

68   (Seated, front, L to R) President of Tanzania Julius Nyerere; President of Mozambique Samora Machel; President of Zimbabwe, Robert Mugabe. At a press conference held by President Nyerere during the Front Line States Summit meeting in Roan House. Lusaka, Zambia, March 9, 1985

In April 1985, I got to know the son of my good friend, the late Indira Gandhi, when Rajiv Gandhi, the new Indian Prime Minister, chaired an extraordinary meeting of the Co-ordinating Bureau of the Non-Aligned Movement in New Delhi. The meeting began on 19 April and was also the occasion to celebrate the 25th anniversary of the foundation of SWAPO.

Much had happened since that day when a few of us had adopted the first constitution of the Ovamboland People's Organization in 1959, which became SWAPO in April the following year. Our struggle and the support we had received from many countries and international organizations had forced South Africa to change too, at least in Namibia, albeit superficially. Apartheid and white "baasskap" were still unchanged in South Africa itself.

On 18 April 1985, on the eve of the New Delhi meeting, we heard the news that South Africa was to introduce an "Interim Government", in violation of so many UN resolutions and finally collapsing the efforts of US and the Western Contact Group of the past seven or eight years. Our support by the Non-Aligned Movement was as solid as ever, and Rajiv Gandhi's response to South Africa's move was to announce that the Government of India had decided to accord full diplomatic status to the South West Africa People's Organization representative in New Delhi. He called on other member states to do the same and, though we always steered clear of ideas of becoming a "government-in-exile", we were given full diplomatic recognition by many states in the years that followed. The puppet Interim Government in Windhoek was, of course, recognized by no other country but South Africa.

The Co-ordinating Bureau of the Non-Aligned Movement issued a special communiqué which recalled that this "manoeuvre by the racist regime of South Africa like any unilateral measure taken by the illegal occupation regime in Namibia is null and void".

I have visited almost every country in the world, while remaining always based in Africa, during our years of international campaigning: the Americas, the Far East, Middle East and Europe. From 1985 we had a SWAPO of Namibia Embassy in New-Delhi, India. I later made a state visit to India, when the then British opposition leader, Neil Kinnock, was also there with his wife. My wife and I invited them for tea to the Indian State House in New-Delhi and they expressed their pleasure at finding us there. He promised that the Labour Party would mobilize the British people to support SWAPO to liberate Namibia.

69 (Left and below) Flagraising and inauguration of the first SWAPO Embassy. New Delhi, India, 24 May 1986

On the same visit we went to Kashmir, the most beautiful part of the world I have ever seen. The Indian Government put an Executive Official Boeing 737 at our disposal and though we were a small delegation the whole Boeing was for our use. We flew over those magnificent mountains, the Himalayas, and saw Everest, the highest mountain in the world. But Kashmir itself, with wonderful greenness due to its high rainfall, was memorable.

We were very grateful to the late Rajiv Gandhi for providing such concrete recognition to SWAPO and our just cause. He did a lot for SWAPO where we needed it most — in the supply of arms. For instance, the Indian Government supplied SWAPO with 106mm artillery guns mounted on Mahindra-Mahindra Jeeps and transported to Angola, with other weapons which were highly effective against enemy tanks and other armoured vehicles.

We were recognized diplomatically by Cuba, Nicaragua, Peru, Iran, Yugoslavia and, before Gorbachev took over, by the USSR and most of the socialist countries. In addition, I was always given full VIP treatment in the African and Nordic countries and in France.

When the Non-Aligned members met again at the UN in June 1984 they worked hard, led by the African group and SWAPO, to get a sanctions resolution through the Security Council. In the end, Resolution 566 issued a very strong condemnation of the racist regime for its installation of a so-called Interim Government as "a direct affront to the Security Council and a clear defiance of its resolutions." Resolution 566 also declared the Interim Government null and void. Again linkage was rejected and South Africa was strongly warned that failure to implement Resolution 435 would mean the Security Council considering the invoking of Chapter VII of the Charter to ensure South Africa's compliance. The sanctions clause was watered down until it was a set of "voluntary measures" urged upon member states. It was that clause that the US gave as its reason for abstaining, not the rejection of linkage.

At the end of the debate I thanked member states for their support but attacked Pretoria's policies, because "their objective is to entrench apartheid ... to delay the independence of Namibia and to weaken the independent African states in the region in an effort to make them dependent on South Africa." I identified "the primary interest of the United States of America in collaboration with the Afrikaner regime" as "to perpetuate the status quo, namely the continued, unfettered plunder of natural resources by the transnational corporations and the enslavement of the African majority in South Africa and Namibia."

These hard words were directed at the US not only after the Cabinda outrage and the Interim Government move, but against a background of South Africa's destabilizing raids on its neighbours, and bloody repression of township uprisings in its own cities. The US policy of "constructive engagement" had done nothing to combat these evils and "linkage" had both prolonged Namibia's enslavement and greatly increased the number of Cuban troops needed to protect Angola from South African aggression.

P. W. Botha tried to promote the Interim Government but this regime managed to undo its own propaganda by their brutal behaviour. A typical example was the end of the legal actions in 1984 which achieved the release of over 100 civilian SWAPO exiles who had been "captured" at the Cassinga massacre on 4 May 1978 and flown to a prison camp at Kaiganachab near Mariental, where they were held without charge for six years. The South African Minister of Justice, Coetzee, had stopped the legal proceedings brought by the Namibian bishops, saying it was "not in the national interest", but the lawyers finally won their case.

Our churches paid dearly for their part in the struggle. Church ministers and deacons were detained and tortured, the Anglican seminary and school at St Mary's mission at Odibo were partly destroyed in June 1981 as was the ELOK printing press at Oniipa, as well as the headquarters in Windhoek of the Council of Churches in Namibia (CCN). A commentator at the time of the Odibo destruction said: "It is clear that whoever did the destruction ... belongs to the anti-church forces in our country who can only act ... under the cover of the night curfew". The General Secretary of the CCN spoke for the people when he said in October 1984: "The South Africans tell the world they are protecting the Namibian people from 'terrorists' — but in reality they are the ones who are causing a lot of deaths. They are the ones who are destroying the humanity of Namibia". The churches in Namibia also played an important role in gaining us the lasting support of the World Council of Churches in Geneva, as well as the Lutheran World Federation and other international church bodies.

In May 1984 a barbecue was held outside Windhoek to celebrate the release of the Cassinga prisoners. The Security Police arrived and arrested 35 SWAPO leaders and members. This happened while P. W. Botha was touring Europe, being received by the British Prime Minister Mrs. Thatcher, Chancellor Helmut Kohl of West Germany and others. He was trying to convince them that he was a man of peace and willing to set about reforming the apartheid system. But incidents like the barbecue raid and arrests spoke louder than his words.

70 (L to R) President of Zambia Dr. Kenneth Kaunda; Bishop Makulu, South Africa (Anglican Church); President of SWAPO Sam Nujoma; addressing the World Church Conference during a commemoration of the Cassinga massacre. Lusaka, Zambia, 4 May 1987

The South Africans imposed a very complicated constitution under the Interim Government — or Transitional Government of National Unity. This collapsed, but it was quite dangerous for us because they were aiming at the Transkei–Bophutatswana kind of bantustan government, which had gone through in South Africa because the South African government had stooges like Lucas Mangope (Bophutatswana), Lennox Sebe (Ciskei), Patrick Mphephu (Venda) and Kaizer Matanzima (Transkei) in those areas who would collaborate effectively. Such people would even go to Europe and be received by people like Prime Minister Thatcher and President Reagan who recognised their political status. Their supporters in Britain and other countries would attack us because we would not recognize the same sort of puppet regime in our own country. I had to deal, at a press conference in the House of Commons in London, with one of their chief spokesmen, Nicholas Winterton, a Conservative MP. When he asked a hostile question, I replied:

"It is a shameful thing that you, a British MP, should support the illegal occupation of our country by South Africa which supported Nazi Germany during the Second World War that bombed the very House of Commons where we are sitting now. Your constituents should disown you because you are on the payroll of our racist enemy!."

The journalists of the international press corps enjoyed this very much indeed.

There were other British Conservative Party MPs supporting the DTA, but the Namibia Support Committee and the Anti-Apartheid Movement were effective in neutralizing them and gaining support for us throughout Great Britain, despite Prime Minister Thatcher's hostility to SWAPO. It gave us much pleasure after leaving from Heathrow feeling we had been pushed out by Mrs. Thatcher, to then be met at Glasgow airport by the city's highest officials, given luncheon by the Lord Provost, put up in the best hotel and given a big reception at the City Hall, with the SWAPO flag flying over it in our honour. Glasgow and Edinburgh were among a number of cities that flew the SWAPO flag in recognition of our struggle for freedom and independence in Namibia.

Final consolidations on the international diplomatic front

Through 1986 and 1987 our international status became ever more firmly established, and South Africa's credibility was destroyed, even among the Western powers that had for so long tried to shield it in the interest of their investments, and in the case of the US, also because of the Reagan Administration's obsession with the Cold War.

Our second Brussels Conference, 5–7 May 1986, 15 years after the first, reflected not only SWAPO's right to be recognized as the unproclaimed government-in-exile but also the confidence that enabled us to bring so many people from Namibia, including some who were not there to represent SWAPO. This was to be seen in the presentation to King Baudouin of a magnificent wooden carving of a lion — Belgium's national symbol. The gift was handed over by Bishop Dumeni (ELOK), Bishop Ausiku (Roman Catholic) and Bishop Kauluma (Anglican), all of whom attended the conference. The Belgian Foreign Minister was at first reluctant to approve the presentation, but we heard of His Majesty's pleasure at receiving the lion carving. SWAPO kept in the background throughout.

In 1985 the UN General Assembly had called for a conference to address the question of removing the obstacles in the way of implementation of Resolution 435. The UN Council for Namibia organized the UN Conference for the Immediate Independence of Namibia. It was held in Vienna, 7–11 July 1986, presided over by the Tanzanian Foreign Minister, the Hon. John Malecela. Among the distinguished guests were the UN Secretary-General, Mr Javier Pérez de Cuéllar; the Presidents of the UN General Assembly and the UN Council for Namibia; the Austrian Foreign Minister; Mr Yasser Arafat, the PLO chairman; Archbishop Trevor Huddleston, President of the British Anti-Apartheid Movement; and Randolph Vigne, Head of the Namibia Support Committee in the UK.

We were at the climax of an intensive two-month European campaign — first Brussels, then a preparatory UN Seminar in Malta; then Oslo and London where the oil and arms embargoes were our objectives respectively. We were also encouraged by a meeting in Rome of AWEPA (the Association of West European Parliamentarian for Action against Apartheid). It was entitled "Namibia — breaking the stalemate, a Western responsibility". As I reminded the delegates in Vienna, the parliamentarians:

> "... unanimously agreed on the urgency of the intensification of the Western states' sanctions policies, both collectively and severally, as a further impetus for concerted action in terms of the non-implementation of Security Council Resolution 435 and to halt internal repression and state terrorism inside South Africa itself, and Pretoria's repeated acts of aggression and destabilization against the Front Line States in the region."

Sanctions indeed seemed to be coming near.

The last of the solidarity meetings before Vienna was the World Conference on Sanctions against racist South Africa, held 16–20 June 1986 in Paris, at which I also spoke on a brief visit. Other meetings were held, as well as rallies and demonstrations in Washington DC, New York, London, Stockholm and elsewhere.

In Vienna I tried to identify the impediments which the Reagan Administration and the Botha regime were putting in the way of the implementation of Resolution 435, and urged that we find "effective ways and means of removing them. This is the single task of this timely and crucial conference". I went on, "Let us move forward; let us turn away from this place, to act!". My final plea was for the cease-fire:

"In 1978 I expressed, to the UN Secretary General, SWAPO's readiness, which I have repeated several times, to sign a cease-fire with Pretoria as a final step to the implementation of Resolution 435. As we approach 1 August, which is offered as a possible date for implementing the UN Plan, I wish to state, once again, that SWAPO is ready, provided that no irrelevant or diversionary elements are introduced."

The Botha regime remained determined to 'destroy' SWAPO, and to deceive the world into believing that they had brought about democracy without SWAPO. Victory was an impossibility for them as we continued to inflict heavy casualties on their side and attacked their military bases, patrols and shot down their military aircraft, as well as causing disruption to electricity power supply, water and telecommunication networks. We had better weapons than before, and a larger force of highly trained men and women. South Africa had to pretend that they were winning, but their strict control of the media, which were supplied only with their communiqués, did not tell the true story of the war.

Morale was at its peak among our Namibian labour force and our students. Trade unionists made great strides, with the Mineworkers Union of Namibia being launched in 1986 as well as the Namibian Food and Allied Workers Union and others. To respond to intense world criticism of the lack of workers' rights in South Africa itself, tentative steps were taken towards allowing black unions the right to collective bargaining, and leaders of the workers in Namibia were quick to take advantage of this and build up new unions, under the umbrella of the National Union of Namibian Workers, which SWAPO had created and maintained close contact with those inside the country. There were mass student and school boycotts and the country was becoming ungovernable, while South Africa obstinately imposed its Interim Government despite its lack of a single black participant of any credibility at home or internationally.

Amidst all the civilian upsurge and state repression of those closing years of South African colonial rule, I will mention only the killing at a SWAPO rally in Katutura on 11 November 1986 of one of our first freedom fighters, who had joined SWAPO military wing in Omugulu-gOmbashe at the beginning, Immanuel Shifidi. He had been released after Ya Toivo, having served 18 years on Robben Island, and obtained employment with the Council of Churches in Namibia. He was at a peaceful pro-UN rally which was attacked by men of the 101 Battalion in civilian clothes, and was stabbed to death by one of them. A colonel, three white officers and a black sergeant by the name of Eusebius Kashindi 'Jack ja Jack' were brought to trial for having planned and carried out the attack, only to have the charge withdrawn on orders from P. W. Botha on the grounds that they had acted "in good faith while combating terrorism in an operational area". The Windhoek Supreme Court cancelled the intervention of Botha, who lodged an appeal. The accused were never brought to trial but the tragic incident made it clear that the South Africans could do as they pleased, despite the existence of a so-called Interim Government.

The more enlightened element in the white community knew by now where their future lay, and we did all we could to give them confidence in the independent Namibia that was soon to come. Gatherings in Lusaka and Sweden in 1986 and in Kabwe, Zambia in 1988 convinced many that a SWAPO government would not mean "the Red Flag flying over Windhoek" as many, from Vorster to US Secretary of State General Alexander Haig, had warned.

I particularly remember the occasion at Kabwe when we learned that Advocate Frank, a former Nationalist Party member of the white Parliament for the south of Namibia, was celebrating his birthday. We sang "Happy birthday to you" and he was noticeably moved. His wife is now a DTA member of the National Assembly and I have appointed his son, a judge, as a commissioner to investigate official corruption.

One particular white Namibian who came over to us in 1984 was advocate Anton Lubowski. I met him that year when he came to Paris, bringing a sculptured stone dove sent by community members in Lüderitz for presentation to the French Foreign Minister Claude Cheysson. The South African government had refused permission for the French Ambassador to collect the gift in Namibia. We wished to honour Monsieur Cheysson for opposing the Western Contact Group's acceptance of 'linkage', as did the Canadians, as I learned in advance from Prime Minister Trudeau. It was the French government, led by President François Mitterand under the Socialist Party, in coalition with the Communist Party of France, which suspended its participation from the Western Contact Group, later followed by the Canadian government of Prime Minister Trudeau. The French and Canadians realised that the Reagan administration wanted to use the Western Contact Group to impose a bantustan government that would be controlled by Botha's government.

Lubowski did a lot for SWAPO in the next four years and showed himself worthy of our trust. He was detained with other SWAPO leaders in Windhoek in 1987 and before that his car had been badly hit by another vehicle, which he then chased until he lost it at a police station. He was himself too trusting, and had not the experience of so many of us who had been through hell itself in the struggle. He was gunned down on 12 September 1989 by an assassin who was almost certainly acting on police orders. General Magnus Malan slandered this dead patriot in the South African parliament by alleging that he was working for South African army intelligence services, but that was a lie.

The South Africans spent a lot on hiring people to spread such stories, as was later revealed by defectors. We were being strongly criticized for the measures we had to take to catch the spies and agents outside the country. A party of the so-called Parents' Committee (led by Ms. Stella Boois and Mr. Philemon Festus Iipumbu, who for reasons known only to himself was disguised as "Mr Phil ja Nangolo"), unwittingly financed by one of the factions within the South African security system, came to Europe to protest against the detention of suspected infiltrators. As I arrived with members of parliament and our own security people to address the European Parliament in Strasbourg, I was confronted by a group shouting "Where are our children?". No sooner had we passed by the group than one of them issued a ready-prepared text, claiming that I had physically assaulted a woman protester. This was a complete fabrication, but was well organized and widely publicized, especially by the West German newspapers who financed the Committee, and despite my denial that I had struck this woman, nor any other in my entire life. Those women and "Phil ja Nangolo" returned to Namibia and continued to be used by the South African apartheid intelligence apparatus.

The "detainee" issue was the main weapon used against SWAPO in the Independence election in 1989. It is true that we detained individuals who had been detected to be South African agents, or for whom there were strong grounds for suspicion. Some of them had caused the deaths of many of our people in Shatotwa in the Western Province of Zambia in 1976 and at the Cassinga massacre in May 1978. The discovery of these sites was the work of spies the South Africans had sent to infiltrate SWAPO rank and file. They spent millions of rand in their undercover operations, part of the web of secret activities which led to the scandal called 'Muldergate'. People accused SWAPO of detaining these people unjustly, but we had to detain enemy spies.

71 *Photographic evidence, published in* The Namibian *in January 1987, of the parading of corpses by South African security forces in Ondobe, in the Oshikango region of northern Namibia. Such brutal killings, and display of the innocent dead, were committed by SADF as anti-SWAPO scare tactics*

We were at war against a powerful and cruel enemy. In many wars, such people would have been eliminated by their captors. If we are accused of ill-treating detainees, this was very little compared to the killing, cruel torture and brutal treatment the apartheid South African regime inflicted on our people over so many years — from major atrocities such as the Shatotwa and Cassinga massacres, to the murder of innocent individuals and the disappearance without trace of many SWAPO members — in an effort to further their anti-SWAPO propaganda campaigns. We know that some of the torturers are still serving in the Namibian police and army, but we have pledged ourselves to reconciliation. We prefer to leave that sad history behind us and concentrate on national reconciliation, economic reconstruction, nation-building and a better future for all Namibians.

Those in the opposition who bring up this matter think that they will gain some sympathy, but they forget that the people are not easily misled by their deceitful tactics and statements. The people knew that there were blacks who were agents of the South African apartheid regime, who were as aggressive as their white masters, beating, torturing and killing people. Others betrayed their comrades for money, as Leonard Phillemon Shuuya ('Castro') had done at the beginning of the struggle.

Diplomatic missions in Europe, Cuba and South America

SWAPO worked extremely hard to maintain our strong position politically through mass mobilisation inside the country, and through all its allies and associates in the labour movement, education sector, churches and other groups. The military sphere had become of paramount importance as we faced the unaltered hostility of the Reagan Administration, who continued to impede progress of the implementation of UN Security Council Resolution 435.

On the international diplomatic front, as I had done from the earliest days of my commitment to the struggle for Namibian independence, I travelled almost without pause, seeking at all times to encourage support for the cause where it was less than strong, and increase involvement where it already existed. As in earlier years, during the 1970s and 1980s I continued at times to travel *in cognito*, for example during a period from 1984 to 1989 when I sometimes travelled on a Tanzanian passport as "Mr. Sam Mwakangale". In the guise of "Mr. Mwakangale" I was a teacher born in Dodoma, and travelled to Angola, Botswana, India, Kenya, Kuwait, Sierre Leone, Zambia and Zimbabwe.

I also travelled on passports issued by the Republics of Algeria, Liberia and Sierra Leone. For example, from 1985 to 1987 under my own name but with a diplomatic passport issued by the Republic of Sierra Leone, I visited Angola, Argentina, Belgium, Brazil, China, Columbia, Congo (DRC), Cuba, Czechoslovakia, Denmark, East Germany, France, Gabon, Ghana, Hungary, India, Iran, Nicaragua, Nigeria, Panama, Peru, Senegal, Spain, Sweden, Switzerland, The Netherlands, Uruguay, Venezuela, West Germany, Zambia, Zimbabwe, and others.

In all these places I met with heads of government and other political and military leaders whose interest and influence could be focused to the benefit of SWAPO's purposes.

Before describing my part and SWAPO's in the final period of the war, I should recall, in particular, one of the major diplomatic journeys I undertook to keep the world-wide support as a solid as it had become.

In March 1987, I went with colleagues to Spain and had a very good meeting with Prime Minister Felipe Gonzalez. This was the springboard for a tour of Latin America from whose countries, through the Non-Aligned Movement, we had received so much support over the years. We flew to Brazil, first to Rio de Janeiro, and then travelled to the capital city Brasilia, where the President received us cordially.

72 Passport issued by Tanzania recording the travels of "Mr. Sam Mwakangale" during the mid-1980s

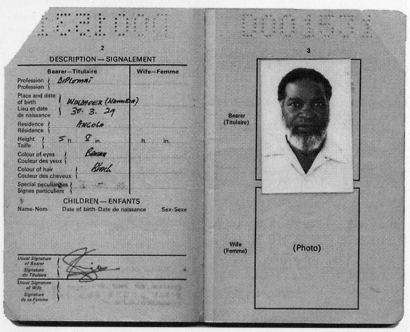

73 Diplomatic Passport issued by the Republic of Sierra Leone, recording the travels of Mr. Sam S. Nujoma in 1985, 1986 and 1987

Uruguay followed, and in Montivideo we were received by officials from the Ministry of Foreign Affairs. I thanked the Uruguayan Government for their votes at the UN, and I laid a wreath at the grave of the late Professor Febregat who had led the Committee on South West Africa at the UN in the early days when we were petitioning.

Our visit to Argentina followed but was for less than a day. We were given an official lunch and ate their delicious beef, which is like our own, as their grass and vegetation is similar to ours. We then went on to Colombia, which was a strange experience. The Foreign Minister came to the airport and invited us to stay over in the country, on condition we deposited a sum of money with them. We politely replied that we were not tourists.

We travelled next to Peru, a country which since 1985 had accorded SWAPO full diplomatic status, as Rajiv Gandhi had appealed for in that year. We were given an official reception, toured government ministries with the President, and were guests at a State banquet given in our honour in the evening. I was treated as a head of state throughout the two-day visit. Venezuela, our next stop, also gave us an official reception, in Caracas. The conservatives were in office but we met also the leader of the opposition, who later was elected President. Panama, where we spent only six hours, I remember mainly for the intense heat on the equator. We were officially received and taken to see the Panama Canal. One could almost feel the sun's rays burning into one's skin.

Our last visit on the mainland was to Nicaragua, where I was met at the airport by President Daniel Ortega, and driven with him in his jeep to the State House for talks. He too was fighting a war, against the Contras coming in from El Salvador with the backing of the US Reagan administration.

This was not, of course, my first visit to South America, where some countries, Guyana in particular, had long been very good friends of SWAPO. This 1987 tour was undertaken to show our appreciation of such support and to brief governments on the situation we now faced, as the struggle began to near its end.

It was now April 1987. Real business was done at our final visit to Havana, the capital city of the Republic of Cuba. Here our delegation was received heartily by President Fidel Castro, one of our closest allies, from whom SWAPO received political, diplomatic and military support. With Comrades Moses Garoeb and Peter Tsheehama (SWAPO Chief Representative based in Havana), I met with General Raúl Castro, the Minister of Defence of the Revolutionary Forces of the Republic of

74 (L to R) Division General Arnaldo Ochoa Sánchez; interpreter; Sam Nujoma, President of SWAPO; Jorge Risquet Valdès, Head of the Department of International Relations of the Central Committee of the Communist Party of Cuba; Army General Raúl Castro, Minister of Revolutionary Armed Forces of the Republic of Cuba and Second Secretary of the Communist Party of Cuba. Havana, Cuba, April 1987

Cuba. Without delay we went into a six-hour meeting chaired by Raúl Castro, the brother of Fidel. Together, we critically analysed the political, diplomatic and military situation. In particular, I informed General Raúl Castro that it was extremely urgent for the Cuban Government to reinforce its internationalist forces on the ground in Angola, and especially to provide them with effective air cover.

My case was simple: "You are there in Angola, but far from the action. You cannot come in and finish off the war while South Africa dominates the air space in the south. What is needed is that you should both greatly increase the war materials and the complement of men and women you already have there, and bring in your MiG 23s to take on the South African war planes. Once Botha is forced to fall back militarily," I told them, "he will collapse politically and everything will be altered."

75   With President Fidel Castro. Havana, Cuba, 1987

President Fidel Castro then agreed and approved SWAPO's proposal to reinforce Cuban internationalist forces in Angola, including MiG 23 jet-fighters. Within three months, new airports at Kahama, Matala and Xangongo were built by Cuban engineers and specialists, thus providing Cuba, FAPLA and PLAN ground forces with effective air cover and superior dogfight capabilities against Botha's war planes.

My urging had been heeded and my prophecy proved correct.

◆ ◆ ◆

24

In Sight of Victory

South Africa claimed that its invasion of southern Angola in September 1985 was aimed at pursuing PLAN fighters. Their spokesmen issued communiqués claiming the destruction of PLAN bases and the killing of large numbers of our fighters. In fact, as some of their disillusioned officers are now writing, they went into Angola to rescue Jonas Savimbi and UNITA, in which they had invested so much. Savimbi's job was to keep SWAPO fighters out of Namibia, which he failed to do. The South African regime's political motive was to bring down the MPLA government and replace it with a puppet UNITA regime, which would totally deny support to SWAPO and the ANC.

FAPLA had been much strengthened by the acquisition of helicopters and ground-to-air missiles and were in a strong position to capture Mavinga and its airstrip, 150 km north of Jamba. Their MiG 23s, also from the Soviet Union, and their radar provided air cover so that their land forces could attack Jamba. The South Africans had air superiority nevertheless, and were able to attack the FAPLA columns while bringing up their mechanized brigades to assist UNITA militarily.

The threat to the survival of UNITA, which South Africa could not have avoided indefinitely, was lifted dramatically early in October 1985 when the US House of Representatives passed a bill giving $35 million 'humanitarian aid' to Savimbi of UNITA. Early the following month President Reagan himself announced the granting of $30 million 'covert aid' (meaning that this was an executive decision which did not have to be approved by the legislature).

We lobbied the UN Security Council, which condemned South Africa's occupation of southern Angola, with only the US abstaining. The UN could make no impression on US policy, which was still strongly pro- UNITA. Savimbi visited the US in January 1985 and was received by President Ronald Reagan who gave him a hero's welcome in Washington. Our own standing remained very low, though it was to get even worse when the House of Representatives tried to limit SWAPO to New York, where we had an office at the UN, and Washington where we had just appointed a representative. The State Department was behind this, but luckily the Senate did not pass the measure, partly due to the strong support we had from the anti-apartheid support groups and from the American Committee on Africa. Our old friends like George Houser, Bill Johnstone, Elizabeth Landis and others stood by us at this critical time.

Our friendships in the US with non-Governmental organizations were as strong as ever, and in April-May 1988 I made a very worthwhile and significant tour there, to which I will return.

Beginning of the end of the armed liberation struggle

The early months of 1986 were a time of strengthening of PLAN. Comrade Peter Mueshihange had taken over as Secretary for Defence in January, and our headquarters in Lubango were militarily solid and all plans were in place.

Later in 1986 there were considerable PLAN military initiatives within Namibia. Our guerrillas carried out many successful operations and attacks, such as on the military base at Okahao in Ongandjera where our 82-mm mortar shells and B10 artillery did great damage, and also killed a lot of Boers at Elundu and Eenhana bases. The attack on a key petrol station at Gobabis by fighters who had come over the border from Botswana in the beginning of 1987 was the first of a series of PLAN actions far from the northern war zone. These included raids on farms near Tsumeb and in the Mangetti triangle east of the Etosha game park in March, mortar attacks on military camps in May, the destruction of electricity pylons as far south as Keetmanshoop also in May, and in July a car park bomb on top of the Kalahari Sands Hotel in Windhoek. This bomb caused millions of rand worth of damage, and among the 48 cars destroyed was that of Sean Cleary, a South African diplomat who had been seconded to the puppets as their chief propagandist. The explosion was only 500 metres from the closely-guarded SADF headquarters in Windhoek. A PLAN sabotage team in Oranjemund did much damage the same month. The 1987 offensive saw further bomb attacks — two in Walvis Bay, another in Windhoek, and the blowing of the Windhoek-Okahandja railway line, along which South African troops and armaments were railed to the north. Such actions destroyed not only military targets but also the credibility of the South African army and police and their puppet Interim Government.

The most significant of the more conventional military engagements was the attack by PLAN fighters on a South African military convoy, 57 km north-east of Ondangua in October 1987. Thirteen South African troop carriers were destroyed and two captured by PLAN. We were able to show photographs of this successful military operation. The South Africans made extravagant claims about PLAN casualties, claiming that they had killed 160 of our combatants in a 'pre-emptive strike' in Angola at this time. I was in Dublin, meeting the Taoiseach (Prime Minister) Mr Charles Haughey, and was able to refute this claim as "deceit and lies used by apartheid South African regime as a pretext for its aggression against the People's Republic of Angola".

Towards the end of 1987, one of the fiercest battles in the history of PLAN was waged against the SADF and Koevoet counter-insurgency unit at Iimbundu (Trida) in Southern Angola. During this battle, the PLAN military Commanders and their forces displayed the full maturity of their powers in dealing with the enemy, even with the odds stacked heavily against them. The SWAPO cadres were under the command of the Regional Chief of Operations, Comrade Nghilifavali Thomas Hamunjela, popularly known as *"Oundjuu ua-Ngundumana Nopoundjuu"*, who was Acting Regional Commander of the northern front at that time, with his Deputy, Comrade Ben Shilongo (*"Shikovelo Onaanda Yeengulu"*). Both proved in this extended battle that PLAN combatants were better trained and equipped to confront and defeat the enemy.

On 31 October 1987, a PLAN reconnaissance unit detected the movement of SADF and Koevoet SADF elements inside the Angolan borders, aiming to attack PLAN headquarters at the northern front, then stationed in the Cuando Cubango province. With this early intelligence, PLAN commanders prepared for battle, analysing the enemy's movements and strength. They worked out countermoves to make it difficult for the enemy to retreat, and divided their troops into platoons equipped with various weapons including ground-to-ground rocket launchers, B-10 and 82mm mortar shells, Sterile 2mm and DZK

76 President Nujoma (in lighter clothing), with SWAPO Secretary for Defence Peter Mueshihange, inspecting Casspir captured in battle. Lubango, Angola, 28 December 1987

77 Comrade Nghilifavali Thomas Hamunjela, Acting Regional Commander of the northern front (1987)

machine guns. The enemy attack was expected to be launched from the east, so mines were laid in that direction. On the western side, an observation post located about 7km from the Commanding Regional Headquarters was prepared to monitor the movements of the enemy.

At about 11 a.m., the PLAN combatants locked horns with the SADF and Koevoet, and the fighting continued fiercely throughout the day and into the night and pre-dawn hours of the next day.

SADF received regular reinforcements which were directed and aided by the colonial South African air force. PLAN reinforcements under the command of Chief of Reconnaissance Comrade Malakia Nakanduungile and his fellow combatants could not reach the base because they were blocked by movements of the enemy.

At 4 a.m. on 1 November 1987, PLAN combatants withdrew from their base. Fighting continued as the enemy continued to attack PLAN positions, relying heavily on air cover. On the same day, two enemy Bucaneers dropped bombs on positions that had already been vacated. PLAN combatants continued the fight and repelled the enemy forces on the ground. PLAN suffered the loss of 8 cadres who sacrificed their lives in that battle, while 30 were wounded. The colonial forces lost more than 200 soldiers. PLAN combatants also destroyed about 4 armoury vehicles and captured 2 Casspir combat vehicles. We counted this protracted and fierce battle as a success, of course, for it contributed significantly to the conclusion of the armed liberation struggle. But the battle was just another of the hundreds of heroic battles fought in those years, by brave sons and daughters whose goal was the independence and sovereignty of their beloved motherland. It is a great sadness to me that not all their names can be recorded in this written account.

Another battle, at Okanghudi, was particularly important for the part played by PLAN's women fighters, of whom we were very proud. In March 1988 I addressed a rally of the SWAPO Women's Council in Luanda, just after touring the war front inside Namibia, and paid tribute to our women fighters. I said:

> "We have adopted equality of the sexes and we are committed to ensuring that this equality is fully exercised in our movement in the interest of promoting the unity of purpose and action towards the total liberation of our motherland."

Much more could be said of the role of women in our struggle — from feeding and caring for the combatants in the war zone, which they did unstintingly, to actual military duties. And they were not alone in this. I still remember with great pride the Cuban women's anti-aircraft regiment who were stationed in and around Lubango who expressed their dismay at returning to Cuba without having fired at the enemy. Then news broke out of P. W. Botha's Presidential Regiment defeat and of its air-force which had been wiped out by Angolan and Cuban MiG 23s. I thus addressed the Cuban Women's anti-aircraft regiment in Lubango at a reception hosted in their honour by the SWAPO Women's Council. The SWAPO Women's Council, led by Comrades Putuse Appolus, Natalie Mavulu, Elen Musialela, Pendukeni Emvula Ithana, Hangapo Veiccoh, Dr. Libertina Amathila, Pashukeni Shoombe, Susan Nghindinua, Teckla Shikola, Febronia Kamati, Ailly Shikuambi, Gertrude Kandanga-Hilukilua and Idda Jimmy (one of the first women to be imprisoned, and who gave birth while in Windhoek prison) — to mention but a few — had set a fine example. I also pay tribute to those who sacrificed their lives in many battles.

Air superiority was the essential element in the war and South Africa had upgraded its Mirage 3 ground-to-air combat aircraft, with Israeli technology, to maintain its superiority. They called the new aircraft Cheetahs and claimed that they would evade the Angolan ground-to-air missiles and radar. South Africa's new long-range helicopters also increased their strength, as did the hundreds of anti-air missiles, called Stingers, with which the US supplied UNITA bandits as 'cover aid' from Mobuto's Zaire, early in 1986.

The Angolans were able to hold on to the territory FAPLA had won back from UNITA, and they strengthened their main bridgehead between the Cuito and Lomba rivers approximately 320 km north-west of Jamba. The final turning point came about from the South African attempt to capture or destroy Cuito Cuanavale.

From early August 1987 for nearly nine months they shelled what they thought were FAPLA positions, largely destroying the town but making no progress in their attempt to advance and take over the FAPLA bridgehead. Their 32 Battalion, commanded by Colonel Breytenbach, spearheaded the South African troops. He has since condemned the whole South African strategy that lost them this crucial battle. They also sent in 101 Battalion, Namibians, who suffered heavy losses. In October 1987, 500 of these SWATF puppet troops mutinied. A spokesman told a South African reporter at Oshakati that the SWATF forces were being used "as UNITA mercenaries against their will". He said:

"To go and fight SWAPO in Angola is a crime against our society; to go and fight against FAPLA in their own country is against God's will."

The mutineers were detained in Walvis Bay and white South African troops had to be sent in their place. They too soon began to suffer serious losses. Later, at the time of the UN implementation of Resolution 435 in 1989, some of these Koevoet/SWATF members were forcibly transferred to South Africa with their families, contrary to my directives to South African Administrator-General Luis Pienaar not to transfer Namibian nationals to South Africa. Pienaar claimed that they had responsibility over those who were fighting on their side. However, the fact of the matter was that the apartheid South African regime had a secret hand in using Namibian black puppets in the killings of ANC members and supporters under the guise of so-called 'black-on-black' violence there in 1990–92.

P. W. Botha could then no longer keep up the pretence that South Africa was not involved, and in the same month his Minister of Defence, Malan, admitted a 'limited presence' of South African troops in Angola. In November 1987, P. W. Botha and several of his ministers, including 'Pik' Botha, publicly visited their troops in Angola, as they had done secretly several times before.

This produced a very strong reaction at the UN. Secretary-General Pérez de Cuéllar had submitted to the Security Council a highly critical report, which gave the lie to South Africa's claims, made at the end of 1987, that they were withdrawing their forces from Angola. Their presence was strongly and unanimously condemned by Resolution 606 on 23 December 1987. The Security Council was instructed to monitor the "total withdrawal" and obtain confirmation of its completion "at their earliest date".

While the US was supplying UNITA bandits and even training its soldiers in the usage of Stinger missiles in Zaire, Chester Crocker was continuing his talks with the Angolans and Cubans about the latter's withdrawal. The MPLA Government was willing to be flexible, but the South Africans continued to make an end of the war and implementation of Resolution 435 impossible by making completely unacceptable demands for rapid withdrawal of the Cuban internationalist forces from Angola. The reverse was happening, with the arrival at Port Namibe late in 1987 of massive Cuban reinforcements, the first contingent being the labour force needed to construct the essential air bases

78   Technicians servicing a MIG-23 ML-type in preparation for a mission in Cuito Cuanavale (January, 1988)

79   Arrival of helicopters in Cuito Cuanavale (January, 1988)

80   MIG-23 being readied for a mission in Cuito Cuanavale.

at Kahama and Matala so that Cuban MiG 23s could engage the South Africans, even over northern Namibia itself, without refuelling.

By the beginning of the year 1988, South African air dominance was over. Their troops were suffering heavy casualties among the white troops, which lacked air cover. Botha had to admit that the South Africans were fighting battles against FAPLA deep inside Angola. Our own 2nd Mechanized Infantry Brigade fought alongside FAPLA at Cuito Cuanavale, but South African propaganda could not admit that we had such forces, after telling the world that we were engaged only in a 'low intensity bush war'. Other PLAN units provided cover for the Cuban forces now poised to move south.

The serious shelling of Cuito Cuanavale began after the South Africans lost so many Mirage jet fighters, irreplaceable due to the arms embargo under UN Security Council Resolutions. Their G5 and G6 artillery, with a range of 40 km, had little effect on the Cuban positions, and four separate advances by South African ground troops failed.

As a counter-offensive, the attack on Cuito Cuanavale not only failed, but it brought about South Africa's ultimate defeat both in the long war against SWAPO and in the heavy fighting against FAPLA.

By the end of 1987, I knew that we must be on the brink of victory. The South Africans were in their worst plight, with an estimated 4,000 troops cut off in the marshy country near the confluence of the Lomba and Cuito rivers, the Angolan front line having moved so far and so rapidly south as to cut them off from their bases to the south-west, such as Ondangua and Oshakati in Namibia. Nor could they move southeast and cross the Kavango River to Rundu. They had many hundreds killed and wounded, their black troops having mutinied.

P. W. Botha was under heavy pressure at home to tell the truth about the war situation. Above all, FAPLA now had the Cubans with them and in the early months of 1988, 15,000 Cubans and Angolans, with PLAN units included, advanced south with their artillery and tanks. The crucial MiG 23s were less than 100 km from the border with Namibia.

South Africa made a final assault on Cuito Cuanavale in late March 1988, but its tanks were destroyed with heavy loss of life. The FAPLA bridge-head succeeded in pushing the enemy back, and that enabled them to keep and maintain Cuito Cuanavale as before.

The end was now in sight.

P. W. Botha's main aim had been to divide Angola into two parts: northern and eastern; and south and eastern Angola under the control of the puppet Jonas Savimbi, with the clear purpose of preventing SWAPO from entering Namibia. This attempt had resulted only in disaster for the minority white South African politicians and army generals. The Angolans, Cubans and SWAPO had defeated the South Africans and their surrogate UNITA. The Reagan Administration's long-drawn-out attempt to score a Cold War victory by removing Cuban internationalist forces from Angola and securing a puppet regime in Namibia had failed. After the South African military defeat, they had to realise that there would never be a compliant SWAPO taking part in a puppet interim government. At last they had to accept the full implementation of Resolution 435. The Cuban withdrawal would now follow after the South African's military defeat.

Battles on the political front continue

At the end of April 1988, negotiations to end the war in Angola were announced and Angola, Cuba and South Africa had their first meeting in London on 3–4 May, under American chairmanship.

I first heard about South Africa's preparedness at last to negotiate in Moscow during my visit at the end of April and beginning of May. I had talks with President of the Soviet Union Mr. Andrei Gromyko, Secretary of the Central Committee of the Communist Party of the Soviet Union Mr. Anatoly Dobrynin, and senior Deputy-Minister of Foreign Affairs Mr. Anatoly Admishin.

This was the time of the first summit meeting between President Reagan and the General Secretary of the Communist Party of the Soviet Union, Mr. Gorbachev. Our confidence in a successful outcome to the process which had begun in London was increased by the agreement between these two Cold War leaders on 29 September 1988 (the 10th anniversary of the passing of Resolution 435), and the deadline for resolving the situation in Angola and Namibia. It did not matter that the date was an over-optimistic one. What encouraged us was the knowledge that South Africa could no longer continue playing delaying tactics with such a commitment from the Reagan Administration.

I flew from Moscow to Atlanta, Georgia in the USA when the London talks were announced. I was kept in close touch with developments there by our long-serving United Kingdom SWAPO Chief Representative, Shapua Kaukungua, who was also Chief Representative for Western Europe. The Cubans gave us detailed briefings on all meetings from then on.

Interviewed in New York on 8 May 1988, I gave *The Namibian* newspaper in Windhoek my views on this vital new development. About our non-participation in those talks, I said:

"As far as SWAPO is concerned, the only role we are interested in playing is to sign the cease-fire with South Africa and start the implementation of Resolution 435. As far as Namibia is concerned a formula is already agreed upon. It is up to the other parties to resolve all the other hurdles in order for us to proceed. The negotiation process is on, but the first phases of the negotiating process have nothing to do with us. We will be around when the time comes for the signing of the cease-fire and the implementation of Resolution 435."

In Atlanta I talked with the former US President, Jimmy Carter, who had long been very supportive of the cause of Namibia's freedom and independence. He promised that if a Democratic administration took over from Ronald Reagan after the upcoming Presidential election in November 1988, he would seek to get Namibian independence based on Resolution 435 accepted as part of US foreign policy. He and the Atlanta Mayor, Andrew Young, with whom we had worked in the Western Contact Group days, agreed to raise the question at the Democratic Convention in July 1988. Had there been such men in power throughout the 1980s, nearly a decade of war and suffering might well have been avoided.

With Theo-Ben Gurirab and Hidipo Hamutenya I travelled on to California — Los Angeles, San Francisco and Oakland — and then to Chicago. Everywhere I talked with state and city representatives and newspaper editors. We did all we could, as we had in Atlanta, to get the US media to give proper attention to our case, to counter the version of events the South Africans had put across through their huge international propaganda offensive.

In Washington on 4 May 1988, I made a point of announcing the policy of national reconciliation, neutrality and non-alignment which the SWAPO Central Committee had adopted. 'National reconciliation' was not a policy designed merely to win votes in the elections, or to buy Western support in the implementation process. On 4 May we had no certainty that South Africa was this time negotiating seriously and not, as on so many previous occasions, simply buying time. I nevertheless emphasized that, in our future non-racial democracy, even 'traitors' who fought on the side of the South African forces of occupation would be equally treated as citizens.

4 May 1988 was also the 10th anniversary of the Cassinga massacre, which P. W. Botha's regime had claimed as a great victory that had

"broken SWAPO's backbone" from which PLAN would never recover. They celebrated with a big military parade in Oshakati. But they were countered by students in marking what we called 'Cassinga Day': thousands of students held a demonstration in Katutura in protest against the South African military parade, and then marched to the Augustineum College. When some of them headed for the centre of Windhoek they were attacked by police with rubber bullets and tear-gas. Police in their Casspirs and military vehicles chased the peaceful young demonstrators, many of them school children, through the streets. That day reflected the situation of the moment. It could be no surprise to anyone that we did not trust the South Africans to negotiate in good faith.

My main engagement in Washington, D.C. was to be present as the principal witness and participant in hearings on Namibia held by the World Council of Churches. The former Nigerian head of state, General Olusegun Obasanjo, took the chair and among the other distinguished members were Mrs. Palme, widow of the late Swedish Prime Minister who had stood by all oppressed peoples from the 1960s onwards. Many leading churchmen were also present, including Bishop Kauluma and Vice-Bishop Kameeta from Namibia. It was at this hearing that I announced SWAPO's 'National Reconciliation' policy.

At the State Department I talked with officials, headed by Mr. Sam Armacost, Under Secretary of State, to whom Chester Crocker was responsible. He spoke about the US–Soviet discussions on regional problems, in which, he said, "there appears to have been progress on Angola-Namibia related issues". We talked also with the campaign office of Governor Michael Dukakis, the Democratic front-runner for the forthcoming presidential election, and directly with an old friend of SWAPO's, the Reverend Jesse Jackson.

Our final meeting was with the UN Council for Namibia in New York. I thanked them for all they had done as the *de jure* government of Namibia, especially in these final years of the struggle. I said that we considered them a "fighting Council for Namibia" and our partners in the long campaign for Nambia's independence. I also urged them to emphasize their legal authority over Namibia at this crucial time and to increase their activities at the international level. The Council for Namibia, with which the office of the UN Commissioner had recently been merged, had indeed done much but they were not supported by the Western powers — the United Kingdom did not even recognise their authority. The Special Representative of the Secretary-General, Martti Ahtisaari, who was much less favourably disposed towards SWAPO, was seen by the Western powers as the man to handle the implementation of Resolution 435, leaving the Council with virtually no role in the implementation.

After New York, we flew to Havana. In a three-hour meeting with Fidel Castro, I was given the strongest assurance of support, in spite of the changes that were taking place in the Soviet Union. Cuba was determined that its sons and daughters who had given their lives in Angola should not have died in vain. We urged the closest coordination between their forces, FAPLA and PLAN in the months ahead, when we were all in so much stronger a position than before. The big increase in Cuban troops, aircraft and armour which I had urged in 1987 had helped to militarily defeat the South African occupation army.

The final meeting was in Luanda with President José Eduardo dos Santos, whose assurances we fully accepted that there would be no compromise in the talks. At that stage their tactic was to call South Africa's bluff; to offer withdrawal in return for immediate implementation of Resolution 435. Hidipo Hamutenya, as Secretary for Information, issued an immediate statement to the effect that SWAPO had been consulted and constantly briefed by Angola and Cuba, despite what was being said in the Western media, and that we saw no need to take part in the talks since they were dealing with South African interference in Angola's internal affairs: "SWAPO will join the process when the stage of implementation of Resolution 435 is reached". In the new international atmosphere resulting from the improvement in Western and Soviet relations, "combined with the impact of military defeats and setbacks, South Africa would find it hard to back away from the negotiations".

From Luanda I travelled to our military headquarters in Lubango where I remained, fulfilling my duties as Commander-in-Chief of PLAN in what was still a very critical phase of the war. The process of "consultation and constant briefing" was delegated to Comrades Theo-Ben Gurirab and Hidipo Hamutenya. They travelled from Brazzaville to Cairo and on through all the 13 rounds of talks between Angola, Cuba and South Africa's representatives.

The South Africans had initiated the process by letting the Americans know that they wanted the war to end, after their military defeats at Cuito Cuanavale. They nevertheless wrecked the second round of talks, held in Cairo on 24-25 June 1988. General Malan, P. W. Botha's Minister of Defence, threatened further action, claiming that their forces were still militarily strong. On 27 June there was a clash at the Calueque Dam near Ruacana, in which Cuban, FAPLA and PLAN troops engaged the South Africans very effectively. The South African Army had built a bunker over the Kunene River Bridge, which received a direct hit by Cuban air force killing and injuring many enemy soldiers who were sheltering there, and others drowned in the river. This forced the South Africans back to the negotiating table. Botha's regime feared that the Cuban internationalist forces would make a hot pursuit across the border and enable SWAPO to seize power in Namibia.

There were no more serious delays except at Brazzaville on 4 December, when 'Pik' Botha suddenly stalled as the protocol was about to be signed. He said South Africa had some important point to consider. He was always one to talk big, to walk out of meetings, and generally behave like a badly brought-up child. He wanted South Africa to appear important, to give the impression that his Government was making the decisions. The Americans told him that the South African government was making a big mistake and that the West wanted them to complete the negotiations, or they would face a big military defeat.

My prediction to the Cubans about the end of P. W. Botha began to become a reality.

In February 1988 he had sent the South Africans' 82nd Battalion, the so-called Presidential Regiment, to cross the Kavango river, in typical Boer style by artificial bridge. They joined in the attack on Cuito Cuanavale, only to be defeated by heavy air attacks by Cuban and Angolan MiG 23s, as South Africa had no air cover. The Angolan and Cuban air attacks had knocked out the South African ground troops, who found themselves completely exposed after their tanks and armoured cars coming across the Kavango river were destroyed, and there was nothing the South African generals could do. In classical, conventional war, once you no longer have air cover it is inevitable that your infantry will be wiped out. The whole South African war machine was in imminent danger of annihilation.

P. W. Botha surely had many sleepless nights at this time. Information had it that after he learned of the heavy defeat of his presidential Regiment at Cuito Cuanavale, he began drinking heavily of Mellow-Wood Brandy. In the end he suffered a serious stroke, which caused him to be permanently paralysed, and which finished him politically. He held on to power until early in 1989 when one of his Ministers, F. W. de Klerk, went to Lusaka to meet President Kaunda, without Botha's knowledge, as he claimed. Botha had lost his authority. In August 1989 he resigned.

Vorster's collapse in 1978 had been partly the result of the war in Namibia, which he could not win. P. W. Botha had been appointed in his place because he had been Minister of Defence. He saw to it that the whole South African economy and that of Namibia, was geared to the war efforts with a view to defeat SWAPO so that they could continue their occupation of Namibia.

Not only did SWAPO bring about the political fall of Vorster and Botha, but at the time of Cuito Cuanavale we were militarily very strong. We had more trained men and women than ever before and new recruits were crossing the Angola–Namibia border in great numbers to join our movement. PLAN units were with the Cubans and Angolans at Calueque and in other engagements along the border. The South African propagandists continued to belittle PLAN and its achievements, but the truth was beginning to emerge. The *New York Times*, in a 'military analysis' in July 1988, were not fooled by their South African sources. "Despite major efforts by South Africa over 20 years, the Namibian rebels' strength, now estimated at 8,000, appears undiminished", they wrote. While South Africa was claiming that SWAPO–PLAN, with the Cubans and FAPLA, were on the border to invade Namibia, the *New York Times* wrote that we were "trying to build up combat power to prevent South African air and ground forces' free movement into Angola, if there is no settlement of the war".

Inside Namibia our fighters never ceased attacking. SADF and SWATF bases at Omahenene, Okankolo, Okongo and the Koevoet base at Ogongo all came under heavy attack. At Onavivi, west of Oshakati, white conscripts had fled the burning base and the South Africans admitted 19 dead. Our own information, from the hospitals, put the figure close to 40.

PLAN intelligence operations inside the country brought a lot of information about South Africa's forward military plans. There was much evidence of disagreement among the South African politicians and army generals in these final months of the war. Colonel Breytenbach has said that General Geldenhuys and he would have attacked Menongue and not Cuito Cuanavale, but "apparently it was because of political pressure that we were prevented". The South Africans could advance no further: "as a result of 'Pik' Botha's activities over the years, the war was allowed to escalate to the point when it was beyond our power to control it". As Breytenbach put it, when the Cubans moved south and "took a position right across the northern border ... there was nothing between them and the Orange River, they could have gone right through if they had chosen to do so". General Malan still claims that Cuito Cuanavale, "the biggest, the greatest battle to have been fought in the history of South Africa", was one of the highlights of his career. He also claims that South Africa "had a limited number of 3,000 troops and lost 31, and the enemy lost between 7,000 and 10,000". But Breytenbach puts such a view down to the South African army's "Com-ops organization ... concerned with influencing the climate of opinion. Basically this means that they were engaged in lying. Pure propaganda". Brytenbach also blames the army spokesmen for spreading the story that SWAPO would lose the elections in Namibia. I told them at the time: "You are talking lies ... SWAPO will win. The fight depended on whether or not we could get the people on our side, and if you failed to do so you would lose". The war — he ended this interview — using coarse language, achieved "absolutely nothing".

The South African propaganda directed at our people often had the opposite effect from what was intended. Our bombing campaign inside the country showed that we had PLAN units as far south as Windhoek, Keetmanshoop and even Oranjemund, and the PLAN combatants in the war zone timed their attacks to coincide with major international developments or local political events in which we were involved. When Frans Joseph Strauss, the right-wing West German leader, visited Namibia we exploded a bomb in the Suiderhof military base, Windhoek. The explosion, on 28 January 1988, was heard all over Windhoek and the news was carried world-wide by the media.

Three weeks later in February 1988, to discredit SWAPO, the South Africans exploded a bomb in the First National Bank in Oshakati, killing 27 and wounding 70 of the crowd who were there to deposit their end-of-the-month pay cheques, most of them hospital workers. Among those killed was the daughter of Bishop Dumeni.

The Council of Churches in Namibia immediately issued a statement listing the evidence for South African perpetration of this atrocity. We called it "part of the dirty propaganda campaign to smear the name of SWAPO". I was able to tell a delegation of white Namibians from "Namibian Peace Plan 435" shortly afterwards that it was "against SWAPO policy to attack so-called soft targets" and that "SWAPO denies involvement in the Oshakati bank bombing massacre".

The following month, March 1988, PLAN fighters made successful attacks on South African bases at Okatope and Eenhana, and fought their way out of a confrontation with the South Africans at Kongo. This came on top of other engagements in January and February, including the bringing down of two army planes inside Namibia, all of their crews meeting their deaths.

Battles at Onesi and Okalongo brought the South African losses in Namibia to 159 in those months, when the tide of war was turning against them in Angola.

South Africa's undertaking to withdraw was finally carried out, eight months later, on 30 August 1988, in the presence of 90 journalists flown to Rundu to see and photograph columns of armoured cars carrying banners inscribed: "Welkom wenners — welcome winners". Even the most prejudiced against us must have asked, when they saw those pictures, "If they are the winners, why are they pulling out and agreeing to independence under Resolution 435 and a three year period of Cuban withdrawal from Angola?".

International communication and internal unity

My role in the second half of 1988 was to keep a firm control of military actions, with our Commander, Comrade Dimo Hamaambo, and Secretary for Defence Peter Mueshihange, while staying in close touch with all the stages of the implementation process. We had to start preparing also for our return home to participate in the elections under UN Security Council Resolution 435.

The South African propaganda against us and the military censorship which had also enabled them to misrepresent our military campaign over many years, and the 1987-8 war in Angola, had to be dealt with. In December 1987 I announced the launching of NAMPA — the Namibian Press Agency — to cover the liberation struggle from bureaux in Europe, the Americas, Asia and in Africa in Harare, Dar-es-Salaam, Brazzaville and Addis Ababa. The UN Council for Namibia helped this campaign with a London conference to get the truth of our situation into the world press, as did the Conference of the National Alliance of Third World Journalists. I attended as principal guest in Atlanta, Georgia (USA) in April 1988. We also valued the good work of the Namibia Communications Centre in London, which relayed news from Lutheran and other church sources in Namibia to reflect the true facts of the situation in Namibia.

Early in June 1988, I issued a statement through NAMPA fully supporting the Angolan and Cuban positions in the peace talks with South Africa and the US, which had just begun. The BBC reported this,

81   Sam Nujoma addressing the NAM Summit. Harare, Zimbabwe, 1986

contradicting the false propaganda that we resented not being included in the talks. The failure of the Cairo meeting that followed showed that as usual it was South Africa creating obstacles to the peace process and not SWAPO. From Geneva I flew to Stockholm to meet the large delegation of white Namibians for the productive meeting already referred to. Another keynote speech was at the 23rd UNIP Congress in Kabwe, Zambia on 18 August 1988, at which I confirmed our agreement to concessions we had made in the negotiations, and before then, including for example that we would seek "as cordial as possible relations with Pretoria" and would not undertake large-scale nationalisation of enterprises without compensation. I emphasised also our continued "support for the ANC, through the OAU, the UN and the Non-Aligned Movement".

As so often before our diplomatic position was solidly endorsed in Namibia itself. The students, in particular, led by the Namibian National Student's Organization (NANSO), acted with great courage and determination. In the first week of June 1988, 75,000 school students boycotted the schools throughout the country and protested at the army and police repression against students. The boycott and demonstration had begun with the protest by the Ponhofi Secondary School in Ovamboland, demanding that an army base be removed from the school vicinity, as the enemy made the school its shield against PLAN attacks. This demonstration led to the arrest of pupils, student leaders and teachers, and increased repression and ill-treatment. The unity of the students, despite South Africa's attempts at bantustan indoctrination, from Ovamboland in the north to Namaland in the south, was demonstrated beyond doubt.

On 20 and 21 June 1988 the National Union of Namibian Workers called a general strike among its affiliated unions in support of the students. The Trade Union demanded the removal of military bases from the vicinity of schools, the release of political prisoners, and the removal of Koevoet units from the townships. More than 60,000 workers supported the strike. The Administrator-General and the puppet Interim Government responded very harshly against the demonstrators. It was clear to us that the people of Namibia were demanding, in no uncertain terms, their freedom and that independence was now inevitable.

South Africa forced to withdraw from Angola

The 29 September 1988 date which had been set by Reagan and Gorbachev for the arrival of UNTAG in Namibia had come and gone, replaced by 1 November 1988. The South Africans made the 29 September date impossible by further obstructive maneouvres at the Geneva talks on 2 August 1988, over the dates for the withdrawal of Cuban troops and — a new obstacle — the demand that Angola cease assisting the ANC of South Africa.

The Boers nevertheless agreed to start withdrawing their troops from Angola on 10 August and to complete the process by 1 September. The most likely explanation of this seems to be that it enabled them to fly out secretly, straight after the 8 August cease-fire, the thousands of their soldiers trapped in Cuando Cubango province after being cut off by the advancing Cuban, FAPLA and PLAN troops.

The newly constructed Cuban airports close to the Namibian border enabled Cuban fighter planes to overfly the northern Namibian enemy bases, causing heavy South African losses in lives and aircraft, and the forces of freedom which now ranged along the Namibian frontier forced P. W. Botha to stop the war. The South Africans continued to try to supplement and update their aircraft and armour, and the US, through Chester Crocker, made it clear that military aid to UNITA would not be cut, again calling on the MPLA Government to share power with UNITA. South Africa was already threatening to raise other obstacles to the start of the transition to elections. One of these was that the UN peacekeeping force was too large. This was in due course to raise even higher the price that was paid in human lives on 1 April 1989.

We had no option but to move on as rapidly as possible to the cease-fire, our hopes raised also by the prospect of a change of administration in the US, where Governor Michael Dukakis had promised, if elected, to lead the effort for sanctions against South Africa. Dukakis also said: "We've got a situation where we are supporting the UNITA group, whose principal partner is South Africa, which attacks American oil companies that are defended by the Cuban army ... I think if we are serious about getting tough with South Africa, this policy has got to end". But Dukakis lost the election and George Bush's very first foreign policy action on becoming President in January 1989 was to announce a massive further aid package to UNITA, spelling death, misery and destruction to millions of Angolans for years to come.

It was a real advantage that the US House of Representatives passed, on 11 August 1989, an Act which warned of a major extension of sanctions. Pik Botha, who had always poured scorn on the sanctions threat, claiming that South Africa was more than self-sufficient, immediately threatened to withdraw from the negotiations if sanctions were enforced. Congress went into recess in October so his words were not put to the test.

The talks moved from Brazzaville to Cairo to New York to the August Geneva meeting. Still wriggling, the South Africans proposed through the Interim Government, to UN Secretary General Pérez de Cuéllar, when he visited South Africa in October, the holding of an all-party conference in Namibia before Resolution 435 came into force. I replied at once that the proper arena for debate was the elections under the UN supervision and control which Resolution 435 would soon bring about. On 15 November 1988, the Cuban withdrawal timetable was agreed at Geneva, the protocol to be finalised in Brazzaville in December. It was then that 'Pik' Botha tried to show that the South Africans were still in control by delaying the signing of the protocol until 13 December, though he described the process itself as "irreversible".

82 Bernt Carlsson, addressing Namibia Day celebration in SWAPO settlement, 26 August 1987 in Angola

The tripartite and bilateral agreements were signed at the UN in New York on 22 December 1988 and, at long last, 1 April 1989 was established as the date for the implementation of the (1978) UN Resolution 435. SWAPO had every reason to feel elated, but the need for caution was never dispelled.

It was increased, in fact, by the tragic death of our Swedish true friend at the centre of these events, Bernt Carlsson, the new UN Commissioner for Namibia, who was killed in the Pan-Am air disaster at Lockerbie in Scotland on 21 December 1989, while on his way to the signing ceremony in New York. At the time, reliable sources indicated that both 'Pik' Botha and General Magnus Malan had been booked on that same Pan-Am flight but had suddenly cancelled their journey.

Understandably, it was speculated that there was a connection between these circumstances and the disaster — that it might have been planned by apartheid South Africans because of their hatred against Sweden, which supported the national liberation movements of both SWAPO and ANC with both humanitarian and diplomatic assistance. The UN Commissionership had been somewhat marginalised by the powers of the Special Representative of the Secretary-General leading the UNTAG operation. Bernt Carlsson was a man of great determination who, if he had survived to continue as Commissioner for Namibia, might have counter-balanced some of the actions of the former, which sought to put us at a disadvantage in the months ahead. We mourned Bernt Carlsson's death, at meetings in London and New York, as did the Swedish Government and people, and the members of Socialist International, of which he had earlier been Secretary-General.

Issues had already come up at the talks which meant difficulties to come, such as the postponement of a decision over the return of Walvis Bay to Namibia, and the 750 million rand debt to international banking institutions which had been incurred in Namibia by the South African regime, purchasing weapons to conduct the war and delay the independence of Namibia.

In spite of these worries we were ready to return and call upon the people to join with us in SWAPO to building a new Namibian nation. In November 1988 we presented an economic policy document aimed at "bringing about a balance between just economic returns to the Namibian people on the one hand and reasonable profits for foreign and local private investors on the other".

But, ominously, the claim was being widely made that the military component of UNTAG was too large at 7,500 troops, with 2,500 civilian components. We had never ceased to demand a strong and effective peace-keeping force and the figure of 7,500 had been agreed since the early days of the Western Contact Group more than 10 years earlier.

The calamity that followed from this could still not deny the Namibian people the fruits of the diplomatic, political and military victory, which was at last to bring about the implementation of UN Security Council Resolution 435 and the achievement of genuine freedom and independence, for which they had struggled for 106 years.

❖ ❖ ❖

25

Final Days of the Struggle for Independence

Since 1987 publicly, and privately long before that, I had been convinced that we had won the war and would soon be returning home to carry out economic reconstruction and the rebuilding of a new Namibian nation based on social justice.

But as the time drew nearer we still had to consolidate our victory. In June 1988 while South Africa was still manoeuvring to delay our victory, SWAPO worked to mobilize its support inside the country through the SWAPO Youth League, SWAPO Elders Council, SWAPO Women's Council, SWAPO Pioneer Movement, the National Union of Namibian Workers (NUNW), other progressive organizations and Chiefs and Headmen.

At the final stage of the military effort, PLAN combatants with the FAPLA forces and Cuban internationalist forces launched the final assault and Cuban MiG 23s bombed Calueque Dam where South African built its military bunker. Now the enemy realized that its war machinery was broken and its soldiers demoralized — they had neither capacity nor stamina to match the well-prepared combined forces of PLAN, FAPLA and the Cuban internationalist forces. It was obvious that the enemy was defeated both militarily and politically, and diplomatically totally isolated, despite the Reagan Administration's financial package to DTA and the South African regime's continuing efforts through bogus organizations such as Ezuva, Etango and Koevoet which aimed to create the impression that they had won the hearts and minds of the Namibian people.

Some top military brass trained by the CIA in counter insurgency techniques were more trusted by P. W Botha, and they were really the rulers and decision-makers while Cabinet members were simply 'rubber stamps'. Major decisions were made by army generals like Minister of Defence Magnus Malan, Van der Westhuizen, Van Tonder and Herman who were authorized by P. W. Botha to expend the resources of both South Africa and Namibia in order to strengthen their military intelligence and propaganda war machinery against SWAPO. Even though a huge amount of money had been spent in order to defeat SWAPO, it was obvious by now that no success could follow from it. The fact of the matter was that the defeat of the South African army at Cuito Cuanavale, Chipa and at Calueque had great psychological effect and was a severe shock to the South African white settlers.

In February 1989, P. W. Botha suffered a stroke and after that his political demise was inevitable.

The end of P. W. Botha did not mean the end of the South African regime's manoeuvres to block the implementation of Resolution 435 and stop SWAPO coming home to participate in a free and fair democratic election. The Generals were still determined to wreck Resolution 435 and they made detailed plans to achieve this diabolical aim. 'Pik' Botha, pleaded with the Reagan administration, which was following the same line at this time. To him must go some blame for persuading the Western Security Council members to downgrade the UN peace-keeping force from the original 7,500 to 4,000. At the very same time he was funding the DTA and other puppets to the tune of over 100 million South African rand to support their manipulation of the election against SWAPO.

On 16 January 1989, the Security Council passed enabling Resolution 628, endorsing the Tripartite Agreement signed at the UN on 22 December 1988, and setting down 1st April 1989 for the commencement of the implementation of Resolution 435. By that date, UNTAG forces were to be in place including, of course, those to man the reception points at which PLAN combatants were to be confined to bases in Namibia, in accordance with Resolution 435. The South African troops were to be confined to bases at Grootfontein or Oshivelo, or both, commencing on 1 April 1989.

We had repeatedly informed the UN Secretary-General that SWAPO had forces inside the country, but there was no written detailed information or instruction in the UN plan as to the procedure our combatants should follow in handing themselves over to UNTAG for confinement to bases on the designated date. The South Africans always pretended that they were not fighting a large-scale war against SWAPO inside the country. In the words of the "legal analysis" put out by the US State Department in favour of South Africa:

> "South Africa categorically rejected any implication that SWAPO bases existed on Namibian territory and made it crystal clear that the South African Government would not permit such bases to be established as part of the UN Plan."

That referred to South Africa's position as it had been in 1978–79, and did not take into consideration our own account that PLAN, the SWAPO military wing, had grown in strength from battalions to mechanized brigades — but all of which we deliberately kept mobile.

Though our forces had been engaged in many fierce battles with the South African troops and local counter insurgency units such as SWATF and Koevoet, they had never, since the launching of the armed liberation struggle at Omugulu-gOmbashe on 26 August 1966, been overrun. They had adopted scientific guerrilla tactics and maintained absolute vigilance and mobility, moving in sections and platoons. They constantly carried out surprise attacks, and caused heavy enemy casualties with minimum losses on our side. In later years this mobility was achieved not only by their tough training in covering long distances rapidly on foot, but was also aided by the use of bicycles which enabled them to move even faster, and even to carry heavy weapons such as 122mm rocket launchers and ground-to-air missiles.

Nevertheless, as 1 April 1989 drew nearer, the South Africans were in a better position than ever before to identify the location of PLAN fighters. In October 1989, a journal called *Top Secret*, quoting London press sources, wrote:

> "At the beginning of March the CIA had provided the South African military intelligence service with the latest surveillance data gathered by 'plane and satellite concerning SWAPO bases within Namibia. It was clear to both Washington and Pretoria that there were already SWAPO units in Namibia. Moreover, some of their bases had been clearly identified."

Our men lay low even after South Africa had separately, on 22 March 1989, signed the cease-fire letter drawn up by the UN Secretary-General's office. They would not meet us to sign the cease-fire jointly in a proper manner because South Africa still pretended that SWAPO did not exist. Not for one moment did we trust the South African government to honour its undertakings under the Tripartite Agreement or Resolution 435 without attempting to derail the UN Plan. We always expected that South Africa would use more delaying tactics and dirty tricks. We had prepared several options, each with its alternatives and fall-backs, to ensure that South Africa would be kept in line with the UN plan.

One of these options was to retain our combatants in their northern and eastern regions inside the country, ready in their positions, while the UN peace-keeping force of UNTAG military and civilian components commenced with the process of full implementation of UN Resolution 435. However, I made it categorically clear that if the South African apartheid regime were allowed to continue to torpedo the implementation, the armed liberation struggle would continue and would intensify.

Some critical arithmetic: 7,500 minus 3,500 = 4,000

We struggled hard, assisted by many friendly governments and support groups, to defeat the proposal that the peace-keeping force be reduced. It was the Americans who initiated the reduction of the UN peace-keeping force from the full complement of 7,500 down to 4,000. They claimed that the UN had no money to pay for a force of that size, and succeeded in getting all the permanent members of the Security Council on their side. The Reagan administration took advantage of the changes in the new USSR leadership: Gorbachev leaned towards the West and was less supportive of the national liberation movements in Africa, in contrast to his predecessors who would have opposed any attempt at torpedoing the implementation of UN Resolution 435.

All the Western Permanent Members of the Security Council made it clear that their governments were not prepared to pay for the cost of the full 7,500 UNTAG military and civilian components to remain in Namibia unless the Chinese government was prepared to share the expenses. Thus, the Chinese were compelled to concur with the rest of the Permanent Members of the Security Council.

In an attempt to prevent further delay in the implementation of Resolution 435, SWAPO approached the UN and offered to repay the full UNTAG operational costs after independence — for both military and civilian components— repaying the UN with its own resources. Our offer was not accepted. Our campaign against the reduction of UNTAG peace-keeping forces was fought and lost. This reduction, of course, seriously down-graded the potential effectiveness of the peace-keeping forces in an emergency situation, given the sheer size of the land which Namibian territory constituted.

On 16 February 1989, the implementation of Resolution 435 was finally authorized by UN Security Council Resolution 632. Although the Security Council agreed to the reduction of the UNTAG military component, we had won the concession that the 3,500 forces which had been subtracted from the full original strength of 7,500 would be held in reserve. Resolution 640, later in the year, required the disbandment of Koevoet, but this, unlike the cut in UNTAG numbers, was not carried out.

The weeks we had lost while we and our friends had done all in our power to retain the full strength of the peace-keeping force inevitably delayed UNTAG's arrival in Namibia, with further consequences that assisted those intent on torpedoing the implementation of Resolution 435. General Prem Chand, in command of the military component of UNTAG, arrived in Windhoek on 26 February 1989. But by the end of March, on the eve of the final cessation of hostilities, fewer than one quarter of the 4,650-strong UNTAG force were in place, and of these scarcely a handful were in the northern Namibian war zone.

My own movements were restricted in the early months by the need to be with our military forces at Headquarters in Lubango and with the SWAPO Political Headquarters in Luanda. So much of our fighting had been done by men and women politically motivated, that we had to do all in our power to explain to them the full implications of their approaching demobilization. Some of the commanders expressed strong misgivings about our agreeing to the demobilization of PLAN and the ending of the armed liberation struggle.

There was a huge task awaiting us back home and we could lose no time in preparing the way, particularly in facing the economic problems confronting the country. I addressed the Council of Ministers of the Southern African Development Co-ordinating Conference (SADCC) in Luanda on 3 February 1989, and outlined the future role we could play in co-operation with Angola, Botswana and Zambia, particularly in dealing with the region's transport problems. I also warned that apartheid South Africa would do all in its power to "undermine and predetermine the outcome of the transition to independence" in its favour and install a puppet government in Namibia.

An international businessman arranged for me to meet, in London, senior directors of the Anglo-American Corporation, which I did at the Ritz Hotel on 9 February. The Consolidated Diamond Mines (CDM) of South West Africa, a key subsidiary of DeBeers, is a major contributor to the Namibian economy through its gem diamond mining operation north of the Orange River mouth. CDM had made scarcely any attempt in the past to show any interest either in contact with SWAPO or in the democratic future of the country. Nevertheless, we wanted to make it clear to the directors of such major companies that we had no wish to disrupt their operations, only to ensure that a proper return went to the Namibian people, through taxes, wages and the localizing of subsidiary activities. I found Mr. Nicholas Oppenheimer and his colleagues receptive and friendly and relations have been cordial since independence.

Perhaps because Rio Tinto Zinc (RTZ) had so flagrantly defied UN Decree No. 1 in exporting Namibian uranium from the mine that they managed and mined at Rössing, near Swakopmund, this company had done much more for the country than CDM. They had set up the Rössing Foundation, which contributed to research, education and training in agriculture and other fields, and seemed much more interested in the future of the country than was CDM, despite the latter's much longer involvement in exploitation of Namibian resources.

It was not true, however, as was reported from time to time, that I had had personal meetings with RTZ Chairmen over the years. This rumour must have come from their own public relations officials, or was at least kept alive by them, as they never contradicted it, though SWAPO did. Their breach of UN Decree No. 1 took place under the Labour administration in Britain. They claimed that they were dependent on the uranium from Rössing and that the ore they extracted illegally at Rössing was the richest and was indispensable to Britain's nuclear power programme.

Though my meeting in February 1989 with RTZ was off the record, the Press got wind of it. I gave an interview to the *London Times* in which I announced that independent Namibia would join the OAU, SADCC and UN and that we were also considering membership of the Commonwealth. There was never any doubt that we would join the Commonwealth, simply that the procedures had to be followed. We valued the great support SWAPO had received over many years from the Commonwealth Fund for Technical Co-operation, which has continued since our independence to fund and administer training programmes over a wide field.

83   President of SWAPO Sam Nujoma with Secretary for Defence
      Peter Mueshihange, reviewing parade in Lubango, where about 20,000
      SWAPO combatants were gathered. 18 February 1989

For me, the most important event of the first three months of 1989 took place on 29 and 30 March when I inspected huge parades of our PLAN combatants at the Hainjeko Military Academy in Lubango, Kahama, Xangongo and other SWAPO military training camps, and read out to them the terms of the cease-fire which would come into full effect on 1 April 1989. I told them that from that day most of them would become civilians again and would be returned to Namibia to take part in "the political mobilization of the masses, to vote for SWAPO, and thereby consolidate the revolutionary gains for which SWAPO had fought, for so many years".

It was a deeply moving occasion as I stood with Comrades Hidipo Hamutenya, first Minister of Information and Broadcasting; Peter Mueshihange, first Minister of Defence; Dimo Hamaambo, the Army Commander; the Chief of Staff Charles Namoloh, known as "Ho Chi Minh"; and the Field Commanders, among them Patrick Iyambo Lungada, who had fought heroically since the launching of the armed liberation struggle at Omugulu-gOmbashe. Over 9,000 men and women combatants of PLAN marched past as I took the salute.

84   SWAPO troops gathered at a rally in southern Angola, just north of the Namibian border, to listen to a speech by Sam Nujoma announcing the UN cease-fire to come into effect on the following day. 31 March 1989

85   (L to R) SWAPO President Sam Nujoma greeting senior PLAN combatants Madame Ottilie Todenge and Laimi Uunona, at SWAPO rally to announce the UN ceasefire. Lubango, Angola, 31 March 1989

86   *(L to R) Governador da Provincia du Cunene-Angola, Pedro Mutindi; President Sam Nujoma; Hidipo Hamutenya, at SWAPO rally to announce the UN ceasefire. 31 March 1989*

I announced the demobilization of all but a basic security force that would be needed if South Africa and its western allies, as we anticipated, were to try a last minute trick to destroy the process of withdrawal and implementation of Resolution 435. This reserve included those fighters who were still deployed further south. We could not afford to disband those in the forward positions that would be the front-line if South Africa were to violate the cease-fire agreement.

From the demobilization parade I hurried to Zimbabwe to attend the meeting in Harare of the Association of West European Parliamentarians Against Apartheid, a commitment which I had made earlier. Margaret Thatcher, then British Prime Minister, had been on a state visit to Zimbabwe only two days before and had flown on to Malawi. She had given a press conference before leaving and had refused to confirm or deny that her last stop would be Windhoek. We were suspicious of what she had in mind. She had met 'Pik' Botha in London a fortnight before, and clearly meant to be part of the Namibian "settlement" though she had been a major obstacle by supporting Reagan's policies since 1981. President Mugabe told me that she did not inform him that she was going to fly from Blantyre, Malawi to Windhoek, Namibia.

Ahtisaari and a serious step backwards

The war was to end on 31 March 1989 and the cease-fire was to commence exactly at midnight on 1 April 1989. However, I was woken with the news that our PLAN combatants inside Namibia — who were waiting to report to UNTAG reception points as they had been instructed in accordance with the UN Resolution 435 — had been fired on by South African forces. Within hours, PLAN combatants, right across from the Eastern Caprivi to Kaokoveld, were engaged in heavy battles with the enemy, in which they fought back heroically and inflicted heavy damage and many enemy casualties. Many dead enemy soldiers being eaten by vultures were found by locals where battles between our PLAN combatants and the enemy had taken place. This bolstered confidence among the people that PLAN fighters were indeed capable of defending them and liberating the country.

The sequence of events soon became clear. Prime Minister Thatcher had arrived in Windhoek from Blantyre early on the morning of 1 April 1989 and had met 'Pik' Botha, the Administrator-General Louis Pienaar, and the UN Special Representative Ahtisaari, who had himself reached Windhoek on the previous day. Botha announced that 600 PLAN fighters had made an "incursion" over the border in clear breach of the cease-fire agreement. South Africa would therefore withdraw from the Tripartite Agreement and cancel the implementation of Resolution 435 if these troops were not immediately driven back over the border or captured and held, pending an inquiry. Mrs. Thatcher is said to have supported Botha fully, without the slightest inquiry being made as to the truth of his claims. There were only a few hundred UNTAG military personnel in the war zone and, though our combatants did not know this, they had not even prepared the reception points to which our combatants were supposed to report themselves and be confined, in accordance with the terms of Resolution 435.

The UN representative, Mr. Martti Ahtisaari, had for some time shown himself to be more concerned with his career at the United Nations than with his responsibilities towards the oppressed people of Namibia under illegal South African occupation. This had meant his becoming very much a collaborator with the US and British over such issues as "UN supervision and control" of the forthcoming elections, and over South African charges of UN partiality towards SWAPO.

He had greatly disappointed us in recent months when we heard rumours that he had tried to persuade the Nordic governments to withhold the funds that they, Sweden most of all, had given SWAPO for humanitarian assistance for a number of years. He had failed, except with his own country, Finland, but this action had made it clear to us that this man, whom we had sponsored to succeed Sean MacBride in 1976, and who was now in charge of the most critical phase of the implementation of Resolution 435, was prepared to bow to the Reagan and Thatcher governments in the US and the UK, whose economic interests in Namibia were primary, and who were therefore prepared to assist in South Africa's violations of the cease-fire agreement. Ahtisaari allowed himself to be convinced that there were no SWAPO forces in Namibia before 31 March 1989. When fabricated evidence of PLAN "incursions" was produced, Ahtisaari swallowed the lie and agreed to permit the South African re-deployment of its 101st Battalion, who were in combat readiness. This diabolical secret plan had the full support of both the Reagan administration and British prime minister Thatcher.

At this crucial and critical hour for Namibia's freedom, Ahtisaari's action betrayed our cause and resulted in the deaths of many innocent civilians. These deaths included those who were killed on the road between Tsumeb and Namutoni while returning from a celebration of the implementation of Resolution 435 in Windhoek. Buses and cars were shot at by soldiers in plain clothes, organized by South African military intelligence. Other fighting that day was the fiercest that had been seen in some sectors of the country since the launching of the armed liberation struggle on 26 August 1966.

Ahtisaari then had to convince the UN Secretary-General by sending a report to the UN headquarters in New York. This he plotted with British prime minister Mrs. Thatcher, who had made trips to Namibia under the pretence of visiting Rössing Uranium Company, a subsidiary company of British Rio Tinto Zinc, or RTZ, which had exploited Namibian uranium for so long. Prime Minister Thatcher cared little about the massacre of the Namibian people, placing more importance on the economic exploitation and profits the company was making. The UN Secretary-General Mr. Pérez de Cuéllar was thus put in a difficult situation and was compelled to report to the Security Council, with the Reagan administration pressurizing and blaming SWAPO as the violator of Resolution 435. South Africa's threat to discontinue the implementation of Resolution 435 would send Ahtisaari back, as well as expelling the UNTAG personnel components from Namibia.

After the defeat of P. W. Botha's presidential regiments at Cuito Cuanavale and Calueque, the minority white South African regime was compelled to accept that Resolution 435 must be implemented, even if only partially. As their next and final option, they quickly moved on to manoeuvres and intrigues in the attempt to destroy SWAPO in the eyes of the Namibian people. One of these manoeuvres was a diabolic scheme to massacre our fighters and innocent civilians in full view of the people, to create the impression that South Africa was still superior despite the fact that they had accepted the implementation of Resolution 435. South Africa also continued to imagine that it was possible to frighten the people away from association with SWAPO and from supporting the Party and its leadership during the forthcoming UN supervised and controlled election under Resolution 435.

Even though PLAN combatants had been attacked by surprise while waiting to be confined to bases by UNTAG, true to their bravery they repelled the enemy fire and caused heavy enemy casualties. The people gained even more confidence in SWAPO as they saw the fighting power of our soldiers in direct combat. As fighting continued after the South African violation of the cease-fire agreement, their casualties were heavy and the South Africans' reported number of white dead soldiers was extremely high day after day.

Our casualties included many who were captured and simply shot at point blank in the back of their necks. This was revealed by a reporter and photographer from the London *Sunday Telegraph* who climbed a wall to photograph a mass grave near Oshakati and identified 19 such bodies. Forensic experts later wrote that the photographs proved that they had been killed in cold blood. Apartheid South Africa had never observed the Geneva Convention in its treatment of captured PLAN war prisoners, though SWAPO had adhered strictly to it on all the occasions when we captured their soldiers. It must be said that the extreme cruelty of the minority white soldiers was based on racial hatred, and horrific crimes were committed by them against the masses during the war of liberation. I must also put on record that white South African commanders often killed wounded PLAN fighters and even overran civilian homesteads with combat vehicles such as Casspirs in their attempts to reduce SWAPO's popularity. Both SWATF and Koevoet insurgency puppet units were guilty of these crimes.

However, gallant PLAN fighters actually reversed the situation, as the battles they fought in response to enemy provocation enhanced SWAPO's reputation as a liberator in the eyes of the people. As a matter of fact, when SWAPO leaders returned to Namibia in the months that followed, we did so as heroes and heroines. Even though we had left the country in hiding and travelled many winding roads to avoid interception and capture, now we returned as heroic victors in the eyes of the people, and we received a warm welcome by thousands of Namibians across the country.

In Harare, I did my level best to show that SWAPO and the UN had been the victims of a well-planned, western-supported, South African conspiracy. Over the Zimbabwean radio I immediately stated that the provocation behind the fighting that had broken out was South Africa's, and I repeated the information we had received about the attacks on civilians on the road between Tsumeb and Namutoni. The same day over the radio, I also rejected the false South African claim that there had been an "incursion" by PLAN combatants. I condemned the South Africans for engineering this incident as a scheme to prevent the implementation of Resolution 435. I expressed our shock that Ahtisaari was violating the UN plan by allowing South African forces out of their bases to attack our people. I reaffirmed that SWAPO was fully committed to the cease-fire agreement, which I had signed on behalf of SWAPO and the oppressed people of Namibia, and which I had ordered all members of PLAN to honour.

In Harare, I also addressed the ambassadors of the USSR, USA and France and the British High Commissioner for an hour and a half. I tried to convince them that further UN troops should be sent to Namibia at once. I asked them why they were siding with the apartheid South African oppressors, who were killing our people. I said:

> "While now Resolution 435 is being implemented there is a war going on, deliberately provoked by apartheid South Africa with the purpose of torpedoing it because there is no effective presence of UN peace-keeping forces. You reduced the numbers of UNTAG military components and this is what has happened as a result."

They denied this, of course, but I could see that the American ambassador was embarrassed since it was the US who had initiated the reduction of the UN peace-keeping forces in Namibia.

President Robert Mugabe, the then Chairman of the Non-Aligned Movement, supported the SWAPO position very strongly. It was at the point when Zimbabwe was serving as a member of the UN Security Council, and this gave its representative the opportunity to effectively support our stands in the Security Council debate and, together with other members of the movement of the Non-Aligned countries, to champion Namibia's freedom and independence.

I knew that the people would support us once we had returned and that we must not allow the South African regime to get away with the torpedoing of Resolution 435. We were totally vigilant. 'Pik' Botha, though, continued to insist that the "SWAPO terrorists" all be sent north of the 16th parallel in Angola, as the Geneva Protocol laid down and we had agreed, knowing that we would win the independence elections whatever the manoeuvres and intrigues the Boer regime would deploy in an attempt to put SWAPO in a disadvantaged position.

On 8 April 1989, I ordered our forces to re-deploy and cross the border into Angola. But the South Africans continued to attack, and the fighting went on bitterly until 24 April 1989. It was not until 26 April 1989 that the South African forces were confined to their bases for 60 hours to enable PLAN fighters to cross at certain agreed points, this time under the observation of the UNTAG military component.

Implementation of the UN Security Council Resolution 435 — The Joint Military Monitoring Commission (JMMC), the Mount Etjo Accord, and Ruacana meeting

The violation by the South Africans of the ceasefire agreement led to meeting of a Joint Military Monitoring Commission (JMMC) comprised of Angola, Cuba and South Africa. On 8 April, before this meeting began, I had already announced that our troops were withdrawing, so all they had to do was to agree on arrangements for our troops to gather and move without further South African attacks. We had had to withdraw from our earlier intention of confining them to bases in Namibia, as contained in Resolution 435. South Africa's lies, and the huge propaganda campaign that followed the 1 April 1989 attacks, obliged us to adopt a tactical retreat and move all our forces to Angola. So through their lies the apartheid regime did convince its western allies of our guilt, as Chester Crocker was quoted as saying after the meeting, "Anybody who thought that South Africa would tolerate an incursion of 1,500 to 1,800 men in violation of all the provisions of the settlement plan was very unrealistic".

The JMMC, in a meeting at a luxury holiday farm at Mount Etjo near Otjiwarongo on 8–9 April 1989, tried to control the movement of our forces north of the 16th parallel. The US and USSR were represented by

Chester Crocker and Mr. Anatoly Adamishin respectively. Messrs. Pienaar and Ahtisaari also attended. Throughout the negotiations, the South Africans, Angolans and Cubans put themselves in charge of our affairs.

At first the JMMC failed to agree on terms acceptable to PLAN and the SADF. But after a series of meetings the 'Mount Etjo Accord' was signed by Angola, Cuba and South Africa. This provided for an immediate ceasefire under which PLAN combatants in Namibia would be given 'free passage' to Angola through designated crossing points controlled by the United Nations. But the Mount Etjo Accord failed because the SADF continued with the fighting and because the UN-monitored assembly points had been used as interrogation centres by the South Africans. In the process, PLAN combatants were blocked from crossing into Angola, and a dozen of them were killed while attempting to report to the assembly points.

When South Africa had repeatedly broken the Mount Etjo Accord, the Angolans and Cubans became annoyed. They refused to mediate between South Africa and SWAPO any longer and encouraged the two parties to talk directly to each other. At this point SWAPO sent signals to South Africa that the ceasefire agreement would collapse unless immediate and direct practical talks took place between parties at the technical level. South Africa communicated to SWAPO through diplomatic channels their readiness to hold direct talks between the field commanders without further delay.

The failure of the Mount Etjo Accord raised serious concerns among PLAN combatants. Comrade Erastus Negonga, who at the time was North Western Front Commander and a member of the PLAN Military Council, recalls that he was expecting new instructions from PLAN Command Headquarters to mobilise forces and renew fighting. Instead, as Commander in Chief of PLAN, I called Comrade Negonga to PLAN Defence Headquarters and presented him with the task of meeting the South African generals at Ruacana in Namibia, and telling them to choose between continued fighting or complying with the Mount Etjo Accord. Comrade Nahas Angula, the SWAPO Secretary for Education, led the delegation to Ruacana, which also included Comrade Andrew Intamba, a member of the PLAN Military Council, and Comrade Kondja Kambala from the Office of the President. Comrade Martin Shalli, the PLAN Chief of Operations and a member of the PLAN Military Council, was also nominated to attend, but could not make it due to other engagements at the front.

On the morning of 18 April 1989, the SWAPO/PLAN delegation arrived at the Ruacana border post in two Angolan helicopters. Except for Comrade Angula who preferred civilian clothes, the delegation were dressed in camouflage uniforms similar to those used by the Angolans and Cubans, and each was equipped with a side-worn makarrov pistol.

The border post was known as 'Beacon 1', and was manned by Angolan Armed Forces on the Angolan side and by the South African Defence Force on the Namibian side. On the ground, everything looked unusual, with no sign of the South African generals on the Namibian side. An Angolan sergeant who welcomed the SWAPO/PLAN delegation on the Angolan side was unable to give any briefing about the meeting, and there was no intermediary to communicate their arrival to the South African delegation. Further, there was no protocol reception whatsoever.

After an hour on the Angolan side of the border, Comrade Angula requested the Angolan sergeant to find out whether there was a South African delegation on the Namibian side to meet the SWAPO delegation. The sergeant reported back that the meeting was organized to take place at the SADF border post inside Namibia. He showed the SWAPO delegation the entrance to the border post and then quickly returned to his own position. The delegation proceeded to the SADF border post, still unmet and undirected. They located a small dining hall in the post which they suspected might be the venue of the meeting, and waited there for some time.

When the South African delegation did arrive at the venue, from behind thick bushes, their six military officers were in brown uniforms and all were heavily equipped with R-4 assault rifles. Comrade Angula immediately recognised the head of the delegation as Major General Willie Meyer, the Commanding Officer of the SWATF. Another delegate who looked very tired indeed was Brigadier Serfontein, the Commanding Officer of Sector 10 at Oshakati which had suffered much from the PLAN rockets at the North Western Front. Other members of the South African delegation were Mr. Carl von Hirschberg from the Office of the Administrator General, Commandant Bolsler, Major Vasaliwo, and another Commandant who did not display his name tag, presumably from the SADF military intelligence.

As the South Africans entered the hall where the SWAPO delegation were already waiting, they kept their eyes fixed on the Angolan side of the border. Then one of them said, "Good day. Where is SWAPO?

Are they coming or not?". It became apparent that the South African delegation thought our men were the Angolans preceding the SWAPO delegation for the talks.

After a silence in the hall, Comrade Angula declared himself as chairman of the meeting and moved to introduce himself as the leader of the SWAPO delegation, which was of course the host delegation on Namibian soil, their country of birth. "I am a civilian, a member of the SWAPO leadership come to talk with you, not to fight", he teased. But he continued sternly, "We are instructed by our President to ask you to choose whether to continue fighting or to grant PLAN combatants free passage back to Angola in compliance with the Mount Etjo Accord".

At first the meeting was tense, with the South Africans in an anxious mood. But this was gradually relieved by humorous remarks made by Comrade Angula and by the able manner in which the SWAPO chairman led the fragile talks. In reply, Major General Meyer thanked Comrade Angula for the mature and diplomatic manner in which he introduced the agenda items of the meeting. General Meyer then introduced Mr. Carl von Hirschberg as the representative of the Administrator General Mr. Louis Pienaar, and assured the SWAPO delegation that South Africa would comply with the Mount Etjo declaration without harassment by the SADF. The South Africans had already undertaken to confine SADF forces into bases during the withdrawal of the PLAN combatants, and now they reiterated their commitment to honour the ceasefire agreement. They promised to convene the JMMC meeting again in the shortest possible time and to assure the commission of South Africa's commitment to the Mount Etjo Accord.

At the closing of the meeting, the South African delegation requested the SWAPO delegation not to disclose the 18 April 1989 meeting to the media, due to its sensitivity. The SWAPO delegation accepted their appeal in principle, on condition that the South African would comply with the resolutions of the meeting. After Comrade Angula dissolved the meeting, he initiated hand-shaking between the two delegations and both parties returned to their headquarters.

This was the first time in the history of the armed liberation struggle that the two warring parties came together at the negotiating table, and the outcome was constructive.

The 18 April 1989 meeting at Ruacana had set the agenda for a meeting of the JMMC on 20 April 1989, also at Ruacana. Subsequent to the JMMC meeting, the then South African Minister of Foreign Affairs 'Pik' Botha announced that the SADF would return to bases as from

Wednesday 26 April 1989 at 4 p.m., for a period of 60 hours. He also again gave assurances that PLAN combatants would be allowed unhindered passage to Angola during the same period.

The story of the 18 April 1989 meeting at Ruacana leaked to the media 5 days later. *The Namibian* ran headlines on Monday 24 April: "SADF/PLAN Meet"; and "South Africa accused of breaking Mount Etjo Declaration and given ultimatum — fight or withdraw". Although the meeting was confirmed by a spokesman from the South African Department of Foreign Affairs, the SWATF Headquarters in Windhoek denied that the meeting had taken place, describing the story as "nonsense and clearly purposeful disinformation...". Mr. Carl von Hirschberg also refused to confirm or deny his presence at the meeting.

In its attempt to convince the public, *The Namibian* insisted that the meeting had taken place. They reported:

> "The two PLAN commanders who attended the April 18 talks on Namibian soil with South African officers and diplomats are Mr. Erastus Negonga and Mr. Andrew Intamba, both members of the SWAPO military council. The SWAPO delegation was headed by Mr. Nahas Angula, assisted by Mr. Kondja Kambala of the President's office and two technical cadres."

The Namibian also revealed that Mr. Hidipo Hamutenya, SWAPO Secretary for Information, had also confirmed the meeting. Mr. Hamutenya was quoted from London as saying that the meeting of 18 April 1989 was prompted by the state of deadlock concerning the implementation of the Mount Etjo Accord:

> "At the Ruacana meeting, SWAPO had spelled out its bottom line and had given the South Africans an ultimatum; either they decided to fight or they decided to allow the PLAN combatants unhindered return to Angola. They couldn't have both."

South African propaganda

South African propaganda was given publicity by the western journalists — some of whom were on the pay-roll of the apartheid regime to condemn SWAPO for the lives lost after the cease-fire. I was personally attacked in the western media as a warmonger and violator of the implementation of Resolution 435. Our replies were deliberately ignored by the western journalists inside Namibia who were more than willing to accept SADF propaganda and disinformation as it was given to them, rather than go and find out the truth for themselves.

The main attack on me and on SWAPO was that we had broken faith with the terms of Resolution 435 and with a later undertaking I had given to accept the terms of the Geneva Protocol. With few exceptions, the media and many western politicians refused to accept our statements since they revealed the South African position of aggression against the Namibian people. SWAPO's position was always as follows:

1. Under the UN Secretary-General's Report of 26 February 1979 (one of the three documents on which Resolution 435 was based), that all PLAN and South African forces were to be confined to bases within Namibia at the commencement of the cease-fire.
2. The references in 'Pik' Botha's letter to the UN Secretary-General of 15 March 1979 to another key document, the Western proposal of January 1979 (S/12636), demonstrated South Africa's initial agreement to SWAPO bases within Namibia and the UN Secretary-General's reply confirmed this arrangement as necessary "to solve the practical problems".
3. The provisions of the Geneva Protocol by which our forces were to be north of the 16th parallel applied only "within the context of the cessation of hostilities between the two warring forces".
4. The Geneva Protocol did not and could not interfere with the agreements between SWAPO and South Africa as incorporated in Resolution 435.

With the insistence of South Africa, actively supported by the Reagan administration and by other western powers in the Security Council, no reference was made with regard to the confinement of SWAPO forces to bases inside Namibia, nor of South Africa troops mentioned in the final document. This was a deliberate and calculated manoeuvre by South Africa and its western allies, with the clear aim of destroying SWAPO.

We never departed from our agreement that our troops would be confined to bases at the cessation of hostilities. When they assembled for this purpose on 1 April 1989, and the South Africans broke the cease-fire agreement and attacked our forces, UNTAG failed to report these violations to the Security Council. Instead, Ahtisaari and South Africa shifted the blame for this disaster onto SWAPO, thereby doing us a great injustice, while SWAPO forces and civilians were dying at the hands of the illegal occupiers of our country. I announced in the subsequent days that we would be willing to submit to the findings of an inquiry into what had happened because the racist South Africans could not have let the truth of their treachery come out.

We held a memorial service for our dead Comrades in Harare before I left, at which I put in simple terms the four points stated above. I reiterated them to the UN Secretary-General in New York, as did my colleagues to UN officials. We repeatedly denied that we had sent our soldiers over the border in an "incursion" on the night of 31 March/1 April 1989. But the western media were gathered in Namibia where the South African propaganda machine told them what they wanted to hear. Statements put out in support of our case by Namibians with access to the truth of what was happening, such as by the Council of Churches in Namibia, were ignored by all but a very few independent-minded journalists.

South Africa's treachery was also successful in gaining certain advantages for the campaign of reducing SWAPO to the level of the puppets. Koevoet was not disbanded in spite of Resolution 632 and Resolution 640 which followed it. Ahtisaari allowed the South Africans a greater role in the arrangements for our return and in the registration of voters that was to follow, and their profile was considerably raised in the western world at our expense. Nevertheless, we remained in a stronger position than ever before.

Pienaar's crucial blunder

However, a blunder was now committed that had the effect of ending all South Africa's threats about cancelling the agreements and backing out of Resolution 435. On 7 April 1989, Administrator-General Pienaar announced in Windhoek what he called "a de facto suspension of the application of Resolution 435", saying that "as a result of the continuing incursions from Angola by heavily armed members of the People's Liberation Army of Namibia it has become impossible to contemplate such elections under prevailing circumstances". 'Pik' Botha had to quickly reply, contradicting Pienaar, with a statement that South Africa remained fully committed to Resolution 435.

Pienaar continued to work with Ahtisaari on the arrangements for voter registration, elections, the constituent assembly and other matters arising out of 435 — but his position as one of the South Africans deciding policy was ended by that blunder.

87 Sam Nujoma speaking to SWAPO followers at a SWAPO star rally in Keetsmanshoop, 4 November 1989

On the same day P. W. Botha announced that he would retire after the General Election to be held in South Africa in September 1989. He in fact resigned even before that, in August 1989. Any pretence that South Africa could hold on to Namibia went at the same time as Pienaar's loss of authority as a result of his 7 April 1989 political blunder.

In my own case, in spite of unceasing attacks on me by three successive South African Prime Ministers — H. F. Verwoerd, B. J. Vorster and P. W. Botha — and more recently by the western media, whipped up by South African propaganda, I had lived to see these three architects of apartheid fall in various ways, while I survived as President of SWAPO to lead our movement to the final victory after nearly three decades of bloody struggle against white minority South African occupation of Namibia.

88 SWAPO President Sam Nujoma with South African Colonial Administrator-General, Louis Pienaar. Windhoek, 24 September 1989

89 (L to R) General Opande of Kenya UNTAG Military component; President of SWAPO Sam Nujoma. Kahama Airport. 20 April, 1989

Final preparations for homecoming

Arrangements were now being made for the return of the large Namibian community in exile under SWAPO's care. There were about 40,000 of them in Angola, with the UN High Commission for Refugees responsible for their repatriation. Early in June 1989, I instructed Dr Nickey Iyambo (first Minister of Health and Social Services) to get ready to return with a few colleagues to prepare the way for the large numbers that were to follow. This first party flew from Luanda on 12 June, only a few weeks after the withdrawal of our forces into Angola as finally agreed with the UN.

Comrade Hage Geingob, who had been appointed by SWAPO Central Committee to lead the forthcoming election campaign, then followed only six days later with a large group which included Dr. Libertina Amathila, Theo-Ben Gurirab and Hidipo Hamutenya, Pendukeni Ithana and many others; and a second Zambian Airways planeload reached Oshakati the same day. From then on, the numbers of our "returnees" increased rapidly, and the stage began to be set for the democratic process in which we were all to participate.

The South African apartheid regime still did not let up in the propaganda attacks and continued with their vicious anti-SWAPO campaign. The Radio South African Co-operation (RSAC) sub-station, located on the top floor of Kalahari Sands Hotel in Windhoek, as we later discovered, daily attacked and slandered SWAPO. RSAC was lubricated, as we now know from 'Pik' Botha's admission, by a massive 'slush fund' of 100 million South African rand which Botha set up to fund all the opposition parties in an effort to defeat SWAPO in the elections.

At the end of May 1989 we called the press to Lubango, Angola to observe the release from detention of a number of SWAPO members who had been held as suspected spies and South African agents. Andimba Ya Toivo and Moses Garoeb, then respectively our Secretary-General and Administrative Secretary, were present, as were a reporter and photographer from *The Namibian* in Windhoek. All those ex-detainees, who complained of harsh treatment and protested their innocence, were returned to Namibia where some of them also became recipients of Botha's massive slush funds, and they duly formed a political party which joined the DTA in opposition to SWAPO. This was their democratic right, which they were free to exercise in the first democratic election, supervised and controlled by the UN. Though there was bitterness against them because of accusations that some had given information to the enemy, they were nevertheless received back into the community.

As I prepared for my return home, numerous issues still caused me to maintain the maximum vigilance. There was much to worry us about the preparation for the elections and in August 1989 I put these concerns very forcefully to the British Government at a press conference in London. I had already found, on a visit two months earlier, that a very changed climate existed at the British Foreign Office, which now gave me 'red carpet' treatment. I had talks with the Foreign Secretary, Sir Geoffrey Howe, and was assured of development aid "without preconditions".

In August 1989, I stressed the bad situation in the north where, in defiance of Resolution 632, Koevoet was still in existence, terrorizing the people in Ovambo, Kavango and Kaokoland. There had been abductions, assaults and the killing of a SWAPO election official, Petrus Joseph, in the Kavango region. A key provision of the implementation was being violated without any protest from the UN. I called on the British government to demand the complete withdrawal of Koevoet insurgency units and also to expose the threatened rigging of the elections by the South Africans, through mass immigration of UNITA bandits from Angola and white South Africans to swell the anti-SWAPO vote, and through the snail's pace registration of voters in SWAPO-supporting areas.

I said it would be the "scandal of the century" if the South Africans rigged the elections "while the UN looks on", and I was well supported by our friends campaigning on this issue. Nevertheless very little media attention was paid to my words, and our sense of alarm grew. That same month, however, the five Permanent Members of the UN Security Council sent a strongly-worded protest on Koevoet to the South African government. Koevoet were "recalled to base", though they remained a constant threat to our people.

The menace under which we all now lived were South Africa's hit squads, "dirty tricks" operators and undercover agents carrying out the orders of their military and political bosses in Pretoria. This was displayed tragically on 12 September 1989, 48 hours before I was due to return, when Comrade Anton Lubowski, then acting as Deputy Head of Administration in the Election Directorate, was shot dead as he was entering his home at Klein Windhoek by a gunman using an AK-47 rifle.

Anton Lubowski, Hartmut Ruppel and other prominent white Namibians such as editor of *The Namibian* Gwen Lister, the human

90   Farewell to Hage Geingob, leading the first large group into Namibia during the UN repatriation programme, with SWAPO leadership in the background. Luanda Airport, Angola, 18 June 1989

91   With Libertina Amathila; Nahas Angula; Patrick Ijambo Lungada in background, 18 June 1989

rights lawyer David Smuts, and the photographer John Liebenberg had been receiving death threats for some time, certainly coming from South African military intelligence and the Special Branch police in Windhoek. Comrade Anton Lubowski had many enemies among the right-wing whites, who hated him for being a SWAPO member and participating in the liberation struggle. It soon became clear, however, that his murderer was a professional killer, organized by one of the units in the South African security apparatus. The murderer has never been brought to justice, and may well still be employed by the State, perhaps even here in Namibia. I expressed my deepest sympathy and condolences to the Lubowski family at their tragic loss, which was also Namibia's, as Comrade Lubowski had much to give our country at its rebirth. SWAPO's official statement described him as "a tireless cadre, selfless fighter and skilled lawyer, whose services this country will always miss".

It was a cause of much concern to my colleagues, as well as to the UNTAG authorities, and the South Africans, who now wanted the independence process to be completed with credit to themselves, that I was returning only two days after an assassination plot against a SWAPO leader had been successfully carried out. Martti Ahtisaari issued a statement warning that any further assassinations or widespread violence would halt the implementation of Resolution 435. SWAPO Director of Elections, Comrade Hage Geingob, was more specific and said:

> "If anything happens to our President there will be no election; the whole process will stop."

~~~~~

Despite the cold-blooded murder of Comrade Anton Lubowski, my wife and I meanwhile were looking forward to our homecoming to Namibia, which we had left so many years before and in very different circumstances.

◆ ◆ ◆

26

Return to Windhoek, Independence and a New Beginning

In early September 1989, before my return home, I attended the Summit of the Movement of Non-Aligned Countries in Yugoslavia outside Belgrade. From there I proceeded to Tehran, the capital city of the Islamic Republic of Iran, one of the countries who accorded SWAPO full diplomatic status. I was met at the airport by SWAPO Chief Representative, Comrade Titus Mwailepeni, and other government officials with whom we had fruitful discussions. They provided us with a special direct flight from Tehran to Luanda.

On 12 September, I flew to Kinshasa where I met with President Mobutu Sese Seko, and then with the new American Assistant Secretary of State for African Affairs Mr. Herman Cohen, who had replaced Mr. Chester Crocker. I urged him to support the implementation of UN Resolution 435 and not to sabotage it as his predecessor had done.

The following day I returned to Luanda. On the eve of my departure I received the sad news from Comrade Hage Geingob of the assassination of Comrade Anton Lubowski by an unknown assailant.

On the morning of 14 September 1989, my wife and I, accompanied by Comrade Moses Garoeb, then SWAPO Administrative Secretary, and other SWAPO senior officials embarked on a chartered Ethiopian Airline Jet 767, flown by an Ethiopian captain accompanied by Namibian co-pilots whom SWAPO had trained with Ethiopian Airline. At Luanda airport, President José Eduardo dos Santos, cabinet ministers and high ranking officials from the MPLA Party saw us off and wished us a successful electioneering campaign. After two and half hours flight, we touched down at 12.30 p.m. at the J. J. Strijdom Airport (now Hosea Kutako International Airport).

Immediately after we landed, I ran into conflict with the South African Colonial Administrator who was still in control, even though UNTAG military personnel and civilian components were also at the airport. He refused to allow photographers to take pictures on the runway, as I disembarked from the plane. I told the South African and UNTAG officials that I was not going to leave the plane until the press and all those who were there to witness my historic return home had gathered on the tarmac. For my part, I had not fought for nearly 30 years for the freedom of my country to return to it now as if sneaking in through the back door. I wished the event to be freely covered by the media, which would spread worldwide the words and pictures of this triumph.

After 20 minutes of delay and consultation, my demand was accepted and I stepped down from the plane, to be greeted first by the internal Acting President of SWAPO, Nataniel Maxuilili, Vice President Hendrik Witbooi and Comrade Hage Geingob. Comrade Geingob held high the same SWAPO flag that I had handed to him on 18 June 1989 as he embarked on the Zambian Airways DC10 en route to Windhoek, and then handed it back to me. Then followed by my dear mother Helvi-Mpingana Kondombolo, 89 years of age and still bright-eyed and upright. I then knelt and kissed the soil of my beloved country — Namibia, "The Land of the Brave".

We were taken quickly through the airport building into a waiting motor-car to begin the 45 km drive into Windhoek. Our capital, a settlement of the Hereros, Nama and Orlams long before the Germans came, was built among hills and the nearest sufficiently flat area for an international-standard airport was at such a distance. Nevertheless, the road was lined all the way to Windhoek by cheering well-wishers and welcoming SWAPO members, supporters, fellow-countrymen and women who were yearning for freedom and independence.

I later learned that after my arrival at the airport there was a commotion when SWAPO security officials detected a South African intelligence officer with a rifle, waiting to assassinate me as I disembarked from the plane. The South African agent was forcibly removed from the airport buildings. This was one of the reasons the press was refused access during my disembarkation from the plane. Windhoek was very tense after the assassination of Comrade Anton Lubowski on 12 September. The Boers were so vicious that even after they agreed to and signed the cease-fire, they wrote on the wall of a car park in the middle of Windhoek, "We are waiting for murderer Nujoma". However, Nigeria and the Front Line States — Angola, Botswana, Zambia, Tanzania, Mozambique and Zimbabwe — and other OAU member states who had established their offices in Windhoek (later on to become embassies and high commissions), coupled with SWAPO security officers, had foiled the assassination plan.

It is a fact that, even though I had lived for some years with the certainty of my return to Namibia on the threshold of independence, come what may, my arrival and the journey to Windhoek and on to Katutura were moments of supreme joy.

By then many thousands of Namibians had returned from exile as I had, and we shared this wonderful feeling of homecoming. I had lived for ten years in Tanzania, nine in Zambia and a further ten years in Angola, and scarcely a month had passed during that whole period without travel to the four corners of the earth, or to be with our freedom fighters or refugees in the SWAPO Education and Health Centres in Angola, Cuba, GDR (East Germany), Congo-Brazzaville and Zambia. Now I was to be in my own home, with my wife and family, and no longer a guest or bird of passage seeking support for Namibia's freedom and independence. This was indeed a joyful and historic homecoming.

Katutura again

Like all the returning exiles I had problems to face, but I was confident that none of them was insurmountable. The first of these was the apartheid policy of separate development — inferior 'bantu' education which created disunity and racial and tribal hatred in the entire Namibian society. This policy of the apartheid regime had affected all our lives. In Katutura, straight after arriving from the airport, I made a statement at a press conference in which I appealed strongly for national unity: "The struggle has been long and bitter. My comrades and I return in a spirit of peace, love, and above all, national reconciliation". I urged:

> "Let us from this day work in unison, forget and leave the sad chapter behind us. These memories of bitter and long years of conflict, racial hatred and deep mistrust among us Namibians must be buried forever. Let us open a new page and a new chapter based on unity, peace, human rights, patriotism, respect for one another and genuine reconciliation."

Our earliest struggles in the Old Location had been based on the demand for human rights and an end to racial discrimination, as well as freedom from colonialism — these goals were now within our grasp. There was in my mind another comparison with those early days: elements in the police and among their friends had meant to assassinate me then but had not succeeded. The threat had been the same on my return, but again their plots had failed. I would now be able to devote myself to some of the tasks we had set ourselves in those early days.

My family and I stayed in Wanaheda, a section of Katutura black townships, in a modern house, recently bought by SWAPO. Katutura, like the sprawling town of Oshakati in the north, had not existed when I had crossed the border into Botswana in 1960. It was many times larger than the Windhoek Old Location where we had lived, but with poor facilities and with the same poverty imposed on our people by the apartheid colonial administration which it was going to be our task to eradicate.

I went to bed filled with such thoughts and it was wonderful to awake early the next morning with the knowledge that I was at home, with my primary task, as set by Chief Hosea Kutako, Samuel Witbooi and SWAPO, almost complete. It was always in our minds that a part of our country, Walvis Bay and the off shore islands, was not yet free from minority white South African occupation.

My first duty the following morning was to register as a voter and then to meet my colleagues in the Election Directorate to discuss the serious difficulties we were facing. Already the South Africans were singling me out for abuse, with an angry reaction by 'Pik' Botha to my press statement the day before in which I had blamed Pretoria for the carnage in the north on and after 1 April 1989, and for the assassination of Comrade Anton Lubowski. To this day I still hold F. W. de Klerk and his military intelligence officers of the South African white minority regime responsible for the cold-blooded murder of Comrade Anton Lubowski.

We mourned him the following day in a packed congregation of thousands in the Lutheran church in Katutura. I and my colleagues sat with the deceased man's widow, children and parents. He was a symbol of the national unity and reconciliation that the SWAPO Central Committee had decided two years earlier would be SWAPO's chief priority. Anton Lubowski's life, tragically though it had ended, inspired many people, both black and white, to bury the bitterness of the past.

Election — progress and anti-progress

The election campaign was well under way and I launched the biggest political rally in Windhoek the country had ever seen, nine days after my return. I spoke for two and half hours to more than 100,000 people in the now Windhoek Independence Stadium, with another 10,000 listening to the loudspeakers outside. As at other such 'Star Rallies', as we called them, to follow in Swakopmund, Oshakati, Katima Mulilo, Keetmanshoop and Gobabis, I called upon the audience first to stand for two minutes of silence in remembrance of the tens of thousands of Namibians who had sacrificed their lives in the fight for freedom and independence. Each time, with varying words, I called on everyone to "work hard to heal the deep wounds which have been inflicted on our people in the past". I also addressed the difficulties we were facing in the election — the violent behaviour of the DTA supporters backed clandestinely by the CCB and other South African military apparatus in the country, without any apparent restraint by the South African police who, of course, were part of the conspiracy of South Africa to torpedo the implementation of Resolution 435.

The South African Administrator-General Mr. Louis Pienaar was in charge of the registration of voters, and the UN Secretary-General Representative was supposed only to certify that the registration process was in accordance with UN Security Council Resolution 435. However, the Administrator-General conspired and registered a large number of UNITA supporters from Angola, along with whites and coloureds from South Africa. These were brought in by planes and buses hired by the apartheid South African Government, to swell the DTA votes.

We had been fully conscious of plans to prevent SWAPO from winning the elections since June 1989 when *The Namibian* published the leaked minutes of a South West African Security Council meeting in Windhoek the previous September. Various tactics had been discussed by DTA leaders, civil service and military chiefs. The minutes recorded the wish of the military chiefs that "the department heads and cabinet must work together as a team to give urgent attention to an overall strategy". The chairman, Dirk Mudge of the DTA, wished to have "all political parties to stand together in the fight against SWAPO".

It was partly to reassure us, and in response to fears expressed by UNTAG and monitoring groups from the Commonwealth and elsewhere, that the Administrator-General had appointed a commission under Advocate (now Judge) Bryan O'Linn, to hear complaints of intimidation in the election. I met Louis Pienaar myself for our first discussion on 24 September 1989, and was aware of him wanting to give me the impression of being impartial in the election, and wanting to make concessions so that it would later be judged as "free and fair".

Pienaar appeared to be a sophisticated man, more than some of his predecessors had been, but we knew enough about him to judge his real attitude and political motives. This was made clear by his action at the beginning of October 1989 in transferring the civil service pension fund from the local administration to trustees who could move it to South Africa, with an estimated capital outflow of 1.2 billion rand. We protested against this, at the continuing election irregularities, and at the continuance of Koevoet, but received only empty reassurances.

I also had to deal with the failure of the authorities to rectify the many complaints from SWAPO supporters who had been targets of South African intimidatory tactics. There was in fact a very serious climate of violence surrounding our campaign and we had many complaints to make about attacks on our supporters and properties. The Commission was unable to find against the culprits for want of evidence, mainly due to the refusal of the police, still under their old command, to make arrests and investigate the attacks.

An ugly incident occurred when the UNTAG office at Outjo was bombed by the CCB (Civil Co-operation Bureau), a hit squad of the South African Military Intelligence aimed at the elimination of political opponents. One local policeman was killed, and the culprits, all known white South Africans, managed to escape the country through the assistance of South African under-cover agents. From the DTA — which the Pretoria racist regime, the Reagan/Bush administration and Thatcher's Conservative British Government all expected to win — came threats that, after the election, SWAPO members would be forced to swallow the SWAPO flags that were flying all over the country.

Shots were fired at our election headquarters building in Windhoek and mob violence was stirred up in Katutura (where there was still the so-called ethnic zoning and, consequently, blocs of party supporters who could be mobilized for such action). Justifiable complaints against SWAPO members and supporters were non-existent.

The UN Security Council was still watchful of the situation and determined that the process should not be wrecked at this final stage.

At the end of October 1989 a resolution introduced by a group of seven member states of the Non-Aligned Movement achieved an unanimous vote for Security Council Resolution No. 643 (October 31, 1989), which demanded full compliance with Resolutions 435 [1978], 632 and 640 [1989], especially the "complete disbandment" of Koevoet, SWATF and "their command structures", the repeal of all laws and regulations inhibiting free and fair elections and that the local police (SWAPOL) collaborate with the UNTAG police.

The only dissent came from the British permanent representative who voted for the resolution but threatened a future veto if the Constituent Assembly attempted to adopt a constitution omitting the 'Constitutional Principles' and without the two-thirds majority requirement that the American and British had imposed on us in 1982. It has to be said that the Constitutional Principles document was formulated by the Americans and British to favour the interests of individual white settlers who had, 'by hook or by crook', acquired and occupied Namibian land during the colonial era (as I have described in the first chapter of this book). It must be clearly stated that the inclusion of a clause in the constitution concerning commercial lands — the so-called "willing seller, willing buyer" clause, which serves to perpetuate the status quo of inequity in land distribution in Namibia — was never in line with SWAPO's position in addressing the land question in Namibia. The inclusion of this clause has resulted in the problem of lands we have after the turn of the millennium.

Nevertheless, at the time, we were fully confident that we would win enough seats, and would work with other parties if necessary, to bring in the constitution we wanted.

The last attempt by the South Africans to block SWAPO's inevitable election victory came a week before the poll.

Once again 'Pik' Botha flew into Windhoek, on the day after Resolution 643 was adopted in New York — 1 November 1989. With Magnus Malan, the Minister of Defence, and General Geldenhuys, he had called a press conference in Pretoria the night before and revealed copies of what he alleged were intercepted UNTAG radio messages referring to the infiltration of 600 PLAN fighters from Angola between 23 and 31 October 1989. We instantly described these allegations as "without a shred of truth". By the evening, Martti Ahtisaari and the UNTAG spokesman Fred Eckhard had examined the messages and found that they "did not conform to any known form of UNTAG communication", and that "there are no PLAN fighters below the 16th parallel to our knowledge". Secretary-General Pérez de Cuéllar simply described the messages as "forgeries".

Botha was accused in the South African parliament of making South Africa a "laughing stock", and the opposition demanded his resignation. He had to admit that he had been the victim of a hoax, what was known as "dirty tricks" from inside South African military intelligence. I met him with colleagues at the office of the Administrator-General in Windhoek (what we now call State House) and confirmed Ahtisaari's assurances that our troops had not crossed the border but were confined to their bases in Angola, in accordance with our earlier undertaking.

What astonished me at this meeting, only the second I had had with him, was that he told me that the messages had been communicated through General Geldenhuys from the same source that had given them information on 31 March 1989 which had led to the unprovoked attack and death of our soldiers and civilians on 1 April 1989. We decided not to reveal what he had said, in the interests of our national reconciliation policy and of preventing further destabilization just before the elections. I told the press:

> "It does not pay any of us now to dwell on sad historical events. We must leave them behind us and start working afresh together towards a bright future for this country."

Botha claimed later that he had no choice but to accept our assurances that our fighters had not crossed the border in November 1989.

I did take the opportunity of telling Botha and General Geldenhuys that our election headquarters had been fired at almost every night and that many other such attempts were being made to destabilize and derail the election process. I told Botha that we were determined not to respond to violence with violence. As I have already mentioned, though we had our suspicions as to the level of their support, we did not know until a year after the elections that the South Africans had poured money — over 100 million rand, according to 'Pik' Botha's own statement in the South African parliament — into the DTA and the smaller parties in their hopeless attempt to try and defeat SWAPO.

We campaigned hard, and between what we called the 'Star Rallies', where I spoke, I met many groups of Namibians, church leaders, members of the business community, and on my first return to Ovamboland, the remaining traditional rulers and headmen of the old kingdoms: the Kwambi, Mbalantu, Kolonkadhi, Kwanyama, Ndonga, Ngandjera and Kwaluudhi. I had lengthy talks with all of them on separate occasions. I visited their traditional royal homesteads to assure them that the future SWAPO government would recognise their traditional authorities. I was a guest of the Ndonga Chief, Elifas Kauluma, at Onamungundo near Ondangwa who had been a strong supporter of SWAPO during the struggle for independence. Despite threats on his life and the destruction of his royal homestead at Onamungundo, burned down by South African military intelligence officers, Koevoet and CCB in 1988, he never gave up supporting SWAPO.

I was encouraged by their unanimous agreement to support SWAPO in the elections and to give their backing to the new government we would form when independence was achieved. Their traditional leadership still means a lot to the people of Ovamboland, as does that of the Kavango, the Kaoko, the Tswana and East Caprivian chiefs, despite some of them having been turned into puppets by the Boers, to carry out their apartheid policy of separate development of bantu education, and homeland administration, aimed at keeping the South African white minority in control and thus depriving indigenous Namibians from working together as a united people to fight for their freedom and independence.

I was able on this occasion to revisit my mother at Etunda, near Okahao, and was pleased to find her in our traditional homestead. Despite her advanced age, the death of my father and the absence of all her five sons, she had with the aid of my sister Nandjala Frieda, who is a widow, kept it up well, and continued to work in the fields. My two other sisters, Naapopye Sofia and Namukuwa Julia had married and were living with their husbands, and both of them have children. That enlarged the family and gave our mother the pleasure of grandchildren to look after, thus helping to keep her strength and morale high.

I also visited the Okahao Lutheran Church Mission where I had attended primary school before I went to Walvis Bay in 1946. I was delighted to find that some of the church buildings, built by Finnish missionaries, were still standing. However, I was saddened to find that some of the church building walls were bullet-scarred, attacked by South African forces who had a military base nearby. This military base was attacked by PLAN combatants on many occasions. According to local people, the enemy normally fired indiscriminately towards the church and school buildings to terrorize church-goers and students in hostels.

This was also the occasion to pay my respects at the resting place of my father Daniel Utoni Nujoma in the Lutheran Church graveyard at Oneeke, where the Finnish missionaries established the first church in Ongandjera district.

Another visit I paid, with full solemnity, was to the grave of the founder of modern Pan-African politics in Namibia, Chief Hosea Kutako. He is buried with the Herero chiefs Samuel Maharero and Frederick Maharero at Okahandja, the traditional Herero royal establishment before the Germans invaded and colonized the then South West Africa.

I addressed Star Rallies around the country. My final Star Rally in Gobabis was attended by more than 5,000, including white farmers who came to listen and who received me well. I urged both blacks and white farmers that we must reconcile, unite and work together as one nation. I went further to say Namibia is a big country and there is room for all of us to live together and build a strong foundation for our common goal, to work together to eradicate poverty, disease and ignorance. By so doing, we will build a solid foundation in which the future generations will live in peace, harmony and prosperity.

Election Day, 16 November, 1989

Next morning, I spoke to the press before leaving the house in Wanaheda. Despite all the provocation from the opposition parties and the violence from the undercover CCB and Koevoets who were still operating under the direction of the South African military intelligence apparatus, it was vital that we have a democratic election worthy as contained in the UN Security Council Resolution 435. I said:

> "We owe it to those who sacrificed their lives in the war, to ourselves and our children, to conduct ourselves in a dignified and disciplined manner. Don't fall prey to violence, disruptive behaviours and disorder and alcoholism. This first democratic election demands us to make sober choices for the future of our country as well as for ourselves."

When the polls opened, my wife and I went to vote in Katutura.

The election was, with very few exceptions, conducted freely and fairly, with a poll of over 95 per cent. For a while there was concern among SWAPO supporters as the results started to come in from the central and southern constituencies, where the opposition parties were strong because of the power of white farmers to compel their workers to vote against SWAPO, and because of the thousands of Angolans and white South Africans who had crossed the Orange River or been flown into Windhoek airport and registered by Louis Pienaar as voters to increase the number of DTA votes.

92 Informing members of the press of SWAPO victory in the first democratic elections. (L to R) Lucas Hifikepunye Pohamba; Hage Geingob; Hidipo Hamutenya; Sam Nujoma; Toivo ya Toivo. Windhoek, November 1989

The whole country had suffered in the war and all but the very oldest had spent their lifetime first under German colonialism and then South African minority white oppression. The worst sufferers had been the more than 50 per cent of the population who lived in Ovamboland, who had been in the front line in the war zone and had suffered Koevoet and South African army and police atrocities, and had supported our freedom fighters as best as they could. When their votes came in, last of all the constituencies, 92 per cent had voted for SWAPO, and this gave us 57.3 per cent of the total vote. We were the leading or second party in 15 out of the 25 electoral districts. Outside Ovamboland, we gained 48.7 per cent of our support, which showed that this was widespread throughout the country.

All South Africa's dirty tricks and propaganda, and the more than 100 million rand and other large financial contributions from right-wing sources in West Germany, USA, Britain and others abroad spent on trying to prevent the SWAPO victory, had failed.

The media, influenced by the heavy propaganda against SWAPO, had made it a contest as to whether or not SWAPO would get two-thirds of the vote (as required by the Constitutional Principles) to give us a free hand in drafting the Constitution, but this had not been our target in any way.

The duly elected Constituent Assembly was made up of 41 SWAPO members, 21 DTA and 10 from among the four smaller parties which qualified by the size of their vote. Our objective now was to move as rapidly as possible, consistent with making proper decisions, so that we could at last achieve our independence without delay and within the period stipulated for the duration of UNTAG.

Making of the Constitution

The Constituent Assembly duly met in the old debating chamber of the Tintenpalast ("Palace of Ink'), the government buildings built by the German colonialists. One of our first actions was the proposal by Theo-Ben Gurirab that the Assembly adopt the 1982 Constitutional Principles as a framework for the Constitution, and so we agreed without argument that Namibia would be a multi-party democracy with an independent judiciary and a strong bill of rights which would protect civil liberties and oppose "arbitrary expropriation of private property without justification".

A Standing Committee, chaired by Comrade Hage Geingob and consisting of eleven SWAPO members and nine from other parties, was appointed to draft the rules of procedure, which was done, despite difficulties with the DTA, by the end of November 1989.

A number of procedural issues had already been resolved by the various parties through consultation, and published in the Constituent Assembly Proclamation of 6 November 1989, i.e., just before the elections. This proclamation dealt with preliminary issues such as the date of coming into force of the Constitution, the adoption of certain rules for the conduct of the Constituent Assembly meetings, and provisions to prevent defection by members of one party to another.

This proclamation also stipulated that the task of the Constituent Assembly was to draw up the Constitution of Namibia, to adopt the Constitution by a two-thirds majority, and to fix a date for the independence of Namibia. After the 1989 Constituent Assembly elections supervised and controlled by the United Nations, the Constituent Assembly duly met on 21 November 1989.

At its first meeting, the Constituent Assembly elected Comrade Hage Geingob as Chairman. His task was not only to conduct the meetings but also to build confidence between diverse parties. He carried out both the tasks remarkably well. The first order of business for the Assembly was to constitute a Drafting Committee. SWAPO as the majority party nominated 12 members to this committee; DTA four members; NNF, FCN, NPF, ACN and UDF one member each.

Of course, before and during the elections, certain perceptions had been created that SWAPO was a socialist organization and was not committed to such ideals as democracy, right to property, etc. Therefore, when Comrade Theo-Ben Gurirab moved that the Constituent Assembly adopt the Contact Group's 1982 Constitutional Principles, it came as a complete surprise to non-SWAPO members of the committee.

Before the process started, each party had prepared its own draft Constitution. The committee was to consider provisions of each draft on specific topics, and come up with a final version for inclusion in the Constitution. However, at that time, a very healthy development took place when, to the surprise of everyone, DTA chairman Mr. Dirk Mudge proposed that SWAPO's draft should be accepted as the basis for drafting the Constitution.

The SWAPO draft had, of course, included provisions such as the protection of basic human rights, and commitment to democracy. All these provisions further facilitated the work of the committee.

Procedurally, the drafters first identified the areas they agreed upon, and set those aside. At the end of this exercise, we were left with those topics where there were material differences between the various parties. Specifically, three major differences had emerged: the type of executive, the type of legislature, and the type of electoral system.

On the question of the type of executive, SWAPO was committed to a strong executive and a unitary system of government, while others preferred to have a loose federal system with a weak central government. As Comrade Geingob put it, they preferred a federal system because they were used to apartheid divisions, but SWAPO wanted a strong, unitary central government to counter the damage done by apartheid. A federal system, we felt, would have only perpetuated the economically non-viable, divisive bantustans. SWAPO sought unity in diversity, but others sought to perpetuate bantustanisation of the country.

Given the political principles of SWAPO, it stood its ground in demanding a strong executive. However, in order to break the impasse and to avoid delaying independence, it was decided that negotiations should take place on the issue, in the spirit of 'give and take'

On the powers of the executive, after long discussions, we agreed that there should be 'checks and balances' on the powers of the President, that executive power be shared between the President and the Cabinet consisting of the Prime Minister and 16 Ministers, and that the President could be elected for two five-year terms. We also included in the Constitution a provision that the President would chair the Cabinet, and would address the parliament at the start of the budget session. In order to enhance transparency and accountability, the Constitution also stipulated that the President would answer questions posed to him after his address.

On the question of legislature, again, SWAPO and other parties were driven by very different principles. Given the small population of the country, SWAPO wanted a unicameral legislature elected on the basis of proportional representation, but others wanted a bicameral parliament. Their thinking was that SWAPO might win the popular vote throughout the country under proportional representation but would not be able to win elections in and control all the regions, and therefore the second legislature was required. Their perception was that the north would be just one constituency or one region, and in their calculations, SWAPO would win in the north, leaving the rest of the regions voting according to their tribal allegiance. Their perception was, however, flawed as it was based on the fact that constituencies would be created according to the size of the population in a given area, and not along the old bantustan lines of tribes as created by South African apartheid policy.

Further, their thinking that SWAPO would win only in the north was also to be proved wrong when regional council elections took place in the thirteen regions. These were the issues that prompted non-SWAPO members of the Constituent Assembly to push for a bicameral legislature. As a compromise, SWAPO accepted the concept of a second house as the 'house of regions'. Each one of the 13 regions — Ohanguena, Caprivi, Oshana, Omusati, Oshikoto, Kunene, Kavango and Otjozondjupa in the north; Erongo, Omaheke and Khomas in the central region; Hardap and Karas in the south — would elect two regional councillors as representatives in the National Council, the 'house of review'. It was also agreed that Namibia would have a three-tier government, constituted in the central government, regional governments, and local authorities.

On the third question of what type of electoral system Namibia should adopt, after a long debate it was agreed that proportional representation would be used for the election of the National Assembly, and a 'first past the post' system would be used for the election of regional councillors.

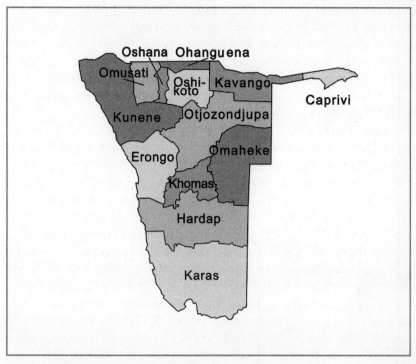

93   Thirteen Administrative Regions of the Republic of Namibia

With these three contentious issues out of the way, the members of the Drafting Committee turned their attention to drafting proper of the Constitution. It goes to their credit that they pulled off this difficult task in just 80 days. At least one author has dubbed this effort an "80 day miracle". The final document, the Constitution of Namibia, was adopted on 9 February 1990. It would come into force on the day of the country's independence.

Further, the Constituent Assembly designated 21 March 1990 as the day on which Namibia would become independent. This day, which is also United Nations Day, was chosen to emphasize international linkages of the people of Namibia during their long years of struggle.

94 The Namibian Constituency Assembly

[The names of the Honourable members read from left to right]

First row: JM de Wet, V Rukoro, MK Katjiuongua, President Sam Nujoma, HG Geingob, MA Muyongo, M Kerina, J Garoeb

Second row: JWF Pretorious, LH Pohamba, P Mueshihange, M Garoeb, A Toivo Ya Toivo, D Meroro, Rev H Witbooi, DF Mudge FJ Kozonguizi, D Luiperd, RR Diergaardt

Third row: WO Aston, P Ithana, Dr E Tjiriange, Rev Z Kameeta, HM Hausiku, N Bessinger, H Hamutenya, Dr L Amadhila, TB Gurirab, JM Haraseb G Dan, C Kgosimang Dr B Africa, A Majavero, E Biwa

Fourth row: Dr PH Katjavivi, N Maxuilili, A von Wieterheim, H Ruppel, SP Wöhler, N Angula, Dr K Mbuende, Dr M Tjitendero, Dr N Iyambo, LJ Barnes, M Barnes, G Siseho

Fifth row: MMEH Huebschle, RK Kapelwa, J Ya Otto, Dr B Amadhila, Rev M Amadhila, DP Botha, JW Wentworth, G Kashe, A Matjila

Last row: Rev W Konjore, P Shoombe, AP Tshirumbu, H Hausiku, W Biwa, HT Hishongwa, J Hoebeb, J Ekandjo, B Ulenga, A Gende, J Gaseb, J Jagger, NK Kaura, A Nuule, CAC van Wyk, AE Staby

Finally, the Constituent Assembly decided that its members would become the first National Assembly, and would put in place transition mechanisms, and mechanism for the election of the first President by the National Assembly. National Council was, however, to come later.

The Constitution of Namibia is, in many ways, a unique document. The oppressed, the disenfranchised who at last won their struggle for freedom, argued for the enshrining of the fundamental human rights in the Constitution. These rights cannot be diluted. Further, ours is perhaps the only Constitution that commits the government to environmental protection. We are proud that our Constitution has been applauded all over the world by scholars and politicians alike, and we are proud that during the first ten years of independence Namibia has lived up to the letter of this supreme law.

Transition

The full implementation of Resolution 435 had been achieved with the conclusion of the elections, and the people realized that at last we were to have our own government and to be masters of our own destiny. Nevertheless, after the election, in the transition period, there were a lot of manoeuvres by our enemies and we had to deal with these.

Above all, we had to produce a constitution in collaboration with the opposition. It was extremely difficult but in the recess that followed, a Constitutional Commission, including three experienced and trustworthy South Africa legal experts, drafted the Namibian Constitution. We had to make a number of concessions to get the constitution, which was based on a SWAPO draft, adopted by the Constituent Assembly. When adopted by the Constituent Assembly in January 1990, it was acclaimed worldwide as the model for a modern multi-party democratic system. It was fitting that our new nation joined those other African states who adopted a democratic system.

My own position had been established in February 1989. Later, when I first spoke in the Constituent Assembly in November 1989. I said:

> "I feel humbled and honoured to take part in proceedings that happen only once in a lifetime. As the son of an ordinary labourer, I feel humbled and honoured to be leading the country towards nationhood."

By the unanimous vote of the Constituent Assembly that leadership, as President of the Republic of Namibia, was conferred upon me.

It was on that occasion that I felt most strongly that my service to Namibia was only now beginning. What I had spent my adult life doing was struggling to break the chains which bound us, as oppressed subjects of a foreign power which scarcely treated us as human beings. The chains of slavery and colonialism were at last broken, but for the future there were other chains to be wrenched apart.

The first of these held in place the deep divisions that make the various population groups strangers, sometimes even enemies, in their own country. I told our people repeatedly that we had a huge country and a very small population: there was more than enough room for all of us to live together as brothers and sisters.

Then there were the old enemies of poverty, ignorance and disease that so reduced the quality of life for a large majority of the Namibian people. These could be defeated only by providing better education and health services, which were to be our first targets and priorities as we implemented the SWAPO political manifesto, which clearly spelt out our policy on economic development in the country.

For me it was essential that our people should understand and play their parts in the political life of the country. We are a democratic country and all Namibians should be able to participate in the democratic process and economic development.

It is also essential that Namibian citizens must embark upon a sound programme of agricultural production, not just to produce adequate food for themselves but also surplus for export to other countries. This is what is meant by freedom and independence — self-reliance, accountability, and the accord of respect to your neighbours and to fellow citizens.

These aims are best summed up in the Address I gave when independence day finally arrived, the full text of which is to be found at the end of this book. My keenest wish is that in time to come, we and our children will be able to look back and see that we have been true to the objectives set out then.

On 9 February 1990, the Constitution was unanimously adopted. The Constituent Assembly had agreed on a Namibian flag, chosen from 400 entries in a national competition. A shadow cabinet had been found to facilitate the transition, with the ministers-to-be shadowing the appropriate government officials to learn more about their future tasks and to identify the policy directions of the incoming government.

The thorny question of forming our own Namibian defence force from a merging of PLAN and SWATF had been tackled. As a result of

95   Signing of the Constitution of Namibia. Tintenpalast, Windhoek

96   (L to R) Toivo ya Toivo; David Meroro; Hendrik Witbooi; Sam Nujoma during ceremonies marking the adoption of the Constitution of Namibia. Windhoek, 9 February 1990

97   SWAPO President Sam Nujoma during Constitution ceremonies, with the new Namibian flag

98   On the steps of the Tintenpalast. Windhoek, 2 February 1990

99 The Cabinet of the Republic of Namibia

Presidency
President
Sam Nujoma

Office of the Prime Minister
Prime Minister
Hage Geingob

Ministry of Defence
Minister
Peter Mueshihange

Ministry of Finance
Minister
Otto Herrigel

Ministry of Health and Social Services
Minister
Nickey Iyambo

Ministry of Labour, Public Service, Manpower Development and Energy
Minister
Hendrik Witbooi

Ministry of Local Development
Minister
Libertina Amathila

Ministry of Wildlife Conservation and Tourism
Minister
Nico Bessinger

Ministry of Works, Transport and Communications
Minister
Richard Kapelwa

Ministry of Lands, Resettlement and Rehabilitation
Minister
Marco Hausiku

Return to Windhoek, Independence and a New Beginning

Ministry of Home Affairs
Minister
Hifikepunye Pohamba

Ministry of Foreign Affairs
Minister
Theo-Ben Gurirab

Ministry of Education, Culture and Sport
Minister
Nahas Angula

Ministry of Information and Broadcasting
Minister
Hiidipo Hamutenya

Ministry of Mines and Energy
Minister
Andimba Toivo ya Toivo

Ministry of Justice
Minister
Ngarikutuke Tjiriange

Ministry of Trade and Industry
Minister
Ben Amathila

Ministry of Agriculture, Fisheries, Water and Rural Development
Minister
Gerhard Hanekom

Government Service Appointments

Deputy Minister of State Security
Peter Tshirumbu

Attorney General
Hartmut Ruppel

National Planning Commission
Director General
Zedekia Ngavirue

The Signatories of the Constitution of the Republic of Namibia

SWAPO OF NAMIBIA

S NUJOMA	REV. H WITBOOI	D MERORO
A TOIVO YA TOIVO	M GAROEB	P MWESHIHANGE
H G GEINGOB	H POHAMBA	T-B GURIRAB
DR L AMATHILA	H HAMUTENYA	N BESSINGER
DR Z KAMEETA	DR E TJIRIANGE	P ITHANA
DR N IYAMBO	DR M TJITENDERO	DR K MBUENDE
N ANGULA	M M HAUSIKU	S P WOHLER
H RUPPEL	A VON WIETERSHEIM	DR P KATJAVIVI
J W WENTWORTH	P BOTHA	REV. M AMADHILA
H T HISHONGWA	B AMATHILA	J YA OTTO
R KAPELWA	I G NATHANIEL	M M E K H HUEBSCHLE
B U UULENGA	J EKANDJO	J HOEBEB
W BIWA	H HAUSIKU	P SHOOMBE
	REV W KONJOREA	P TSHIRUMBU

D.T.A OF NAMIBIA

M MUYONGO	D F MUDGE	F J KOZONGUIZI
D LUIPERT	J M HARASEB	G DAN
P M JUNIUS	DR B J AFRICA	L J BARNES
C KGOSIMANG	A MAJAVERO	G KASHE
N K KAURA	M BARNES	A MATJILA
H E STABY	A GENDE	J JAGGER
J GASEB	A NUULE	C A C VAN WYK

UNITED DEMOCRATIC FRONT OF NAMIBIA

J GAROEB	R R DIERGAARDT	G SISEHO
	E BIWA	

AKSIE CHRISTELIK NASIONAAL

J M DE WET	J W F PRETORIUS	W O ASTON

NATIONAL PATRIOTIC FRONT OF NAMIBIA

M K KATJIUONGUA

FEDERAL CONVENTION OF NAMIBIA

M KERINA

NAMIBIA NATIONAL FRONT

V RUKORO

my request to the British Government, four British military experts visited Namibia and saw all the appropriate individuals and groups in order to put forward a proposal for the integration and training of our future defence force, as they had done in Zimbabwe. Despite their continued unhelpfulness in the past, Britain now appeared anxious to help, and proposals for training the unifying Namibian Defence Force, Namibian Police and for English language training were put forward. It had been decided by SWAPO many years earlier that English would replace Afrikaans as the medium of instruction and as the official language of the Government. We had had much help from Britain and the Commonwealth in raising the SWAPO teachers' standard of English instruction in SWAPO Education and Health Centres and colleges in exile.

My own unanimous election by the Constituent Assembly as President took place on Friday 16 February 1990. I was the sole candidate and the acclamation that followed my election was evidence that SWAPO's policy of national reconciliation was already bearing fruit. In the gallery on this occasion was the prominent American political activist Reverend Jesse Jackson, who exclaimed: "Mandela's out of gaol and Sam Nujoma is in office!" Nelson Mandela had been released the previous Sunday, 11 February, and the two events did indeed symbolize the new era, in which southern Africa was moving towards the final defeat of colonialism, apartheid and the total liberation of the African continent.

It was also the decision of the Constituent Assembly that I should be sworn in by the UN Secretary-General, Javier Pérez de Cuéllar, on the day now fixed for the independence celebrations. This was to be 21 March 1990, a date of poignant memory as it was the anniversary of the Sharpeville massacre in 1960, news of which had reached me soon after my arrival in Dar-es-Salaam, and which was to have an electrifying effect on the freedom movement throughout the continent. It had also been chosen by the United Nations as Human Rights Day.

The white South Africans oppressors, whose role in the transition had already been so much greater than had been envisaged under UN Security Council Resolution 435 (29 September 1978), wanted to perform the ceremony. But we made it absolutely clear that it was the United Nations, as the *de jure* government of Namibia since the termination of the mandate by the General Assembly Resolution 2145 in 1966, that should, through the UN Secretary-General, swear-in the first President and that South Africa had no status in the matter at all.

The ministers were all to be sworn in by the Namibian-born Chief Justice Hans Berker, whose position, together with that of the other judges, we had accepted in the change-over.

Departures without dignity

There was a lot happening around the country that showed that the South African elements, at all levels, were not going to move out without doing all the damage they could. In the north, armed men whom we knew to be under Koevoet command destabilized wherever they could the fragile peace that had succeeded 23 years of war. It came out that General Dreyer, their commanding officer, was accommodating his men on a farm, Manheihm, near Tsumeb, and that they had a large supply of arms. In the south too, arms caches were discovered and the under-cover units such as that which had assassinated Anton Lubowski had not been apprehended.

Our relations with the South African Administrator-General Louis Pienaar grew increasingly strained. As his remaining time in the country shortened, he set about doing all he could to benefit those who had run the country with him during the illegal occupation of the apartheid South African regime, by promoting them beyond their proper rank, increasing their pay, and, as already mentioned, transferring pension funds out of the country and even making it possible for officials to take out lump-sum pensions there and then. In the closing days of the South African colonial administration it became necessary for the Minister of Finance, Dr. Otto Herrigel, to dash from one bank to another telling managers not to honour cheques made out on instructions from the Administrator-General.

The South African colonial officials were determined that they would not leave Namibia empty-handed. Pre-fabricated houses at all South African military bases were dismantled and transported to South Africa. Even the contents of what is now State House were not safe from the grasping hands of the departing South African administrators. In the old residence which had been the home of the German governors and South African administrators, many historically interesting objects, paintings and ornaments, which had accumulated over the preceding century, disappeared along with the former occupants. As a result of a tip-off, our officials found that these had been secretly moved to a warehouse, in readiness for being transported by rail to South Africa.

We were able to reclaim much of that collection, but many other valuable items were stolen from government offices by the departing white South African administrators.

It was not a dignified departure from the country which they had exploited for so long, but it was consistent with the way they had behaved towards the Namibian people — as was their stated repudiation of Resolution 432 which had required the "early re-integration" of Walvis Bay and the off-shore islands after independence.

This thieving should be contrasted to the demand they made, in which they were supported by some Western governments, that SWAPO should inherit the 800 million rand debt owed to South African commercial banks for expenditures in Namibia. Since some of this was spent on civilian infrastructure such as schools and hospitals, we eventually accepted the debt. A government with a sense of honour and jealous of its national reputation might have made the gesture of writing off such a sum, especially to help a new country get on its feet.

I attended Louis Pienaar's farewell banquet on 20 March, after a long day spent at the airport receiving heads of state and government, and where possible talking with prime ministers, foreign ministers and politicians who had been invited to attend our independence celebration, in recognition of their support for the struggle of the liberation of Namibia. The last to arrive was Comrade Nelson Mandela and I felt that meeting him at the airport must take precedence over my attendance at Pienaar's banquet, though I did manage to arrive while it was still in progress. I saw Mr. Pienaar off at the airport the day after South Africa's illegal rule was finally terminated.

Independence Day, 21 March 1990

Independence Day itself, 21 March 1990, has been the subject of countless reports and has been thoroughly recorded in many commemorative books and videos. On that historic day, the invited guests who attended the Independence Day ceremonies, with more than 50,000 Namibians and others, witnessed the raising of the Namibian flag in the Windhoek Independence Stadium, as did many millions of television viewers all over the world, at a few minutes after midnight.

In addition to the thousands of Namibian patriots who celebrated with us in Windhoek there were independence celebrations throughout the country, such as the one presided over by Mzee Simon Kaukungua in Oshakati, where independence was also fittingly celebrated.

100 Arrival of heads of state for the Independence Day ceremonies, Windhoek.
(Top) President of Tanzania Mwinyi; (Centre) President of Egypt Hosni Mubarak
(Bottom) President of Angola José Eduardo dos Santos

I was proud and honoured to welcome foreign dignitaries to our country, who came to join us in celebrating our victory and independence. Among them were representatives of anti-apartheid movements, support groups from all parts of Africa, Asia, Europe, the Americas and Australia, who had actively supported our cause, sometimes in the face of official political opposition in their own governments, and for no reward other than the goal finally achieved. This was their day as well as ours and it was proper that they should share it with us.

We also remembered that night those who had not lived to see the day of our freedom, those who had sacrificed their lives for freedom and Independence:

— at the Windhoek Old Location;

— at the Shatotwa and Cassinga massacres;

— in the war zone after the South African Army violation of the 1 April 1989 cease-fire agreement;

— on the battlefield over the 23 years of armed liberation struggle;

— as political prisoners of the South Africans on Robben Island and in other torture camps and prisons;

— as victims of the atrocities of the SWATF, Koevoet and the bantustan "home guards";

— as victims of assassination by under-cover agents of the South African military intelligence;

and many other compatriots who disappeared without a trace and went to their graves, while our country was still in colonial bondage. The blood of all these sons and daughters of Namibia watered the tree of our liberty and will always be remembered by present and future generations of the Republic of Namibia.

It was in the spirit of SWAPO's policy of national reconciliation that we also remembered those of our countrymen and women who had died in defence of South African rule, or while opposed to it but alienated from the liberation movement.

~~~~~

101   *UN Secretary-General Javier Pérez de Cuéllar, handing over the reins of state power to President-Elect Sam Nujoma at swearing-in ceremony. Windhoek, 21 March 1990*

The tasks ahead

As that great day of our independence drew to a close, there was one thought above all others in my mind: *Tomorrow the history of independent Namibia begins*, and we owe it to all who have gone before, as well as to all who will come after, to make it one worthy of them and of the heroic struggle in which we were able to triumph at last.

We had, through this heroic struggle, attained political freedom, the essential first goal of SWAPO. But immense tasks lay ahead.

After independence we would be faced with the challenges of nation building, of economic reconstruction and of unifying a population that had been torn along racial and ethnic lines during centuries of colonial oppression, apartheid and 'bantustanization'. We would be working to provide for the well-being of all our people, to improve educational and health services, and the infrastructure needed for the building of a modern, just society.

Finally, it was my firm belief, and so it remains, that the Independence victory of SWAPO would enable the Namibian people to participate in the wider Pan-African movement to attain the ultimate goal of a united continent, in which the aspirations of the African people on the continent and those in the Diaspora as whole will be achieved.

❖❖❖❖❖❖❖

Appendix 1   Inaugural Speech, 21 March 1990

INAUGURAL SPEECH BY HIS EXCELLENCY SAM NUJOMA, FIRST PRESIDENT OF THE REPUBLIC OF NAMIBIA
Windhoek, 21 March, 1990

Honourable Master of Ceremony,

Your Excellencies, Heads of State and Government, Distinguished Guests,

Dear Compatriots,

Ladies and Gentlemen,

For the Namibian people and for myself, this day, the 21st of March, 1990, is the most memorable and indeed the most emotional moment in the annals of our history.

This solemn hour is the moment which our people have been waiting for, for more than a century. This is the day for which tens of thousands of Namibian patriots laid down their lives, shed their precious blood, suffered imprisonment and a difficult life in exile. Today, our hearts are filled with great joy and jubilation because our deepest and longest yearning has been realised.

Honourable Master of Ceremony, Sir, for the past 43 years or so, this land of our forebears has been a bone of contention between the Namibian people and the international community, on one hand, and South Africa, on the other. The Namibian problem has been at the centre of bitter international dispute over the last four decades. The United Nations and other international bodies produced huge volumes of resolutions in an attempt to resolve this intractable problem.

However, it pleases me to state that we are gathered here today, not to pass yet another resolution, but to celebrate the dawn of a new era in this land and to proclaim to the world that a new star has risen on the African continent. Africa's last colony is, from this hour, liberated.

It is, therefore, profoundly momentous and highly joyous, for the Namibian people and myself, that the highest representative of the international community, the Secretary-General of the United Nations, together with the State President of South Africa, and the Namibian nation, which I am honoured to lead, are able to announce, here today, to the world that a definitive and final solution to the protracted Namibian problem has, indeed, been unanimously reached by these three parties.

For the Namibian people, the realisation of our most cherished goal, namely, the independence of our country and freedom of our people, is a fitting tribute to the heroism and tenacity with which our people fought for this long-awaited day. We have been sustained in our difficult struggle by the powerful force of conviction in the righteousness and justness of our cause. Today history has absolved us; our vision of a democratic state of Namibia has been translated into a reality.

With regard to the international community, the achievement of Namibia's independence today is, we believe, a welcome and laudable culmination of many years of consistent support for our cause. The world's demand for our country to be allowed to exercise its inalienable right to self-determination and independence has been achieved. We express our most sincere gratitude to the international community for its steadfast support.

As for the government of South Africa, it can be said that the decision to accept the implementation of Resolution 435 has been the first demonstration of political will to find a negotiated solution to the problems of our region. Furthermore, President de Klerk's proclamation here today that South Africa has reached a final and irreversible decision to relinquish control over Namibia is an act of statesmanship and realism. This, we hope, will continue to unfold in South Africa itself.

Compatriots, Ladies and Gentlemen, I seize this opportunity to point out that the protracted process of negotiating an agreement on Resolution 435 and struggling for its implementation has been difficult and, at times, acrimonious. It was only perseverance, forbearance and commitment which helped us to see the process through to its logical conclusion, namely, the birth of the Namibian nation we are here to witness.

Against this background, it is heartening for the Namibian people and I, to know that our independence has been achieved under conditions of national consensus and international unanimity. The impressive presence here today of so many world leaders and other dignitaries is a clear testimony to the fact that Namibia's achievement of independence is an event of great world importance. For us, this is yet another reason for celebration.

With respect to the important question of national consensus, I am glad to announce that, following the independence election last November, the various Namibian political parties have been able to work together in the Constituent Assembly, where we formulated and adopted a Constitution acceptable to the broad majority of our people.

Against this background, Honourable Master of Ceremony, Distinguished Guests and Dear Compatriots, I am indebted to the Namibian electorate for giving SWAPO an absolute majority, thereby enabling it to form the first government of the Republic of Namibia. In the same vein, I am grateful to the members of Namibia's Constituent Assembly for the confidence they have placed in me in electing me as the first President of the Republic of Namibia. I pledge to do my utmost to uphold the Constitution of the Republic, and to honour the trust which the Namibian people have bestowed upon me to lead this new nation at this critical juncture.

To the Namibian people, I would like to state, on this solemn and historic occasion, our nation blazed the trail to freedom. It has arisen to its feet. As from today, we are the masters of this vast land of our ancestors. The destiny of this country is now fully in our own hands. We should, therefore, look forward to the future with confidence and hope.

Taking the destiny of this country in our own hands means, among other things, making a great effort to forge national identity and unity. Our collective security and prosperity depend on our unity of purpose and action. Unity is a pre-condition for peace and development. Without peace, it is not possible for the best and talented citizens of our country to realise their potential.

Our achievement of independence imposes upon us a heavy responsibility, not only to defend our hard-won liberty, but also to set for ourselves higher standards of equality, justice and opportunity for all, without regard to race, creed or colour. These are the standards from which all who seek to emulate us shall draw inspiration.

Master of Ceremony, Sir, in accepting the sacred responsibility which the Namibian people have placed on me, as the first President of the Republic of Namibia, I would like to bow and pay homage to our fallen heroes and heroines, whose names Namibia's present and future generations will sing in songs of praise and whose martyrdom they will intone.

In conclusion, I move, in the name of our people, to declare that Namibia is forever free, sovereign and independent!

Sam Nujoma

Appendix 2.1 Letter: 14 March 1989, Javier Pérez de Cuéllar to Sam Nujoma assigning cease-fire date of 1 April 1989

THE SECRETARY-GENERAL

14 March 1989

Excellency,

In paragraph 60 of my report of 23 January 1989 to the Security Council concerning the question of Namibia (S/20412), I stated that, as regards the cease-fire envisaged in resolution 435 (1978), both South Africa and the South West Africa People's Organization (SWAPO) had agreed to a de facto cessation of hostilities, with effect from 10 August 1988, as provided for in the Geneva Protocol of 5 August 1988. It had been foreseen in resolution 435 (1978) that the cease-fire between South Africa and SWAPO would take effect on the date of the beginning of implementation of the Settlement Plan. I accordingly intended to send identical letters, at the appropriate time, to South Africa and SWAPO proposing a specific date and hour for the formal cease-fire to begin.

My report of 23 January 1989 was approved by the Security Council in its resolution 632 (1989) of 16 February 1989.

I accordingly propose that the formal cease-fire should begin at 0400 hours Greenwich Mean Time on 1 April 1989. At that time the comprehensive cessation of all hostile acts is to take effect.

I request you to assure me in writing no later than 22 March 1989 that you have accepted the terms of the cease-fire and that you have taken all necessary measures to cease all warlike acts and operations. These include tactical movements, cross-border movements and all acts of violence and intimidation in, or having effect in, Namibia.

Please accept, Excellency, the assurances of my highest consideration.

Javier Pérez de Cuéllar

His Excellency
Mr. Sam Nujoma
President
South West Africa People's
   Organization
Luanda

Appendix 2.2 Letter: 14 March 1989, Javier Pérez de Cuéllar to Botha (as copied to Nujoma) assigning cease-fire date of 1 April 1989

14 March 1989

Excellency,

In paragraph 60 of my report of 23 January 1989 to the Security Council concerning the question of Namibia (S/20412), I stated that, as regards the cease-fire envisaged in resolution 435 (1978), both South Africa and the South West Africa People's Organization (SWAPO) had agreed to a de facto cessation of hostilities, with effect from 10 August 1988, as provided for in the Geneva Protocol of 5 August 1988. It had been foreseen in resolution 435 (1978) that the cease-fire between South Africa and SWAPO would take effect on the date of the beginning of implementation of the Settlement Plan. I accordingly intended to send identical letters, at the appropriate time, to South Africa and SWAPO proposing a specific date and hour for the formal cease-fire to begin.

My report of 23 January 1989 was approved by the Security Council in its resolution 632 (1989) of 16 February 1989.

I accordingly propose that the formal cease-fire should begin at 0400 hours Greenwich Mean Time on 1 April 1989. At that time the comprehensive cessation of all hostile acts is to take effect.

I request you to assure me in writing no later than 22 March 1989 that you have accepted the terms of the cease-fire and that you have taken all necessary measures to cease all warlike acts and operations. These include tactical movements, cross-border movements and all acts of violence and intimidation in, or having effect in, Namibia.

Please accept, Excellency, the assurances of my highest consideration.

Javier Pérez de Cuéllar

The Honourable Roelof F. Botha
Minister for Foreign Affairs
  of the Republic of South Africa
Pretoria

Appendix 2.3   Letter: 18 March 1989, Sam Nujoma reply to Javier Pérez de Cuéllar accepting cease-fire date of 1 April 1989

South West Africa People's Organisation
SWAPO OF NAMIBIA
OFFICE OF THE PRESIDENT

Solidarity — Freedom — Justice

P.O. Box 953,
LUANDA,
ANGOLA.
Tel: 39234/30937
Telex: 3069

Your Ref: ....   Our Ref: OP/OND/03/89

18 March 1989

H.E. Javier Perez de Cuellar,
Secretary-General of the United Nations,
New York, N.Y. 10017.

Excellency,

<u>SWAPO'S REPLY</u>

This is to acknowledge receipt of Your Excellency's letter dated 14 March 1989, in which you, <u>inter alia</u>, indicated that a similar letter would be sent to South Africa, proposing a specific date and hour for the formal ceasefire to begin in accordance with Security Council Resolution 435 (1978); and that the ceasefire comes into effect on 1 April 1989 at 0400 hours Greenwich Mean Time.

In this connection, I would like to recall that I sent a letter to Your Excellency (S/20129) dated 12 August 1988, in which I stated, <u>inter alia</u>, SWAPO's acceptance of the <u>de facto</u> cessation of armed hostilities in and around Namibia between South Africa and SWAPO, in accordance with the Geneva Protocol of 5 August 1988.

I accordingly hereby declare SWAPO's acceptance of the terms of the ceasefire as stipulated in Your Excellency's letter dated 14 March 1989. Furthermore, I would like to reiterate SWAPO's commitment scrupulously to work in earnest for a peaceful and successful implementation of Security Council Resolution 435 (1978), leading to the genuine independence of Namibia.

In this context, I wish, once again, to urge Your Excellency to continue to exert your best efforts with a view to ensuring that violence and intimidation would be avoided at all cost.

Accept, Your Excellency, renewed assurances of my highest consideration.

Sam Nujoma
PRESIDENT OF SWAPO

Appendix 2.4 Letter: 21 March 1989, Botha reply to Javier Pérez de Cuéllar accepting cease-fire date of 1 April 1989

MINISTER VAN BUITELANDSE SAKE
MINISTER OF FOREIGN AFFAIRS

21 March 1989

Excellency

I refer to your letter dated 14 March 1989 regarding the establishment of a formal cease-fire in South West Africa/Namibia as foreseen in United Nations Security Council Resolution 435 (1987).

Your Excellency will recall that in my communication to you on 8 August 1988, I conveyed to you the acceptance of the provisions of the Geneva Protocol by the South African Government. I also confirmed, in terms of the provisions of paragraph 5 of the Protocol, the South African Government's commitment to adopt the necessary measures of restraint in order to maintain the existing de facto cessation of hostilities.

In addition I wish to confirm that the de facto cessation of hostilities should be formalised as soon as possible and not later than 04h00 Greenwich Mean Time on 1 April 1989.

Please accept, Excellency, the assurance of my highest consideration.

R F BOTHA

His Excellency Javier Perez de Cuellar
Secretary General of the United Nations
NEW YORK

Appendix 3 Resolutions of the United Nations Security Council, pertaining to South West Africa / Namibia

****

RESOLUTION 385 (1976)
Adopted by the Security Council at its 1885th meeting on 30 January 1976

The Security Council,

Having heard the statement of the President of the United Nations Council for Namibia,

Having considered the statement by Mr. Moses M. Garoeb, Administrative Secretary of the South West Africa People's Organization,

Recalling General Assembly resolution 2145 (XXI) of 27 October 1966, by which the Assembly terminated South Africa's Mandate over the Territory of Namibia, and resolution 2248 (S-V) of 19 May 1967, by which it established a United Nations Council for Namibia as well as all other subsequent resolutions on Namibia, in particular resolution 3295 (XXIX) of 13 December 1974 and resolution 3399 (XXX) of 26 November 1975,

Recalling its resolutions 245 (1968) of 25 January and 246 (1968) of 14 March 1968, 264 (1969) of 20 March and 269 (1969) of 12 August 1969, 276 (1970) of 30 January, 282 (1970) of 23 July, 283 (1970) and 284 (1970) of 29 July 1970, 300 (1971) of 12 October and 301 (1971) of 20 October 1971, 310 (1972) of 4 February 1972 and 366 (1974) of 17 December 1974,

Recalling the advisory opinion of the International Court of Justice of 21 June 1971 that South Africa is under obligation to withdraw its presence from the Territory,

Reaffirming the legal responsibility of the United Nations over Namibia,

Concerned at South Africa's continued illegal occupation of Namibia and its persistent refusal to comply with the resolutions and decisions of the General Assembly and the Security Council, as well as with the advisory opinion of the International Court of Justice,

Gravely concerned at South Africa's brutal repression of the Namibian people and its persistent violation of their human rights, as well as its efforts to destroy the national unity and territorial integrity of Namibia and its aggressive military build-up in the area,

Strongly deploring the militarization of Namibia by the illegal occupation regime of South Africa,

1. Condemns the continued illegal occupation of the Territory of Namibia by South Africa;

2. Condemns the continued illegal and arbitrary application by South Africa of racially discriminatory and oppresssive laws and practices in Namibia;

3. Condemns the South African military build-up in Namibia and any utilization of the Territory as a base for attacks on neighbouring countries;

4. Demands that South Africa put an end forthwith to its policy of bantustans and the so-called homelands aimed at violating the national unity and the territorial integrity of Namibia;

5. Further condemns South Africa's failure to comply with the terms of Security Council resolution 366 (1974);

6. Further condemns all attempts by South Africa calculated to evade the clear demand of the United Nations for the holding of free elections under United Nations supervision and control in Namibia;

7. Declares that, in order that the people of Namibia may be enabled freely to determine their own future, it is imperative that free elections under the supervision and control of the United Nations be held for the whole of Namibia as one political entity;

8. Further declares that, in determining the date, timetable and modalities for the elections in accordance with paragraph 7 above there shall be adequate time, to be decided upon by the Security Council, for the purpose of enabling the United Nations to supervise and control such elections, as well as to enable the people of Namibia to organize politically for the purpose of such elections;

9. Demands that South Africa urgently make a solemn declaration accepting the foregoing provisions for the holding of free elections in Namibia under United Nations supervision and control, undertaking to comply with the resolutions and decisions of the United Nations and with the advisory opinion of the International Court of Justice of 21 June 1971 in regard to Namibia and recognizing the territorial integrity and unity of Namibia as a nation;

10. Reiterates its demand that South Africa take the necessary steps to effect the withdrawal, in accordance with Security Council resolutions 264 (1969), 269 (1969) and 366 (1974), of its illegal administration maintained in Namibia and to transfer power to the people of Namibia with the assistance of the United Nations;

11. Demands again that South Africa, pending the transfer of power provided for in paragraph 10 above:

(a) Comply fully in spirit and in practice with the provisions of the Universal Declaration of Human Rights;

(b) Release all Namibian political prisoners, including all those imprisoned or detained in connexion with offences under so-called internal security laws, whether such Namibians have been charged or tried or are held without charge and whether held in Namibia or South Africa;

(c) Abolish the application in Namibia of all racially discriminatory and politically repressive laws and practices, particularly bantustans and homelands;

(d) Accord unconditionally to all Namibians currently in exile for political reasons full facilities for return to their country without risk of arrest, detention, intimidation or imprisonment;

12. Decides to remain seized of the matter and to meet on or before 31 August 1976 for the purpose of reviewing South Africa's compliance with the terms of the present resolution and, in the event of non-compliance by South Africa, for the purpose of considering the appropriate measures to be taken under the Charter of the United Nations.

RESOLUTION 431 (1978)
Adopted by the Security Council at its 2082nd meeting on 27 July 1978

The Security Council,

Recalling its resolution 385 (1976) of 30 January 1976,

Taking note of the proposal for a settlement of the Namibian situation contained in document S/12636 of 10 April 1978,

1. Requests the Secretary-General to appoint a Special Representative for Namibia in order to ensure the early independence of Namibia through free elections under the supervision and control of the United Nations;

2. Further requests the Secretary-General to submit at the earliest possible date a report containing his recommendations for the implementation of the proposal for a settlement of the Namibian situation in accordance with Security Council resolution 385 (1976);

3. Urges all concerned to exert their best efforts towards the achievement of independence by Namibia at the earliest possible date.

RESOLUTION 432 (1978)
Adopted by the Security Council at its 2082nd meeting on 27 July 1978

The Security Council,

Recalling its resolutions 385 (1976) of 30 January 1976 and 431 (1978) of 27 July 1978,

Reaffirming in particular the provisions of resolution 385 (1976) relating to the territorial integrity and unity of Namibia,

Taking note of paragraph 7 of General Assembly resolution 32/9 D of 4 November 1977, in which the Assembly declares that Walvis Bay is an integral part of Namibia,

1. Declares that the territorial integrity and unity of Namibia must be assured through the reintegration of Walvis Bay within its territory;
2. Decides to lend its full support to the initiation of steps necessary to ensure early reintegration of Walvis Bay into Namibia;
3. Declares that, pending the attainment of this objective, South Africa must not use Walvis Bay in any manner prejudicial to the independence of Namibia or the viability of its economy;
4. Decides to remain seized of the matter until Walvis Bay is fully integrated into Namibia.

RESOLUTION 435 (1978)
Adopted by the Security Council at its 2087th meeting on 29 September 1978

The Security Council,

Recalling its resolutions 385 (1976) of 30 January 1976 and 431 (1978) and 432 (1978) of 27 July 1978,

Having considered the report of the Secretary-General submitted pursuant to paragraph 2 of resolution 431 (1978) and his explanatory statement made in the Security Council on 29 September 1978 (S/12869).

Taking note of the relevant communications from the Government of South Africa to the Secretary-General,

Taking note also of the letter dated 8 September 1978 from the President of the South West Africa People's Organization to the Secretary-General,

Reaffirming the legal responsibility of the United Nations over Namibia,

1. Approves the report of the Secretary-General on the implementation of the proposal for a settlement of the Namibian situation and his explanatory statement;
2. Reiterates that its objective is the withdrawal of South Africa's illegal administration from Namibia and the transfer of power to the people of Namibia with the assistance of the United Nations in accordance with Security Council resolution 385 (1976);
3. Decides to establish under its authority a United Nations Transition Assistance Group in accordance with the above-mentioned report of the Secretary-General for a period of up to 12 months in order to assist his Special Representative to carry out the mandate conferred upon him by the Security Council in paragraph 1 of its resolution 431 (1978), namely, to ensure the early independence of Namibia through free elections under the supervision and control of the United Nations;
4. Welcomes the preparedness of the South West Africa People's Organizatoin to co-operate in the implementation of the Secretary-General's report, including its expressed readiness to sign and observe the cease-fire provisions as manifested in the letter from its President of 8 September 1978;
5. Calls upon South Africa forthwith to co-operate with the Secretary-General in the implementatoion of the present resolution;
6. Declares that all unilateral measures taken by the illegal administration in Namibia in relation to the electoral process, including unilateral registration of voters, or

transfer of power, in contravention of resolutions 385 (1976), 431 (1978) and the present resolution, are null and void;

7. Requests the Secretary-General to report to the Security Council not later than 23 October 1978 on the implementation of the present resolution.

❖ ❖ ❖

RESOLUTION 439 (1978)
Adopted by the Security Council at its 2098th meeting on 13 November 1978

The Security Council,

Recalling its resolutions 385 (1976) of 30 January 1976, 431 (1978) of 27 July and 435 (1978) of 29 September 1978,

Having considered the report of the Secretary-General submitted pursuant to paragraph 7 of resolution 435 (1978),

Taking note of the relevant communications addressed to the Secretary-General and the President of the Security Council,

Having heard and considered the statement of the President of the United Nations Council for Namibia,

Taking note also of the communication dated 23 October 1978 from the President of the South West Africa People's Organization to the Secretary-General,

Reaffirming the legal responsibility of the United Nations over Namibia and its continued commitment to the implementation of resolution 385 (1976), in particular the holding of free elections in Namibia under United Nations supervision and control,

Reiterating the view that any unilateral measure taken by the illegal administration in Namibia in relation to the electoral process, including unilateral registration of voters, or transfer of power, in contravention of the above-mentioned resolutions and the present resolution, is null and void,

Gravely concerned at the decision of the South African Government to proceed unilaterally with the holding of elections in the Territory from 4 to 8 December 1978 in contravention of Security Council resolutions 385 (1976) and 435 (1978);

1. Condemns the decision of the South African Government to proceed unilaterally with the holding of elections in the Territory from 4 to 8 December 1978 in contravention of Security Council resolution 385 (1976) and 435 (1978);

2. Considers that this decision constitutes a clear defiance of the United Nations and, in particular, the authority of the Security Council;

3. Declares those elections and their results null and void and states that no recognition will be accorded either by the United Nations or any Member States to any representatives or organ established by that process;

4. Calls upon South Africa immediately to cancel the elections it has planned in Namibia in December 1978;

5. Demands once again that South Africa co-operate with the Security Council and the Secretary-General in the implementation of resolutions 385 (1976), 431 (1978) and 435 (1978);

6. Warns South Africa that its failure to do so would compel the Security Council to meet forthwith to initiate appropriate actions under the Charter of the United Nations, including Chapter VII thereof, so as to ensure South Africa's compliance with the aforementioned resolutions;

7. Calls upon the Secretary-General to report on the progress of the implementation of the present resolution by 25 November 1978.

RESOLUTION 532 (1983)
Adopted by the Security Council at its 2449th meeting held on 31 May 1983

The Security Council,

Having considered the report of the Secretary-General (S/15776),

Recalling General Assembly resolutions 1514 (XV) of 14 December 1960 and 2145 (XXI) of 27 October 1966,

Recalling and reaffirming its resolutions 301 (1971), 385 (1976), 431 (1978), 432 (1978), 435 (1978) and 439 (1978),

Reaffirming the legal responsibility of the United Nations over Namibia and the primary responsibility of the Security Council for ensuring the implementation of its resolutions 385 (1976) and 435 (1978), including the holding of free and fair elections in Namibia under the supervision and control of the United Nations,

Taking note of the results of the International Conference in Support of the Struggle of the Namibian People for Independence, held at UNESCO House in Paris from 25 to 29 April 1983,

Taking note of the protracted and exhaustive consultations which have taken place since the adoption of resolution 435 (1978),

Further noting with regret that those consultations have not yet brought about the implementation of resolution 435 (1978),

1. Condemns South Africa's continued illegal occupation of Namibia in flagrant defiance of resolutions of the General Assembly and decisions of the Security Council of the United Nations;

2. Calls upon South Africa to make a firm commitment as to its readiness to comply with Security Council resolution 435 (1978) for the independence of Namibia;

3. Further calls upon South Africa to co-operate forthwith and fully with the Secretary-General of the United Nations in order to expedite the implementation of resolution 435 (1978) for the early independence of Namibia;

4. Decides to mandate the Secretary-General to undertake consultations with the parties to the proposed cease-fire, with a view to securing the speedy implementation of Security Council resolution 435 (1978);

5. Requests the Secretary-General to report to the Security Council on the results of these consultations as soon as possible and not later than 31 August 1983;

6. Decides to remain actively seized of the matter.

◆ ◆ ◆

RESOLUTION 539 (1983)
Adopted by the Security Council at its 2492nd meeting on 28 October 1983

The Security Council,

Having considered the report of the Secretary-General (S/15943) of 29 August 1983,

Recalling General Assembly resolutions 1514 (XV) of 14 December 1960 and 2145 (XXI) of 27 October 1966,

Recalling and reaffirming its resolutions 301 (1971), 385 (1976), 431 (1978), 432 (1978), 435 (1978), 439 (1978), and 532 (1983),

Gravely concerned at South Africa's continued illegal occupation of Namibia,

Gravely concerned also at the tension and instability prevailing in southern Africa and the mounting threat to the security of the region and its wider implications for international peace and security resulting from continued utilization of Namibia as a springboard for attacks against and destabilization of African States in the region,

Reaffirming the legal responsibility of the United Nations over Namibia and the primary responsibility of the Security Council for ensuring the implementation of its resolutions, in particular, resolutions 385 (1976) and 435 (1978), which call for the holding of free and fair elections in the Territory under the supervision and control of the United Nations,

Indignant that South Africa's insistence on an irrelevant and extraneous issue of "linkage" has obstructed the implementation of Security Council resolution 435 (1978),

1. Condemns South Africa for its continued illegal occupation of Namibia in flagrant defiance of resolutions of the General Assembly and decisions of the Security Council of the United Nations;

2. Further condemns South Africa for its obstruction of the implementation of Security Council resolution 435 (1978) by insisting on conditions contrary to the provisions of the United Nations plan for the independence of Namibia;

3. Rejects South Africa's insistence on linking the independence of Namibia to irrelevant and extraneous issues as incompatible with resolution 435 (1978), other decisions of the Security Council and the resolutions of the General Assembly on Namibia, including General Assembly resolution 1514 (XV) of 14 December 1960;

4. Declares that the independence of Namibia cannot be held hostage to the resolution of issues that are alien to Security Council resolution 435 (1978);

5. Reiterates that Security Council resolution 435 (1978), embodying the United Nations plan for the independence of Namibia, is the only basis for a peaceful settlement of the Namibian problems;

6. Takes note that the consultations undertaken by the Secretary-General pursuant to paragraph 5 of resolution 532 (1983) have confirmed that all the outstanding issues relevant to Security Council resolution 435 (1978) have been resolved;

7. Affirms that the electoral system to be used for the elections of the Constituent Assembly should be determined prior to the adoption by the Security Council of the enabling resolution for the implementation of the United Nations plan;

8. Calls upon South Africa to co-operate with the Secretary-General forthwith and to communicate to him its choice of the electoral system in order to facilitate the immediate and unconditional implementation of the United Nations plan embodied in Security Council resolution 435 (1978);

9. Requests the Secretary-General to report to the Security Council on the implementation of this resolution as soon as possible and not later than 31 December 1983;

10. Decides to remain actively seized of the matter and to meet as soon as possible following the Secretary-General's report for the purpose of reviewing progress in the implementation of resolution 435 (1978) and, in the event of continued obstruction by South Africa, to consider the adoption of appropriate measures under the Charter of the United Nations.

RESOLUTION 566 (1985)
Adopted by the Security Council at its 2595th meeting on 19 June 1985

The Security Council,

Having considered the reports of the Secretary-General (S/16237 and S/17242),

Having heard the statement by the Acting President of the United Nations Council for Namibia,

Having considered the statement by Dr. Sam Nujoma, President of the South West Africa People's Organization (SWAPO),

Commending the South West Africa People's Organization for its preparedness to co-operate fully with the United Nations Secretary-General and his Special Representative, including its expressed readiness to sign and observe a cease-fire agreement with South Africa, in the implementation of the United Nations Plan for Namibia as embodied in Security Council resolution 435 (1978),

Recalling General Assembly resolutions 1514 (XV) of 14 December 1960 and 2145 (XXI) of 27 October 1966,

Recalling and reaffirming its resolutions 269 (1969), 276 (1970), 301 (1971), 385 (1976), 431 (1978), 432 (1978), 435 (1978), 439 (1978), 532 (1983) and 539 (1983),

Recalling the statement of the President of the Security Council (S/17151) of 3 May 1985, on behalf of the Council, which, inter alia, declared the establishment of the so-called interim government in Namibia to be null and void,

Gravely concerned at the tension and instability created by the hostile policies of the apartheid regime throughout southern Africa and the mounting threat to the security of the region and its wider implications for international peace and security resulting from that regime's continued utilization of Namibia as a springboard for military attacks against and destabilization of African States in the region,

Reaffirming the legal responsibility of the United Nations over Namibia and the primary responsibility of the Security Council for ensuring the implementation of its resolutions, in particular resolutions 385 (1976) and 435 (1978) which contain the United Nations Plan for Namibian independence,

Noting that 1985 marks the fortieth anniversary of the founding of the United Nations, as well as the twenty-fifth anniversary of the adoption of the Declaration on the Granting of Independence to Colonial Countries and Peoples, and expressing grave concern that the question of Namibia has been with the Organization since its inception and still remains unsolved,

Welcoming the emerging and intensified world-wide campaign of people from all spheres of life against the racist regime of South Africa in a concerted effort to bring about an end to the illegal occupation of Namibia and of apartheid,

1. Condemns South Africa for its continued illegal occupation of Namibia in flagrant defiance of resolutions of the General Assembly and decisions of the Security Council of the United Nations;

2. Reaffirms the legitimacy of the struggle of the Namibian people against the illegal occupation of the racist regime of South Africa and calls upon all States to increase their moral and material assistance to them;

3. Further condemns the racist regime of South Africa for its installation of a so-called interim government in Windhoek and declares that this action, taken even while the Security Council has been in session, constitutes a direct affront to it and a clear defiance of its resolutions, particularly resolutions 435 (1978) and 439 (1978);

4. Declares that action to be illegal and null and void and states that no recognition will be accorded either by the United Nations or any Member State to it or any representative or organ established in pursuance thereof;

5. Demands that the racist regime of South Africa immediately rescind the aforementioned illegal and unilateral action;

6. Further condemns South Africa for its obstruction of the implementation of Security Council resolution 435 (1978) by insisting on conditions contrary to the provisions of the United Nations Plan for the independence of Namibia;

7. Rejects once again South Africa's insistence on linking the independence of Namibia to irrelevant and extraneous issues as incompatible with resolutions 435 (1978), other decisions of the Security Council and the resolutions of the General Assembly on Namibia, including General Assembly resolution 1514 (XV) of 14 December 1960;

8. Declares once again that the independence of Namibia cannot be held hostage to the resolution of issues that are alien to Security Council resolution 435 (1978);

9. Reiterates that Security Council resolution 435 (1978), embodying the United Nations Plan for the independence of Namibia, is the only internationally accepted basis for a peaceful settlement of the Namibian problem and demands its immediate and unconditional implementation;

10. Affirms that the consultations undertaken by the Secretary-General pursuant to paragraph 5 of resolution 532 (1983) have confirmed that all the outstanding issues relevant to Security Council resolution 435 (1978) have been resolved, except for the choice of the electoral system;

11. Decides to mandate the Secretary-General to resume immediate contact with South Africa with a view to obtaining its choice of the electoral system to be used for the election, under United Nations supervision and control, for the Constituent Assembly, in terms of resolution 435 (1978), in order to pave the way for the adoption by the Security Council of the enabling resolution for the implementation of the United Nations Independence Plan for Namibia;

12. Demands that South Africa co-operate fully with the Security Council and the Secretary-General in the implementation of the present resolution;

13. Strongly warns South Africa that failure to do so would compel the Security Council to meet forthwith to consider the adoption of appropriate measures under the United Nations Charter, including Chapter VII, as additional pressure to ensure South Africa's compliance with the above-mentioned resolutions;

14. Urges Member States of the United Nations that have not done so to consider in the meantime taking appropriate voluntary measures against South Africa, which could include
    (a) Stopping of new investments and application of disincentives to this end;
    (b) Re-examination of maritime and aerial relations with South Africa;
    (c) The prohibition of the sale of krugerrands and all other coins mined in South Africa;
    (d) Restrictions in the field of sports and cultural relations;

15. Requests the Secretary-General to report on the implementation of the present resolution not later that the first week of September 1985;

16. Decides to remain seized of the matter and to meet immediately upon receipt of the Secretary-General's report for the purpose of reviewing progress in the implementation of resolution 435 (1978) and, in the event of continued obstruction by South Africa, to invoke paragraph 13 above.

◆ ◆ ◆

RESOLUTION 601 (1987)
Adopted by the Security Council at its 2759th meeting on 30 October 1987

The Security Council,

Having considered the reports of the Secretary-General of the United Nations of 31 March 1987 (S/18767) and 27 October 1987 (S/19234),

Having heard the statement by the President of the United Nations Council for Namibia,

Having also considered the statement by Mr. Theo-Ben Gurirab, Secretary for Foreign Affairs of the South West Africa People's Organization,

Recalling General Assembly resolutions 1514 (XV) of 14 December 1960 and 2145 (XXI) of 27 October 1966 as well as resolutions S-14/1 of 20 September 1986,

Recalling and reaffirming its resolutions 269 (1969), 176 (1970), 301 (1971), 385 (1976), 431 (1978), 432 (1978), 435 (1978), 439 (1978), 532 (1983), 539 (1983), and 566 (1985),

1. Strongly condemns racist South Africa for its continued illegal occupation of Namibia and its stubborn refusal to comply with the resolutions and decisions of the Security Council, in particular resolutions 385 (1976) and 435 (1978);

2. Reaffirms the legal and direct responsibility of the United Nations over Namibia;

3. Affirms that all outstanding issues relevant to the implementation of its resolution 435 (1978) have now been resolved as stated in the Secretary-General's reports contained in documents S/18767 of 31 March 1987 and S/19234 of 27 October 1987;

4. Welcomes the expressed readiness of the South West Africa People's Organization to sign and observe a cease-fire agreement with South Africa, in order to pave the way for the implementation of Security Council resolution 435 (1978);

5. Decides to authorize the Secretary-General to proceed to arrange a cease-fire between South Africa and the South West Africa People's Organization in order to undertake the administrative and other practical steps necessary for the emplacement of the United Nations Transition Assistance Group;

6. Urges States Members of the United Nations to render all the necessary practical assistance to the Secretary-General and his staff in the implementation of the present resolution;

7. Requests the Secretary-General to report to the Security Council on the progress in the implementation of the present resolution and to submit his report as soon as possible;

8. Decides to remain seized of the matter.

RESOLUTION 629 (1989)
Adopted by the Security Council at its 2842nd meeting on 16 January 1989

The Security Council,

Reaffirming its relevant resolutions, in particular resolutions 431 (1978) of 27 July 1978 and 435 (1978) of 29 September 1978,

Taking note of its resolutions 628 (1989) of 16 January 1989,

Noting that the parties to the Protocol of Brazzaville, contained in document S/20325 of 14 December 1988, agreed to recommend to the Secretary-General that 1 April 1989 be established as the date for the implementation of resolution 435 (1978),

Recognizing the progress in the south-western African peace process,

Expressing concern at the increase in the police and paramilitary forces and the establishment of the South West Africa Territory Force since 1978 and stressing the need to ensure conditions under which the Namibian people will be able to participate in free and fair elections under the supervision and control of the United Nations,

Noting also that these developments make appropriate a re-examination of the requirements for UNTAG effectively to fulfil its mandate which include, inter alia, keeping borders under surveillance, preventing infiltration, preventing intimidation, and ensuring the safe return of refugees and their free participation in the electoral process,

Recalling the approval by the Security Council of the Secretary-General's statement on 28 September 1978 to the Security Council (S/12869),

Emphasizing its determination to ensure the early independence of Namibia through free and fair elections under the supervision and control of the United Nations, in accordance with its resolution 435 (1978) of 29 September 1978,

Reaffirming the legal responsibility of the United Nations over Namibia,

1. Decides that 1 April 1989 shall be the date on which implementation of resolution 435 (1978) will begin;

2. Requests the Secretary-General to proceed to arrange a formal cease-fire between SWAPO and South Africa;

3. Calls upon South Africa to reduce immediately and substantially the existing police forces in Namibia with a view to achieving reasonable balance between these forces and UNTAG so as to ensure effective monitoring by the latter;

4. Reaffirms the responsibility of all concerned to co-operate to ensure the impartial implementation of the settlement plan in accordance with resolution 435 (1978);

5. Requests the Secretary-General to prepare at the earliest possible date a report to the Council on the implementation of resolution 435 (1978), taking into account all relevant developments since the adoption of that resolution;

6. Requests also the Secretary-General, in preparing his report, to re-examine requirements necessary for UNTAG in order to identify wherever possible tangible cost-saving measures without prejudice to his ability fully to carry out its mandate as established in 1978, namely, to ensure the early independence of Namibia through free and fair elections under the supervision and control of the United Nations;

7. Calls upon Members of the United Nations to consider, in co-ordination with the Secretary-General, how they might provide economic and financial assistance to the Namibian people, both during the transitional period and after independence.

◆ ◆ ◆

RESOLUTION 632 (1989)
Adopted by the Security Council at its 2848th meeting on 16 February 1989

The Security Council,

Reaffirming its relevant resolutions, in particular resolutions 431 (1978) of 27 July 1978, 435 (1978) of 29 September 1978 and also 629 (1989) of 16 January 1989,

Further reaffirming that the United Nations plan contained in its resolution 435 (1978) remains the only internationally accepted basis for the peaceful settlement of the Namibian question,

Confirming its decision contained in paragraph 1 of resolution 629 (1989) of 16 January 1989 that 1 April 1989 shall be the date on which implementation of resolution 435 (1978) will begin,

Having considered the report submitted by the Secretary-General (S/20412) and his explanatory statement of 9 February 1989 (S/20457),

Taking into account the assurances given to the Secretary-General by all its members as contained in paragraph 5 of his explanatory statement (S/20457),

Reaffirming the legal responsibility of the United Nations over Namibia until independence,

1. Approves the report of the Secretary-General (S/20412) and his explanatory statement (S/20457) for the implementation of the United Nations plan for Namibia;

2. Decides to implement its resolution 435 (1978) in its original and definitive form to ensure conditions in Namibia which will allow the Namibian people to participate freely and without intimidation in the electoral process under the supervision and control of the United Nations leading to early independence of the Territory;

3. Expresses its full support for and co-operation with the Secretary-General in carrying out the mandate entrusted to him by the Security Council under its resolution 435 (1978);

4. Calls upon all parties concerned to honour their commitments to the United Nations plan and to co-operate fully with the Secretary-General in the implementation of the present resolution;

5. Requests the Secretary-General to keep the Security Council fully informed on the implementation of the present resolution.

RESOLUTION 640 (1989)
Adopted by the Security Council at its 2882nd meeting, on 29 August 1989

The Security Council,

Having critically reviewed the implementation process of resolution 435 (1978) since its commencement and noting with concern that all its provisions are not being fully complied with,

Concerned at reports of widespread intimidation and harassment of the civilian population, in particular by Koevoet elements in SWAPOL,

Recognizing the efforts being exerted by the United Nations Transition Assistance Group (UNTAG) to carry out its responsibilities in spite of obstacles thus placed in its way,

Recalling and reaffirming all its resolutions on the question of Namibia, particularly 435 (1978), 629 (1989) and 632 (1989),

Reiterating that resolution 435 (1978) must be implemented in its original and definitive form, to ensure conditions in Namibia which will, allow the Namibian people to participate freely and without intimidation in the electoral process under the supervision and control of the United Nations leading to early independence of the Territory,

Recalling and reaffirming its firm commitment to the decolonization of Namibia through the holding of free and fair elections under the supervision and control of the United Nations and in which the Namibian people will participate without intimidation or interference,

1. Demands strict compliance by all parties concerned, especially South Africa, with the terms of resolution 435 (1978) and 632 (1989);

2. Further demands the disbandment of all paramilitary and ethnic forces and commando units, in particular Koevoet, as well as dismantling of their command structures as required by resolution 435 (1978);

3. Calls upon the Secretary-General to review the actual situation on the ground with a view to determining the adequacy of the military component of UNTAG in relation to its ability to carry out its responsibilities as authorized under resolutions 435 (1978) and 632 (1989) and to inform the Security Council;

4. Invites the Secretary-General to review the adequacy of the number of police monitors in order to undertake the process for any appropriate increase that he may deem necessary for the effective fulfilment of UNTAG's responsibilities;

5. Requests the Secretary-General, in his supervision and control of the electoral process, to ensure that all legislation concerning the electoral process is in conformity with the provisions of the Settlement Plan;

6. Further requests the Secretary-General to ensure that all proclamations conform with internationally accepted norms for the conduct of free and fair elections and, in particular, that the proclamation on the Constituent Assembly also respects the sovereign will of the people of Namibia;

7. Requests the Secretary-General to ensure the observance of strict impartiality in the provision of media facilities, especially on radio and television, to all parties for the dissemination of information concerning the election;

8. Appeals to all the parties concerned to co-operate fully with the Secretary-General in the implementation of the Settlement Plan;

9. Expresses its full support for the Secretary-General in his efforts to ensure that Security Council resolution 435 (1978) is implemented in its original and definitive form and requests him to report to the Council before the end of September on the implementation of the present resolution;

10. Decides to remain seized of the matter.

RESOLUTION 643 (1989)
Adopted by the Security Council at its 2886th meeting, on 31 October 1989

The Security Council,

Reaffirming all its relevant resolutions on the question of Namibia, especially resolutions 435 (1978) of 29 September 1978, 629 (1989) of 16 January 1989, 632 (1989) of 16 February 1989 and 640 (1989) of 29 August 1989,

Also reaffirming that the United Nations plan for the independence of Namibia, contained in resolution 435 (1978), remains the only internationally accepted basis for the peaceful settlement of the Namibia question,

Having considered the report of the Secretary-General of 6 October 1989 and the addendum thereto of 16 October 1989,

Noting with deep concern that, one week before the scheduled elections in Namibia, all the provisions of resolutions 435 (1978) are not being fully complied with,

Noting the progress made so far in the implementation of the settlement plan and the remaining obstacles placed in its way as well as the efforts being exerted by the United Nations Transition Assistance Group to carry out its responsibilities,

Reaffirming the continuing legal responsibility of the United Nations over Namibia until the full attainment by the Namibian people of national independence,

1. Welcomes the report of the Secretary-General of 6 October 1989 and the addendum thereto of 16 October 1989;

2. Expresses its full support for the Secretary-General in his efforts to ensure that Security Council resolution 435 (1978) is fully implemented in its original and definitive form;

3. Expresses its firm determination to implement resolution 435 (1978) in its original and definitive form in order to ensure holding of free and fair elections in Namibia under the supervision and control of the United Nations;

4. Reaffirms its commitment in carrying out the continuing legal responsibility over Namibia until its independence to ensure the unfettered and effective exercise by the people of Namibia of their inalienable rights to self-determination and genuine national independence in accordance with resolutions 435 (1978) and 640 (1989);

5. Demands immediate, full and strict compliance by all parties concerned, in particular South Africa, with the terms of resolutions 435 (1978), 632 (1989) and 640 (1989);

6. Further reiterates its demand for the complete disbandment of all remaining paramilitary and ethnic forces and commando units, in particular the Koevoet and the South-West Africa Territorial Force as well as the complete dismantling of their command structures, and other defence-related institutions as required by resolutions 435 (1978) and 640 (1989);

7. Requests the Secretary-General to pursue his efforts to ensure the immediate replacement of the remaining South African Defence Forces personnel in accordance with resolution 435 (1978);

8. Demands the immediate repeal of such remaining restrictive and discriminatory laws and regulations as inhibit the holding of free and fair elections and that no such new laws be introduced and endorses the position of the Secretary-General as expressed in his report that Proclamation AG 8 should be repealed;

9. Invites the Secretary-General to keep under constant review the adequacy of the number of police monitors in order to undertake the process for any appropriate increase that he may deem necessary for the effective fulfillment of the United Nations Transition Assistance Group's responsibilities;

10. Demands that the South West Africa Police extend full co-operation to the United Nations Transition Assistance Group civil police in carrying out the tasks entrusted to it under the settlement plan;

11. Mandates the Secretary-General to ensure that all necessary arrangements are made in accordance with the settlement plan to safeguard the territorial integrity and security of Namibia in order to ensure a peaceful transition to national independence, and to assist the Constituent Assembly in the discharge of responsibilities entrusted to it under the settlement plan;

12. Requests the Secretary-General to prepare appropriate plans for mobilizing all forms of assistance, including technical, material and financial resources for the people of Namibia during the period following the elections for the Constituent Assembly until the accession to independence;

13. Urgently appeals to Member States, United Nations agencies, intergovernmental and non-governmental organizations to extend, in co-ordination with the Secretary-General, generous financial, material and technical support to the Namibian people, both during the transitional period and after independence;

14. Decides that, if the pertinent provisions of the present resolutions are not complied with, the Security Council shall convene as required before the elections to review the situation and consider appropriate action;

15. Requests the Secretary-General to report on the implementation of the present resolution as soon as possible;

16. Decides to remain seized of the matter.

RESOLUTION 652 (1990)
Adopted by the Security Council at its 2918th meeting, on 17 April 1990

The Security Council,

Having examined the application of the Republic of Namibia for admission to the United Nations (S/21241),

Recommends to the General Assembly that the Republic of Namibia be admitted to membership in the United Nations.

Photograph Acknowledgements

Where it has been possible to identify the sources of picture illustrations reproduced in this volume, specific acknowledgements are as given below (listed by the Illustration number).

Personal Collection of Sam Nujoma	Front Cover, 7, 8, 9, 10, 12, 13, 17, 18, 72, 73
The Namibia Press Agency	19, 22, 25, 55, 56, 58, 59, 60, 66, 67, 68, 70, 76, 81, 82, 83, 85, 87, 88, 92, 95, 96, 97, 98, 100, 101
The United Nations	36 [UN photo no. 127,943]
	38 [UN photo no. 132, 642]
	39 [UN photo no. 132,975]
	40 [UN photo no. 136,189]
	43 [UN photo no. 138,268]
	45 [UN photo no. 138,279]
	46/7 [UN photo no. 145,511]
	53 [UN photo no. 161,794]
Angolan Ministry of Information	33
Mattias Aberg/Afrikabild, Stockhold	Back Cover
Middle East News Agency	15
National Archives of Namibia / IDAF/Mayibuye Centre	42 [no. 13185] 84 [no. 350]
PIB Photo Division, New Delhi	52

The remaining illustrations included in this volume (and many others which have been omitted due to constraints of space) were offered from the collections of numerous individuals; from the archives of SWAPO and other governmental and educational bodies of Namibia and elsewhere; and from other sources, all of which are gratefully thanked for their contributions to this volume.

Index

A

Abdel-Wahab, Mustafa Rateb 187
Abrahams, Kenneth 129
Adamishin, Anatoly 401
Address to the UN Security Council, 5 October 1971 206–212
Adjei, Ako 103
Admishin, Anatoly 374
African Liberation Committee (of OAU) 124
African Party for the Independence of Guinea and Cape Verde Islands (PAIGC) 124
African Pioneer Movement 104
Afro-Asian People's Solidarity Organization 213
Ahtisaari, Martti 257, 266, 287, 288, 293, 376, 396, 401, 412, 419
Akuenye, Thobias 73
Akumbe, Mateus 327
Akwenye, Onesmus Shikongo 50
Alexander, Ray 54, 242, 243
Algerian National Liberation Front (FLN) 95, 97, 119
All-African People's Conference 113, 114, 152
Aluteni, Abel Shuudeni 173, 178
Amathila, Ben 161, 190, 435
Amathila, Libertina 370, 409, 411, 434
American Committee on Africa 104
Ammoun, Judge 202
Amukuaja, James 164, 183
Amungulu, Naftalie (Kombandjele) 179
African National Congress (ANC) 52, 54, 91, 93, 121, 122, 124, 128, 152, 159, 243, 245, 275, 277, 365, 371, 382, 383, 386
Andrew Intamba 401
Anglo-American Corporation 51
Angula, James Hamukuaoja (Shoonjeka) 160, 161, 162
Angula, Nahas 299, 401, 403, 404, 411, 435
Angula, Penehafo 328
Anti-Apartheid Movement 123, 213
Appolus, Emil 127, 128, 131, 147
Appolus, Meekulu Putuse 77, 107, 113, 117, 118, 370

Arafat, Yasser 308, 353
Armacost, Sam 335, 376
Ashipala, Danger 317
Ashipala, Jack 142
Auala (Bishop) 203, 209
Augustinas, Abiatar 328
Augustineum College 376
Aune, Meme Katangolo 27
Ausiku, Bishop 352

B

Baddawi (Judge) 143
Banda, Hastings 59, 86, 101
Banderanaike, Mrs. 119
Bantu Education 209
Baudouin, King 106, 352
de Beers, David 248
Belgian Congo (now DRC: Democratic Republic of the Congo) 18, 88, 97, 101, 103
Bella, Ahmed Ben 129
Berker, Hans 438
'Berlin Conference' 8
Bessinger, Nico 344, 434
Beukes, Hans 50, 104
Bismark, Otto von (German Chancellor) 8
Blaauw (Special Branch Chief Captain) 43, 61, 62
Blignaut, Brewer (Chief Native Commissioner) 52, 62, 62–69, 63, 64, 65, 74, 80, 105, 107, 120, 126
Bolsler (Commandant) 402
Boois, Stella 356
Botha, P. W. 243, 266, 267, 271, 285, 288, 293, 294, 297, 322, 340, 344, 350, 355, 370, 371, 373, 375, 377, 378, 379, 384, 388, 407
Botha, 'Pik' 268, 306, 371, 378, 379, 384, 385, 388, 395, 396, 400, 403, 405, 409, 416, 419, 420
Bottomley, Arthur 153
Brazzaville Group 114
Breytenbach, Col. 370, 379, 380
Brezhnev, Leonid 332
Broederbond 244, 334
Brooks, Angie 102

Bulawayo, Fines 88
Bunting, Brian 243
Bush, George 307, 384
Bushmen Battalion 293

C

Caetano, Marcello 169
Caprivi African National Union (CANU) 133, 135, 136, 191, 244
Caradon, Lord 212
Carlsson, Bernt 385, 386
Carpio, Victor 118, 217
Carsten Veld 42, 61
Carter, Jimmy 280, 288, 291, 295, 375
Casablanca Group 114
Cassinga 263, 264, 265, 266, 272, 284, 315, 316, 323, 332, 350, 356, 357, 375, 441
Cassinga Day 376
Castro, Fidel 105, 256, 309, 333, 361, 363, 377
Castro, Raúl 361, 362
CCB (Civil Co-operation Bureau) 418, 421, 422
Chand, Prem 288, 391
Chande, Ali 90, 91
Cheysson, Claude 307, 355
Chief Iipumbu ja Tshilongo 14, 15
Chief Johannes Kambonde 54, 55, 63, 64, 65, 66, 67, 68, 195
Chief Kahimemua Nguvauva 6
Chief Johannes Kambonde 120
Chief Mandume ja Ndemufajo 11, 13, 14, 29
Chief Muaala 107
Chief Munjuku Nguvauva 85
Chief Nikodemus Kavikunua 6
Chief Samuel Maharero 8, 10, 17
Chief Samuel Witbooi 34, 43, 48, 49, 68, 78, 118
Chief Tshekedi Khama 17
Chipenda Column 231
Chitepo, Herbert 95
Chitunda, Daniel 88
CIA (Central Intelligence Agency) 152, 230, 388, 389
Clark Amendment 232, 290
Clark, William 306
Cleary, Sean 366
Cohen, Herman 413
Commission of Inquiry into South West African Affairs 131
Congo-Brazzaville 154, 415

Congo-Kinshasa (now DRC: Democratic Republic of the Congo) 124
Consolidated Diamond Mines 57, 392
Constituent Assembly 424, 430, 431
Constitution Drafting Committee 424, 430
Constitutional Principles 424
Constitution Signatories 436
'constructive engagement' 276, 289, 350
Consultative Congress July 1976, Nampundwe, Zambia 247
Contract system 50–52
Council of Churches in Namibia 380
covert aid 306, 365
Crocker, Chester 283, 287, 289, 295, 306, 335, 343, 371, 376, 384, 400, 413
Cuban Women's anti-air regiment 370
de Cuéllar, Javier Pérez 310, 353, 371, 384, 397, 419, 437, 442
Cuito Cuanavale 370, 373, 377, 378, 379, 380

D

Dadoo, Dr. 99
Davis, Hurbert 41
Democratic Republic of the Congo (DRC) 3, 4, 124, 151, 152, 154, 358, 415 [see also Belgian Congo, Zaire]
Democratic Turnhalle Alliance (DTA) 245, 262, 286, 306, 322, 334, 409, 417, 424, 425
de Wet, Nel 71, 72, 73, 75, 126
Diefenbaker, General George 117
DMZ 16th parallel 325
Dreyer, "Sterk Hans" 325
DuBois, W. E. B. 103
Dukakis, Michael 376, 384
Dumeni (Bishop) 352
Duncan, Patrick 54, 243

E

Eckhard, Fred 419
Eilo, Malakia (Kamati-ka-Eilo) 317
Ekandjo, Eino Kamati 170, 178
Ekandjo, Jerry 157, 241
Elago, Isak Shoome 173
Emvula, Ruth 328
Erasmus, Celine 328
Escher, Alfred 218, 219, 261

Index

F

Fanon, Frantz 97
FAPLA 35, 236, 243, 322, 329, 363, 365, 370, 371, 373, 377, 378, 379, 383, 387
FCN 425
Febregat, Professor 118, 361
Festus, Philemon 356
floggings 228
Ford, Gerald 277
Ford, Martha 272
Fortune, Ismail 104, 118
Fourie, Brand 276, 297
Frank (Advocate) 355
Front for the Liberation of Mozambique (FRELIMO) 121, 123, 124, 152, 159, 275, 277

G

de Guiringaud, Louis 269, 280
Gandhi, Indira 308, 309, 347
Gandhi, Rajiv 346, 347, 349, 361
Gariseb, August 72
Garoeb, Moses 73, 104, 117, 190, 191, 316, 361, 409, 413
Garvey, Marcus 104
de Gaulle, Charles 107
Geingob, Hage 142, 147, 150, 409, 411, 412, 413, 414, 423, 424
Geldenhuys (General) 322, 324, 344, 379, 419, 420
Genscher, Hans-Dietrich 246, 269, 280
German Lutheran Church 249
Gichuru, James 114
Goldblatt, Lucian 80
Gonzalez, Felipe 358
Good Offices Commission 48–49
Gorbachev, Mikhail 290, 374, 390
Government of Angola in Exile (GRAE) 237
Gowaseb (Pastor) 203, 209
Grimes, James 102
Gromyko, Andrei 257, 374
Gross, Ernest 132
Gurirab, Theo-Ben 254, 259, 262, 272, 299, 342, 375, 377, 409, 424, 425, 435
Gutsche, Bernhardt 76, 79

H

Hager, C. L. 72
Hahn, Hugo "Shongola" 15, 27, 228
Haiduua, Jonas 173, 318
Haig, Alexander 355
Haimbodi, Thomas 162, 164, 173
Hainjeko Military Academy 393
Hainjeko, Tobias 149, 158, 159, 160, 161, 172, 179, 180, 182, 190
Haitembu, Vilho 158
Hall, Justice 78
Hamaambo, Dimo 159, 232, 234, 236, 316, 381, 393
Hambija, Petrus 158, 159
Hamulemo, Simeon Namunganga 178
Hamunime, David (Keenongoja) 170, 178
Hamunjela, Nghilifavali Thomas 367, 368
Hamutenya, Aaron 34, 36, 126, 157, 174
Hamutenya, Hidipo 125, 262, 272, 299, 342, 375, 377, 393, 395, 404, 409, 423, 435
Hamutumbangela, Theophilus (Reverend) 49, 51, 52–58, 54, 104
Hanekom, Gerhard 435
Haufiku, Nghidipo Jesaja (Kambua) 170, 178, 317
Haughey, Charles 367
Hausiku, Marco 434
Heimerikx, Gerard 328
Heita, Festus 161, 162
Helmut, Paul 190
Henock, Johannes 64
Heptulla, Najma 308
Herbert, Frans 328
Herman (General) 272, 388
Herrigel, Otto 434, 438
Himumuine, Batholomeus 47
Hipangelua, Akapeke 164
von Hirschberg, Carl 402, 403, 404
Hishongua, Hadino 299
Homateni, Natanael Lot 161, 178
Hough, Danie 297
Houser, George 104, 366
Howe, Geoffrey 410
Huddleston, Trevor 353
Hugo, J.P. 37
Human Rights Day 75, 437

I

Iihuhua, Thomas 157
Iimbili, Shihepo 241
Iipinge, Aaron 60
Iita, Sakeus Petrus 136
Iithete, Lamek 161
Iitula, Simeon 178

Iileka, Shikalepo *162, 163, 164*
Independence Day, 21 March 1990 *439–443*
Indongo, Iyambo *190, 230, 264*
Intamba, Andrew *401, 404*
International Court of Justice *98, 100, 132, 133, 138, 143–155, 158, 159, 173, 198*
International Labour Organization *222*
Ipinge, I. *173*
Israel, Kali Ki' *63*
Ithana, Pendukeni Emvula *370, 409*
Ithete, Nangolo *124*
Itika, Sakeus Philipus *164, 178, 183*
Iyambo, Nickey *124, 190, 409, 434*
Iyambo, Patrick Israel (Lungada) *158, 160, 161, 162, 166–171, 180, 229, 393, 411*

J

Jackson, Rev. Jesse *376, 437*
Jacob, Henok (Malila) *162*
Jacobsen *199*
Jimmy, Idda *370*
Johannes, Axel *299*
Johnstone, Bill *366*
Joint Military Monitoring Commission (JMMC) *400, 400–404*
Joint Monitoring Commission (JMC) *329–334*
Joseph, Matthew *178*

K

Kadhikua, Rudolph *173, 178*
Kahana, Johannes *190*
Kahimise, Josaphat *149*
Kakuambi, S. *173*
Kakuva, Johannes *136*
Kalangula, Peter *105, 306*
Kaluenja, Homateni *190*
Kamati, Febronia *370*
Kamati, Petrus *178*
Kambala, Kondja *404*
Kambonde, Timothy *41*
Kameeta (Vice-Bishop) *376*
Kampala, Fanuel *73*
Kanjeule, Mathias Elia (Shimbungu) *178*
Kapelwa, Richard (Kabajani) *137, 190, 299, 434*
Kapere, Aaron *76*
Kapeuasha, Martin *241*

Kapolo, Efraim *178, 179, 183*
Kapuuo, Clemens *47, 49, 74, 75, 254*
Kapwepwe, Simon *127*
Karuaihe, Johannes *83*
Kasavubu, Josef *88, 97*
Kashea, Joseph *241*
Kashindi, Kasino, Johannes Akaupa *304*
Kandanga-Hilukilua, Gertrude *370*
Katjavivi, Peter *128, 310*
Katjiuongua, Moses *118, 340*
Katjivena, Edwald *124, 148, 174, 190*
Katutura *38, 43, 64, 65, 71, 72, 73, 74, 75, 77, 224, 335–338, 376, 415, 416, 418, 422*
Kaukuetu, Watja *72, 75, 78*
Kaukungua, Shapua *124, 148, 299, 374*
Kaukungua, Simon *124, 126, 128, 148, 157, 190, 441*
Kauluma (Bishop) *352, 376*
Kauluma, Elifas *421*
Kaunda, Kenneth *86, 88, 101, 122, 125, 152, 153, 208, 230, 247, 272, 273, 340, 341, 342, 351, 378*
Kavela, Nelson (Sadrag) *160, 161, 162*
Keita, Modibo *119*
Kembale, Kakuwa *316*
Kenya African Democratic Union (KADU) *112, 114*
Kenya African National Union (KANU) *112, 114, 121, 124*
Kenyatta, Jomo *101, 121, 122*
Kerina, Mburumba *42, 50, 54, 78, 80, 81, 84, 101, 102, 104, 113*
Khan, Zafrullah *202*
Khrushchev, Nikita *106*
King Shihetekela Hiudulu *13–14*
Kinnock, Neil *347*
Kirkpatrick, Jeanne *306, 345*
Kirschnereit, Kurt *248*
Kissinger, Henry *228, 251–260, 276, 277, 278, 279, 280, 281, 282, 289*
de Klerk, F. W. *378, 416*
Koevoet *224, 293, 321, 325, 326–328, 332, 336, 371, 383, 387, 389, 391, 406, 410, 419, 421, 422*
Kohl, Helmut *350*
Koinange, Mbiyu *122*
Kondombolo, Hiskia *34, 36*
Kondombolo, Mpingana-Helvi *22, 414*
Kongwa military training camp *158, 159, 160, 171*
Kooper, Rev. Markus *104, 119*

Kovambo Katjimune, Theopoldine 38, 39, 40
Kozonguizi, Fanuel 42, 49, 53, 78, 81, 84, 97, 100, 104, 118, 119, 243
Kuhangua, Jacob 54, 55, 78, 104, 107, 127, 128, 131, 146, 192, 345
Kutako, Hosea (Chief) 17, 34, 43, 46, 48, 49, 51, 68, 78, 99, 106, 107, 118, 132, 193, 194, 207, 332, 422

L

Landis, Elizabeth 366
League of Nations Article 22 (1920) 16
Lelyveld, Joseph 322
Liebenberg, John 412
linkage 250, 283, 290, 306, 307, 308, 313, 339, 340, 349, 350, 355
Lister, Gwen 410
Lombard, Hans 145
Louw, Eric 51, 105, 205, 332
Lowenstein, Allard 50
Lubowski, Anton 355, 410, 412, 413, 414, 438
Lüderitz, Adolf 6
Ludwig, Hugo 31
Lumumba, Patrice 88, 97, 151
Lutheran World Federation 248

M

MacBride, Sean 220, 221, 222, 257, 259, 397
Machel, Samora 346
Macmillan, Harold 105, 106
Maharero, Frederick 422
Makarios (Arch-Bishop) 119
Makulu (Bishop) 351
Malan, Daniel F. 33, 37, 71, 104, 244, 388, 419
Malan, Magnus 197, 293, 356, 371, 377, 380, 385
Malecela, John 187, 353
Mandate for German South West Africa (1920) 16
Mandela, Nelson 80, 437, 439
Mangope, Lucas 351
Marenga, Jacob 8
Marianga, Morton 87
Martinez de Alva, Salvador 118
Matanzima, Kaizer 351
Matheus, Josef (Jo'burg) 161
Matongo, Crispin 344

Mavulu, Natalie 370
Mau Mau 92, 101
Mawema, Michael 87, 95, 101
Maxuilili, Nathaniel 157, 174, 178, 195, 218, 341, 414
Mbaeva, Nathaniel 73, 77, 78, 79, 107
Mbidi, Gabriel 157, 174
Mboya, Tom 114
Mbuende, Gabriel 47
Mbuende, Kaire 47
Mbumba, Erastus 161
McBride, Sean 281
McHenry, Donald 267, 273, 275
Meiring, (General) George 336
Menon, Krishna 212
Meroro, David 76, 86, 122, 138, 139, 157, 195, 202, 218, 240, 316, 432
Meyer, (General) Willie 402
Middlewick, C. S. 37
Mifima, Solomon 118, 129, 145, 190
Mitterand, François 290, 355
Mize (Bishop) 248
Mobutu, Sese Seko 237, 413
Mondlane, Eduardo 159
Moses, Michael Nghifingila 178
Mount Etjo Accord 400–404
Mphephe, Patrick 351
Mpingana, Nehale Ija 11, 13
Muaala, Festus 162
Muashekele, Leevi 58, 59, 62
Muatale, Eliader 125, 127, 158, 159, 173
Mubarak, Hosni 440
Mudge, Dirk 295, 306, 322, 323, 325, 341, 417, 425
Mueshihange, Peter 115, 117, 118, 174, 366, 368, 381, 393, 434
Mugabe, Robert 295, 346, 395, 399
Muhamed, Murtala 287
Muleko, Johannes 61
Muller, Hilgard 205, 209, 210, 217
Mulonda, Crispin 136
Multi-Party Conference (MPC) 327, 329, 338, 340, 342, 344
Munamava, Daniel 85, 86, 118
Mundia, Nalumino 136
Mungunda, Anna "Kakarukaze" 76, 262, 272
Musheko, Johannes 162
Mushimba, Aaron 157
Mushimba, Hilma 26
Musialela, Elen 370
Mutindi, Pedro 395

Mutongolume, Maxton Joseph *126, 128, 174, 190*
Mutumbangela (Reverend) *79*
Mutumbulua, Jason *178*
Muyongo, Albert Misheke *136, 138, 190, 191*
Muzorewa, (Bishop) Abel *215, 295*
Mwaanga, Vernon *187, 199*
Mwailepeni, Titus *159, 413*
Mwashekele, Kathrina *62*
Mwinyi (President of Tanzania) *440*

N

Namuandi, Messah Victory (Shiuayanga) *161, 162*
Naholo, Festus *272*
Nakale, Jonas *164*
Nakanduungile, Malakia *369*
Nakanjala, Johannes *65*
Nakawa, John *136*
Nambinga, Rehabeam Olavi *162, 164, 179*
Nambinga, Usko *299*
Namholo, Charles Philip Dixon *318*
Namibia Communications Centre, London *381*
Namibia National Convention (NNC) *242*
Namibia, naming of *187*
Namibia Support Committee *123, 145, 213*
Namibia National Convention (NNC) *202, 244*
Namibia National Front (NNF) *425*
Namibian Heroes' Day *172*
Namibian National Student's Organization (NANSO) *382, 385*
Namibian Press Agency (NAMPA) *381*
Namibian Defence Force *431, 437*
Namoloh, Charles *393*
Namuandi, Messah Victory (Shiuayanga) *160, 161, 162*
Namuganga, Simeon *162*
Nandi-Ndaitwah, Netumbo *299*
Nandjule, Julia Gebhard *26, 31, 34*
Nangolo, Andreas *60, 61*
Nangombe, Martin *42, 43*
Nangula, Shindjuu sha *318*
Nanjolo, Festus *162*
Nanking Military Academy *159*
Nankudhu, John Otto (Koshiuanda) *158, 159, 161, 162, 164, 166, 172, 178*

Nanyemba, Peter (Ndilimani) *130, 142, 160, 161, 190, 191, 192, 247, 299, 310, 311, 316*
Nashivela, Jonas *161, 178*
Nasser, Gamal Abdel *98, 100, 114, 119, 154, 193, 194*
National Alliance of Third World Journalists *381*
National Convention *222*
National Front for the Liberation of Angola (FNLA) *230, 231, 232, 236, 237*
National Front for the Liberation of Angola (MPLA) *124, 150, 152, 159, 229, 230, 231, 232, 234, 236, 277, 365, 371, 384*
National Party *37*
National Patriotic Front of Namibia (NPF) *425*
National Reconciliation policy *376*
National Union of Namibian Workers (NUNW) *383, 385, 387*
National Union for the Total Independence of Angola (UNITA) *229, 230, 231, 232, 235, 236, 237, 270, 272, 278, 289, 290, 306, 322, 325, 329, 331, 332, 335, 365, 366, 370, 371, 374, 384, 410, 417*
Naunyango, B. *173*
Nauyala, Kapuka *262, 272, 299, 342*
Nawa, Joseph *136*
Ndadi, P. Hamalua *173*
Ndadi, Vinia *58, 190*
Ndafenongo, Jekonia *190*
National Democratic Party of Southern Rhodesia (NDP) *85, 87*
Ndume, Elia *170*
Negonga, Erastus *401, 404*
Negongo, Epapharas *149*
Nehale, Festus *170, 178, 179, 183*
Nehru, Jawaharlal *117, 119*
Nelengani, Louis *55, 79, 118, 146, 191*
Nepaya, Thomas *149*
Nepolo, Erastus *328*
Nepolo, Gisela *328*
Neto, Antonio Agostinho *159, 231, 232, 234, 236, 283, 287, 296*
Ngala, Ronald *114*
Nganjone, Levi *75*
Ngavirue, Zedekia *75, 104, 118, 119, 435*
Nghaamua, Salatiel *31, 58*
Nghindinua, Susan *370*
Niekerk, Van *81*

Nienhaus, P. *297*
Niilenge, Petrus Simon *164, 179, 183*
Niilenge, Shinima 'Harakatyi' *164, 178*
Nixon, Richard *253*
Nkrumah, Kwame *46, 97, 103, 117, 119, 139, 140, 151*
Non-Aligned Movement (NAM) *119, 123, 150, 286, 382*
North Atlantic Treaty Organization (NATO) *221, 223, 227*
Nujoma, Daniel Utoni *174, 300, 421*
Nujoma, John Ndeshipanda *41, 229*
Nujoma, Nelago *41*
Nujoma, Noah *129*
Nujoma, Sakaria Nefungo *41, 229*
Nujoma, Stephen *304*
Nujoma, Utoni Daniel *41*
Nujoma, Utoni *229*
Nuunjango, Bethuel *178*
Nuuyoma, Yoliindje *327*
Nyerere, Julius *18, 45, 46, 90, 92, 93, 101, 117, 121, 124, 125, 152, 153, 158, 180, 256, 273, 283, 346*

O

Obasanjo, Olusegun *376*
Ochoa Sánchez, Arnaldo *362*
Odinga, Oginga *124*
Olympio, Sylvanus *45, 46*
Omugulu-gOmbashe *129, 142 146, 155, 162–163, 174–183, 389*
Onguediva Training College *337*
Opande (General) *408*
'Operation Zulu' *231, 236*
Oppenheimer, Nicholas *392*
Organization of African Unity (OAU) *121, 122, 123, 124–125, 147, 150, 152, 211, 213, 215, 220, 223, 224, 243, 253, 257, 268, 286, 300, 382, 392*
    OAU Liberation Committee *152*
    OAU Liberation Committee Fund *129*
Ortega, Daniel *361*
Oshakati bombing, Feb. 1988 *380*
Oshikuku massacre *326–328*
Ya Otto, John *122, 139, 178, 195, 218, 224, 229*
Ovamboland People's Congress (OPC) *42, 45–69, 54, 347*
Ovamboland People's Organization (OPO) *43, 45, 101, 107*

OPO Constitution (aims and objectives) *55*
OPO name change to SWAPO *101*
Owen, David *267, 269, 275, 280*
Oxford Conference (1966) *142*

P

Palme, Mrs Olof *376*
Palme, Olof *142, 154*
Pan-African Freedom Movement of East, Central and Southern Africa (PAFMECSA) *121, 122, 123, 125, 188*
Pan-African National Congress (PAC) *99, 119, 120, 121, 122, 123, 124, 128, 145, 152, 159*
Pan-African Women Organization *107*
Patriotic Front *277*
Peoples' Liberation Army of Namibia (PLAN) *20, 22, 170, 180, 192, 194, 197, 227, 229, 231, 232, 234, 235, 236, 244, 246, 247, 250, 300, 315, 324, 363, 365, 366, 367, 369, 373, 376, 377, 378, 379, 380, 383, 387, 396, 398, 399*
Pienaar, Louis *371, 396, 401, 406–407, 408, 417, 418, 422, 438, 439*
Pierson-Mathy, Paulette *212*
Platt, David *140*
Pohamba, Lazarus *148, 190*
Pohamba, Lucas Hifikepunye *124, 125, 127, 128, 138, 139, 141, 148, 158, 173, 190, 423, 435*
Pohamba, Lukas Hifikepunye *174*
Pointe, Paul Andre la *269*
Pokkesdraai Compound *55, 65, 74, 75*
Police Zone *48, 52, 68*
Policia International Defence d'Estate (PEDE) *236*
Ponhofi Secondary School, Ovamboland *383*
Pope John Paul II *345*
Pre-Implementation Meeting (PIM) on Namibia *288*
press and publicity campaign (1950s) *66–69*
Proclamation AG26 (South African) *263*
'Proclamation R17' *216*
'Proximity Talks' *263*

R

Radio South African Corporation (RSAC) *409*

Rahman, Tung 117
Rawlings, Jerry John 99
Reagan, Ronald 288, 291, 351, 366, 375
Rio Tinto Zinc (RTZ) 392, 397
Risquet Valdès, Jorge 362
Robben Island 164, 172, 179, 182, 183,
    200, 216, 224, 240, 241, 344, 354, 441
Roberto, Holden 231
Rogers, William D. 208, 278, 279
Rössing Foundation 392
Rössing Uranium 222, 392
Royal Institute of International Affairs,
    London 145
Ruacana meeting 400–404
Ruppel, Hartmut 410, 435

S

Sakaria, Lazarus 158
dos Santos, José Eduardo 340, 377, 413, 440
Savimbi, Jonas 236, 237, 278, 280, 289, 290, 322, 325, 326, 365, 366
Schaufele, William 278, 279
Schultz, Ursula 122
Scott, Reverend Michael 17, 34, 42, 47, 48, 49, 51, 54, 78, 80, 81, 84, 97, 104, 119, 194, 207, 252
Sebe, Lennox 351
Segal, Ronald 93, 99
Serfontein (Brigadier) 402
Shalli, Martin 318, 401
Shaningua, Ndjaula ('Mankono') 164, 178
Shelungu, Kornelius 162
Shidika, Jacob 241
Shifidi, Immanuel August 162, 178, 183, 354
Shiguedha, Frans 73
Shihungileni, Simeon 149, 178
Shiimi, Uushona 63, 66, 195
Shikola, Teckla 370
Shikolalje, Paulus 162
Shikomba, David 183
Shikuambi, Nikanor 63
Shikuku, Martin 114
Shikwambi, Ally 370
Shilongo, Ben 367
Shilongo, Julius ('Kashuku') 164, 170, 178
Shilongo, Toivo 136
Shimbama, Bathlomeus 78, 80
Shimbambi, Magdalena 26

Shimueefeleni, Jonas 170, 179, 183
Shipanga, Andreas 129, 242, 246, 247, 344
Shipena, Ananias 63, 79
Shiponeni, John 178
Shitilifa, Phillemon (Kakwalindishishi) 164, 178
Shitilifa, Titus Mwailepeni 158
Shityuwete, Helao Joseph 170, 178
Shixungileni, Simeon Linekela (Kambo) 160, 161, 162, 166
Shoombe, Pashukeni 370
Shoome, Isak 162
Shoopala, Leo 142
Shultz, George 290
Shuuya, Leonard Phillemon ('Castro') 163, 170, 172, 180
Silas, Johannes 328
Simbwaye, Brendan 135, 136
Simons (Professor) 243
Simons, Jack 54, 242
Singh, Natvar 309
Sipalo, Munukayumbwa 136
Sir Zafrullah Khan 143
'Skeleton Coast' 228
Smith, Ian 152, 153, 215, 245, 250, 253
Smuts, David 412
Smuts, General Jan 17, 33, 48, 244
South African Defence Force (SADF) 230, 291, 293, 321, 332, 335, 367, 369, 379, 405
South African Nationalist Party 334
South African Railways (SAR) 34, 36, 38, 41
South African Terrorism Act 174
South West Africa Liberation Army (SWALA) 170, 179, 177, 190, 192
South West Africa Native Labour Association (SWANLA) 25, 27, 28, 34, 38, 49, 52, 63, 71, 72, 73, 97, 108, 118, 119, 121, 122, 123, 188, 243, 340
South West Africa People's Organization (SWAPO) 22, *and throughout*
    SWAPO Elders' Council 387
    SWAPO, formation of 108
    SWAPO Health and Education Centres 257, 415, 437
    SWAPO Pioneer Movement 387
    SWAPO Women's Council 107, 246, 369, 370, 387
    SWAPO Youth League 240, 387
South West Africa Territorial Forces (SWATF) 224, 293, 321, 325, 332, 370, 371, 379, 389, 419

Southern African Development Co-
   ordinating Conference (SADCC) *391,
   392*
Special Committee of 24 *147*
Spencer, Judge Percy C. *143, 144*
St. Barnabas Night School *34, 47*
Steenkamp, Willem *331*
Steyn, Martinus Theuns *261*
Stockwell, John *232*
Strauss, Frans Joseph *380*
Strijdom, J. G. *43, 71, 244*

T

Taapopi, Israel Nashilongo *183*
Taapopi, Nashilongo E. *241*
Tambo, Oliver *78, 80, 93, 99, 100*
Tanzania-Zambia Railway *153*
Tanga Consultative Congress (1969–
   1970) *189–196*
Tanganyika African National Union
   (TANU) *88, 89, 90, 91, 92, 93, 95, 117,
   121*
'Tar Baby option' *253*
Telli, Diallo *145*
Thant, U *68, 145, 187*
Thatcher, Margaret *287, 288, 294, 312,
   350, 351, 352, 395, 396*
Tito, Josip Broz *114, 119*
Tjafenda, Dometrio *140*
Tjipahura, Kaleb Hanganee *173, 178, 183*
Tjiriange, Ngarikutuke *190, 272, 435*
Tjitendero, Moses *124*
Tjombe, Moice *152*
Tjongarero, Daniel *272, 344*
Tlhabanello, Mokganedi *272*
Tobias, Benedicts *328*
Tobias, Bernadete *328*
Todenge, Ottilie *394*
Toivo Ya Toivo, Andimba Herman *42,
   54, 55, 62, 63, 67, 104, 157, 161, 163,
   172, 174, 175, 178, 344, 345, 409, 423,
   432, 435*
van Tonder (General) *272, 388*
Touré, Sékou *119*
Trans-Africa Correspondence College *36*
Transition *430–431*
Tripartite Agreement *388, 390, 396*
von Trotha (German Governor) *10*
Trudeau, Gary *355*
Tsheehama, Peter Tshirumbu *230, 321,
   361, 435*
Tshombe, Moice *88*

Tuhadeleni, Eliaser (Kaxumba ka Ndola)
   157, 160, 161, 162, 174, 178
Turnbull, Sir Richard *93*
Turnhalle 'conference' *253*
Turok, Ben *242, 243*

U

Undery, Sir Charles *48*
Unilateral Declaration of Independence
   (UDI) *153, 215, 245, 250*
United Democratic Front *425*
United Nations (UN) *41 and throughout*
United Nations Committee Against
   Apartheid *205*
United Nations Council for Namibia *381*
United Nations General Assembly
   Resolutions:
   1514   *106, 108–111, 113, 276*
   2145   *150, 151, 175, 186, 192, 198,
          222, 269*
   2248   *185, 269*
United Nations High Commissioner for
   Refugees (UNHCR) *230*
United Nations Security Council
   Resolutions:
   276   *198, 199*
   310   *203*
   385   *251–260, 261, 265, 273, 274,
          281, 291   (full text 452–453)*
   387   *276*
   431   *269 (full text 453)*
   432   *266, 269, 285, 292 (full text
          454)*
   435   *170, 263, 266, 268, 271, 275,
          285, 291, 292, 294, 295, 306,
          307, 308, 313, 325, 343, 371,
          374, 375, 377, 381, 384–386
          (full text 454–455)*
   439   *293 (full text 455)*
   532   *334 (full text 456)*
   539   *339 (full text 456–457)*
   566   *349 (full text 458–459)*
   606   *371*
   628   *388*
   632   *391, 406, 410 (full text 452–
          453)*
   640   *391, 406*
United Nations Transition Assistance
   Group (UNTAG) *283, 285, 286, 290,
   315, 383, 386, 388, 390, 391, 396, 397,
   399, 400, 412, 414, 417, 418, 419*

United National Independence Party (UNIP) 33, 41, 43, 86, 88, 93, 95, 101, 120, 121, 122, 135, 136, 382
Universal Declaration of Human Rights 75
Urquhart, Brian 274, 288, 293, 296, 297
US Policy towards Namibia 277–290
Uunona, Laimi 394
Uupindi, Gisela 326, 328
Uushona, David 59
Uushona, Malakia Shivute 178

V

Van der Watt (Special Branch Police) 61
Van der Westhuizen (General) 272, 342, 388
Van Niekerk, Willie 340, 341, 342, 343
Vance, Cyrus 267, 269, 280, 281, 282, 288, 292, 296
Vasaliwo (Major) 402
Veiccoh, Hangapo 370
Versailles Treaty 16
Verwoerd, Hendrik F. 33, 37, 71, 73, 140, 142, 143, 144, 146, 175, 197, 209, 215, 228, 244, 407
Vigne, Randolph 54, 145, 353
Viljoen, Daan 72, 77, 120
Viljoen, Gerrit 262
de Villiers (Advocate) 138
Vincent (Bishop of Damaraland) 52
Vorster, B. J. 179, 180, 197, 203, 208, 215, 219, 228, 242, 243, 246, 248, 250, 253, 285, 293, 355, 379, 407
Vorster, John 210, 279

W

Waldheim, Kurt 216, 222, 227, 257, 261, 275, 276, 284, 297
Walvis Bay 5, 256, 263, 266, 269, 275, 285, 386
Wath, J. G. van der 107

Watja Kaukwetu, Willy 73
Welensky, Sir Roy 87, 88
Western Contact Group 261–276, 293
Whiteman, Herbert 103
Williams, Mennen 296
Wilson, Harold 152, 153
Windhoek Old Location 38, 71, 72, 73, 74, 75, 77, 79, 83, 99, 122, 126, 174, 182, 416
Windhoek Uprising 71–81, 102, 104, 107
Winter (Bishop) 216, 248
Winterton, Nicholas 351
Witbooi, Hendrik 8, 157, 272, 344, 345, 414, 432, 434
Witwatersrand Native Labour Association (WENALA) 18, 28, 51, 85
Woods (Bishop) 248
World Council of Churches 248, 376
World Court 114, 118, 131, 132, 133, 140, 142, 143, 145, 146, 147, 150, 181, 196, 197, 198, 199, 202, 203, 323
World Health Organization (WHO) 222

Y

Young, Andrew 267, 275, 306, 375

Z

Zachariah, Lazarus Haiduua (Shakala) 170, 178
Zaire (now DRC: Democratic Republic of the Congo) 35, 103, 129, 230, 231, 236, 370, 371
Zimbabwe African National Union (ZANU) 150, 152, 245
Zimbabwe African National Union — Patriotic Front (ZANU-PF) 87, 152, 159, 245, 277, 288, 295
Zimbabwe African People's Union (ZAPU) 87, 121, 152, 159
Zyl, Van 297